ZIONISM, ISRAEL
AND
ASIAN NATIONALISM

ZIONISM, ISRAEL
AND
ASIAN NATIONALISM

by

G. H. JANSEN

THE INSTITUTE FOR PALESTINE STUDIES

Beirut

1971

The Institute for Palestine Studies is an independent non-profit Arab research organisation not affiliated to any government, political party or group, devoted to a better understanding of the Palestine problem. Books in the Institute series are published in the interest of public information. They represent the free expression of their authors and do not necessarily indicate the judgement or opinions of the Institute.

Monograph Series No. 29

THE INSTITUTE FOR PALESTINE STUDIES
Ashqar Building, Rue Clémenceau, P.O. Box 7164
Beirut, Lebanon

CONTENTS

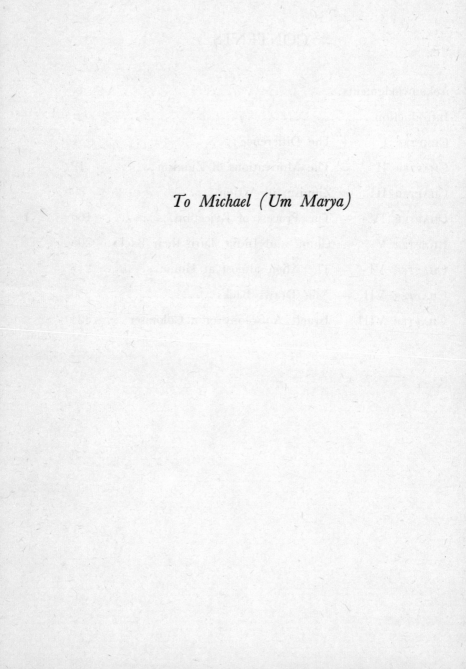

To Michael (Um Marya)

ACKNOWLEDGMENT

I am happy to acknowledge the help of many individuals and institutions in the writing of this book. Thanks to Albert Hourani's distinguished sponsorship, St. Antony's College, Oxford, helped to make it possible for me to take time off from my journalistic duties to write this book, and the Middle East Centre of the College, once again, provided me with living and working space. The hospitable helpfulness of Mrs. Josephine Ward and of Lionel Dix at 137 Banbury Road made my stay there that much more pleasant. In London, Chandra and Suviraj Grubb provided a base which was at once stimulating and restful.

I received much assistance from the libraries of Chatham House, especially its invaluable press-clipping section, the Indian School of International Studies, New Delhi, and the Institute for Palestine Studies and the Palestine Research Centre, Beirut.

This book has benefitted greatly from the suggestions of many people who took the trouble of reading it in typescript: Albert Hourani, Walid Khalidi, who was particularly painstaking, Soraya Antonius, and Michael Simpson. Michael Jansen contributed in this and many other ways by typing, researching and, above all, by her encouragement and patience.

INTRODUCTION

In this book Zionism and the State of Israel are seen as an intrusive force, which is not the case with most books on the subject. This is at least partly due to the fact that my angle of vision is different from that of most other writers. As an Indian I look westwards towards Israel from the east; as Europeans or Americans they look east to Israel from the west. I see Zionist Israel coming towards my point of observation; for them it is moving away. It is one thing to look down the length of the Mediterranean and see Israel on its eastern non-European shore; it is quite another thing to view, from across the Persian Gulf and the mountains of Moab, this dynamic new state that has established itself on the western rim of Asia.

One may, with reason, wonder whether the powerful Western friends and supporters of Israel would not feel quite differently about that country if it were located, say, on the coasts of Portugal or of New England; but the fact is that it is located in quite a different continent.

The central theme of this book is that Israel is in Asia but not of it. For a very brief period after her foundation Israel tried to become a part of Asia, but she failed and has now almost abandoned the attempt. Indeed that attempt was foredoomed to failure because of the very nature of the Zionist movement which, in several essential ways, was non-Asian or anti-Asian.

At this point it may be feared that I am uncritically accepting the familiar Arab accusations that Israel is "foreign" and "colonial". I think not. It is curious that the Israelis concede that on this one aspect of the problem the "Arab propaganda machine" has been successful in "leading people astray". For many years, and at very close range, I have observed the pathetically inept efforts of Arab propaganda and I am not prepared to concede it any persuasive power. It is the facts that I have found convincing and, especially, the words of the Zionists themselves; thus it is on the words of the Zionists rather than the Arabs that this book is based.

To come to my present point of view I moved counter to my upbringing and to my own earlier views on the Palestine problem itself.

Zionism, so it is claimed, is based on and is a continuation of the history of the Jewish people as recorded in the Old Testament, and the political programme of that movement merely purports to fulfil the Promise of the Return that Jehovah made to His "Chosen People". As is now well known, anyone who sincerely accepts the teachings of the Old Testament is half-way to being a Zionist. Both my parents were devout adherents of the more fundamentalist denominations of Protestant Christianity, for which the Old Testament is far more important than the New; and they insisted that their children share their own certitude that the return of the Jews to the Holy Land was a divinely ordained preliminary to the End of the World, which, for them, was very nigh. After 1947 my father, who was a completely convinced Gentile Zionist, roundly condemned the Arab antagonists of Israel for trying to frustrate the Will of God; this remained his conviction till his death in 1964.

At the missionary school I attended, the study of the scriptures and various religious observances were almost the most important part of the curriculum. A few Jewish boys attended the school and I clearly recall that our feeling towards them was one of awed respect that they should be the descendants of the great Patriarchs and Prophets about whom we knew so much. This is fairly typical of the attitude towards the Jews in India where there has never been the slightest trace of anti-Semitism.

Like most young Indians at that time I was obsessed with the Indian national struggle and, after World War II, held it to the credit of the Jews of Palestine that they should be fighting the British at the same time as the Indian movement was going through its final struggles against the same imperial power. Furthermore, as a believer in socialism, I was powerfully drawn towards the Palestinian kibbutz which seemed to be the perfect blend of socialist idealism and practicality.

For all these various reasons I was so enthusiastically a pro-Zionist in 1947 that one of the first pieces I wrote as a journalist was an article pointing out the necessity and the justice of the U.N. Partition plan. Such was my desire to have direct contact with this movement of which I so strongly approved that, for a brief period, I was the correspondent in India for the well-known Tel Aviv newspaper *Ha'aretz*.

During my first diplomatic assignment to the Indian Embassy in Cairo in the years 1948 to 1952 I remained pro-Israel, although the Indian Government had adopted the pro-Arab policy to which it still adheres. Such reports as I made, at my particular hierarchical level, and they were numerous, were contrary to official policy. It was not very difficult to be anti-Arab and pro-Israel during those years: the Arab armies had made a miserable showing in the 1948 fighting largely because of corruption and even downright betrayal at home. Egypt itself was passing through the last, loathsome years of Farouk's reign and for a time the King gave a free hand to the Muslim Brotherhood, one of whose main propaganda targets was India.

I first felt that the Arabs could be decent, self-respecting people, determined to do something about their problems, when I passed through Cairo early in 1953 not many months after the expulsion of Farouk. And that the Arabs had a case, and a good case, on Palestine was borne in on me when I was posted to the Permanent Indian Delegation to the U.N. at New York. Several incidents came up for debate in the Security Council at that time and the Arab point of view was most ably presented by Dr. Charles Malik of Lebanon and the much lamented Dr. Mahmoud Azmi of Egypt. Between them they effectively countered the arguments of that glossy orator, Mr. Abba Eban. These debates sent me back to the basic documents on Palestine and on re-reading them I could not resist the conclusion that the Arabs were in the right and the Israelis in the wrong.

But no one operates entirely on the plane of cold reason, least of all with regard to the Palestine problem, which is perhaps more heavily charged with emotion than any other continuing international question. It was on the emotional level that I

reacted against the perfervid, persistent, highly-organised support given by American Jewry, very conspicuous in New York,
to the State of Israel. This seemed then, and seems to me now,
a clear case of extra-territorial loyalty, which is to be deplored,
not admired or encouraged. I also felt that a country that
depended heavily on such loyalty was fundamentally flawed.
Subsequent events have only confirmed these feelings.

The small, single incident that marked the break with my
former Zionist sympathies was when, in front of a theatre off
Broadway, I refused to buy theatre tickets from lady volunteers
of the Hadassah movement which supports hospitals in Israel.
This improbable connection seemed to link politics with hydro-
ponics, and Israel appeared akin to one of those plants normally
rooted in soil, but which are actually grown suspended in chemi-
cally-fertilised water.

I was fortunate enough to attend the Bandung Conference in
1955 at which, in private session, Mr. Nehru warned the Arabs
that the danger to them came not so much from Israel itself
as from the larger, more powerful forces behind that state.
Mr. Nehru's thinking was so far ahead of the Arab delegations
that they jointly protested to the Indian Prime Minister. It
took him some little time to assure them that he had been pro-
claiming the justice of the Arab cause for twenty-five years.

In my case a similar conviction has survived such incidents
and a fifteen-year residence in Beirut since late 1955—first as
a diplomat and then as a foreign correspondent for an Indian
newspaper. Anyone who believes that living with the Arabs is
likely to influence one's thinking in their favour should try doing
so as a journalist; we have to endure a special combination of
unwarranted suspicions and wearying frustrations at the hands
of Arab governments.

A few years back some newspapers in Lebanon denounced
me, and some of my other foreign colleagues, for being "Zionist
agents," and at least one publication in Israel has dubbed me
an "anti-Semite".

I have visited Israel five times in all, and received every
assistance from officials of the government. I have met with
several of the leaders of Israel, though not with all I would have

wished to have seen. I have travelled over most of the country from Metullah and Dan in the north beyond Beersheba to Eilat in the south.

One cannot, and should not, withhold admiration for what has been achieved in Israel, though it must never be forgotten that this was with lavish, unstinted financial help from abroad. I especially recall the calm confidence of the families living in the kibbutz of Dan, less than a mile from the Syrian frontier; as well as the devotion and energy of the young pioneers in a new frontier kibbutz, thirty miles north of Akaba, in the hot depths of the Wadi Araba, where they were growing gladioli for the florist shops of northern Europe. Much of what goes on in Israel can only be described as a tour de force.

If only, I have often thought, if only Israel were located somewhere else! Because Israel is in the wrong country—for this country belonged to another people who have been ejected and replaced. And Israel is in the wrong continent for it is foreign to Asia. But just how foreign I discovered only when I made the abrupt transition from Jordanian Jerusalem to Israeli Jerusalem by walking through the Mandelbaum Gate.

CHAPTER I

THE DIFFERENCE

Surface impressions

Walking through the Mandelbaum Gate one passed, within a distance of two hundred yards, not merely from one state to another but to a different civilisation and culture, in a different continent, brought there by a different racial group which, it may be added, is living in a different century.

The policemen at the checkposts on the Jordanian and on the Israeli side of the barriers looked alike, at first glance, because they still wear the same dark blue serge uniform inherited from the British Mandatory regime. But there the resemblance ended, for the Jordanians were brown-skinned Arabic-speaking Semites, while what was striking about the Israelis was the predominance of pink-skinned Hebrew-speaking Slavs or Teutons. In their checking the Jordanians were slow-moving but polite, the Israelis quick but abrupt. And these were only the first indications of difference.

It was thanks to Pope Paul that I, a resident in an Arab country, was able to make a double crossing, back-and-forth, between Jordan and Israel. During his pilgrimage to the Holy Land in January 1964 the Pope visited shrines on both sides of the frontier, so as an exceptional case journalists (excluding Arabs and Israelis) were allowed to move freely both ways. On two previous visits to Israel, as well as on two subsequent occasions, I travelled via Cyprus so that I did not pass directly, and in a matter of minutes, from one of its neighbours into Israel. The removal of the political-geographic gap between them helped to bring home the gap that existed on every other plane.

1

Because of the difference in race (which Arab propagandists incorrectly deny) it was natural that the size and shape of the faces and bodies of the inhabitants of the two Jerusalems should not be the same. But what was noticeable was that the normal expression on the faces was different too: on the Arab side there was more lively openness while the Israeli countenance was more withdrawn and worried. Clearly the Israeli has brought the tensions and complexes of Europe with him in his baggage.

In dress, too, there was a contrast between the colourful and varied garb of the Arabs with the more uniform, the more drab and utilitarian dress of the Israelis. For instance, no one in Jordanian Jerusalem wears peaked caps or brimmed felt hats; no one in Israeli Jerusalem wears anything else. The pace of life is also different. The Israeli pedestrian, more so in Tel Aviv than in Jerusalem, hurries along at a pace unseen in any Arab city and he pushes his way brusquely through crowded streets. The speed and impatience of Europe infects the Israeli to a far greater degree than it does the Arab.

This is just one of the easily-observed differences in public behaviour. Perhaps the most striking one is that in the relation of the sexes. Where else in Asia will one see, at all hours of the day, but especially at night, young men and women publicly holding hands or walking with their arms linked, kissing and caressing each other? One sees this even in conservative Jerusalem; in Tel Aviv and Haifa it is common form but not, I believe, in any other major town or city on the mainland of Asia; and only probably in the off-shore islands like Singapore or Hongkong. In the relation of the sexes, that basic element in any society, Israel is unlike any other society in Asia.

There was one recent occasion when the clear differences in appearance, dress and behaviour between Arab and Israeli were singularly apparent. In July 1967, some weeks after the Second Battle for Palestine, I happened to be in Jerusalem on the day when, for the first time in twenty years, the people of the new city were allowed to visit the old city, and it seemed as if the whole population of the Israeli sector emptied itself into the Arab half. Packed tight into the narrow streets of the walled city was a representative mass of the citizenry of Israel, and by no standards could they be described as merging unobtrusively into the surroundings. The men wore unbuttoned shirts and brief shorts, the women transparent, sleeveless blouses, shorts or tight trousers; they held hands or put their arms around each other's waist or shoulders. Under normal circumstances before the Israeli occupation it would have been inconceivable for foreign tourists to dress or behave in this fashion in the old city. Nor was the behaviour of the Israelis very different in front of what is for them the holiest of holy places—the Wailing Wall. I visited the area twice during a Sabbath and for every one Israeli who came to pray there were nine others who came to buy souvenirs or have their photographs taken. The normally devout Jordanians were more perplexed than shocked.

The point to be stressed is that the Israelis I observed were not being deliberately careless or provocative; they were simply being themselves; yet when they behaved in the Arab area as they normally did in the Israeli side they seemed more foreign than the most provincial tourist from the Middle West.

Seldom, if ever, anywhere in Asia, does one cross as abrupt a language barrier as when one crosses into Israel from the landward, Asian approach. At most other frontiers there is some affinity between the languages spoken on each side: but although Arabic and Hebrew belong to the same language family and have some words in common, the European intonations of Hebrew as spoken in Israel make a simple conversation in that language unintelligible to an Arab. The observer is also struck by the wide use of Yiddish among former East European immigrants, and by the way in which many Polish, Hungarian, Rumanian and other former European Jews still keep up their native languages in Israel.

The road from the Mandelbaum Gate into the centre of Israeli Jerusalem skirts the area where it is quite customary to see men dressed in a fashion that, vaguely, recalls the cossacks of the steppes: large, flat hats generously trimmed with fur, a flowing outer robe over a figured waist-coat, and knee-boots. The younger boys also catch the eye with their black hats, black suits and black stockings, and ringlets around the ears. These, of course, are the Orthodox Jews who still wear this seventeenth-century Polish costume that was the uniform of the ghettos in Eastern Europe. They serve as vivid reminders, if the six-pointed Star of David on the flag at the Israeli check-point has not already done so, that Israel has its distinctive religion in Judaism. Distinctive in the sense that while Islam, Hinduism and Buddhism are spread over many Asian countries, Judaism, except for minute colonies, is practised only here. Christianity, like Judaism, was born here in Palestine but later found its main base in Europe. Partly because of the powerful sponsorship of the imperial powers of Europe, Christianity is now found, in some strength, in several Asian countries, seven millions in India alone; Judaism, without such whole-hearted support throughout Asia, is found in strength only in Israel so that it constitutes yet another point of difference from the rest of the continent.

The outward aspect of Israel's largest city, Tel Aviv, as is notorious, partakes of nothing indigenous and the same is true of Israeli additions to Arab towns such as New Nazareth or New Safad. Since modern architecture is wedded to the glass-sided shoebox this is, perhaps, inevitable. But the foreign, grafted-on quality of Israel is observable even in the rural landscape. Arthur Koestler has said that the Israeli kibbutzim reminded him of the Ukraine or Poland;[1] they reminded me of parts of Yugoslavia and Hungary. They also reminded me of another instance where the landscape of part of one continent was made-over to resemble the landscape of a part of another: that was in the Metidja, the rolling plain to the south and east of Algiers, which the French colons had converted into a passable imitation of the Côte d'Or in Burgundy.

So far I have dealt with surface impressions, but as I travelled back and forth across the length and breadth of Israel I could not escape the feeling, pervasive but not easily explicable, that here was a country which in its essential spirit, its basic organisation, in the texture of its daily life, was European. I recalled the remark of a discerning Israeli acquaintance who said of his country "our politics are on the French model, our culture is

---

[1] A. Koestler: *Promise and Fulfilment*, London, 1949, p. 325.

Central European, our civil service is Anglo-Saxon and our people are now mainly European". Setting aside the final phrase for the moment I felt that the preceding remarks, though correct, did not go to the heart of the matter. But after going through the illuminating tables of that voluminous publication *The Statistical Abstract of Israel* I had to admit, however reluctantly, that perhaps Marx supplied the key with his assertion that the economic foundations of a society determined what its cultural and sociological superstructure would be.

According to those tables the economic life of Israel is over 80% non-agricultural and less than 20% agricultural, while the rest of mainland Asia is the exact reverse—over 80% agricultural and less than 20% non-agricultural. During one of my visits to Israel I met with General Moshe Dayan who was then, oddly enough, the Minister of Agriculture and quoted these figures to him. He expressed surprise that agriculture had even that high a percentage in his country and added that if he had his way he would bring it down to 10%. (He commented, with some pride, that in the mechanisation of agriculture Israel came just behind Italy). And when I remarked that this division of labour meant that there was inescapably a wide gap between the socio-economic structure of Israel and that of the rest of Asia he retorted that it was for the Asian countries to try and catch up with Israel. Whether they will and whether they want to is another question, but the fact remains that the gap exists, because the very thought-processes and the fundamental value-judgements of an agricultural society are quite different from those of a non-agricultural country.

What Israel does not have sets her apart from Asia as much as what she does have. The Asian countries may not be as generously endowed with industrial organisation or technical skills but undoubtedly (and perhaps because of that lack) they are gifted with their own many-sided indigenous cultures, which Israel lacks. There is in Israel today (and many Israelis deplore it) no distinctive native food or dress or dance or handicrafts or architecture. Perhaps because the people of Israel are drawn from half a hundred different countries it would be too much to expect a single composite culture, but there is no mosaic of

separate cultures either. The national dance, the Hora, is
Ukrainian and the Israeli national anthem, the "Hatikvah" is
an old Central European folk melody: a waiter once proudly
asked me to partake of an Israeli breakfast, but its bread and
butter, cheese and olives have been eaten in the Levant for
millennia.[2] The Jews who came to Israel did not bring bits
and pieces of culture with them because for the most part they
were not those assimilated to the culture of their countries of
origin—the assimilated Jews did not, and still do not, feel the
need to come to Israel. The vacuum of this cultural anonymity
has to some extent been filled by the one Jewish community
which, moving en bloc, did bring its native culture with it, the
ancient Jewish community of Yemen, which is why Yemeni
dances, jewellery and other handicrafts are so noticeable in
Israel today.

The Yemeni immigrants are a part of Israel's Oriental population, which on paper slightly outnumbers its Occidental
population. In view of this, it has sometimes been argued that
Israel is inevitably an Oriental, or Afro-Asian state.[3] This may
be statistically correct, but it is not the Oriental Jews who give
the state its surface coloration or its essential political and
economic character. The leadership, economic organisation,
political system, cultural life, outlook and dress are all Occidental, with the Oriental majority constituting an internal
proletariat. And, as we shall see later, the Oriental Jews protest,
vigorously and vocally, against this situation. Indeed in the
main towns and cities of Israel the Orientals are barely visible,
especially in Tel Aviv—which may explain the following occurrence. As a brown-skinned Indian I have walked, obviously a
foreigner, through a score of cities from Japan to California but

---

[2]On the other hand Israel's diet is more "Western" than most Western
countries: it has the highest per capita consumption of poultry in the world
and, in 1956, came third in the consumption of eggs, after the U.S. and
Canada. Its consumption of fish is also very high. A. Rubner, *The Economy
of Israel*, London, 1960, p. 103.

[3]J. Parkes: *Arab and Jew in the Middle East*, London, 1967 and "Israel's
Oriental Problem", *Bulletin of the Council of the Sephardic Community*, Jerusalem, vol. II, no. 7–9, pp. 3 – 4.

never have I been stared at so much, because of my foreign-ness, as in the streets of Tel Aviv.

In one way, this did not surprise me. Across the vast breadth of Asia, on one plane of life or another, there is a continuous shading of one country into its neighbour and that into the next; there is never an abrupt and total change into "foreignness". Pakistan is linked to the Arab World and to Iran by religion and its written language, and to India by similarities of race, culture, and spoken language. Buddhism is a bond between India and the whole of South-East Asia and Japan, while Burma has ties of race and language with Thailand and Laos. But between Israel and its Asian neighbours there is just a total difference of outward dress, behaviour, language, food, religion and social organisation. Tel Aviv and Beirut may seem akin, but only at first glance. In essentials, in the daily life of its people, Beirut is not very different from Bombay or Saigon; in the same way Jordanian Jerusalem has much in common with Ispahan or Benares or Kyoto. But Israeli Jerusalem or Tel Aviv are truly similar only to Budapest or Frankfurt.

At the Mandelbaum Gate Asia stopped and Middle Europe began.

The non-Asian origins of Israel

Why, it may be asked, should the Jewish State in Asia be so alien and so non-Asian? There is a simple demographic and mathematical answer: for many centuries the Jews have been a non-Asian people.

In the world today outside Israel there are about thirteen and a half million Jews; thirteen millions are to be found in Europe, North and South America and Australia; the remaining half million are located in the continents of Africa and Asia, and of them a mere 100,000 are in Asia, the mother-continent of the Jewish people.

In any representative collection of Jews the Asian Jews would be in a small minority. It is surprising that in Israel the Oriental Jews should amount to half the population, but that is due partly to an accident of history and partly to the creation, by European Jews, of the State itself.

That Jewry should be so heavily non-Asian is part of the long tragedy of the Jewish people. After the expulsion of the Jews from Palestine by the Emperor Hadrian in the second century the majority of adherents to Judaism, nevertheless, continued to live in "the Orient", that is, in the Levant and along the Mediterranean littoral of North Africa. It was only in the 12th century that the demographic balance was tipped and the majority of Jews, by large-scale conversion or by a higher birth-rate, came to be found in Europe. Since that time, and despite the new concentration of Jews in Israel, Judaism has remained a non-Asian religion.

When they first entered Europe the Jews spread throughout that continent but in their subsequent history we see them, because of persecution, moving across Europe in waves, some slow, some of tidal force and speed, first from west to east and then from east to west.

On two occasions in the history of European Jewry survival was due to the protective hospitality of Islamic rulers. The first time was in the 8th century when the Moorish Conquest of Spain put an end to Christian persecution there. From the 10th century onwards pressure on the Jews in Western Europe slowly increased so that by the 16th century the whole of that area was cleared of Jews, except for small and scattered pockets. The Jewish communities had moved east and found refuge in the Ottoman Empire, Poland and Russia, in whose western provinces, later known as The Pale of Settlement, the main mass of Jewry was assembled.

Under Ottoman rule the Jews lived peaceably, but in Eastern Europe there was always discrimination and active dislike erupting from time to time in pogroms. Despite this, European Jewry, along with all other European peoples, contributed to the population explosion that Europe witnessed in the 19th century. In 1800 European Jewry numbered between 2½ and 3 millions; by 1850 this figure had increased to 5 millions; and by 1914 to more than 12 millions.

And this increase came about despite a massive migration from Eastern to Western Europe and across the Atlantic to America that followed the pogroms in Russia in 1881. Between

1881 and 1914 more than a quarter of the Jewish population of the world was violently displaced, and as a result a new centre of Jewry was created: in these 33 years the Jewish population of the United States increased from less than a quarter of a million to over two millions.

It is a curious fact that while the Jewish population in West European countries trebled in the 19th century, mainly by immigration from the east, in Eastern Europe, despite the outflow, the Jewish population multiplied by five or six times. In 1772 there were 600,000 Jews in Russia, by 1917 they numbered 4 millions.[4]

This great increase in numbers confirmed the trend towards a definite non-Oriental majority within world Jewry. Nor was this trend reversed by yet another violent change in its numbers that took place in Europe in World War II. Six million Jews (out of a total of 25 million civilian victims) were liquidated by the Nazis so that along with emigration, in 1959, European Jewry was reduced to less than 4 millions. But by that date the Jewish community in North America had increased to five and a half millions. Jewry today, according to its main agglomerations, is North American, then European and South American; Africa comes next in the list, followed by Asia (excluding Israel) and Australasia.

Israel, therefore, is necessarily foreign to Asia because it is a state created by European Jews and, after its creation in 1948, was almost exclusively inhabited by them; since then it has been sustained by Jewry in America and Europe.

The circumstances of the creation of the State of Israel in 1948 ensured that the 1948 population should be almost entirely foreign to Asia. This came about through the expulsion of the overwhelming majority of the original native Arab inhabitants of Palestine, who, had they stayed on in the new Jewish state in any numbers, would have provided a link between it and the neighbouring Arab area of West Asia. The figures relative to

[4]These figures are drawn from H. Sacher: *Zionism and the Jewish Future*, London, 1916, pp. 12–14. See also J. Parkes: *The Emergence of the Jewish Problem*, London, 1946, Introduction.

this violent change in population are these: in 1919 when Britain took over the administration of Palestine its population of 700,000 was 8% Jewish, and of that 56,000, about 30,000 had immigrated since 1880. In 1948, through immigration from Europe, the Jewish community had increased to about 600,000 as against 1.2 million Arabs, both Moslem and Christian. By the end of 1949 the Arabs numbered only about 150,000, and with the Jewish population increasing rapidly they were too few, and in too subordinate a position, to be able to give any sort of local colouring to the Jewish State. Before the expansion of Israel following the hostilities in June 1967, it was the Arabs who then formed 10% of the population, an exact reversal of the 1919 figures.

In referring to the movement of the Palestine people out of their country in 1948 I have advisedly used the word "expulsion". For many years and up to the early 1960's, general credence was given to the allegation, put about by the Israelis, that the Palestinians left of their own free will on orders broadcast to them by their leaders who promised that they would be able to return home in a matter of weeks. The painstaking research of such scholars as Erskine Childers[5] and Walid Khalidi[6] has finally disproved this story: they have shown that not only were no such broadcasts made but that, on the contrary, broadcast appeals were directed to the Palestinians urging them not to leave their homes. If they left it was because of military pressure and because of well-publicised acts of terrorism, of which the massacre at the Arab village of Deir Yassin is the best known. Subsequent to the establishment of these facts the then Foreign Minister of Israel, Mrs. Golda Meir asserted, in an interview with me in 1961, that the Palestinians left on Arab orders; but the Israeli Ministry of Foreign Affairs, despite my repeated requests, was unable to provide any documentary proof to support the claim of the Foreign Minister.

Thus the State of Israel, as we know it today, came into existence by the taking-over of an inhabited territory by foreign

---

[5]Erskine Childers, *The Spectator*, May 12, 1961.
[6]Walid Khalidi, *Middle East Forum*, Beirut, November 1959.

immigrants followed by the expulsion of the vast majority of its indigenous inhabitants. There are few parallels in history for such an occurrence. Arab propagandists frequently assert that Israel resembles the white settler regimes in South Africa and Rhodesia. This is an inaccurate comparison. In those two countries the entire state apparatus is in the hands of the settlers but the native inhabitants have remained, and in a very large majority. The same is true of Liberia, even though the newcomers were more or less of the same racial stock as the native inhabitants. The only two precedents in world history would seem to be the expulsion of the Red Indians from their territory by the settlers of North America[7] and that of the German population by the Poles and Russians from the territory east of the Oder-Neisse Line in 1945-46.

Because the creation of Israel produced this drastic population-shift a new and dynamic element was added to all the other constituents of its foreignness to which reference has been made. It meant that Israel was not just an inert foreign body in Asia but an active antigen which the host body was both unwilling and unable to accept. But that Israel should have this quality was inherent in the Zionist movement that brought it into existence.

The present condition of Israel and the ultimate objectives of Zionism have been accurately described in these words of a persuasive advocate of Zionism: "The Crusaders, after all, were the last to attempt what the Israelis have attempted—the transplantation of an European society on to the shores of the Eastern Mediterranean. It is as well to make no mistake about the fact that the Israelis wish to remain European, that their political and social objectives are those of the European Welfare State."[8]

---

[7]Herzl, the founder of political Zionism, refers to his Diaries as being "the log-book of the new *Mayflower*", (*Diaries* p. 574); the American Zionist leader, Judge Louis Brandeis, frequently referred to the settlers in Palestine as "the Jewish Pilgrim Fathers". A. Hertzberg: *The Zionist Idea*, New York, 1959, p. 519.

[8]Max Beloff: "Time, Space and Israel" in *The Mission of Israel*, (ed.). J. Baal, Jeshura, New York, 1963, p. 176.

CHAPTER II

THE MOTIVATIONS OF ZIONISM

The Return

It must have been a powerful force indeed that impelled the Jews of Europe to come to that stretch of the eastern coast of the Mediterranean known as Palestine in order to establish themselves there in a country of their own. The newly independent states of Asia, that came into existence at about the same time as Israel, were the product of nationalist movements. According to the Israelis their state, too, had nationalist roots which, they claim, is one great point of similarity between Israel and the new states of Asia. This nationalist movement among the Jewish people was Zionism.

The word "Zionism" was coined in 1893, which would seem to indicate that the movement is a relatively modern one, like several other nationalisms, especially those of Asia.

The Jewish movement, however, is bound to differ from the Asian nationalisms in one very obvious respect: the latter were freedom movements by people living in certain territories to remove foreign rulers and thus become masters of their own destiny. Jewry in the lands of Dispersion had no single territorial base for all or most of its people—though in the Pale of Settlement it had a large area in which a large number of them lived. A territorial base was the starting point of all the Afro-Asian nationalist movements; to achieve a territorial base was the end, the prime objective, of Zionism.

It is fairly well known that in several countries, India or Algeria for instance, the national movement was not the expression of an already existing nationality or national feeling: rather the national movement created that feeling. Zionism's

task was more complicated: it did not merely have to shape a
people which was there into a nationality, it had to bring a
scattered people into a territory that had to be taken over and
also, simultaneously or subsequently, create out of them a
nation.

At this point three major questions need to be posed. The
first, relatively less important one, is whether a specifically
nationalist feeling did or did not exist in the Jewish people prior
to the organised Zionist movement. The second, far more crucial, question: does the sentiment subsequently engendered by
Zionism truly deserve the name of "nationalism". Thirdly,
and just as important: if Zionism was not a nationalist movement
—what were its actual motivations?

As has been said, the nationalisms of Asia each had a "territorial base," but they had far more than this to work on. This
was so because these "territorial bases" were the sites of ancient
civilisations, whether they were the mountain-girdled plateaux
of Anatolia, Persia and Afghanistan, or the peninsulas of Arabia,
India and Malaysia, or the river-valleys of Tigris-Euphrates,
Irrawaddy, Mekong and Yangtse, or the island groups of
Japan, the Philippines and Indonesia. Within these distinct
geographic entities there were established races with their own
religions, cultures, languages, traditions, and history. These
factors, as well as common territory, were the raw materials
that the Asian nationalists had available from which to build
new national structures. They were all cemented together by
that basic, indispensable, emotion—a love of the motherland.
We have to see whether all, or any, of these factors were available
to the Zionists.

To establish the motivations of Zionism is of more than mere
historical interest. The character of the Asian nationalist movements has been passed on, in some measure, to the nation-states
they produced, even if these states seem disappointingly different
from the original aspirations of the nationalist leaders. This is
true also of Zionism and the State of Israel: the internal day-to-
day politics of Israel, her relations with her neighbours, her
foreign policy, are all still to a large extent determined by the
character and motivations of the Zionist movement.

Because of the peculiar situation of the Jewish people, it is very difficult, if not impossible, to define precisely what sort of a movement Zionism is, and this differentiates it from other nationalist movements in Afro-Asia.

One Zionist has said "Zionism is an ideal and, as such, indefinable",[1] another asks "What is Zionism? Certainly in its essence and aim it is Palestine; but at the same time it is all that is strongest, deepest, most vital in the Judaism of the whole world",[2] an answer which, in itself, is an excellent example of how Zionism swings between the particular and the general, between politics and religion.

The Encyclopaedia Britannica defines Zionism, quite simply, as "Jewish reaction to Gentile anti-Semitism".[3]

Thus, at the outset it can be seen that the motivations of Zionism could be either religious or racial feelings, a political idea, or the desire to escape from anti-Semitic persecution, or a combination of these.

Within most nationalist movements there were various, even antagonistic, schools of strategy. But these divided on the same two, rather simple, issues: should the methods to be used be violent or constitutional, and should independence be demanded in toto and forthwith or by stages over a period of time. Within Zionism, however, there were differences not only over methods but even over the principal objective.

Hence the surprisingly large number of varieties of Zionism that crop up in its history: philanthropic Zionism, practical Zionism, political Zionism, synthetic Zionism, cultural Zionism, spiritual Zionism and religious Zionism; also socialist Zionism, as well as minimal Zionism, folk Zionism, and messianic Zionism; nor is this a complete listing, for there was also non-Zion Zionism.

It is especially bewildering to discover that the principal founder of Zionism as a large-scale organised movement, Theo-

[1]S. Schechter in Hertzberg, *op. cit.*, p. 505.
[2]N. Sokolow in *Zionism: Problems and Views*, eds. Goodman and Lewis, London, 1916, p. 31.
[3]1943 Edition.

dor Herzl, began as a wholly non-Zion Zionist, moved through a partial non-Zion stage and became a fully Zionist Zionist in the last year of his life.

But perhaps these numerous appellations are all only new names for a very ancient feeling, the desire of the Jewish people to fulfil the prophecy of the Return to the Holy Land as enunciated in the books of the Old Testament. It may seem strange, even to some Jews, that a 20th century movement should be based on religious texts dating from the Later Bronze Age. Yet because of the part they play in Zionist apologetics, if not in the Zionist movement itself, one has to take note of the Covenant entered into by the Jewish people with their God Jehovah who made them His "Chosen People" and gave them the Promised Land of Palestine. These happenings are recorded in the book of Genesis. In later prophetic books, especially Isaiah, there is the further promise that the scattered Jewish people shall be gathered together again in Palestine which will presage the arrival of the Messiah.[4] The Promise and the Return are the religious bases of Zionism.

Jewish and Christian theologians have debated these texts interminably, arguing over the exact geographic limits of the Promised Land and as to whether they are to be applied literally to the Jewish people alone or in a metaphorical sense to all mankind.[5] These discussions are of little practical value and less interest, except to fundamentalist Christians.

What is truly relevant is the fact that the emotion surrounding the idea of The Return was sustained through the centuries by two powerfully evocative sayings, or slogans. The first comes from the 137th Psalm, describing the Jews in exile in Babylon, where they raise the cry "If I forget thee, O Jerusalem, let my right hand forget its cunning". These words occur in the prayers which Jews are expected to repeat three times a day. The second

[4]A representative selection of these Biblical texts is given by N. Barbour in his *Nisi Dominus*, London, 1946, pp. 12–15.

[5]A mercifully brief example of these disputations is A. Guillaume, "Zionists and the Bible", in *Palestine and the Bible*, Institute for Palestine Studies, Beirut, 1967.

sentence is the toast drunk during the observance of the Passover festival—"Next year in Jerusalem". In their own, less obvious, fashion these words have had as great an impact on the course of history as "Liberty, equality, fraternity" or "Workers of the world, unite".

Perhaps because of the strength of the feelings about The Return in popular Judaism, in all lands and at all times, it has even been said that Zionism began with the Exodus from Egypt and the Return from the Babylonian Exile.[6]

Those words are a fine rhetorical flourish, with a grain of truth in them. A more sober estimate of the part played by religion in the Zionist movement and in the creation of the State of Israel has been provided by that learned Gentile Zionist, the Reverend James Parkes.[7] Setting out to describe the five roots of Israel Dr. Parkes begins with the cautionary words: "Whereas the Arab case is a normal one, and easy to understand, for it rests on the normal association of a people with the land in which it has lived for centuries, the Jewish case is not easy to appreciate"[8] (notwithstanding which the Arab case has not been so well understood as the Jewish one). The first root of Israel is Judaism, for "secularist Zionism cannot alter the fact that the deepest root from which the State of Israel has sprung is the Jewish religion".[9] The second root is the Messianic Hope that the Jewish people would be summoned home by the Messiah's coming. Jewish history, with its record of persecution, is given as the third root, and the continuity of Jewish life in Israel as the fourth. The fifth and last root is the relation of Palestine Jewry to the Jewish World. It is doubtful whether the hard-headed politicians who are now the leaders of Israel would give the same primacy to the religious motivation, though very many Zionist theoreticians do include the age-old aspiration for The Return as among one of the major impulses of the Zionist movement. To use the words of the first President of Israel:

[6]N. Sokolow: *History of Zionism*, vol. 1, London, 1919, p. xiv.
[7]J. Parkes: *Five Roots of Israel*, London, 1964.
[8]*Op. cit.*, p. 3.
[9]*Op. cit.*, p. 5.

"Palestine has this magic and romantic appeal for the Jews."[10]

Fortunately or unfortunately magic and romance play a very small part in the lives of ordinary human beings, Jews included. Hence it is that though Jewry pledged every day not to forget Jerusalem and nursed the longing to return to it, very few Jews actually went there either on pilgrimage or to settle even when there were no obstacles in the way of The Return.

Herzl himself seems to have had little patience with such romantic ideas. Writing to the Chief Rabbi of Vienna in 1896 he said: "And how was this revaluation of the symbolism of the The Return, so frequently mentioned in Jewish prayer, to be understood? Why, whenever the Return to Zion is spoken, the very opposite is to be read into it".[11] Those were harsh words, but not far from the truth, because through the ages only a very thin trickle of Jews made the journey of return to Palestine. Indeed, even in Hellenistic times, at least as many Jews had lived outside Palestine as in it. In later ages the number of Jews in the country "must have sunk to a very few thousands" and indigenous Jews who could claim that their ancestors had never known exile dwindled to a single village by the 19th century—the remote hill village of Pekiin in Galilee.[12]

There was no political obstacle in the way of Jewish immigrants because "The Moslem rulers seem at no period to have refused to allow Jews from foreign countries to enter and settle in Palestine. This (i.e. settlement) was not a permission granted to Western Christians".[13] It was only in 1885, after the arrival of the first Zionist settlers from Rumania in 1882, that the then Sultan Abdul Hamid for the first time in history ordained that Jews might enter as pilgrims only, not as settlers, "though the law was never strictly enforced". But even this, and subsequent restrictive laws, applied only to foreign Jews; Jews who were citizens of the Ottoman Empire, and there were many hundreds of thousands of them in countries neighbouring on Palestine,

[10]Chaim Weizmann: *Trial and Error*, London, 1950, p. 143.
[11]*Diaries*, p. 221.
[12]J. Parkes: *History of Palestine*, London, 1949, p. 182.
[13]*Op. cit.*, p. 179.

could at all times settle in Palestine.[14] In 1814 it is estimated
that there were only about 10,000 Jews in Palestine and by 1914
a mere 35,000 Jews out of 12 millions had obeyed the thrice-daily
injunction not to forget Jerusalem to the extent of making The
Return to The Promised Land. This is conclusive proof that
"after all that has been written as to the place occupied by Palestine in the heart of the Jewish people, Palestine as a land to live
in has but little hold upon the individual Jew".[15] Indeed one
Zionist writer made mention of "the reproach that Palestine is
less visited by Jews than by any other denomination".[16]

    In earlier ages, it could of course be argued, Jews were
deterred from going to Palestine by the dangers and difficulties
of the journey. No such barrier stood in the way of Jews in
nearby Egypt or in what is now Syria and Lebanon, but they
seem to have preferred to remain in Cairo, Damascus and Beirut.
Nor, in fact, did physical barriers prevent Jews making ready to
go to Palestine, and even travelling part of the way thereto, when
they were seized with the conviction that the Messiah's return
was imminent. No less than three of these false Messiahs presented themselves to the Jewish people and as early as 1096 we read
of Jews from all the countries of Europe gathering at Salonika
to take ship to Palestine; there were similar scenes of enthusiasm
in 1665.[17] These incidents would seem to show that occasional
gusts of messianic expectation were able to uproot Jews and,
despite difficulties of travel, move them towards Palestine but
that, over the centuries, there was no correspondingly strong
steady and continuing urge to make The Return.

    If the religiously-motivated call of The Return to the Holy
Land brought very few Jews to Palestine, the secular urgings of
the Zionist movement to return to the Land of Israel had only a
slightly greater degree of success. In the years between 1885
and 1914 about 30,000 Jews emigrated to Palestine, of whom
12,000 were working on the land. The majority of these were

[14]*Op. cit.*, pp. 267–271.
[15]P. Horowitz: *The Jewish Question and Zionism*, London, 1927, pp. 74–75.
[16]H. Bentwich, letter to *The Jewish World*, 21.1.1897.
[17]Parkes, *op. cit.*, p. 175.

probably only escaping persecution and Tsarist conscription, and not following the call of Zion. The Zionists reproached themselves bitterly for this lack of response. In 1914 one prominent Zionist leader commented: "if only a handful of young men can be found among 12 million people to give their sweat, then this is a sign, the sign of Cain, that the hucksters cleave to their huckstering because they lack strength for anything better".[18]

The positive reluctance of Jews to go to Palestine in any numbers, to respond to the call of the Land, whether emanating from Judaism or from Zionism, is even more noticeable after 1919 when Britain became the administering power in Palestine. From then on the British authorities promoted and facilitated immigration. Travel had become very much easier and Jewish settlement was financed from abroad. Yet in the twelve years from 1920 to 1932 only 118,000 Jews, 0.75% of world Jewry, entered Palestine. In 1927 more people left Palestine than went in, and for the year 1928 the net gain through immigration was exactly ten persons.

At this point of time, according to one friend of Zion, the Jews lost the chance of settling the Palestine question swiftly and decisively before it became a real problem. R.H.S. Crossman deplores the fact that in 1919-1920 World Jewry failed "to fulfil its share of the task, the provision of half a million immigrants in the first few years".[19] He blames the Russian revolution for cutting off the flow of potential immigrants but there were very large Jewish communities in Eastern and Central Europe—to say nothing of America—which could have provided the needed half million Jews. They did not because the pull of Palestine was just not strong enough.

This has always been so throughout the many centuries of Jewish history: it is well known that most of the Jews who were led away into Babylonian exile, and who first made the promise not to forget Jerusalem, nevertheless remained in Babylon when they were permitted to return to Jerusalem and their mother-

[18]J. H. Brenner in Hertzberg, *op. cit.*, p. 309.
[19]R. H. S. Crossman: *A Nation Reborn*, London, 1960, p. 62.

land.

Difficulties of travel in the Ottoman Empire in its last decades may have stopped some Jews from going to Palestine. But nothing could stop them from going to the Promised Land in their imagination, that is if they did feel the strong urge to return. Yet there is curiously little about Palestine in modern Hebrew art or literature. One looks in vain for "songs of Zion", the note of nostalgic yearning seems to have expended itself with the Psalmist and the prophet Isaiah. Zion was on the lips of the Jewish people every day but, according to the testimony of the artists, it had little place in their imagination or in their hearts.[20]

Accordingly the idea of The Return as such, whether religious or secular, the sheer love of the land of Palestine, cannot be accepted as one of the major motivations of the Zionist movement: it provided an emotional aura, no more. The immemorial magic "romantic" appeal of Eretz Israel for the children of Israel is best summed-up in this epitaph of a distinguished British historian: "the fact remains that in all those years this course (to Palestine) was not much taken... when they left (Russia or Poland) with the Holy Land on their lips, their feet carried them resolutely in the other direction, to Germany or England or America. Even when—like the expelled Sephardim of Spain—they went to the hospitable, tolerant Turkish Empire... it is odd how few of them went to Palestine, which was after all an easily accessible and under-populated part of that empire. There was a trickle, but not a stream... Romantic idealists may look back and discover the origins of this adventure in the dreams of mediaeval mystics, the vaticinations of Polish rabbis. Now that the ground is gained, the myth may safely be incorporated in the title deed".[21]

The myth, however, has not been buried, but instead reincarnated in another form. Instead of its religious aura the

---

[20]R.F. Mintz: *Modern Hebrew Poetry*, Berkeley, 1966; D. Patterson: *The Hebrew Novel in Czarist Russia*, Edinburgh, 1964; appendices on *Modern Hebrew Literature* and *Zionism and Modern Art* in Sokolow's *History of Zionism*, vol. 2.

[21]H.R. Trevor-Roper: *Jewish and Other Nationalism*, the Fifth Herbert Samuel lecture, London, 1962, pp. 13–15.

myth of The Return has been politicised to fit the world of the post-colonial era. Thus it is that the creation of Israel is represented as The Return of a people originally Asian to its old Asian homeland. But this claim, as we shall see, is as mythical as any earlier one.

* * *

The use of religion and race

When expatiating on the influence of Judaism on Zionism many pro-Zionists, both Jews and Gentiles, make the claim that since the Jew is unique, by being simultaneously a member of a race and a religion, so also is Judaism unique by combining religion with nationalism. Thus the holy books of Judaism are not merely religious texts but are also the history of the ancient Jewish race and descriptive of the geography and ecology of Palestine. Lord Balfour, who played a decisive role in the life of modern Jewry, makes the claim for uniqueness in these words: "none suggest that we plant Buddhist colonies in India...or renew in favour of Christendom the crusading adventures of our mediaeval ancestors. The answer is, that the cases are not parallel. The position of the Jews is unique. For them race, religion and country are inter-related as in the case of no other race, no other religion, and no other country on earth"...The Jews' religious aspirations and hopes are "expressed in language and imagery so utterly dependent for their meaning on the conviction that only from this one land, only through this one history, only by this one people, is full religious knowledge to be spread through all the world".[22] Or, put more succinctly "through the life of a nation the revealed will of God was done".[23]

A preliminary comment must be that if Balfour's interpretation of Judaism is correct then that religion displays a dogmatic certainty strikingly at variance with the tolerance and eclecticism that marks the other religions of Asia.

But even the claim to uniqueness in the world cannot be sus-

[22]A. J. Balfour, Introduction to Sokolow's *History of Zionism*.
[23]Parkes, *Five Roots of Israel*, p. 7.

tained because the Hindu and Hinduism have the same inter-mingled characteristics as the Jew and Judaism; provided his mother is Jewish, a Jew, for instance, does not cease to be a Jew if he is an atheist or even converts to another religion: the Hindu also inherits his religion through birth. Likewise, until the fairly recent creation of secular Indian nationalism, Hinduism was a combination of religion and racial or national feeling because the land of India, Bharat Mata, is as intertwined with Hinduism as Palestine is with Judaism.

Yet despite this intertwining of religion and a territorial feeling, Hinduism in the lands of its Dispersion, to which it was carried by Indian settlers, did not develop a "magic" or "roman-tic" doctrine of the Return to the Holy Land of Hindustan. The West Indian novelist of Indian descent, V.S. Naipaul, has described how completely Hinduism was transferred to the West Indies, including the full paraphernalia of caste. The food, dress and the domestic architecture of the Indian community there were all strictly Indian. Yet he adds that the journey from India to the West Indies was final for there was no widespread hankering for a Return[24]—and when Naipaul himself paid a visit to India his feeling was one of revulsion. Thus a religion completely similar to Judaism in its complex mixture of religion and territorial feeling did not produce anything similar to the Zionist longing for Palestine; and, as we have seen, this longing within the Zionist movement was not a force of any great power or practical effectiveness.

Yet the claim to uniqueness and the comparison with Hin-duism does suggest another motivation for Zionism—partly religious, partly political. Is Zionism the political expression of a religious community that is rendered all the more possible because of the peculiar, though not the unique, intertwining of "race, religion and country" in Judaism? Certainly a great many Zionists gave this interpretation to their movement. To put it more bluntly, did Zionism use religion for political pur-poses?

On this matter there were two schools of thought among the

[24]V. S. Naipaul: *An Area of Darkness*, London, 1964, pp. 30-33.

Zionist leaders. The larger and more influential section, including Herzl, simply tried to utilise the link that Judaism provided
with the land of Palestine while denying that Zionism had any
essential links with Judaism. The smaller group claimed that
Judaism was the national religion of the Jewish people and that
it was the task of Zionism to provide that people with a national
territorial base in Palestine, the land consecrated by Judaism.
Leaders in the first group calmly and deliberately utilised
Judaism because it was useful in providing a certain emotional
impulsion; the second group depended on Judaism in their
Zionist work because they linked the "Jewish nationalism" of
Zionism with the "religious nationalism" of Judaism. And not
a few of these leaders propagated both points of view.

Herzl was so little connected with Jewry, let alone with Judaism, that in his writings before he took up the idea of the
Jewish state, there are "scarcely a dozen lines of passing references to Jews".[25] His detachment from Judaism was also shown
in a remark he made in a letter written in 1893: "the real and
definitive solution (of the Jewish problem) could only be in the
complete disappearance of the Jews through baptism and inter-
marriage".[26] Herzl followed up this train of thought in the
quite extraordinary plan he proposed later, in 1893, by which
he would approach the Pope and promise to begin a movement
for the open, mass conversion of Jews to Roman Catholicism in
return for the Pope's help in stemming the rising tide of anti-
Semitism: he envisaged the conversion even of his own children.[27]

It is notorious that Herzl was unmoved by any special religious
appeal emanating from Palestine or Jerusalem. In the most
important of all the Zionist texts, his *Der Judenstaat*, The
State of Jews, or The Jewish State as it is usually and inaccur-
ately translated, he keeps a completely open mind on the comparative merits of Palestine or Argentina as the site of the State:
"we shall take what is given us and what is selected by Jewish
public opinion".[28] Coolly appraising the role of Palestine in

[25]Hertzberg, *op. cit.*, p. 25.
[26]A. Bein: *Theodor Herzl*, London, 1957, p. 89.
[27]Bein, *op. cit.*, p. 94.
[28]Theodor Herzl: *The Jewish State*, London, 1946, 4th Edition, p. 30.

Zionism, he wrote: "Palestine is our ever-memorable historic home. The very name of Palestine would attract our people with a force of marvellous potency"; and "in its favour is the mighty legend".[29] Nor did Herzl display any great warmth for Jerusalem, the pulsing heart of the emotion for The Return. Far from wanting to make it the capital of any future Jewish State, he declared "we shall extraterritorialise Jerusalem which will then belong to nobody and yet to everybody...the great condominium of culture and morality"[30]—but not of religion. Herzl did pay a visit to Palestine and Jerusalem but it was not as a pilgrim. He went there as a politician and only because he wanted to meet the Kaiser for a political discussion; and when recording his brief, hurried visit Herzl complains a good deal about the heat and the discomfort of the Holy Land.

Parodying the ancient invocation, he wrote in his diary: "When I remember thee in days to come, O Jerusalem, it will not be with pleasure. The musty deposits of two thousand years of inhumanity, intolerance and uncleanliness lie in the foul-smelling alleys". He did have what he called "great moments" when he looked down on Jerusalem from the Mount of Olives but his hopes for the city were those of an enlightened town-planner, not those of a religious devotee.[31]

Max Nordau, who was perhaps Herzl's closest collaborator, denied the connection between Zionism and Judaism more explicitly. At the 4th Zionist Congress he asked in a speech: "Why did we become Zionists? Perhaps because of a mystical yearning for Zion? Of that most of us are free".[32] He had earlier referred to talk of a special Jewish "mission" as "claptrap" and "a folly".[33]

Nor were Herzl and Nordau the only Zionist leaders to deny the connection between Zionism and Judaism. Among a large number one can select, at random, people like M.J. Berdichev-ski, who criticised the vagueness of such ideas as Jewish culture

[29]*Op. cit.*, pp. 30, 56.
[30]*Diaries*, pp. 345-346.
[31]*Op. cit.*, pp. 745, 753.
[32]M. Ben Horin: *Max Nordau*, London, 1956, p. 199.
[33]*Op. cit.*, p. 183.

or Jewish nationalism, and also J. Klatzkin who went further and maintained that talk of spiritual uniqueness, of destiny and mission was the mark of the abnormality of an un-nation. "To be a Jew" he declared, "means the acceptance of neither a religious nor an ethical creed".

The Zionist writers who linked Zionism with Judaism as a national religion either asserted this as a bold fact, or else indulged in the circular argument that Zionism, the movement of the Jewish people, was nationalist because the Jews were a "nation"; also that Zionism was nationalist because it obviously was connected with Judaism, the "national" faith of that people; but no clear definition of the word "national" was ever offered. It was one of the earliest Zionist thinkers, Moses Hess, who in his work *Rome and Jerusalem*, published in 1862, first linked the idea of Zionism with national Judaism. "Judaism is... organically related to Jewish nationalism. Judaism is above all a nationality";[34] "the Jewish religion is primarily Jewish patriotism"[35] and "the Jew who does not believe in the national rebirth of his people can work only for the liquidation of his people".[36] These assertions and arguments continued in much the same form for the next 75 years till in 1925 we find no less a person than Albert Einstein saying "Zionism springs from an even deeper motive than Jewish suffering. It is rooted in a Jewish spiritual tradition, whose maintenance and development are for Jews the raison d'être of their continued existence as a community...the re-establishment of the Jewish nation".[37]

To the intertwining of race and religion in Judaism the Zionists added the third strand of nationality so that it became possible for Zionist leaders, who had denied that there was any religious element in Zionism, to assert that it was based on the nationality principle in Judaism. Hence Herzl himself wrote: "We recognize ourselves as a nation by our faith"[38] and "we feel our historic

---

[34]Moses Hess: *Rome and Jerusalem*, New York, 1958, p. 19.
[35]*Op. cit.*, p. 28.
[36]*Op. cit.*, p. 58.
[37]Albert Einstein: *About Zionism*, London, 1930, pp. 56-58.
[38]*Diaries*, p. 56.

affinity only through the faith of our fathers".[39] The linking of religion and politics he expresses thus: "you do not understand imponderables? And what is religion? Bethink yourself what the Jews have endured for two thousand years for the sake of this fantasy...Certainly this national fantasy must rest on practical foundations".[40] And the sceptical atheist Nordau told the 2nd Zionist Congress: "the Zionists are not a party, they are Judaism itself...we must no longer speak of Zionism. What we are now called upon to realize is not Zionism but Judaism".[41] Non-religious Judaism was thus fully incorporated into the political programme of Zionism.

The real ambivalent confusion on this issue is best expressed by Ahad Ha'am (Asher Ginzberg), the founder of "spiritual Zionism", who, writing to Judah Magnes, in 1910, said "you say you want 'to propagate national religion and religious nationalism'. I must confess that this formula is not altogether clear to me. 'National religion'—by all means: Judaism is fundamentally national... But when you talk of propagating 'religious nationalism' I do not know what you mean (unless you are simply saying the same thing in other words). Do you really think of excluding from the ranks of the nationalists all those who do not believe in the principles of religion? If that is your intention, I cannot agree...If it is impossible to be a Jew in the religious sense without acknowledging our nationality, it is possible to be a Jew in the national sense without accepting many things in which religion requires belief".[42]

Perhaps we can arrive at a genuine estimate of the importance of Judaism as a motivating force in Zionism by considering this striking biographical fact: the majority of Zionist leaders, past and present, did not and do not believe in or practise the Jewish faith; they were and are lapsed Jews, agnostics when they are not atheists. In his masterly volume on *The Zionist Idea* Hertzberg anthologises the works of 37 of the most influential Zionists and where he notes their spiritual condition in his

[39] *The Jewish State*, p. 54.
[40] Bein, *op. cit.*, p. 116.
[41] Ben Horin, *op. cit.*, p. 191.
[42] Hertzberg, *op. cit.*, pp. 261-262.

introductory notes we find that no less than 21 abandoned Judaism: these include most of the famous names in Zionist history—Hess, Smolenskin, Pinsker, Herzl, Nordau, Ahad Ha'am, Syrkin, Borochov, Gordon, Weizmann and Ben Gurion. It is noteworthy that of the 21 no less than 13 were either the sons or grandsons of rabbis, or were students in yeshiva religious schools or, in their earlier years, Talmudic scholars. When they abandoned Judaism it was as a conscious action; but nevertheless, their Jewish upbringing left its mark on them so that Judaism coloured their Zionist thinking even when their Zionist activity was not religiously motivated.

It is perhaps the most striking of the many paradoxes in Zionism that the principal leaders of the movement to found a state for the Jews were not Jews in their religious beliefs. As a Zionist historian asks: "what made it possible for the 'neo-messianists' vehemently to deny God and yet insist that they could rebuild the Jewish nation only on the land He had promised to Abraham?"[43] He gave no answer.

Theodor Herzl said of himself "I am a freethinker",[44] and it is in the privacy of the pages of his diary that we may see, with brutal, startling clarity exactly how the author of *The Jewish State* planned to harness Judaism to the tasks of state-building

He was more than a little impatient of the organised faith. His "Jewishness", he wrote, had "nothing to do with affected religiosity."[45] When considering the place of religion in the Jewish State he said "we shall let every man find salvation over there in his own particular way. Above and before all we shall make room for the immortal band of our Freethinkers who are continually making new conquests for humanity".[46] During his visit to Jerusalem he was told that it was forbidden for Jews to enter the Temple area, on pain of being excommunicated by the rabbis: "how much superstition and fanaticism on every

[43]*Op. cit.*, pp. 74-75.
[44]*Diaries,* p. 283.
[45]*Diaries,* p. 111.
[46]*Op. cit.,* p. 155.

side! Yet I am not afraid of any of these fanatics"[47] he commented.

Herzl knew no Hebrew, the sacred tongue, nor anything of the ritual of the synagogue, so when during one of the Zionist Congresses he was invited to pronounce the benediction in the Basle synagogue he had "the few Hebrew words" "drilled into him" and pronouncing them caused him "more anxiety than the Congress speeches".[48] A supremely ironic touch is that when, in the stormy and crucial 5th Congress, Herzl wished to impress the assembly with his devotion to Palestine by reciting in Hebrew the prime slogan of Zionism about not forgetting Jerusalem he had to have the words written out for him in Latin script.[49]

Perhaps because of these occasional ceremonial acts the anti-clerical Weizmann records that at one point he was distressed by Herzl's "excessive respect for the Jewish clergy", while reporting that the Rabbis said of Herzl that "far from understanding true Judaism... (he) considers all great Rabbis, heads of congregations and Jewish scholars, as being valueless".[50]

If Herzl did show the clergy any respect it was because he considered them not at all "valueless" for his programme of arousing the Jews to leave Europe for a new home. In *The Jewish State* he anticipated that "our Rabbis, on whom we especially call, will devote their energies to the service of our idea, and will inspire their congregations by preaching it from the pulpit... an appeal such as this may be uttered in the synagogue".[51] He elaborated on this idea in his diary: "The Rabbis... will impart their enthusiasm to the others from their pulpits. Imagine with what fervour our old saying 'Next year in the Promised Land' will be spoken henceforth. There is no need to call any special assemblies with a lot of blather. This propaganda will be included in the religious service and properly so... The Rabbis will then regularly receive the advices of the Society of Jews and announce and interpret them to their congrega-

[47]*Op. cit.*, p. 747.
[48]*Op. cit.*, pp. 588-589.
[49]A. Bein: *Theodor Herzl*, New York, 1956, plates, pp. 120-123.
[50]Weizmann, *op. cit.*, p. 24.
[51]*The Jewish State*, p. 54.

tions".[52] Herzl also had in mind more specific tasks for the rabbis to fulfil, such as recruiting agents, not only from their normal congregations but from among wealthy Jews whose financial assistance was needed to build up the new Jewish state: "I shall ask the millionaires who still have Jewishness in their hearts to meet with a rabbi who will read my address to them. The rabbis who do not wish to come along will be shunted aside. But the rabbis will be the pillars of my organisation and I shall honour them for it... As a reward they will be formed into a fine proud hierarchy which, to be sure, will always remain subordinated to the State".[53]

Herzl planned to make use of the power of popular Judaism in another way to draw the average Jew to the new country. "Do I need to illustrate the phenomenon of masses and the ways of attracting them to any spot by discussing religious pilgrimages too?" He notes that Christians and Muslims travel in large numbers to Lourdes and Mecca. "So over there we will build a more beautiful Sadagora* for the Wonder Rabbi."[54]

Although he may have thought that the Rabbis would be useful, Herzl's basic dislike for the clergy remained. Later in the diary he gives a satirical analysis of how the Wonder Rabbis gain power over their congregations not through any spiritual qualities but simply by having good connections; they are, he concludes, "simply peddlers of influence".[55]

It could be that Herzl's views on the utility of Judaism and the clergy were not confined to the pages of his diary; it is likely, too, that they were shared by other Zionist leaders, agnostics also, who formed his circle. It is this that may have led Ahad Ha'am to deplore the fact that "almost all our great men,— those, that is, whose education and social position have prepared them to be at the head of the Jewish State—are spiritually far removed from Judaism, and have no true conception of its nature

*Sadagora was a famous centre of Jewish pilgrimage in Rumania.
[52]*Diaries*, p. 151.
[53]*Op. cit.*, p. 103.
[54]*Op. cit.*, p. 155.
[55]*Op. cit.*, p. 641.

and its value".[56] But Ahad Ha'am was himself a non-believer who wanted to use religion, though in a different way, to buttress his non-religious "spiritual Zionism". He advocated the observance of traditional religious practices because they had "a national sanction" and were "the holy things of the nation".[57] This observance without belief recalls a similar idea of that other agnostic, Moses Hess, who decided that since Judaism was "a national cult" he would "observe the fasts and feasts...to keep alive...the Jewish folk traditions".[58]

This anthropological or folklorist approach to Judaism by these Zionists was perhaps less brutal, but also less honest, than that of Herzl, but essentially it was the same thing—an attempt by a political movement not to draw strength from religion but to make use of it.

True religion, with its universalistic appeal, has always been antagonistic to the divisive, particularistic loyalties of nationalism and political movements. This was, and still is, true of that Judaism, both of the Orthodox and the Reform varieties, which has been consistently antagonistic to Zionism and so can hardly be accounted one of the motivations of that movement. It was the Association of German Rabbis who opposed the holding of the 1st Zionist Congress in Munich in 1897, obliging it to be transferred to Basle; and in the same year the Central Conference of American Rabbis "resolved, that we totally disapprove of any attempt for the establishment of a Jewish State".

Even as early a proponent of Zionism as Moses Hess, sensing—quite correctly—the ineluctable antagonism between the politicised Judaism of Zionism and Judaism as such pronounced the doom of Orthodoxy in 1862: "the forms of Orthodox Judaism, which until the century of rebirth were perfectly justified, will disintegrate naturally by themselves, through the power of the living idea of Jewish nationalism and its religious history".[59] This prophecy has not been fulfilled because ordinary, organised Judaism has been taken over and politicised by the Zionists,

[56]Hertzberg, op. cit., p. 268.
[57]Ahad Ha'am: Essays, Letters, Memoirs, Oxford, 1946, p. 45.
[58]Hess, op. cit., pp. 50, 51.
[59]Hess, op. cit., p. 37.

on the lines indicated by Herzl. Large numbers of Orthodox Jews have been brought into Zionism by the Mizrachi Zionist movement, founded 40 years after Hess made his comments on Orthodoxy. Nevertheless religious opposition to Zionism still continues today, both within and outside Israel. Such opposition is not confined only to the ultra-Orthodox (who do not recognise the existence of the State) but is also to be found among pious but modern-minded Jews. The latter are probably nearer to the true spirit of Judaism than are the members of Israel's state-supported Grand Rabbinate who, "as a reward" for supporting Zionism, have been "formed into a fine proud hierarchy".

This account of the relations between Zionism and the Jewish religion will seem familiar, and ominously so, to anyone conversant with the modern history of South Asia, West Asia and Japan. Zionism reminds the Asian observer of the extremist politico-religious groups which mobilise themselves on the fringe of Asian politics.

The form of Zionism that claimed the purely religious idea of The Return as its motivation is similar to the Hindu revivalist movement of the Arya Samaj in India with its harking back to the ancient glories of Hindustan or Aryavarta. It also recalls the glorification of ancient Nippon by the Shintoism of Imperial Japan.

More striking still is the resemblance between politico-religious Zionism and exactly similar movements in present-day Japan and South and West Asia. Here one can list the Sokakgakai in Japan, that bases itself on Buddhism; the Buddhist political movements associated with the names of U Nu and S.W.R. Bandaranaike in Burma and Ceylon, respectively; the Jan Sangh offshoot of the Arya Samaj in India; and the Muslim Brotherhood in Egypt.

A Zionist may argue that if similarities exist between Zionism and these movements in several countries spread across the continent, then clearly Zionism is akin to, or is in tune with, an important element in Asian political thought or feeling.

Such a conclusion would not be valid because these politico-religious movements are not part of the mainstream of Asian nationalism, which is secular; they are in fact in opposition to

nationalist governments. Earlier in the century Ataturk in
Turkey and Reza Shah in Iran had to break the opposition of
the imams and the mullahs. The Buddhist movements in Burma
and Ceylon became so intolerant and violent that they have
had to be pushed aside. In India the militant wing of the Jan
Sangh, the R.S.S., were responsible for killing Mahatma Gandhi
and went into eclipse; and in Japan the Sokakgakai is viewed
with nervous suspicion. The Muslim Brotherhood in Egypt has
had to be strenuously suppressed because of its addiction to con-
spiratorial violence. They are the whirlpools and eddies in the
shallows off the main secular current of Asian nationalism.

The sense of apartness

In India, and also in Belgium and Wales, separatist nationalisms, or, more correctly, sub-nationalisms base themselves on
the claim of a separate language. Herzl was the first to dismiss
language as a possible base for Zionism because of the all-too-
obvious fact that Jews in the Dispersion spoke the various languages of their countries of residence. In his plans for the Jewish
State he envisaged that the immigrants would speak their several
tongues but anticipated that German might become the lingua
franca.[60] Herzl could not foresee the revival of Hebrew as a
living language due to the devoted work of Ben Yehuda. But
that linguistic re-creation came some years after Zionism was
an established movement and was a by-product, not a motivating cause.

After the horrors of racial persecution visited upon the Jews
of Eastern and Central Europe in the last fifty years it may seem
cruelly ironic to even attempt to interpret Zionism as the political
expression of a racial or ethnic community. Herzl, always a
realist, rejected the idea but a few other Zionist leaders did not.
In his diary Herzl describes his first meeting with the British
Zionist, Israel Zangwill, and notes that Zangwill was "a long-
nosed Negroid type, with very woolly deep-black hair... his
point of view is a racial one—which I cannot accept if I so much

as look at him and myself".[61] Zangwill was not alone in his racial ideas. The gentle and idealistic Gordon asked: "what is this national sentiment? Wherein is its strength? We have no country of our own, we have no living national language... Religion? But our religion is on the wane...there is a primal force within every one of us...This is our ethnic self".[62] And the American Zionist, R. Gottheil, claimed that "Zionism has sought and found for us a basis which is broader than the religious one, that of race and nationality."[63]

These, however, were minority views and most Zionists today would accept the scientific finding that by tests based on physical size, colour of hair and eyes, shape of the nose, and of blood "any claim that the Jews have a racial entity cannot be met".[64]

Yet in the writings of the earlier Zionists, before the concept of "race" became sinister and suspect, we have expressions of extreme racialism. The most startling examples of these boastful claims are to be found in that basic Zionist text, *Rome and Jerusalem* by Moses Hess. In it, this former friend and colleague of Karl Marx, writes "every Jew has the makings of a Messiah, every Jewess that of a Mater Dolorosa": "only the Jews could rise to the height on which life and death seem equal"; "the great teachers of the knowledge of God were always Jews."[65] Nordau claimed that the Jew was "more industrious and abler than the average European, not to mention the moribund Asiatic and African."[66] Even the clear-eyed Ahad Ha'am wrote to a friend "you will not understand that our very existence in dispersion is possible only because we feel ourselves to be 'the aristocracy of history' ".[67] And, finally, Herzl himself, in seeming contradiction of his earlier views, noted "our race is more efficient in everything than most other peoples of the earth. This,

[61]*Op. cit.*, p. 273.

[62]Hertzberg, *op. cit.*, p. 380.

[63]*Op. cit.*, p. 498.

[64]Harry Shapiro, *The Jewish People*, UNESCO, Paris, 1960, Chapter VI.

[65]Hess, *op. cit.*, pp. 15-18.

[66]Hertzberg, *op. cit.*, p. 241.

[67]Ahad Ha'am, *Essays, Letters, Memoirs*, p. 268.

in fact, is the cause of the great hatred".[68]

Those are the claims of four of the greatest Zionist leaders of the past. But the feeling continues into the present, for in 1957 Ben Gurion asserted of his people "I believe in our moral and intellectual superiority, in our capacity to serve as a model for the redemption of the human race".[69]

On what are these strong opinions based? In the absence of any satisfactory concept of a Jewish race, they cannot accurately be described as racial chauvinism—rather, perhaps, a Jewish sub-racialism or meta-racialism. Do they provide a valid motivation for Zionism?

Perhaps the answer is provided by Herzl in this assertion from *The Jewish State*: "We are a people—*one* people". But the concept of "a people" is perilously near that of "race" and Herzl later redefined, or obscured, his idea in the words: "we are an historical unit with anthropological diversities. This also suffices for the Jewish State". Be that as it may, it does not suffice to isolate that common element in Jewry which we are seeking; it merely provokes the further question: "in what way have the Jews been 'an historical unit'?" History records the opposite— that even in Hellenistic times as many Jews were scattered outside Palestine as lived inside it.

If the Jews were "*one* people" they would share certain traditions and ways of life. But there is no common tradition binding the Jews in India with those of Poland; the way of life of the Jew in Morocco could hardly be more different than that of the Jew in America: in food, dress, culture and social behaviour they are assimilated to the varied people among whom they have lived. It is precisely this diversity, this lack of a common factor, which presents the government of Israel with problems of assimilation when they arrive there.

It is an Israeli who provides the most suggestive answer. Dov Barnir argues "Thus for 19 centuries we had between Jews 'a history' (it is the history of self-defence against persecution), a 'community of belief' (belief in survival and final redemption),

[68]*Diaries*, p. 1347.
[69]*Forum*, no. 3, 1957, pp. 20-38.

and a 'community of interests' (Jewish solidarity in the face of exactions and atrocities)".[70] The use of quotation marks is noteworthy in itself but even more so is the fact that all the three common elements are defined in negative terms, of Jewish reaction to hostile external forces. Here we seem to be getting to the heart of the matter for Dov Barnir links this negative reaction to Israel, that is, to Zionism. A few pages earlier he writes: "It is not for nothing that Jules Isaac has written, without an exclusive faith, no separatism; without separatism, no survival (but prompt assimilation); and without survival, the end of Israel. To a certain extent the Challenge precedes the Rejection";[71] the Rejection, that is, of the Jew by the Gentile world.

Barnir's suggestion is that the Jews, partly by their own choice, are a group apart. Earlier Zionist writers have noted both the Jewish apartness and the fact that it was partially self-created, but none of them suggested, as Barnir seems to do, that these two factors combine in a common Jewish political attitude, "The Challenge," which could be a possible motivation for Zionism, albeit a negative one.

Hence an examination of how Jewish apartness came about could explain the emergence of Zionism.

The ghettos of Eastern Europe were, of course, the direct, physical expression of the apartness of the Jews. The word "ghetto", (like "race") now has an in-built pejorative connotation, but probably this was not so for all the Jews who lived in these areas. One Zionist writer claims that "the expulsions and the ghettos—these assured our survival".[72] Small wonder then that "in the first instance there can be little doubt that Jewish hands laid its foundations".[73] Perhaps the best analysis of the strange relationship of the Jew to his ghetto was that given by Max Nordau in his address to the 1st Zionist Congress in 1897.

[70]"Le Conflit Israélo-Arabe", Les Temps Modernes, no. 253 bis, p. 423. Barnir is a member of the National Committee of the Histadrut and of the Political Bureau of the Mapam party.

[71]Op. cit., p. 420.

[72]J.H. Brenner in Hertzberg, op. cit., p. 310.

[73]P. Horowitz, The Jewish Question and Zionism, London, 1927.

After saying that for the Gentile "the primary sentiment is the detestation of the Jews", he describes the ghetto Jew in words of angry, almost mocking, pride "wherever the authorities did not shut him up in a ghetto, he built one for himself. He would dwell with his own and would have no other relations but those of business with Christians...The ghetto for the Jew of the past was not a prison, but a refuge...Only the ghetto gave Jews the possibility of surviving the terrible persecutions of the Middle Ages—In the ghetto the Jew had his own world; it was his sure refuge and it provided the spiritual and moral equivalent of a motherland...they had but one care: to make (the ghetto's) existence secure through invisible walls which were much thicker and higher than the stone walls that surrounded it physically".[74]

One of those "invisible walls" was the ritualistic aspect of Judaism: "national apartness is inherent in the many forms and prohibitions of our religion"[75] declared one Zionist writer. And Moses Hess before him had also linked Jewish ritualism with political existence: "the observance of thousands of minute precepts exists in order to preserve the integrity of Judaism in the Diaspora; that is Jewish patriotism".[76] Nordau went further when saying that ritualistic prohibitions in conditions of apartness strengthened Jewish community feeling: he claimed that the prohibitions were deliberately, if unconsciously, introduced in order to maintain the apartness. "All Jewish customs and practices unconsciously pursued one sole purpose, to preserve Judaism by separation from others, to maintain the Jewish community...This impulse towards separateness was the source of most of the ritual laws, which for the average Jew were identical with his very faith."[77]

Thus the ghetto and ritualistic taboos were, at least in part, deliberately created by the European Jew to maintain his apartness, which in turn strengthened his separatist community feeling. And Nordau continues with his line of argument that

[74]Nordau in Hertzberg, op. cit., pp. 237-238.
[75]J. Klatzkin in Hertzberg, op. cit., p. 321.
[76]M. Hess, op. cit., p. 56.
[77]Nordau in Hertzberg, op. cit., p. 238.

this separatist feeling leads naturally to the Zionist programme of establishing a separatist community in a separate state; he even quotes precise figures: two million Jews are happy and contented in their land of birth and have no idea of abandoning it. They are one-sixth of the Jewish people (at that time); but five-sixths or ten million Jews are profoundly unhappy in the countries where they live: these must be given the chance of redemption, through Zionism.[78]

Later Zionist theoreticians, in order to lend weight and dignity to their movement, have tried to insert a fourth link in the causal chain of apartness—community feeling—Zionism so that it becomes apartness—community feeling—nationalism—Zionism. One such effort is to be found in the section on "Jewish Nationalism" by Leon Simon in the Chatham House study on *Nationalism*.[79] After stating that the Jews have "a common subjective sense of distinctness from the rest of the world and community with one another" Simon goes on to state that this "sense of solidarity, aided by the hostility of the outer world, which it no doubt helped to provoke, was always strong enough to secure the continued existence of this peculiar 'nation' ".[80] Here again the use of quotation marks is significant as is the use of the word "peculiar", which greatly weakens the Zionist argument. Another claim on behalf of Zionism for nationalist respectability has been made by Professor Talmon, Professor of History in the Hebrew University. He maintains that "earlier as well as later national movements have shown the same dialectic in their historical development: we are not they—the majority or ruling nation; we are different; we have to show what our distinctness consists of."[81] But Talmon here only re-emphasises that Zionism has

[78]*Op. cit.*, pp. 243-244.

[79]The editor makes it clear that Simon's essay expresses a personal point of view not necessarily in accord with that of the study group that produced the volume. The section on Middle East nationalism was written by an Englishman, an example of the sort of balance between Arabs and Zionists maintained in "objective" Western publications, which continues to the present day.

[80]*Nationalism*, p. 163.

[81]J. L. Talmon, *op. cit.*

an essentially negative motivation—the sense of apartness. As we have seen, Zionism is not motivated by positive factors of religious belief, of culture or race or language; yet some or all of these factors —and not merely a sense of apartness—are what stimulate authentic nationalisms throughout the world.

An historian of Zionism has rightly claimed that "any version of Zionism must necessarily imply some sense of a loss of hope in the future total acceptance of the Jew as an individual by the majority society".

This racialist pessimism is repugnant to Afro-Asian nationalism. A good many Afro-Asian states are, perforce, pluralistic societies—the Philippines and Malaysia, India and Ceylon, Lebanon and Egypt, Kenya and Nigeria—since they comprise a multiplicity of races, religions and languages. In not every case is there a happy reconciliation within the national fold but at least the tendency is towards co-existence and away from the deliberately pessimistic alienation of Zionism.

Thus having isolated the major motivation, though negative, for Zionism and the State of Israel we find that it is yet another element of differentiation between Zionism and Afro-Asian nationalism, and between Israel and the new states of the Third World.

Nationalism or refuge?

Despite this could it be that Zionism is a type of unmotivated self-generating nationalism—a nationalism per se? Such indeed, is the popularity and the undeserved prestige of nationalism in the modern world that almost every Zionist writer does describe the movement as a "national" or "nationalist" one. Most of them accept the definition unquestioningly, as being too obvious to need any explanation. Some, who do try to analyse this definition do it in circular fashion—that the Jewish "people" constitute "a nation" and therefore, a popular Jewish movement like Zionism is "nationalist".

However there are a few theoreticians who scrutinise Zionism's nationalist credentials more closely. It does not take a very searching enquiry to reveal the basic differences between Zionism and the usual types of nationalism, but these writers bridge this gap by saying that Zionism *is* a nationalism—but of a *peculiar* variety. Thus Hertzberg, at the very outset of his study of the "Zionist Idea", concedes that "Zionism cannot be typed, and therefore easily explained, as a 'normal' kind of national risorgimento...It is, therefore, a maverick in the history of modern nationalism."

As far back as 1895 Y.M. Pines concluded that the Jews "cannot be defined as an ordinary 'natural' nationality";[82] and, 60 years later, Berlin agreed that the Jews "were not a nation in any normal sense of the word".[83]

Others subscribe to the idea that since "the objective factors of nationhood, such as territory and language have had partly to be replaced by mental and spiritual substitutes...the Jews became, as it were, a 'spiritual nation'";[84] or, without any 'as it weres': "We have always been a spiritual nation".[85] Yet others claimed that if Israel in exile was a nation, it was not "a living nation".[86] And then there is the famous definition of Pinsker in his *Auto-Emancipation*, one of the great classics of Zionist thinking, that "The Jews are feared because they are a ghost nation, long since dead".[87]

There is also the definition by negation, as in the case of the socialist Zionist, Nahman Syrkin: "It is true, this nationalism does not represent some high national ideal—that is the tragic contradiction of Jewish life. Nonetheless, the enemy has *always* considered the Jews a nation, and they have always known themselves as such. Though they were robbed of all external national characteristics—they were a distinct nation whose very existence was sufficient reason for its being";[88] in other words a self-generating nationalism. A non-Zionist historian, straining at the bonds of the nationalist definition, can only describe Zionism

[82]Hertzberg, *op. cit.*, pp. 15, 412.
[83]Berlin, *op. cit.*, p. 5.
[84]J. Heller, *The Zionist Idea*, London, 1947, p. 19.
[85]P. Smolenskin in Hertzberg, *op. cit.*, p. 147.
[86]Rabbi Abraham Kook, in Hertzberg, *op. cit.*, p. 437.
[87]L. Pinsker, *Auto-Emancipation*, London, 1932, p. 18.
[88]In Hertzberg, *op. cit.*, p. 343.

as "this last, least typical of European nationalisms".[89]

Although an historian of nationalism, Hans Kohn, has declared that nationalities are so complex that "they defy exact definition"[90] this has not deterred him, and a host of other writers, from attempting definitions. The Chatham House study on nationalism lists these as the characteristics of a "nation": the idea of a common government in the past, present or for the future; a community of a certain size, and closeness of contact between individual members; a more or less defined territory; certain characteristics (e.g. language) which distinguish it; certain common interests; a certain degree of common feeling or will, associated with a picture of the nation in the minds of individual members.[91] Kohn himself says that the most usual common characteristics of a nation are: common descent, language, territory, political entity, customs and traditions, traditions and religion: of these six elements, the Jewish people had only the last, religion. Perhaps the most thorough-going study of Zionism as a nationalism is that of J. Heller who lists seven common characteristics of a nation: a common origin; physical and mental peculiarities; historical past and tradition; territory; language; culture; and, in the usual act of circular definition, national consciousness. It would seem that the Jewish people had one half of one of these characteristics—a common historical past, but Heller himself dismisses them all and says that Judaism (which he does not list) "seems to be the only bond of union between all the heterogeneous parts of World Jewry today". The reason why he did not mention religion is contained in his next dispirited sentence: "Yet adherence to the religious law is today no longer a link holding all the Jews together".[92]

However, in a chapter entitled "The Unique Character of Jewish Nationality"—Heller argues against what he calls two erroneous assumptions: that a nation must have *all* the character-

[89]Trevor-Roper, *op. cit.*, p. 23.
[90]H. Kohn, *The Idea of Nationalism*, New York, 1945, p. 13.
[91]*Nationalism*, p. xviii.
[92]Heller, *op. cit.*, pp. 12-17.

istics usually listed, and that the Jewish nation must be like all the other nations or not be accepted as one at all. This contentiousness denotes Heller's uneasy awareness—which any objective observer must share—that as far as the usual characteristics of a nation are concerned the Jewish people were possessed of virtually none, and that therefore the Zionist movement, within this people, cannot be accepted as a form of nationalism: one cannot make the bricks of nationalism without the straws of national characteristics.

Heller is among the Zionist writers who insist on Zionism's national character, but who also admit that it is, in his words, "unusual", "unique", "extraordinary".

But even with all these qualifying and partisan categorisations it is still not possible to fit Zionism even into the most elaborately detailed typology of nationalist movements. The scheme worked out by K. Symmons-Symonolewicz has no less than 9 divisions or sub-divisions:[93]

    I   Minority Movements
        A. Perpetuative
           1. Segregative (ghettos and the *millet* system).
           2. Pluralistic (seeking identity with equality).
        B. Irredentist

   II   Liberation Movements
        A. Restorative (Poland, Hungary)
        B. Revivalist (Catalonians or Lithuanians)
        C. Ethnic (Latvians or Somalis)
        D. Antinomist—Secessionist (the U.S.A.)
        E. Anti-colonialist (India, Burma)
        F. Nativist (the Riff movement).

This scheme finds a place for the ghetto but Zionism does not fit into any of its categories. Symmons-Symonolewicz refers to the work of L. Wirth who broke down the nationalism of minorities into three types: pluralistic, seeking autonomy; seces-

[93]K. Symmons-Symonolewicz, "Nationalist Movements: An Attempt at a Comparative Typology" in *Comparative Studies in Society and History*, vol. VII, no. 2, The Hague, 1965, p. 221 et seq.

sionist or seeking separation from the dominant majority; militant, seeking domination over this majority with support from aggressive co-nationals from across the border.[94] Zionism could possibly be seen as a modified hybridisation of the secessionist and militant types because the Jews in Europe did not seek to secede into an area of Europe but into Palestine where they, successfully, sought to dispossess a native majority, with the help of co-nationals. But such a classification would only emphasise that Zionism cannot be placed among the "normal" categories of nationalism.

Three of the six characteristics mentioned by the Chatham House study could fit Zionism: the Jews had a common interest in surviving persecution, a common will to escape from it, and a desire to form a government in the future. But by themselves these characteristics are so broad that they could be applied to almost any political pressure group, even the smallest subnational section or tribal sub-section.

When dealing with Israeli nationalism, the end-product of Zionism, the Israeli Foreign Minister, Abba Eban, often[95] refers to Renan's eloquent, but vague, definition of nationhood: "A nation is a soul, a spiritual principle. To share a common glory in the past, a common will in the present: to have done great things together; to wish to do them again—these are the essential conditions of being a nation". The first sentence is rhetoric; and as to the second one cannot but ask when were the Jews last "together to do great things"? The recalling of the past is a common theme in the arguments for Zionist nationalism; even the anti-Judaic Klatzkin said that the Jews were "members of one family, bearers of a common history"[96]...necessarily, of course, a remote history.

But the argument from history has been disposed of by another Zionist writer, Y.M. Pines: "True enough, a common past is a national heritage, but it is not the begetter of nationality. It is

[94]*Op. cit.*, p. 266.

[95]As, for instance, in his essay "Reality and Vision in the Middle East" in *Foreign Affairs*, July 1965.

[96]In Hertzberg, *op. cit.*, p. 317.

unheard of for an effect to turn round and become the cause of its own cause!"[97]

The advocates of Zionist nationalism are on surer ground when they refer, as Renan and the Chatham House study do, to "the common will", or, as put by Kohn, "most essential is a living and active corporate will. Nationality is formed by the decision to form a nationality".[98]

Granted that late 19th century European Jewry had this "common will" it still has to be determined whether it was motivated by national feeling and directed towards the creation of a national entity.

Zionist writers take the national quality of their movement for granted because, they say, it was no more than a reflection, within European Jewry, of the nationalist struggle that took place in almost every European country during the last century. If this is correct then the reproach of one Zionist writer is also correct—that the Jews pick up an idea when other people are almost finished with it.[99] The origin of Zionism as an original political movement can be dated at 1896, when Herzl's *The Jewish State* was published, and 1897, the year of the 1st Zionist Congress: the earlier expositions of the Zionist idea were completely forgotten. These two dates are very late in the history of European nationalism, considering that European Jewry was intermingled with all the European peoples who had begun their nationalist struggles much earlier. Greece achieved her independence in 1832, Italy in 1860, Hungary was granted autonomy in 1867, and Bulgaria in 1878, the same year in which Serbia and Montenegro gained independence, a good twenty years before the official foundation of the Zionist movement. Jewish national feelings, if they existed, should surely have responded earlier to the nationalist spirit of the times.

Professor Trevor-Roper has produced an interesting theory to explain this late emergence of "Jewish nationalism".[100] He

[97]In Hertzberg, *op. cit.*, p. 413.
[98]Kohn, *op. cit.*, p. 15.
[99]Ahad Ha'am, *op. cit.*, p. 45.
[100]Trevor-Roper, *op. cit.*, p. 16.

argues that the first wave of European nationalism, in 1859-1869, brought the nationalism of the "historic" nations of Europe, Italy, Germany and Hungary, to victory. These states then began oppressing their minorities which produced a wave of "secondary nationalisms", of Czechs, Slavs, Croats and Jews. But Berlin has denied that the Jews were similar to the Central and East European minorities,[101] who, in any case, began their movements some time before European Jewry. Even Trevor-Roper had to conclude that Zionism was "the last, least typical of European nationalisms".

Zionist theoreticians are still sensitive about this late emergence, particularly since an anti-Zionist Jewish author has recently argued that "it should not have been necessary to wait for Herzl, the end of the 19th century and the development of the Zionist movement to demand the creation of a Jewish state, if among the Jews there existed the will to form a nation".[102]

An answer is given by Dov Barnir who asks why it should have been necessary for the Italian, Hungarian or German peoples to wait for the 19th century?—a slow maturing and a patient incubation is always indispensable for nationalisms. Like most analogies Barnir's analogy is misleading. The nationalist doctrines of the Italians, Hungarians and Germans did not enjoin them three times a day, over the centuries, to do something practical and political as the Jews were enjoined to go to Jerusalem; an injunction, moreover, which a few sometimes obeyed, thus showing the inactive majority that obedience was a practical possibility should they desire it.

An examination of the motivations of Zionism can lead to no other conclusion but that it was, and is, not truly nationalist and was not a part of the main nationalist impulse of its home continent, Europe. The most that can be said for it is that "it was a faith which had to be taken on trust...It was in conformity with the Zeitgeist of nationalism".[103] Still less, therefore, is Zionism akin to the nationalisms of Afro-Asia. It is not only

---

[101]Reference note 92, above.

[102]G. Friedmann, *The End of the Jewish People?* London, 1967, p. 238.

[103]J. Marlowe, *The Seat of Pilate*, London, 1959, p. 35.

that the Zionist leaders were "half-national",[104] assimilated, Westernised Jews. Zionism lacked the essential base of nationalism in that the Jews were not a race, nor really even a people, but merely a group apart. They could not be accounted a race or even a people because there has never been an agreed answer to the question: What is a Jew?

The best summing up of this quest for the motivations of Zionism is given in the words of R.H.S. Crossman, who is warmly sympathetic towards Zionism and Israel. After noting that the Israeli law courts have discovered that it is no easy task to find the common characteristics which differentiate Jew from non-Jew he says: "that characteristic is certainly not religion (at least 80 per cent of the Israelis are agnostic). Nor can we detect either a common race or a common cultural tradition... The Israelis, in fact, are bound together by one salient fact—that they are unwanted in the countries in which they are born".[105]

Here then we come to the true, powerful motive force of Zionism The sense of apartness, a negative factor, is one side of the coin. The being unwanted is the active element, the other side of the coin. The two together result in anti-Semitism. The "common will" of the European Jews to escape from anti-Semitism emerges as Zionism.

The nationalisms of Afro-Asia have been based on the desire of races or peoples, with their own religions, cultures and languages, to be free in their own homelands. Thus positively motivated these nationalisms could hardly have been more different from the anti-anti-Semitism of Zionism which sought not independence but a refuge.

The direct, definite links between the Zionist movement and anti-Semitism in Eastern Europe are clear beyond any shadow of a doubt. Yet every historian of Zionism has denied the link, persistently and sometimes vehemently, because of their determination to present Zionism as some form of nationalist movement, even if only an abnormal variety. The reasons for this re-writing of historical facts will be examined a little later.

[104]Trevor-Roper, *op. cit.*, pp. 20-21.
[105]Crossman, *op. cit.*, pp. 91-92.

In its surface appearance and its basic way of life Israel is a Western state because it has been created by Jews from the West who form the majority of World Jewry. Yet despite that majority Israel could very well have been brought into existence as an Oriental state by the hundreds of thousands of Oriental Jews who lived in countries near to or bordering on Palestine. This did not happen because Israel is the product of Zionism and European Jews became Zionists because they alone were persecuted by European anti-Semitism. Israel is not an Oriental Zionist state because, till the creation of Israel in 1948, Zionism gained no hold on Oriental Jewry[106] because they did not suffer from anti-Semitism in their countries of residence.

Therefore Sartre is wrong when he says that the Jew has been made by anti-Semitism; only the Western Zionist Jew has been made into a Zionist by anti-Semitism, for anti-Semitism is a specifically European Christian disease.

After the French Revolution Western and Central Europe became progressively, if only relatively, free of anti-Semitism. Prejudice, strong and open prejudice, continued but there was no active, physical persecution. However, throughout the 19th century Eastern Europe remained heavily infected with the most virulent form of anti-Semitism.

This factor alone explains why Zionism emerged from Eastern Europe. Its leadership was almost exclusively Eastern European as was the rank-and-file of its mass following. In consequence the leadership-elite of the State of Israel is still very largely drawn from the East European immigrants of the Second and Fourth Aliyot.*

The exegetical apologetics of later Zionist historians, trying to explain away the anti-Semitic origins of Zionism, read very curiously when set beside the original writings of the East European founders. They never hid the fact that they were reacting to anti-Semitism, and that what they urgently wanted was a country of refuge, which might or might not be a nation state, and not necessarily located in Palestine.

---

*Aliyot—waves of immigration.
[106]L. Stein, *The Balfour Declaration*, p. 35.

From its inception and down to the 1920's the Zionist movement was riven with disputes arising from differences of outlook
and aim between Western European and Eastern European
Jewry. But the leaders who engaged in these, often bitter,
disputes were overwhelmingly East European, at least in birth
and early upbringing. If, once again, we glance at the biographies of the 37 leading Zionists included in Hertzberg's *The
Zionist Idea*, which deliberately sets out to be a representative
selection, we find that only 6 of the 37 were not from Eastern
Europe, the most notable of these exceptions being Moses Hess
and Judah Magnes. Even among leaders of American Jewry
we find the well-known names of such East Europeans as Schechter, Brandeis and Rabbi Silver.

It has been noted that not one of the members of Herzl's Inner
Zionist Action Committee was a "Westerner". From the beginning the "Easterners" were always in a great majority in the
Zionist Organisation and at the Zionist Congresses.[107] This
was inevitable because the majority of the Jews of Europe were
to be found in Russia, Poland and the eastern areas of the Austro-
Hungarian Empire.

But it was precisely because of this concentrated massing of
the Jews in Eastern Europe that that area was most afflicted
with anti-Semitism and therefore most productive of Zionism.

The biographies of these 37 leaders, and of others, reveal that
almost all of them, especially the more influential, adopted
Zionism not because of a general political conviction but because
of the direct impact of anti-Semitism, either through some incident in their personal lives or because of some contemporaneous
event. And, what is more noteworthy, the effect of anti-Semitic
happenings on them was so strong and immediate that many
of them switched overnight to Zionism from an advocacy of
anti-Zionist assimilation or agnosticism or socialism.

The Zionism of the earliest leader, Kalischer, who was born
in 1745, sprang from a desire to find a solution for the misery
of East European Jews.[108] Two other early proponents, Alkalai

---

[107]V. K. Rabinowicz, *Fifty Years of Zionism*, London, 1950, pp. 18-19.
[108]Hertzberg, *op. cit.*, p. 110.

and Hess, were influenced by the Blood Accusation brought under French Jesuit instigation against the Jews of Damascus in 1840 by the Ottoman authorities. The pogrom of 1870 converted Smolenskin. The impact of the 1881 pogrom was so decisive that it has been called "a break in modern Jewish history":[109] it had a decisive effect on such famous Zionists as Pinsker, Ahad Ha'am and the young Weizmann. It is well known from their own statements that the anti-Semitic Dreyfus Affair, in 1894, was the decisive factor in converting Herzl and Nordau to Zionism: they were both eye-witnesses of the famous scene of the degrading of Captain Dreyfus while the Parisian mob outside howled "Down with the Jews". The 1903 pogrom of Kishinev was the turning point towards Zionism of Jabotinsky and Ben Gurion. It was anti-Semitic discrimination in America that brought the well known critic Ludwig Lewisohn into the Zionist fold; and the same was true of no less a personality than Albert Einstein.

It is the Zionist leaders themselves who describe, very often in moving words, how anti-Semitism moved them from indifference to active Zionism. Thus Hess, recalling the incident of 1840 declared: "although I was then far from Judaism, I already had the desire to express my Jewish patriotic feelings in a cry of pain...on account of the rudeness and credulity of the Asiatic and European mobs...The grief...now became a prevailing state of mind".[110] Herzl is even more explicit: "I was indifferent to my Jewishness; let us say it was beneath the level of my awareness. But just as anti-Semitism forces the half-hearted, cowardly and self-seeking Jews into the arms of Christianity, it powerfully forced my Jewishness to the surface". And in 1895 he wrote: "How did I discover (the idea of the Jewish State)? I do not know. Thirteen years...the idea took shape. My first notes date from 1882, the year in which I read Duhring's book"[111]—a virulently anti-Semitic work, which appeared a year after the Russian pogroms. Nordau said unequivocally:

---

[109]*Op. cit.*, p. 180.
[110]Hess, *op. cit.*, pp. 31-32.
[111]*Diaries*, pp. 109-111.

"anti-Semitism opened my eyes to a return to my forgotten Jewishness".[112] The always quirky Jabotinsky said that the beginnings of his Zionist activities were connected with the Italian opera (compositions by Jews on Jewish themes) and with the organisation of the Odessa self-defence against the 1903 pogromists; both he and the poet Bialik wrote powerfully denunciatory poems on these massacres.[113] Einstein wrote of his conversion in 1921: "until two years ago I lived in Switzerland and during my stay there I did not realise my Judaism. There was nothing that called forth my Jewish sentiments in me. When I moved to Berlin all that changed. There I realised the difficulties that many young Jews were confronting (especially the refugee students from Eastern Europe who were threatened with expulsion). These and similar happenings have awakened in me the Jewish national sentiment. I am a national Jew in the sense that I demand the preservation of the Jewish nationality as of every other. I look upon Jewish nationality as a fact".[114] Thus we have described the process of how anti-Semitic discrimination drove even so gentle and unwordly a person as Einstein into an assertion of dogmatic Zionism.

The founding fathers of Zionism were perfectly frank and open in stating that for them the object of Zionism was to find, with desperate urgency, a place of refuge for East European Jewry against the anti-Semitic persecution. Pinsker, in 1882, argued that the recent pogroms had caused the national consciousness of the Russian and Rumanian Jews to burst forth "in the shape of an irresistible movement towards Palestine... The Jews have no other way out of their desperate situation".[115] In the same year Lilienblum presented the case even more dramatically: "Eretz Israel...which is our only haven in this time of trouble...is plainly and simply a matter of life and without whose solution we are doomed as a people".[116]

[112]Ben Horin, op. cit., p. 175.
[113]J.B. Schechtman, Rebel and Statesman, vol. 1, New York, 1956, pp. 74-78.
[114]Einstein, op. cit., p. 27.
[115]Pinsker, op. cit., pp. 28-30.
[116]Lilienblum in Hertzberg, op. cit., p. 170.

The words "a refuge for the oppressed Jewish masses"[117] occur like a steady refrain through all the Zionist writings of Herzl. Thus, testifying before a Royal Commission in London in 1902 he argued: "the Jew must either die or get out. The Jews of Eastern Europe cannot stay where they are...where are they to go?"[118] Or again: "My plan calls for the utilization of a driving force, that actually exists. What is this force? The distress of the Jews!"[119] Or, still more bluntly: "No great exertion will be necessary to stimulate the immigration movement. The anti-Semites are already taking care of this for us".[120] In his speech to the 1st Zionist Congress he said: "the feeling of unity among us...was in process of dissolution when the tide of anti-Semitism rose about us. Anti-Semitism has given us our strength again. We have returned home".[121] But if they had, the Jews had also lost their home in Europe: "we shall have to withdraw from Europe. We can stay here no longer".[122] When trying to impart something of his own sense of urgency to Joseph Chamberlain, the then Colonial Secretary, Herzl, pleaded: "I must bring them an immediate help."[123]

Indeed the most bitter criticism directed against Herzl and his "Western" group by leaders of East European Jewry, like Ahad Ha'am and Weizmann, is precisely that for the former, Herzlian Zionism was "the product of anti-Semitism and is dependent on anti-Semitism for its existence", "looking for nothing more in Palestine than a State, a safe refuge for homeless Jews"; and, in the words of the latter, "for Herzl, and perhaps a majority of the representatives of the Jews meeting in Basle, Zionism meant an immediate solution of the problems besetting their sorely tried people,"[124]—and nothing more.

[117]*Diaries*, p. 648.
[118]*Op. cit.*, p. 389.
[119]*Op. cit.*, p. 237.
[120]*Op. cit.*, p. 152.
[121]*Op. cit.*, p. 233.
[122]*Op. cit.*, p. 140.
[123]*Op. cit.*, p. 1360.
[124]Weizmann, *op. cit.*, p. 112 and Ahad Ha'am in Hertzberg, *op. cit.*, p. 266; and Ahad Ha'am, *Essays*, p. 285.

That the main force behind Zionism was simply the expulsive thrust of anti-Semitism in East Europe was perfectly clear to its original founders.

Even in their less practical, more theoretical, argumentation the Zionists worked out a curious and intermingled dialectic between anti-Semitism and Zionism. Herzl accepts without protest the remark of the Grand Duke of Baden that "people have regarded Zionism as a species of anti-Semitism",[125] which is why the German government had hesitated to give support to Zionism. The French Zionist Bernard Lazare believed that it was "because the Jews are a nation that anti-Semitism exists".[126] Nordau was somewhat more subtle in arguing that Zionism was the product both of the nationality principle and the perversion of the nationality principle that is anti-Semitism.[127] Perhaps most subtle of all in his approach to anti-Semitism was Pinsker who contended: "We must prove that the misfortunes of the Jews are due, above all, to their lack of desire for national independence... we must prove that *they must become a nation*";[128] thus he argues that the lack of nationalist Zionism produces anti-Semitism which should produce Zionism.

In fact the Zionists always displayed an ambivalent attitude towards anti-Semitism: they found it useful and at the same time some of them from their hatred and obsession elevated anti-Semitism into a natural instinct to be found in all humanity, thus reinforcing that pessimistic strain in Zionism that has already been noted.

Herzl anticipated that anti-Semitism would assist Zionism in two ways. Firstly, "in the beginning we shall be supported by anti-Semitism through a recrudescence of persecution".[129] That would happen in Eastern Europe, but less obviously and more politely the Central and West European governments would also help because they, too, would like to see the backs of the Jews, if not through persecution then through emigration

---

[125]*Diaries*, p. 657.
[126]In Hertzberg, *op. cit.*, p. 471.
[127]Ben Horin, *op. cit.*, p. 182.
[128]Pinsker, *op. cit.*, p. 17.
[129]*Diaries*, p. 56.

organised by the Zionists. Herzl records this anticipation several times in his diary but he also records that he did not like it when the Kaiser, with imperial bluntness, told Herzl to his face that there were some sorts of Jews he would be happy to see emigrate.[130] Several other Zionist writers express the expectation of this type of polite co-operation between anti-Semitism and Zionist emigration.

But there was one other, practical, fashion in which Herzl thought the anti-Semites would be useful: "it would be an excellent idea to call in respectable, accredited anti-Semites as liquidators of property (of emigrating Jews). The anti-Semites will become our most dependable friends, the anti-Semitic countries our allies".[131] Precisely this has, in fact, come about between West Germany and Israel today.

So long as anti-Semites were "respectable", and "accredited", Herzl was able to come to terms with them and even reach a degree of liking, as with the notorious Russian Interior Minister, Plehve. He records, with wry humour, his cordial meetings with other Jew baiters in the spirit of the latter-day saying: some of my best friends are anti-Semites.

But Herzl's feeling for anti-Semitism went deeper than the political or the personal level. In his own words: "anti-Semitism, which is a strong and unconscious force among the masses, will not harm the Jews. I consider it to be a movement useful to the Jewish character. It represents the education of a group by the masses, and will perhaps lead to it being absorbed. Education is accomplished only by hard knocks". No other Zionist leader shared Herzl's somewhat complacent "Western" views about the educative value of anti-Semitic persecution but some agreed, vehemently, that it was a strong, unconscious force.

Pinsker insisted that anti-Semitism "as a psychic aberration is hereditary, and as a disease transmitted for two thousand years it is incurable...The antipathy (for the Jews) exists in all places and at all times...(Judeophobia) is an hereditary form

[130]*Diaries*, p. 728.
[131]*Diaries*, pp. 83-84.

of demonopathy, peculiar to the human race".[132] Nordau also felt that anti-Semitism was rooted in the psychological peculiarity of man and that it was not temporary; he described it as a form of "misoneism"—the hatred of the new.[133]

This demonological interpretation of anti-Semitism is itself something of an aberration for it is wholly Eurocentric. It is for instance, absurd to allege that "all" the countries of Afro-Asia were afflicted with it at "all" times: on the contrary, the ancient Jewish communities of South India, Iraq and North Africa had good, peaceable relations with the local inhabitants.

In truth there is nothing in the attitudes of Afro-Asian nationalism towards its antagonist, imperialism, remotely comparable to the complex love-hate relationship between Zionism and anti-Semitism: Anti-Semitism created Zionism, and Zionism was then dependent on the expulsive dynamism of anti-Semitism, which it could not but hate. Except in India, the Afro-Asian nationalists, quite simply, hated and opposed imperialism. In India Mahatma Gandhi tried to draw a distinction between hateful imperialism and the imperialist, who was not to be hated. But even he never said that imperialism was useful or that it was a good influence on the Indian character. It is perhaps the masochistic element in Zionism's relation with anti-Semitism which gives it a distinctly different quality from Afro-Asian nationalism. A contemporary Zionist historian has written that "Herzl gives the impression of a man suffering from a toothache. He is told he must not touch it, but touch it he must" but this is true of the feelings of all the other Zionist leaders towards anti-Semitism.

Most curious is the theory, propounded especially by Herzl and Nordau, that Zionism, as Herzl said in *The Jewish State*, is simply "the peacemaker" between Jew and Gentile because it puts anti-Semitism to a "constructive" use. This has been described by Hertzberg as "the subtlest, most daring, and most optimistic conception to be found in political Zionism" for it results in "an offer on the part of the Jew to assure the peace of

---

[132]Pinsker, *op. cit.*, p. 19.
[133]Ben Horin, *op. cit.*, p. 184.

western society by abandoning it for a state of his own, it is the ultimate sacrifice on the altar of his love for the modern world".[134] This might be a dubious sort of poetry but to the baffled Afro-Asian nationalist such sentiments seem either comic or grotesque or sinister; "and what", he might well ask, "what has all this to do with nationalism?"

There was, of course, much more than a psycho-pathological relation between Zionism and its motive force. The rhythm of Jewish immigration from Europe into Palestine was a direct reflection of the presence, or absence, of anti-Semitic pressures, since, as we have seen, there was no steady Jewish movement into Palestine. There was no continuing pull from without, from Palestine, but only spasmodic pushes from within, from Europe.

In the years 1648-1649 the trickle of immigrants into Palestine grew to a stream because of massacres in the Ukraine.[135] While, on the other hand, when in 1840 the future of Palestine was open to discussion not a voice was raised among the Jews for the restoration of the land to them,[136] because, despite the scandal of the Blood Accusation in Damascus, there was no anti-Semitic outburst in Europe.

In the next 40 years some of the classic texts of Zionism were written by Alkalai, Kalischer and Hess but they attracted no attention because of a temporary truce between European Jewry and anti-Semitism: Zionism was not in the air. The pogrom of 1881 after the assassination of Tsar Alexander II immediately resulted in the formation of the Lovers of Zion movement and the establishment of the first Zionist settlement in Palestine in 1882. But once again, because of the absence of anti-Semitic pressures, Zionism by 1896 "faded into the background" and became "a romantic vision". . . "a few years more and the entire movement seemed doomed to extinction".[137] From this fate it was rescued by the Dreyfus Affair and Herzl who maintained the Zionist impulsion, which was given further strength

---

[134]J.L. Talmon, *op. cit.*, and Hertzberg, *op. cit.*, Introduction pp. 48-51.
[135]Parkes, *History of Palestine*, p. 182.
[136]L. Stein, *The Balfour Declaration*, p. 9.
[137]Bein, *op. cit.*, p. 179.

by the pogrom of 1903. Yet again, with the absence of anti-Semitic pressures, and despite the existence of an official Zionist organisation, the movement relapsed into querulous inactivity until 1911.

Zionism, in its origins, was an East European movement not merely because most of its leaders came from that region, where the majority of European Jewry was congregated; there were also two other reasons. The first, as we have seen, was the special susceptibility of East European Jewry to anti-Semitism, which was based on mass prejudice, but was also actively encouraged by insecure regimes to draw discontent away from them. The second reason that favoured the propagation of Zionism among East European Jewry was its size and its strong internal organisation.

The antagonism between "Eastern" and "Western" Jews within the Zionist movement was an accurate reflection of the deep difference between the Easterners living in contact with a predominantly Slav environment and culture, and the Westerners with their contacts with Anglo-Saxon or Latin culture. The latter had more than contacts with their environment; by the later 19th century they were, willingly, assimilated to it. Not so the Eastern Jews who were almost completely unassimilated and who remained strongly and profoundly Jewish, steeped in religion and orthodox tradition. They gave to the Zionist movement not only its leadership but a mass base and the qualities of endurance and idealism.

And they were able to maintain themselves distinctively apart because 6 or 7 million of them lived in one contiguous area, the Pale of Settlement. Within the Pale they were permitted to run their own affairs through an elaborate network of powerful community organisations, the kahals, which had a certain autonomy especially in regard to education; in these organisations leading rabbis had great influence.

Many writers have referred to the Pale of Settlement as if it were some enlarged ghetto. A Zionist historian has talked of the Jews being cooped up in the Pale "leading their own religious life and, one might almost add, their national life, as if they were in their own land, but denied all freedom and rights of citizenship and cut off,—partly by their own desire, and partly by the conditions under which they lived,—from the general scheme of the world's progressive thought and culture... cramped in their lives, narrowed in their vision;"[138] an accurate enough description except for the use of such words as "cooped" and "cramped". They are utterly inaccurate because of the vast size of the Pale. It stretched from the Baltic to the Black Sea and included Warsaw, Kiev and Odessa. Its area, 360,000 square miles, was the same as that of France and comprised 20% of European Russia.

Within the boundaries of the Pale the Jews were, most often, not permitted to live in villages or undertake agriculture. Consequently, though the Jews were one-sixth of the population there was a high percentage of them in the towns and cities: in Mohilev province 94%, Minsk 69%, Vilna 56%, Kiev 49%.[139] Thus it was only too easy for them to live completely self-enclosed lives within a wholly Jewish atmosphere.

Since this large body of Jews was left alone to develop its own institutions, Jewry within the Pale, with the passage of time, "was virtually a nation within a nation with the added feature that it gained the cultural leadership of the farflung Jewish world",[140] or at least was "an authentic national minority settled upon its own ancestral soil".[141]

Thus within the Pale, East European Jewry had achieved two things: something very much similar to an autonomous, organised national existence, and, far more important, a territorial base. It is true that the land was not theirs and that their existence on it was often precarious but the Pale was an area in which the East European Jew could feel at home among his own kith and kin.

Therefore when Herzl propounded the idea of a Jewish State they knew, from their own experience, what he meant because, in however attenuated a fashion, they were living within one

[138]P. Horowitz, *op. cit.*, pp. 20-21.
[139]M. Davitt, *Within The Pale*, London, 1903, p. 38 et seq.
[140]A.S. Eban, *Afterword*, in Pinsker, *op. cit.*
[141]Berlin, *op. cit.*, p. 13.

such state. For these Jews the Zionist programme was merely the transference of the Pale to Palestine, plus the granting of political rights.

To some extent this transference of East European conditions, en bloc, to Palestine has been effected. Hence the visible incongruities of some aspects of Israeli life in their new and contrasting West Asian setting.

For a political reason, too, it was easy for the "Eastern" Jews to give enthusiastic moral support to Zionism. Cut off from Russian life, most of these Jews felt no loyalty to the Russian state and hence they were not troubled by any feelings of double loyalty.

For Western Jewry things were very different: less numerous, dispersed and assimilated, they felt themselves caught in a real struggle of double loyalties; participating in the life and structure of the Western states the idea of a Jewish State was not only new but frightening. The reaction of Edwin Montagu, British Secretary for India, to the Balfour Declaration was a significant reflection of this attitude: "The Government", he wrote, "has dealt an irreparable blow at Jewish Britons and has endeavoured to set up a people which does not exist."

It did not take Herzl very long to discover where his real strength lay. After the 1st Zionist Congress he wrote of his "discovery of East European Jewry...the strength of which he had not even suspected", he was impressed with its "inner unity" and the fact that these Jews were "steeped in Jewish national sentiment".[142]

According to Talmon, Herzl in all his Zionist work "had in mind the Jews of Central and Eastern Europe, certainly not the Jews of the Oriental countries, or for that matter of the West". Writing of emigration to the Jewish State Herzl referred to "our unskilled labourers who will come first from the great reservoirs of Russia and Roumania".[143]

It is, therefore, no more than a plain statement of fact that "Jewish nationalism was given reality almost entirely by the

[142]Bein, *op. cit.*, p. 245.
[143]Talmon, *op. cit.*, and Herzl, *The Jewish State*, p. 37.

Jews of the Russian Empire,... If the Jews of Russia had not existed, neither the case for, nor the possibility of realizing, Zionism could have arisen in any serious form".[144]

And Russian Jewry was so important because anti-Semitism, impinging on the masses of East European Jewry, was the main motivation of Zionism, and those masses were the main instrument for achieving Zionism.

The leaders of the 'Eastern Jews' were well aware of their importance to Zionism and from the beginning they resented the fact that the leadership in those early years was in the hands of "Westerners" like Herzl. Reliving the old battles one "Eastern" leader, Weizmann, somewhat acidly and patronisingly, comments that it was because of Russian Jewry that "Herzl found a movement ready for him. We brought not only our principles to Palestine, but our own population".[145]

However, it was on the issue of whether Palestine—Zion— should be the goal of Zionism that the first big battles were fought within the Zionist movement.

In short the issue was whether Zionism should be based on the principle of "Jewish nationalism" or on the philanthropic need to find a haven for Jews fleeing from anti-Semitism, in any part of the globe.

* * *

The partial solution

Since Zionism, by definition, is the movement of Jews to Palestine, it may seem strange that Palestine as an objective, its eponymous raison d'être, should have become the cause of controversy. It did so because the most influential of the early Zionist leaders were non-Zion Zionists, and the love for the land of Palestine was not inherent in the Zionist movement, nor in its leaders, nor in the Jewish masses.

The very earliest exponents of the Zionist idea, Alkalai, Kalischer and Moses Hess, were all pro-Palestine. But their

[144]Berlin, *op. cit.*, pp. 12, 17.
[145]Weizmann, *op. cit.*, p. 43.

words fell on stony ground and had practically no influence on the Zionist movement during its quiescent period between 1840 and 1880.

Strange as it may appear not even the 1881 pogroms, which did so much to revive Zionism, sufficed to push Jewish emigrants or Zionist thinking definitely in the direction of Palestine. In 1875, before the pogrom, someone like Smolenskin was sufficiently detached to argue: "the foundation of our national identity was never the soil of the Holy Land, and we did not lose the basis of our nationality when we were exiled. We have always been a spiritual nation...".[146] He was one of those Zionists who felt forced to look to Palestine alone by the events of 1881, along with other Russian Jewish leaders such as Ben Yehuda and Lilienblum.

Yet on a more famous Zionist, Pinsker, the pogroms had an exactly opposite effect: they shook him to the depths of his being and turned him away from assimilation towards a fervent Zionism but they also turned him away from Palestine. In his *Auto-Emancipation* he argued: "We finally must have a *home*, if not a *country* of our own. If we would have a secure home...we must above all not dream of restoring ancient Judaea. We must not attach ourselves to the place where our political life was once violently interrupted and destroyed. The goal of our present endeavours must be not the 'Holy Land', but a land of our own. We need nothing but a large piece of land for our poor brothers. Perhaps the Holy Land will again become ours. If so, all the better...," "this piece of Land might form a small territory in North America or a sovereign Pashalik in Asiatic Turkey".[147]

Bitterly attacked by the Zionists, Pinsker allowed himself to be "Zionised" into giving Palestine preference as the goal, but he refused to make this preference a matter of principle. At a Zionist conference he called at Katowitz in 1884 he refused to present alternative choices of homeland: "he chose Palestine because it is realisable since the people want it, why? Simply

---

[146]Smolenskin, in Hertzberg, *op. cit.*, p. 147.
[147]Pinsker, *op. cit.*, pp. 32, 38.

because it wants a home".[148]

East European Jewry also performed the act of Zionisation on the most famous of the non-Zion Zionists, Herzl himself. Herzl's motives in not giving initial preference to Palestine were the same as Pinsker's: both men were moved not by mystical visions but by an urgent humanitarianism which sought the most quickly-available home for East European refugees. Lacking religious feeling for Palestine they did not insist on it because, as a part of the Ottoman Empire, they did not see how it could become quickly available to large-scale, open immigration.[149]

This attitude put them, and the many other Zionists who thought like them, at odds with the East European Jewish leaders on two counts: objective and method.

These "Eastern" leaders, as we shall see, were not all totally committed to Palestine as the objective; but under pressure from the eastern Zionists they insisted on Palestine, and as it was not available to open immigration, they suggested illegal infiltration.

Herzl eventually accepted the goal of the East Europeans but never the method they suggested; and so he spent the few remaining years of his life going from court to court in diplomatic efforts to open Palestine to official, organised Jewish immigration, without success.

Herzl stated his views on Palestine and infiltration clearly in *The Jewish State*: "two territories come under consideration, Palestine and Argentina. In both countries important experiments in colonisation have been made, though on the mistaken principle of a gradual infiltration of Jews. An infiltration is bound to end badly. It continues till the inevitable moment when the native population feels itself threatened, and forces the government to stop a further influx of Jews." In later years this is precisely what happened in Palestine both under the Ottomans and the British.

"Palestine or Argentina?" he asks; "we shall take what is

---

[148]M. Buber, *Israel and Palestine*, London, 1952, p. 128.

[149]The similarity of Herzl's and Pinsker's views is the more striking because Herzl only heard of Pinsker's work after writing *The Jewish State* and finished reading it five years later.

given us and what is selected by Jewish public opinion".[150]
In the privacy of his diary Herzl was much cooler towards the
idea of Zion as a goal for Zionism. In June 1895, in what was
supposed to be an address to the Rothschild family, Herzl quotes
himself as saying: "I shall now tell you everything about the
'Promised Land' except its location. That is a purely scientific
question. We must have regard for geological, climatic, in short,
natural factors of all kinds with full circumspection and with
consideration of the latest research... For a time I had Palestine
in mind. This would have in its favour the facts that it is the
unforgotten ancestral seat of our people, that its very name would
constitute a programme, and that it would powerfully attract
the lower masses. But most Jews are no longer Orientals and
have become accustomed to very different regions... Then, too,
Europe would still be too close to it, and in the first quarter
century of our existence we shall have to have peace from Europe
and its martial and social entanglements, if we are to prosper...
But on principle I am neither against Palestine nor for Argentina".[151]

Pinsker also believed that the site of the Jewish State should
be fixed by experts: not for him, or Herzl, the "magic" and
"romance" of Palestine, spoken of by Weizmann!

Elsewhere Herzl, arguing the pros and cons, notes the lack
of room for expansion in Palestine; but in its favour "the mighty
legend"; while South America would have a lot in its favour
because of "its distance from a militarised and seedy Europe".[152]

The 1st Zionist Congress however resolved that "the object
of Zionism is the establishment for the Jewish people of a home
in Palestine secured by public law." That was in 1897. Herzl
had been publicly Zionised but he had not been really converted.
He continued to feel the urgent need for a place of refuge, and
in 1899 he wrote; "In any case I believe that after the next
Congress we shall proceed in a practical way to the land, any
land". And as late as 1902 he said, privately, that he thought a

[150]Herzl, *The Jewish State*, pp. 29, 31.
[151]*Diaries*, p. 133.
[152]*Diaries*, pp. 56, 69.

plan for settlement in Cyprus was "a reasonable one".[153]

The quarrel over whether or not Palestine should be the Zionist goal had been brewing for years between "Westerners" and "Easterners", with the latter feeling that" the Zionism of the Westerners was...a mechanical and so to speak sociological concept".[154] It came to a head in the 5th Congress in 1904. Herzl then had to report that despite his indefatigable diplomatic efforts the best offer he could extract from the Sultan Abdul Hamid was free Jewish immigration into the Ottoman Empire, in small separate groups to any area—except Palestine. He refused this on the spot. At this juncture the British Government made an offer of a tract of land in Uganda (the actual area was later known as "The White Highlands" and is in Kenya). Herzl was in favour of the Zionist Organisation sending a commission of enquiry to Uganda to consider it as a temporary place of settlement, pending an ultimate Zionist settlement in Palestine which would await more favourable times. The Easterner Weizmann summarises this development in these bitter words: "Palestine had in fact, never been 'available' to the Western leadership. It had been a mirage and when the mirage faded, Uganda... was proposed".[155]

Herzl won on the vote to send the commission; but the vote was 295 affirmative to 177 negative with 100 abstentions. It was a moral defeat and led to a walk-out by the Easterners. In a private meeting with them, and in the closing session, Herzl had to pledge that the final goal was Palestine.

Weizmann represents these happenings as the final victory of the Zion Zionists over the non-Zion Zionists, as the decisive imposition of the will of the East European leadership, speaking for the masses of Eastern Jewry, on the hesitant assimilated Western leaders who had lost touch with the Jewish people. This is true only in a very general sense.

On the details of the struggle within the Congress Weizmann is almost wholly inaccurate. For one thing he gives the impres-

[153]*Diaries*, p. 413.
[154]Weizmann, *op. cit.*, p. 74.
[155]Weizmann, *op. cit.*, p. 75.

sion of a clear-cut division with almost all the Easterners solidly united against Herzl. For another, he ascribes to himself a crucial role. He describes how during the voting, which was by individual roll call, the number of negative votes from the Easterners surprised the gathering. Weizmann's father and brother voted affirmatively but when he called out his own negative vote Herzl went white in the face. From that moment, according to Weizmann, Herzl was finally Zionised.[156] This is high drama but also pure fantasy.[157]

In fact many Eastern Jewish leaders were not committed to Palestine alone nor were all the Westerners against it. In a meeting of the Actions Committee before the Congress the two members who were in favour of the commission of enquiry were both Russians. One of them actually came from Kishinev, the scene of the most recent pogrom, and he remarked that in their present circumstances the Jews of Russia would go anywhere— even to hell. Of the three members who voted against, two were Westerners.

Because of the division an unofficial caucus met the next day to decide whether to lay the British offer of Uganda before the Congress. Herzl left this meeting so as to leave its discussions free. Four Russian representatives were in favour and it was three Westerners who were opposed, so the offer went to the Congress with the result already mentioned.

Before the Congress the Russian Zionists as a whole had taken a vote on Uganda with 146 against, 84 in favour and many abstentions.

In this caucus Weizmann spoke and voted in favour of Uganda but two days later voted negatively in the Congress.[158]

---

[156]Weizmann, *op. cit.*, p. 117.

[157]The usefulness of Weizmann's writings and speeches as sources of historical fact is extremely suspect after the devastating analysis made of *Trial and Error* by V.K. Rabinowicz in his *Fifty Years of Zionism*. He is obviously partisan and sometimes pettifogging but his long listing of Weizmann's inaccuracies of interpretation and of fact, both large and small, has not been questioned. The only possible alternative explanations are that Weizmann either had a very poor memory or that he was mendacious. Rabinowicz's work deserves to be much more widely known.

[158]Rabinowicz, *op. cit.*, pp. 54-63; Bein, *op. cit.*, pp. 453-463.

Herzl was justified in writing, in his diary, of "these petty Russian Actions Committee politicians who at first were in the Action Committee for the immediate acceptance of the East African Project and later dramatically left the hall as if their innermost feelings were hurt."[159]

But he was protesting against something that is all-too-common in political life. Politicians who express sensible opinions in private act and speak foolishly in public because of fear of what their constituents back home might think—in this case the masses of East European Jewry who were supposed by most of their leaders to be devoted to Palestine and Palestine alone.

They were not. But, ironically enough, Herzl himself made the mistake of thinking that they were. When he met, not long before his death, with the Actions Committee, in April 1904, he made his "mea culpa" to it. He confessed that at first he was simply "a Jewish statist" (that is a non-Zion Zionist looking for any refuge). But he had learned much: "first and foremost I learned to know Jews, and that was sometimes even a pleasure. But above all I learned to understand that we shall find a solution to our problem only in Palestine."[160]

The masses of Jewry in Russia at that time, after the Kishinev pogrom, did not think so at all.

When their leaders, smarting from their defeat in the vote at the Congress, returned home they called together a conference at Kharkov and after it despatched an ultimatum to Herzl to take the East African project off the agenda of the next Zionist Congress. The reaction to this ultimatum revealed that the larger half of the Zionist Organisation as a whole opposed the Kharkov decision. More significantly, within Russian Jewry itself protest committees were formed which voted in favour of sending a commission to East Africa and, all over Russia, the Kharkov delegates were denounced as "traitors" and "conspirators". *The Jewish Chronicle* wrote, at that time, that "the East African Project had, without doubt, many more adherents

---

[159]Herzl, *Diaries*, vol III, p. 495 in the German edition. These words are not given in the "complete" four-volume English edition.

[160]Bein, *op. cit.*, p. 496.

among the Russian Jews than Zionism itself."[161]

What is truly surprising is that the Mizrachi, the religious Zionists in Eastern Europe, were, despite the thrice-daily prayer for Jerusalem, mostly in favour of Uganda.[162]

Even more startling was the reaction to this impassioned debate in Palestine itself, the object of the whole quarrel. Koestler quotes an Israeli historian for the view that in 1903 in Palestine, "The passion for Uganda soon became associated with a deadly hatred for Palestine...Nor was this the expression of a few individuals. Indeed it was only a few individuals here and there in the villages and towns who remained loyal and did not associate themselves with the abusive and decrying masses... All opposition to Uganda came from outside Palestine. In Zion itself all were against Zion". Koestler remarks that this episode is "usually slurred over in Zionist histories",[163] quite understandably.

Yet despite the misunderstandings, despite the protests, the East European leaders had their way and in the 7th Zionist Congress, after Herzl's death, it was affirmed that Palestine alone was the goal of the movement, but it was not till the 10th Congress, in 1911, that the Easterners took control of the Zionist Organisation.

In the intervening years the quarrel over Palestine went on. Now the Westerners tried to hinder the colonisation work in Palestine which the Easterners had embarked on in 1908. The non-Zion Zionists, led by Israel Zangwill, left the Zionist Organisation altogether and formed the rival Jewish Territorial Organisation which, unsuccessfully, tried to find a haven for the Jews in such various places as Peru, Ecuador, Kenya, New Guinea and Australia.

It took a wholly external and unexpected event to fix Zionist ambitions firmly on Palestine—that was the First World War and the dissolution of the Ottoman Empire that it brought about.

[161]Rabinowicz, *op. cit.*, pp. 64-66; Bein, *op. cit.* pp. 480, 488.
[162]Weizmann, *op. cit.*, p. 114.
[163]Koestler, *Promise and Fulfilment*, p. 37, quoting S. Zemach, *Introduction to the History of Labour Settlement in Palestine*.

But even many years after that war at least one influential
Zionist questioned the link between Zionism and Zion in exactly
the same terms used by Smolenskin, 55 years earlier. In 1930
Judah Magnes wrote: "I do not at all believe that without
Palestine the Jewish people is dying out or is doomed to destruction; on the contrary, it is growing stronger. There are three
chief elements in Jewish life: the people, the Torah and the Land
of Israel. My view is that the people and the Torah can exist
and be as creative, as they have existed and been creative,
without the Land".[164]

One epitaph on Herzl claims that though he was "quite
ignorant of the tide of thought and feeling that was pulsing
through Russian Jewry...he brought the message and the
teaching of the Russian Jew to the Jew of the West...he taught
more than he knew."

We have seen that in public Herzl admitted that he had learned
about the indispensability of Palestine and we have also seen
that he was primarily moved by the need to find an immediate
refuge for East European Jews pushed out by anti-Semitism.
But it is also very clear from his public utterances and private
diaries that he knew very well that the Jewish people would not
move to the Jewish State whether in Palestine or elsewhere unless
they were forced to do so by anti-Semitism, or induced to do so
by the propaganda of the Zionist movement. He had no illusions
on the pulling-power of Palestine: he knew, and said, that there
was no daring, selfless urge towards Palestine even among East
European Jewry.

In 1904 a French Jew making an enquiry in Russia found
that "in truth Palestine attracted them less than the idea of
emigration." In the years before Herzl was even less optimistic.
In *The Jewish State* he wrote, with almost cruel frankness: "Those
who are in despair at this moment will go first. They will be
led by the pseudo-intellects which we produce so superabund-
antly and which are persecuted everywhere...The anti-Semites
will provide the stimulus...a little despair is indispensable to
a great undertaking...the poorest will go first to cultivate the

<hr>

[164]Magnes, in Hertzberg, *op. cit.*, p. 444.

soil... Higher and yet higher ranks will feel tempted to go over... when our 'desperadoes' increase the value of the land by their presence and by their labour".[165] In his diary he remarks, solicitously, that the initial hard or dangerous work of clearing the land of the new State may have to be done by local people so as not to scare off the new Jewish settlers: "old prisoners don't like to leave prison. They have to be coaxed".[166] His favourite words for the emigration process were drawn from horticulture: "we will dig out the centres and take them across...transplant whole environments in which the Jews feel comfortable"; "we will give the Jews a homeland...by carefully digging them up with all their roots and transplanting them to better soil." "When we journey out of Egypt again we shall not leave the fleshpots behind".[167]

Clearly this was to be no heroic national venture; but then Herzl was a realist about what his people would accept.

Nor were the Zionist leaders any more heroic. The essence of the Zionist movement was the call to Jews to move from Europe to somewhere else, which the East Europeans insisted should be Palestine. But very few of the leaders making the call—most of them East Europeans—followed their own exhortations and set an example to the masses by leaving Europe to settle in Palestine. These men did not face the difficulties that the impoverished masses did; they all had the means to travel to Palestine and could have evaded the immigration restrictions as thousands of others did. Yet Herzl himself paid only one hurried visit of ten days to Palestine because he was scheduled to meet the Kaiser there; he did not bother to see anything more than the country between Jaffa and Jerusalem. Hess did not even do that much, nor Pinsker, nor Smolenskin, Nordau, Syrkin, Schechter. Weizmann admits that he paid his first visit when he was 33, and as a result of a challenge but for which he would only have gone later.[168] This was the attitude of the

---

[165] *The Jewish State*, pp. 28, 29, 57.
[166] *Diaries*, p. 208.
[167] *Diaries*, pp. 41, 149, and *The Jewish State*, p. 101.
[168] Weizmann, *op. cit.*, p. 159.

majority of the leaders. It is, indeed, easier to record the few names of those well-known Zionist leaders who practised in Palestine what they preached about Palestine—Ben Yehuda, Ahad Ha'am, Brenner, Gordon, Jabotinsky, Magnes, Ben Gurion, than to list those who did not.

Here then we have the spectacle of a movement of a unique kind, which it is claimed is nothing if not idealistic but with a simple, practical objective—a relatively short journey from Europe to the eastern Mediterranean coast. But when we examine the words and acts of the leaders and their followers the most fitting description seems to be the lines of Macaulay:

And those behind cried 'forward'
And those in front cried 'back'.

* * *

Political and humanitarian alternatives

Herzl's *The Jewish State* was subtitled "An Attempt at a Modern Solution of the Jewish Problem". In Herzl's mind the problem and its solution were analysed in clear and simple terms: the Jews of Eastern Europe subjected to anti-Semitic persecution must leave Europe for another land somewhere else. We have seen that there was much controversy over the location of that land, and we have also seen that, at the time and later, a variety of prestigious reasons were given to explain, or conceal, the fact of flight. A two-fold complication about objective and motive was thus injected into Herzl's simple solution.

A third complication was accepted by Herzl himself and by every other Zionist leader: Zionism could only be a partial, a very partial solution of the Jewish problem because only a relatively small proportion of European Jewry would want to, or be able to, go to the Promised Land, wherever it was.

Unlike any other nationalist movement the original Zionist leaders did not aspire for their movement to achieve its ostensible goal completely.

It is true that on the earlier pages of his Diary, which reflect his excitement at the "discovery" of the idea of the Jewish State, Herzl wrote of the ceremoniously organised emigration of the whole of European Jewry. But he was soon brought down to earth, for a few months later, when he actually committed the idea to paper, he wrote "Whoever wishes may stay behind... Will people say...only the poor would go with us? It is precisely the poor whom we need at first! Only the desperate make good conquerors."

This was Herzl's public acceptance of a fact which several of his predecessors in the Zionist movement had had to accept: that the rich and assimilated Jews, of Western and Eastern Europe, would not move to the Jewish State, that the poor Jews of the West would probably also not go, and only some, not all, of the poor Jews of the East.

Since even the enthusiastic Smolenskin had had to admit "not all the Jews will go, only those who are destitute or persecuted will look for a place to which to emigrate...It would be enough if only one million of our brethren (out of 10 million) would go, for it would be a relief both to them and to those remaining in the Diaspora"[169]—with this facing of realities the Zionists sought to make a virtue, a divine virtue, of necessity and said, with Rabbi Alkalai, that "We are commanded not to attempt to go at once and all together to the Holy Land. In the first place, it is necessary for many Jews to remain for a time in the lands of dispersion, so that they can help the first settlers in Palestine, who will undoubtedly come from among the poor. Secondly, the Lord desires that we be redeemed in dignity; we cannot, therefore, migrate in a mass...."[170]

With Pinsker we come to another, more subtle and realistic, explanation for Jewry's reluctance to go to Zion in large numbers. Again, it is said to be not necessary, according to what may be called the Zionist's "critical-mass" theory of anti-Semitism or, alternatively, the theory of surplus Jewish anti-value. According to these theories anti-Semitism arises only when the percentage of Jews in the general population rises above a certain critical percentage, and that the Zionist answer to anti-Semitism is to try and get the Jews in surplus to that percentage

[169]Smolenskin in Hertzberg, *op. cit.*, p. 151.
[170]Alkalai in Hertzberg, *op. cit.*, p. 105.

to emigrate, and that surplus would naturally come from the impoverished rootless masses.

Thus Pinsker says "we can mix with the nations only in the smallest proportions...Therefore we must see to it that the *surplus* of Jews, the unassimilable residue, is removed...If the Jews could be equally distributed among all the peoples of the earth, perhaps there would be no Jewish question:" What is needed is "a secure and inviolable home for the *surplus* of those Jews who live as proletarians in the various countries. There can of course be no question whatever of a united emigration of the entire people. The comparatively small number of Jews in the Occident...may in the future remain where they are. The wealthy may also remain, even where Jews are not readily tolerated...It is this surplus which conjures up the evil fate of the entire people. It is now high time to create a refuge for this surplus".[171]

Considering that Herzl was quite unaware of Pinsker's writings it is extraordinary how similar their ideas were on this subject, down to the use of the word "surplus", which, oddly enough, Herzl always emphasised and wrote in English in the German manuscript of his diary.

However yet another theory on possible Jewish immovability was added by Herzl. He claimed that not all European governments would let their Jews go, because of the adverse effect this might have on their economy. Considering the state of European opinion at the time this sounds improbable, but Herzl gives it as a reason for the use of the rather ugly word "surplus": "we must use the word 'surplus' otherwise they (the European governments) will not let us make propaganda and move away"; and, more optimistically: "each country would relinquish only as many Jews as it can spare. In each country, the drainage would come to a standstill along with anti-Semitism itself." The basic idea of how "the surplus was to be drained off" remained: "By no means all Jews would emigrate to Palestine from Russia—no more than they would from other countries—, but only a *surplus* of proletarian and desperate ones...supported by their wealthy

[171]Pinsker, *Auto-Emancipation*, pp. 31-36.

fellow Jews".[172]

Almost every subsequent Zionist writer repeated the idea of Nordau: "no mass immigration is likely. Zionism neither demands nor expects it".[173]

But by the end of the first quarter of this century the new problem posed for Jewry by the very partial solution provided by Zionism to the Jewish Problem had to be faced. In 1927 the Swiss Zionist, Fleg, admitting that Zionism did not imply "the return of all Jews to Palestine—a thing numerically impracticable" still felt that it would be "a miracle" for there to be "three million Jews (who) will speak Hebrew, will live Hebrew on Hebrew soil!!" (a surprising increase on Smolenskin's figures of one million out of ten). But, he asks, "for the twelve million Jews who will remain scattered throughout the world, for them and for me, the tragic question remained: What is Judaism?... How be a Jew? Why be a Jew?"[174]

Fleg would have done well to refer to the earlier writings of Ahad Ha'am who foresaw all the practical and spiritual problems raised by the programme of "political Zionism". In direct criticism of the 1st Zionist Congress Ahad Ha'am, in 1897, pointed out that because of natural increase "the number of those remaining outside of Palestine will by no means diminish" (and, as has been noted, the number of Jews in Europe in the 19th century, despite massive immigration to America, actually increased fourfold). Therefore, he asked "if the Jewish State means not an "ingathering of the exiles" but the settlement of a small part of our people in Palestine, how will this solve the material problem of the Jewish masses of the Diaspora?...it will not be ended by the creation of the Jewish State, and it is, indeed, beyond our power to solve it once and for all."[175] Later on, in 1902, Ahad Ha'am turned to the dangers of the "draining-off" idea: "have we it in our power to diminish the number of Jews in every country to the maximum which the economic

---

[172]*Diaries*, pp. 51, 336, 670, 783.
[173]Ben Horin, *op. cit.*, p. 194.
[174]Fleg, in Hertzberg, pp. 482-483.
[175]Ahad Ha'am, in Hertzberg, *op. cit.* pp. 263-264.

condition of the country can bear without arousing anti-Semitism?" This he referred to as "the Achilles heel of political
Zionism".[176]

And a fatal weakness it was, and is, to Zionist theory if not to
Zionist practice. Fourteen years later we find no less a person
than Weizmann making this pessimistic confession: "to congreg-
ate all the Jews together in one place is obviously impossible,
even if it were desirable. The millions of Jews in Eastern Europe
could not be transplanted by a wave of a wand to a Jewish land,
and any gradual emigration must be more or less counterbalan-
ced by the natural growth of population. The political and
economic problems of the Jews in Eastern Europe must be
settled, for the great mass of them, in the countries where they
live."

What then is Zionism all about? What was it striving for?

Weizmann's answers, necessarily, are circumlocutions since
he has ruled out the Ingathering: "a home for the Jewish
people...in which they can produce a type of life correspondent
to the character and ideals of the Jewish people...the national
centre...the source of all that is most essentially Jewish...
there the Jewish mind and character will express themselves as
they can nowhere else".[177]

Not only are these vague words, they sound very much like
what Ahad Ha'am had advocated, and Weizmann had no
patience with Ahad Ha'am.

Ahad Ha'am's own answer to his question was that Zionism
should not try to solve the Jewish Problem by establishing only
a political state but rather one that would be a spiritual-cul-
tural centre. Five years later still, Einstein reached much the
same conclusion: "Palestine will not solve the Jewish problem
but its development will mean a revival of the soul of the Jewish
people."

Even these ideas were seen as inadequate by one of the famous
later exponents of spiritual Zionism. Judah Magnes, in 1930,

---

[176]Ahad Ha'am, *Pinsker and Political Zionism*, in Pinsker, *op. cit.*, p. 49.
[177]Weizmann, Introduction to *Zionism and the Jewish Problem*, ed. Sacher,
London, 1916.

declared squarely: "Palestine cannot solve the Jewish problem
of the Jewish people. Wherever there are Jews there is the Jewish problem. It is part of the Jewish destiny to face this problem
and make it mean something good for mankind."[178]

Here we have one more of the many tortuous peculiarities
that characterise Zionism as a political movement. Its founders
claimed that it was meant to solve a particularly urgent and
tragic human problem—the apartness of the European Jew that
led to anti-Semitic persecution. Yet many of these leaders, from
the outset, stated that Zionism could provide only a partial
solution. Partial solutions are, of course, better than none; but
some of the Zionists foresaw that it would not suffice at all.
In fact, the State of Israel has not provided the answers to the
Jewish Problem, either numerically or emotionally.

This pessimistic obliquity of Zionist aims is also one more
factor differentiating Zionism from the Afro-Asian national
movements. These had independence as their goal and independence, subsequently, produced problems of its own. But
the national leaders, while engaging in struggle, did not believe
that the movement as such could only be a partial, or complete,
failure, that it might never achieve its objectives and would
always remain incomplete, which would have been a betrayal
of their following.

For a movement based on a lofty humanitarian ideal Zionism
was also singularly alive to the profit motive. Zionist leaders
appealed quite frankly for the support of upper and middle class
Jews on the basis that the Jewish State would be a profitable
investment. According to Marxist analysis the profit hunger of
the national bourgeoisie is the motive force of all national liberation movements, but whether through self-deception or cunning concealment the Asian nationalist leaders did not tell their
followers openly that they should join the nationalist movement
to make profits. The Zionists did. The Holy Land itself became
good business. Pinsker pointed out the advantages of prompt
participation in the Zionist movement because if Palestine was
chosen as the site of the Jewish State land there would rise in

[178]Magnes, in Hertzberg, *op. cit.*, p. 444. Einstein, *op. cit.*, p. 36.

price. Smolenskin argued in favour of Palestine because it could become "a centre of commerce linking Europe with Asia and Africa", and also the site for glass factories, "for the sand of the country is of high quality".[179] In his writings Herzl made a deliberate attempt to harness the business acumen of his people to the Zionist programme. The executive arm of his movement was to be "The Jewish Company", "strictly a business undertaking" meant to "draw enormous profits" from its undertakings. Parts of *The Jewish State* read like a nationalist manifesto but most of the latter half is merely a company prospectus. As to individual supporters, their acquisitiveness was also appealed to. "We shall not lose our acquired possessions; we shall realize them; those only will depart who are sure thereby to improve their position;" "the exodus will be at the same time an ascent of the class." He even foresaw the danger that through the Zionist movement "the moderately rich Jews would have created a new and large business and Jewish emigration would be forgotten".[180]

Most of the calculating and unappealing aspects of Zionism— its exploitation of religious sentiment, its use of, and dependence on, anti-Semitism, its appeal to cupidity—became parts of it when the movement was taken over by "political nationalist Zionism", a process that began in the last year of Herzl's life and was completed in 1911.

In 1905 it was definitely decided that Palestine should be the territorial goal of the Zionist movement. But till 1911, when the Herzlians were displaced from the leadership, it was still not clear what sort of Jewish establishment should be built up in Palestine, whether it was to be cultural or political. The latter was preferred in 1911.

There were two other types of Zionism—philanthropic and humanitarian—which were less objectionable, but political nationalist Zionism pushed aside the former and absorbed the latter. Philanthropic Zionism had existed through the ages in the form of the Hallukah, the charity paid in at synagogues for

[179]Pinsker, *op. cit.*, p. 40 and Smolenskin in Hertzberg, *op. cit.*, p. 153.
[180]*The Jewish State*, pp. 30, 60, 70, 85.

pious Jews who wanted to emigrate to die in the Holy Land. The donations of Baron Hirsch to Jewish colonies in Argentina and of Baron Edmond de Rothschild to similar colonies in Palestine were merely grandiose examples of philanthropic Zionism.

Humanitarian Zionism was best exemplified by Pinsker and Herzl *in the early period* of their Zionist work, when they were still non-Zion Zionists. It is true that Herzl also thought in terms of a state with the full panoply of statehood but this was subordinate to the main objective—of finding a home, quickly, for refugees. To get this Pinsker and Herzl, despite their theorisings, were prepared to accept land anywhere on any terms.

After 1911, during the War years and then during the discussions leading up to the Balfour Declaration in 1917, it was political nationalist Zionism that dominated the movement.

That remained the position during the period of the Mandate in Palestine up to 1932, though the political Zionists kept their nationalist objectives concealed under the cloak of the concept of "The National Home".

Zionism could concentrate on national politics from 1911 to 1932 because there was no great need for philanthropy or humanitarian feelings since there were no large-scale anti-Semitic expulsions from Europe. About 100,000 Jews entered Palestine during this 20-year period; in 1916 the Zionist organisation already had 200,000 members.

After 1932 and until the creation of Israel in 1948 the humanitarian theme was once again placed in the forefront of the Zionist Movement by the political Zionists, but in order to reinforce their nationalist arguments: the Jewish State was a necessity in order to provide a home for refugees from the Nazis.

This remained the case for the first three or four years of Israel's existence, but from the early 1950's, and especially after June 1967, Zionism's main, almost its sole, objective has been political—the sustaining of the nation-state of Israel through financial support, diplomatic pressure, publicity and immigration. The swinging back and forth between the various schools of thought and action within Zionism thus came to an end with the final triumph of the political nationalists.

Veneers of interpretation laid subsequently upon a movement can sometimes be as important, perhaps even more important than the original object, for if there are a sufficient number of layers they can make the original unrecognisable.

This process of interpretative transformation began very early in Zionism and still continues, obscuring the anti-Semitic origins of the movement while high-lighting its "nationalist" aspects.

There has been such a large number of books, essays, and speeches by Zionists arguing the case for Zionism as a nationalist movement that this vehemence in itself leads one to suspect that the Zionists need to convince not only others but themselves as to the validity of their argument.

We have seen how, repeatedly, Zionism was presented as a nationalism by linking it, in circular argumentation, with the "national" Jewish people or the "national" religion of Judaism.

The emphasis on the nationalist aspect became especially noticeable during and after World War I in which the principle of nationality played so large a part. In one book on Zionism, published in 1916, the Table of Contents includes, *inter alia*, these chapter headings: One of the Smaller Nations; Israel a Nation; Zionism and the Revival of Nationality in Europe; The Jews a Nation; England and the Jewish National Movement.[181]

Since the early Zionists made no secret of the fact that, both personally and in general terms, the motivation of Zionism was to be found in anti-Semitism, simple denials of anti-Semitic origins are not enough; they have to be gradually obscured under layers of argument.

Thus even Einstein while admitting that Zionism arose "from the fact of Jewish suffering" (i.e. anti-Semitism) contended that it also arose "from an even deeper motive than Jewish suffering. It is rooted in a Jewish spiritual tradition".[182] Zionism is also presented as a sort of higher avatar of anti-Semitism. Thus A. Eban in 1937: "How far does Zionism go in meeting the

[181]*Zionism: Problems and Views*, eds. Goodman and Lewis, London, 1916.
[182]Einstein, *op. cit.*, pp. 56-58.

challenge of anti-Semitism?...although anti-Semitism was the stimulus for its origin, Zionism has outlived the purely philanthropic motive of its programme." The identification is then made between Zionism and a well-known Asian nationalist movement: "To take a topical instance—Indian nationalists desire their freedom because Imperialism keeps them in the throes of subjection. But they would not desire their autonomy any less if the Imperial Government treated them with the most liberal and kindly tolerance imaginable. Similarly, the actual misery of the Jews in the Diaspora fortifies but does not create the necessity for Zionism."[183] (This comparison was rejected by both Gandhi and Nehru, as will be seen in a later chapter).

Within this general turning-away from anti-Semitism the importance of the impact of certain anti-Semitic happenings, of decisive import to the Zionist movement, is likewise explained away. Thus: " it is often said that the massacres and persecutions of 1880-1881 were a turning point in Russo-Jewish thought, but all that they effected was the crystallisation and clarification of ideas".[184]

Herzl's own words on the importance of the anti-Semitic Dreyfus Affair in converting him to Zionism are discounted and diminished: "Herzl was overstating when he says that the Dreyfus affair made him a Zionist"; and "It is the accepted opinion that anti-Semitism was the cause of Herzl's revelation. Quite true, but this was only an external factor, not the inner motivation."[185]

It avails nothing for Nordau, also deeply affected by Dreyfus, to admit that "anti-Semitism opened my eyes to return to my forgotten Jewishness" for the chapter in his official biography in which these words are quoted is one long argument that Nordau's conversion to Zionism was not a sudden reaction to anti-Semitism.[186] We find the same playing-down of the anti-

---

[183]Eban in *Afterword* to Pinsker, *op. cit.*, pp. 81-82.
[184]Sacher, in *Zionism and the Jewish Future*, p. 56.
[185]D.M. Stamler, *Backdrop To Tragedy*. Boston, 1957, p. 148; and Klatzkin in Hertzberg, *op. cit.*, p. 326.
[186]Ben Horin, *op. cit.*, pp. 175, 177, and Chapter V.

Semitic motive in the official biography of Jabotinsky.[187]

Finally, in the synthesis of the anti-Semitic thesis and the "nationalist" antithesis we find one modern Zionist theoretician arguing: "Neither anti-Semitism nor nationalism, as such, were the preconditions for modern Zionism".[188]

The embarrassment of the Zionists with the anti-Semitic origins of their movement is easily understandable. For one thing Israel claims to be a nation-state and it would be a peculiarity if, unlike other nation-states, it was the product of anything else except a national movement. For another, the motivation of a reaction to anti-Semitism could seem a merely negative response to an external force and not something original springing from within the Jewish people; it could even be interpreted, unkindly, as a form of flight.

But for the past century nationalism has been part of the Zeitgeist and nationalist slogans have been part of the verbal currency of the times. The Zionists could not but conform to current political fashions by presenting their movement as part of the world-wide nationalist tide.

There was also a more practical reason. People who were merely refugees from anti-Semitism could be told that they did not need to have a state of their own. But if Jewry was defined as a nation this gave it a "claim to an inalienable right to self-determination".[189] Its credentials became immensely more respectable.

Though these reasons for the re-interpretation of Zionist origins are understandable there still remains a doubt as to why Zionist theorists are unwilling to accept a simple refugee origin for their movement and for the State of Israel. After all the United States was created by refugees and some Zionist writers have seen the parallel with the Mayflower and Pilgrim Fathers. Australia today is not ashamed of its origins as a penal colony. And although Zionist theorists and historians today play down the refugee origin of the Jewish state, Israeli politicians and

---

[187]Schechtman, *op. cit.*
[188]Hertzberg in his Introduction, *op. cit.*, p. 38.
[189]Hertzberg, *op. cit.*, p. 18.

diplomats have not hesitated to use the concept of the refugee state when this works to their immediate political advantage. In 1947, for instance, the use of this concept was a decisive psychological factor swinging diplomatic support in favour of the United Nations plan for a Jewish state.

Perhaps the reason for Zionist embarrassment is to be found in its claims, based on the Biblical Covenant, to have a special educative role and a redemptive mission in the world—a light to lighten the Gentiles. The gap between these lofty claims and a refugee state may seem dismayingly wide. Hence the more elevating reinterpretation.

But glosses apart, an examination of the motives and origins of Zionism reveals it to be this: a Westernised movement led by agnostic East European Jews who sought a refuge for the Jewish people from anti-Semitic persecution and who, after much controversy, fixed on Zion, Palestine, as their objective for colonisation because of its useful links with religious sentiment, which the leaders did not share.

No amount of reinterpretation can give to a movement of this type a nationalist cast. Zionism is non-nationalist. As such it is quite different from the movement that created the Afro-Asian states of the Third World.

CHAPTER III

ZIONISM IN ACTION

Differences from Afro-Asian nationalism

Zionism as a system of ideas, as a programme for action, could perhaps be mistaken for a nationalist movement because the complicated scaffolding of theory erected around it also serves as an effective camouflage.

Zionism in action could never be mistaken for a nationalist movement by any observer familiar with the principles and methods of movements for national independence from colonial occupation.

The Afro-Asian movements were anti-colonial and directed against the Western Powers. Zionism in action was the exact opposite on both counts—it was colonial and it sought the protection of the European powers.

Because of the fragmentation of the Jews in the Diaspora Zionism obviously could not use the same methods as the Afro-Asian nationalists. Because of the lack of a territorial base of its own we do not find in Zionism the usual Afro-Asian progression from polite requests for self-government on to demands for Dominion or associated status culminating in a declaration of independence (or from the colonial power's point of view, a descent from dissidence through agitation to rebellion). Nor do we come across in Zionist history the successive phases of orderly public meetings passing resolutions, followed later by processions, house arrests and deportations and, finally, sabotage and imprisonment.

To be an ex-jail bird, or at least a deportee, was an indispensable qualification for an Afro-Asian nationalist leader. Very few of the Zionist leaders ever went to jail or needed to.

To succeed, an Afro-Asian movement had to become a mass movement so as to counter the armed strength of the rulers with the sheer weight of the unarmed people, or to make the people the protective background for the freedom fighters. Zionism could not bring the mass of Jews in the Diaspora into full play for fear of arousing anti-Semitic reactions from the surrounding majority. The Zionists relied instead on external allies, such as Britain and the United States, and concentrated upon influencing them by means of persuasive interviews, discreet lobbying, fund-raising and propaganda campaigns and pressure from highly-organised groups whose influence was out of proportion to their actual support from Diaspora Jewry.

These differences were the inevitable consequences of the fact that the Afro-Asians were trying to evict alien rulers from their lands, while the Zionists were attempting to gain a foothold in another country from which the local inhabitants, by force or persuasion, would have to be evicted.

The Zionists, of course, have succeeded in this aim. The sheer physical fact of what has happened in Palestine is that what was, under Ottoman and British authority, an Arab majority and a Jewish minority has been converted into a Jewish majority and an Arab minority under the authority of a Jewish state. This represents the actual physical seizure, the capture, of Palestine by the Zionists. It is a remarkable feat, but it is also colonialism in its simplest, most direct, most brutal form.

Zionism is not only colonial but is, specifically, a form of Western, that is European, colonialism. This is so not only because all the Zionists were European but also because they were part of the general movement of Western colonialism and were Western in their thinking and feeling on the subject of colonisation.

The Zionists were also direct allies, or at least junior partners, of the Western colonial powers. The Zionist leaders were looking for a territory for their refugees from European anti-Semitism; clearly no such territory was available in Europe itself, for no European state would hand over any portion of its land to the Jews. The Zionists never questioned this European refusal. It was the unspoken basis of a tacit agreement between these Europeans, Zionists and Gentiles, who together worked at finding alternative territories anywhere outside Europe. When King Ibn Saud suggested to Roosevelt in 1945 that the Jews should be compensated for their suffering with a piece of German territory, he was accused by Roosevelt of being unhelpful. The Zionist objective was colonial and the Zionist method was pro-colonial.

Under Herzl there were many unsuccessful attempts at collusion between the Zionists and several European governments to find territory for the former in Palestine, Sinai and Uganda.

Under Weizmann there was the successful collusion between Zionism and the British Government which opened the doors of Palestine through the Balfour Declaration, which became practical politics after Britain's military defeat of the Ottoman Empire.

During the Mandatory period the Zionist-British cooperation continued, with the British administration pledged to create conditions—against Arab opposition if necessary—permitting Jews to enter Palestine in such numbers that they would eventually become the majority and take over the country.

Only when the British, after World War II, would not allow immigration at the speed demanded by the Zionists did the latter begin an armed struggle. But this was very different from an anti-colonial struggle. It was not aimed at securing national independence for the indigenous (Arab) majority, but to prevent this by ultimately establishing a Jewish state in the place of British rule. The struggle of the Jews was that of "colons" fearful of ultimate betrayal by their imperial protectors; it had analogies with the French Algerian and Rhodesian rebellions later, but none with the Afro-Asian independence movements.

It is when we examine the basic presuppositions of the Zionist leaders, especially someone like Herzl, on the question of acquiring a non-European territory that we can see how much they share the mental outlook, and the even more important emotional attitudes, of the European colonisers of their day.

It was inescapable that the day-to-day language of Zionism should have been "permeated by the terminology of colonisation".[1] But perhaps too much should not be made of the fact that the Zionists spoke of "colonies" and had a "Jewish Colonial Trust" and a "Colonisation Department". These were merely the verbal expressions of a colonial mentality which the Zionists, almost unthinkingly, shared with the Europeans of their time.

These basic Zionist colonial presuppositions were the following: that Europe and North America represented civilisation and the rest of the world barbarism; that Europe, therefore, had a civilising mission to execute in colonising that outer darkness; that all non-European territories were available for exploitation or settlement and that their inhabitants should be grateful for their lands to be objects of seizure, purchase or barter.

The most striking expression of this fundamental attitude was given in Herzl's *The Jewish State*: "Supposing His Majesty the Sultan were to give us Palestine, we could in return undertake to regulate the whole finances of Turkey. We should there form a portion of the rampart of Europe against Asia, an outpost of civilisation as opposed to barbarism. We should as a neutral State remain in contact with all Europe, which would have to guarantee our existence".[2] Why the "have to", it may be asked? Presumably in return for services rendered by the Jewish State as the defenders of Europe against Asian "barbarism".

In similar vein Herzl noted in his Diary: "It is a river of gold, of progress, of vitality which the Sultan will admit into his Empire with the Jews".[3] In his address to the 1st Zionist Congress he argued: "It is more and more to the interest of the civilised nations and of civilisation in general that a cultural station be established on the shortest road to Asia. Palestine is this station and we Jews are the bearers of culture who are ready to give our property and our lives to bring about its creation".[4]

The same insistence on the civilising mission is found in his remark: "We shall remain part of civilisation while we are

---

[1] Fayez Sayegh, "The 'Non-Colonial' Zionism of Mr. Abba Eban", in *Middle East Forum*, vol. xlii, 4, pp. 43-74.

[2] Herzl, *The Jewish State*, p. 30.

[3] *Diaries*, p. 213.

[4] Herzl, *Congress Addresses*, New York, 1917, p. 24.

emigrating. After all we don't want a Boer state, but a Venice".[5] Which is presumably why Herzl records his odd insistence that when immigrating the Jews should dress for dinner, like the proverbial Englishman wearing a dinner jacket in the lonely outposts of Empire, "to impress the natives".[6]

Herzl felt that he was part of a superior Western civilisation not only vis-à-vis Asia but even as against the backward Jews of Eastern Europe: "The return of even semi-Asiatic Jews under the leadership of thoroughly modern persons must undoubtedly mean the restoration to health of this neglected corner of the Orient. Civilisation and order would be brought there. Thus the migration of the Jews would eventually be an effective protection of the Christians in the Orient"[7]—in short a Jewish-Christian alliance against Islam, which, interestingly enough, Israel is still seeking.

It is very often the off-hand remark that is most revealing, as is the case when Herzl comments: "the Orient is always amusing," or on his acceptance of the claim that "in the Orient everybody was afraid of everybody else. The people were a wild animal that could be unleashed, but also steered in any direction".[8]

Herzl's bland assumption of European superiority, in which Zionism partakes, is revealed in a statement like: "All Palestine talks about our nationalist plan. After all we are the hereditary lords of the land".[9] As also this handsome tribute to the British Empire: "What the English are doing is splendid. They are cleaning up the Orient, letting light and air into the filthy corners".[10] And this was written in 1903 when many thoughtful Englishmen were having doubts about how "splendid" the Empire was, not excluding Rudyard Kipling.

The complete agreement between Zionism and European colonisers that all of the non-European world was "available"

[5]*Diaries*, p. 213.
[6]*Diaries*, p. 212.
[7]*Diaries*, p. 671.
[8]*Op. cit.*, pp. 1355, 803.
[9]*Op. cit.*, p. 517.
[10]*Op. cit.*, p. 1449.

for their use appears from the conversations of Herzl and Joseph Chamberlain, the British Colonial Secretary. Chamberlain remarked that he was prepared to help if he could, for he liked the Zionist idea: "In fact if I could show him a spot in the English possessions where there were no white people as yet, we could talk about that".[11] That there might be non-white people living there already was, naturally, irrelevant. And on his world travels Chamberlain kept the needs of the Zionists in mind: "I have seen a land for you on my travels, and that's Uganda. It's hot on the coast, but farther inland becomes excellent, even for Europeans. You can raise sugar and cotton there. And I thought to myself, that would be a land for Dr. Herzl."[12] Unfortunately there were already Europeans in that territory who made it known that they wanted no Jewish settlers.

Herzl shared these colonialist assumptions with Zionist leaders who came both before and after him. Moses Hess quotes, with full approval, these words addressed to the Jews: "You shall be the bearers of civilisation to peoples who are still inexperienced and their teachers in the European sciences, to which your race has contributed so much. You shall be the mediators between Europe and far Asia, opening the roads that lead to India and China—those unknown regions which must ultimately be thrown open to civilisation".[13] And Nordau, with his usual eloquent vehemence denied that Zionism represented a rejection of European civilisation or a shift towards Asia: "In truth we will become Asians as little as the Anglo-Saxons in America Indians, in South Africa Hottentots, or in Australia Papuans".[14] (It is perhaps a significant pointer to the Zionist future that in all these three cases the Anglo-Saxons expelled or exterminated the local people). The Jews wanted to return to Palestine, according to Arthur Ruppin, "not in order to submerge in Asiatic barbarism";[15] nor would Nordau "admit that the return

---

[11]*Op. cit.*, p. 1361.
[12]*Op. cit.*, p. 1473.
[13]Hess, in Hertzberg, *op. cit.*, p. 134.
[14]Ben Horin, *op. cit.*, p. 197.
[15]A. Ruppin, *The Jews of Today*, p. 350.

of the Jews to the land of their fathers is a relapse into barbarism".[16] Fifty years later the fear of the "relapse into barbarism" is still openly expressed in Israel.

Many years later, too, the Zionist leaders claimed that they had actually played the role of successful conquerors and colonisers. In 1917 Ben Gurion described his fellow-Zionists in Palestine: "we were not just working—we were conquering, conquering a land. We were a company of conquistadors."[17] And Weizmann, in 1919, told the Versailles Peace Conference: "What the French could do in Tunisia,...the Jews would be able to do in Palestine...because the Zionists...even then (had) done more constructive work in Palestine than the French in Tunis." It also compared favourably, he said later, with the colonising work of British settlers in Canada and Australia.[18]

Thus we have the strange and saddening spectacle of the European Jew, expelled from Europe by his fellow-Europeans, and seeking a non-European territory to colonise, yet firmly convinced of the correctness of his colonial claim and his innate continental superiority. Among the pitiful belongings on the back of the Zionist Jewish refugee from Europe was The White Man's Burden; and he *was*, after all, a white man.

Since the Gentile and Zionist colonialists of Europe assumed that the non-European world was their oyster they could not for one moment concede that non-European peoples had any political rights or rights of possession in their homeland; in particular the right to self-determination had to be either ignored or circumvented.

Before World War I it was ignored because the very idea that Afro-Asians had political rights would have been taken as mere impertinence. Thus Herzl felt no qualms on this score.

But after the war, self-determination, thanks to President Wilson's presence at the Peace Conference, was very much in the air, so the Zionists and their Gentile supporters had to take it into account; especially because the Arabs invoked the prin-

[16]Ben Horin, *op. cit.*, p. 204.
[17]Ben Gurion, *Rebirth and Destiny of Israel*, New York, 1954, p. 9.
[18]Weizmann, *Trial and Error*, pp. 191, 244, 277.

ciple to contest the Zionist claim to a National Home in Palestine.

The official Zionist position on self-determination was given in a brochure entitled *Zionism, a Reply to Recent Criticism* published in 1921 by the Zionist Organisation of Great Britain which, as the Zionist group most directly concerned with Palestine, would be fully cognisant of authoritative Zionist argumentation. One of the criticisms replied to is "that Zionism cannot be reconciled with the principle of self-determination." The answer is given in these words: "To admit that self-determination simply means a system under which account should only be taken of the present racial composition of every province and town would mean...leaving the dispossessed dispossessed and the landless landless.... Has it ever been recognised, in the whole history of civilisation, that colonisation of an underdeveloped territory can only be undertaken with the consent of the majority of the actual inhabitants on the spot? Had it been so, hardly any country in the world could have been colonised." "If in every such case the principle of self-determination had been carried to its abstract logical conclusion and, say, a plebiscite of the natives had been taken, all expansion would have been rendered impossible, and the crowded masses of Europe would now suffocate and starve on this side of the Atlantic while a handful of Red Indians would still freely roam in the limitless spaces of America." After this frightening vision, and the damaging confession that the Zionists regarded the Palestine Arabs as the early American settlers had regarded the Red Indians, the Zionist case is clinched thus: "Colonisation is a principle no less important than self-determination and there are cases when the second can only be applied in so far as it is compatible with the free development of the first. It is, of course, not claimed that every land in the world should be open to colonisation: only underpopulated and generally backward territories can be considered appropriate for the expansion of the homeless. But the world has already evolved the conception of a Society of Nations. Whatever may be the further stages of its progress, the idea of a World Council representing the aggregate conscience of civilised peoples, implies, *inter alia*, the competence to sanction the opening up of an undeveloped area for colonisation. This sanction will have to be taken as the expression of a collective will outweighing purely local consideration".[19]

Today the advocates of Zionism and the Israeli Foreign Ministry would refrain from such a public repudiation of self-determination. In 1921 the Zionists did not need to conceal their intentions because they were talking to people who, for the most part, shared their colonialist outlook and who possessed effective power. What the peoples of the "generally backward countries" thought about the issue did not greatly matter, though, even then, it did matter more than the Zionists believed.

The Gentile supporters of the Zionists pushed aside the principle of self-determination perhaps even more unceremoniously. That ardent Zionist and equally ardent imperial statesman, Balfour, wrote in 1919: "The four Great Powers are committed to Zionism. And Zionism, be it right or wrong, good or bad, is rooted in age-long traditions, in present needs, in future hopes of far profounder import than the desires and prejudices of the 700,000 Arabs who now inhabit that ancient land. In my opinion that is right." But unlike the Zionist statement quoted above which claimed the support of the League of Nations, Balfour was honest enough to say that the policy he described could not be "harmonised" with the Covenant of the League, "for in Palestine we do not propose even to go through the form of consulting the wishes of the present inhabitants of the country."[20]

This robust cynicism was meat too strong for the delicate stomachs of the "liberal" variety of Gentile Zionist who had to find some argument to justify the exception to the rule of self-determination made in favour of the Zionists. Thus the famous pacifist, Norman Angell, argued that there could be no question of "majority" or "minority" rights in Palestine because "the homelessness of the Jews... concerns the whole of mankind, the whole of civilisation... are the Arabs a majority in that connection?"[21]

[19]*Zionism, a Reply to Recent Criticisms*, Zionist Organisation, London, 1921, pp. 7-9.
[20]Quoted in Stein, *The Balfour Declaration*, pp. 649-670.
[21]Quoted in Heller, *The Zionist Idea*, p. 68.

Here again we must note the automatic, Eurocentric exaggeration of a purely European peculiarity, anti-Semitism, into a world-wide phenomenon: the considerable portion of mankind that dwelt in Afro-Asia was not as familiar with the concept of Jewish homelessness because in that area the Jews had lived happily at home over the centuries.

Some of the Jewish Zionists with more sensitive consciences also felt the need to justify by argumentation the denial of self-determination. In his "Open letter to Mahatma Gandhi", written in 1939, the Jewish philosopher Martin Buber asks: "What do you mean by saying a land belongs to a population... You obviously mean to say that a people, being settled on a land, has so absolute a claim to that land that whoever settles on it without the permission of this people has committed a robbery." According to Buber this means giving sanctity to some original act of conquest. He goes on "It seems to me that God does not give any one portion of the earth away...The conquered land is, in my opinion, only lent to the conqueror who has settled on it—and God waits to see what he will make of it." Referring to the work of the Jewish settlers Buber says "This land recognises us, for it is fruitful through us".[22]

Just as Zionism has been described as a "spiritual nationalism" here Buber is enunciating a sort of "spiritual colonialism".

The end result of these arguments is the same as the bald, original claim: a people settled in the land can be ignored and pushed aside by foreign settlers if these latter, like the Zionists, claim to be superior to "the natives".

* * *

Herzl and diplomatic bargaining

Since Herzl was solidly embedded in the European colonial movement it would be almost unkind to compare his campaign on behalf of Zionism to the anti-colonialist campaigns waged by the nationalist leaders of Afro-Asia: in type they are mutually exclusive when not antagonistic. But since the Zionists hail

[22]Buber and Magnes, *Two Letters to Gandhi*, Jerusalem, 1939.

him as the founder of the State of Israel—even to the extent of having transferred his remains to Jerusalem—it becomes necessary to examine his diplomatic operations.

Herzl's activities were of a unique and singularly peculiar type, for what he tried to do was to buy a country for Jewry. Considering Zionism as nationalist, then Herzl can only be described as a "commercial nationalist", who tried to strike a bargain through high-level diplomatic negotiations.

Herzl's programme is briefly, and kindly, described in these words of a fellow-Zionist: "Herzl's thinking was very European. He believed that with Jewish money, the sympathy of the Powers, and the consent of the Sultan, the Judenstaat could be created in Palestine as the genii built Aladdin's palace. The Sultan, desperately in need of money and seeing little prospect of averting disintegration, would readily sell a charter transferring Palestine to the Jews, whose loyalty and continued support could be counted on; the Powers would hasten to guarantee an arrangement which relieved them of a distressing political problem; Jewish money would then put the Jews in Palestine."[23] The programme has also been described, succinctly and less kindly, by Weizmann: "There were rich Jews and poor Jews... What was more logical, then, than to get the rich Jews to give the Sultan money to allow the poor Jews to go to Palestine?"[24]

In retrospect the off-hand contempt in Weizmann's words seems justified, for Herzl's hectic efforts, which led to his early death, came to naught. The eight years during which he laboured mightily for the Jewish State are punctuated by journeyings in the Orient Express back and forth between Vienna and Constantinople with the object of persuading Sultan Abdul Hamid to permit unlimited Jewish immigration with an autonomous Jewish area in Palestine in return for Jewish financiers taking on the debts that the Ottoman Empire owed to various European governments. The tortuous negotiations carried on, for the most part, through shady and corrupt intermediaries, went on intermittently though always on the verge of collapse—

[23]H. Sacher, "Zionism and its Programme", *Sociological Revue*, 1912.
[24]Weizmann, *Trial and Error*, p. 62.

not unlike the Ottoman Empire itself.

There was a large element of bluff, on both sides, all through
the negotiations, and each party was well aware of the other's
unreliability. On Herzl's very first visit the Sultan sent the
following categoric and moving message to him: "advise him
not to take another step in this matter. I cannot sell even a foot
of land, for it does not belong to me, but to my people. My
people have won this empire by fighting for it with their blood
and have fertilized it with their blood. We will again cover it
with our blood before we allow it to be wrested away from us...
Let the Jews save their billions. When my Empire is partitioned, they may get Palestine for nothing. But only our corpse
will be divided. I will not agree to vivisection."[25] On the other
hand, it was apparent from quite early on that the one thing
everybody assumed was at Herzl's disposal—Jewish money—was
not going to be forthcoming. The two main Jewish financiers,
Baron Hirsch and Baron Rothschild were philanthropic, not
political, Zionists and consistently refused to back the plan of
the Jewish State. The only reason the negotiations with Herzl
were kept going was that it was more useful for both sides not
to have to admit failure: the Sultan because he used Herzl as
a bargaining counter with other financial interests, and Herzl
because he shrank from dashing the high hopes that he himself
had raised. Only in 1903 could he bring himself to tell his
followers that the Sultan had specifically excluded Palestine
from the area that might be opened to Jewish settlement.

This experience should have taught Herzl the lesson that even
in the venal world of politics there were some things—like one's
native land—which were not for sale. But having failed to buy
Palestine he tried to buy other areas. On one occasion he remarks impatiently: "Those South American republics must
be obtainable for money. We can give them annual subsidies."[26]
He tried again with the Ottoman Empire but this time in
order to acquire the area around El Arish and the Sinai peninsula: this idea failed because the Egyptian Government would

[25] Diaries, p. 378.
[26] Op. cit., p. 92.

not divert enough water from the Nile to establish settlements in the area. Yet his working combination of diplomatic negotiation plus money is explained by him in these words: "Possession, power and right. I shall have the possession assigned to me by the Egyptian government, then I shall demand from the English government as much power as possible, and finally I shall acquire the right to go with it from the Turkish government by means of baksheesh".[27]

He had the same ideas for the Congo: "The Congo State has land enough which we can use for our settlement. We can take over part of the responsibilities, that is, pay an annual tax, which may be fixed later, to the Congo State, in return for which we naturally lay claim to self-government and a not too oppressive vassalage to the Congo State".[28]

Herzl's plans for Mozambique were likewise based on purchasing power but had a more subtle political purpose: "I will try to get this inactive land for a Chartered Company from the Portuguese government, which needs money, by promising to meet the deficit and to pay a tribute later. However I want to acquire Mozambique only as an object of barter in order to get from the English government the entire Sinai Peninsula with Nile water summer and winter, and possibly Cyprus as well—and for nothing!"[29]

The reference to Cyprus is explained in these words: "Once we establish the Jewish Eastern Company with 5 million pounds capital for settling Sinai and El Arish, the Cypriots will begin to want that golden rain on their island too. The Moslems will move away, the Greeks will gladly sell their lands at a good price and migrate to Athens and Crete".[30]

These projects have been described in Herzl's own words to convey the authentic flavour of an approach to nation-building that is a genuine historic curiosity.

The projects are also significant for two other reasons. They

[27]*Op. cit.*, p. 1432.
[28]*Op. cit.*, p. 1512.
[29]*Op. cit.*, p. 1487.
[30]*Op. cit.*, p. 1362.

show that Herzl was incapable of crediting other peoples with national self-respect: for him all that the Zionist had to do was to show the colour of his money and others would move away to make way for the Jews. Was this so because he lacked national feeling himself? He asserted that the Jews were a people, and he worked for them; but did he feel himself to be a part of them? He once wrote: "I am a German-speaking Jew from Hungary and can never be anything but a German."[31]

Secondly, Herzl's idea that economic benefit would reconcile people to Zionist plans became an integral part of Zionist apologetics. Down to the present day the Israelis approach the expellees from Palestine with promises of generous financial aid and the Arab governments with offers of customs unions, free ports and transit rights which they obviously think are tempting, but which the Arabs find insulting and derisory. The Jews should, surely, be the last to expect anyone to follow the sad example of Jacob selling his birthright for a mess of pottage.

Herzl not only tried to buy a country, he tried to buy people into helping him to buy a country. Considering some of the people he tried to tempt his efforts seem ludicrous. Thus he planned to approach the unfriendly Rothschild: "if you go with us we shall enrich you one last time. We shall make you big beyond the dreams of the modest founder of your House. We shall make you rich by tripling your contribution, the billion with which we started"; a less material bait is also thrown out: "we shall take our first elected ruler from your House".[32]

He wrote to Cecil Rhodes: "If you and your associates supply the requested financial aid for this you will...have the satisfaction of making a good profit".[33]

Commenting on Herzl's methods Professor Talmon notes: "Herzl was at bottom compelled to resort to the very, very old Jewish methods of backstairs diplomacy...Wherever he went Herzl had to oil palms".[34] His diary records the details, sometimes amusing, sometimes sordid, of his bargaining over the

[31]*Op. cit.*, p. 171.
[32]*Op. cit.*, pp. 164-165.
[33]*Op. cit.*, p. 1194.
[34]Talmon, *op. cit.*

size of bribes—over 20,000 francs for one interview with the
Sultan.[35]

The intimate linking of purchasing power and politics in
Herzl's mind is revealed in two entries from his diary on plans
for creating the Jewish state:

"1st   stage: The Rothschilds
2nd   stage: The midget millionaires.
3rd   stage: The little people (i.e. wide publicity!). If it
          comes to this stage the first two will rue the
          day."[36]

And with prophetic accuracy: "If there should then be attempts to impede the free passage of the Jews, we shall know
how to mobilize the public opinion of the world (liberals, socialists, anti-Semites) against the imprisonment of the Jews. Then
too our diplomats will be at work (we shall make financial
concessions in the form of loans and special gifts). Once we are
outside, we shall put our trust in our army, our purchased
friendships, and a Europe weakened and divided by militarism
and socialism.

This is Jewish emancipation."[37]

Apart from what can only be called state-purchase the main
object of Herzl's frenetic diplomatic activity was to obtain the
active support or the passive protection of one or the other of
the European powers for the Jewish State. He put this intention
in broad terms into *The Jewish State*: "The Society of Jews will
treat with the present masters of the land, putting itself under
the protectorate of the European Powers, if they prove friendly
to the plan."[38]

Herzl's feelings towards the non-European Ottoman Empire
were extremely ambivalent. He despised the regime and the
Sultan personally; he foresaw the partition of this Empire and
even fitted that eventuality into his plans. At the same time he
did not want it to come about too quickly, at least not before

[35]*Diaries*, p. 861.
[36]*Op. cit.*, p. 44.
[37]*Op. cit.*, p. 51.
[38]*The Jewish State*, p. 30.

he was able to get what he wanted from the Empire. Hence
when hostilities broke out with Greece, fighting to complete
its independence, Herzl sent fulsome messages of loyal support
to the Sultan along with donations of money and promises of
medical aid, but he also did not want Turkey to win too decisively.[39]

Herzl actually suggested that an official delegate or an observer of the Sultan should attend the 1st Zionist Congress.[40]
At the same time he left Palestine, after seeing the Kaiser there,
secretly and hurriedly, because he feared assassination by the
Ottoman authorities, assuming that they knew him to be no
real friend of the Empire: "If the Turkish government had only
a glimmer of political foresight, this time they would have put
an end to my game once and for all."[41]

Towards Germany, Britain and Italy on the other hand he
could be open in his admiration and requests for support, without the need or the desire to play any "game".

Herzl wanted the same things from all the European Powers:
that they should use persuasion or pressure on the Sultan to get
him to accept an area of Jewish settlement, and that that area
should then be brought under the protective wing of these
Powers. In brief, though Herzl assured the Sultan that the
European Jewish settlers would be loyal Ottoman subjects he
was not prepared to put them entirely within the power of a
non-European empire. This was double-dealing, because an
European protectorate over the Jewish area would have been
just one more avenue for European interference in the internal
affairs of the Ottoman Empire. And this is probably why
Herzl feared assassination and why, even more curiously, he
suggested that the European protectorate be exercised *secretly*.
He gives no indication how this strange arrangement could have
been made to work, and perhaps the proposal was due to Herzl's
over-long addiction to secret diplomacy and devious bargaining.

Germany was clearly Herzl's first love. It was to his good

[39]*Diaries*, pp. 537, 541.
[40]*Op. cit.*, p. 545.
[41]*Op. cit.*, p. 760.

friend the Grand Duke of Baden that Herzl first proposed the formation of a Jewish Chartered Company (which would manage the Jewish settlement) with its headquarters in Karlsruhe "and under the protection of His Royal Highness Grand Duke Friedrich. There will automatically result from this a political relationship of protection by the (German) Empire, one to which there can be no objection from third parties. No express declaration on the part of the Imperial Government is required for this; in fact, we could be repudiated without further ado, as operating on our own, just as the English government was able to do with Cecil Rhodes at any time."[42]

Herzl wanted the German protectorate for more than political reasons. He admitted that many would "shake their heads over it". Not he, however: "to live under the protection of this strong, great, moral, splendidly governed, tightly organised Germany can only have the most salutary effect on the Jewish national character."[43] As may be recalled Herzl thought anti-Semitism would have the same beneficial effect.

But the Kaiser was too good a friend of the Sultan to accept Herzl's dubious propositions, so he turned to Britain. From fairly early on Herzl had wanted to get the Prince of Wales (later Edward VII) to become one of the joint protectors of the Jewish State.[44] Herzl was very practical when he wrote to British leaders and in December 1896 he suggested to Lord Salisbury "the creation of an autonomous Jewish vassal state in Palestine, similar to Egypt, under the suzerainty of the Sultan. The matter is possible if we have the backing—and I repeat expressly, the invisible backing—of a Great Power... England's advantage would be that a railroad would be built across Palestine from the Mediterranean to the Persian Gulf... England would have these benefits *sans bourse délier* (without expense) and without the world's learning of her participation... England would have a neutral reserve route to India, in case difficulties arose at the Suez Canal."[45]

[42]*Op. cit.*, p. 794.
[43]*Op. cit.*, p. 693.
[44]Rabinowicz, *op. cit.*, p. 8.
[45]*Diaries*, p. 501.

It was, once more, material gains that he pressed on Lord
Lansdowne, the British Foreign Secretary, in October 1902,
when asking for British support for the El Arish-Sinai plan:
"In some short years the Empire would be bigger by a rich
colony...All other Jews in the world, too, will come into England's fold at one stroke—if not politically, then at least morally...At one stroke England will get ten million secret but loyal
subjects active in all walks of life all over the world. They sell
needles and thread in many small villages all over the East;
but they are also wholesale merchants, industrialists, stock
brokers, scholars and artists and newspapermen and other
things...England will get ten million agents for her greatness
and her influence. And the effect of this sort of thing normally
spreads from the political to the economic. It is surely no exaggeration to say that a Jew would rather purchase and propagate
the products of a country that has rendered the Jewish people a
benefaction than those of a country in which the Jews are badly
off".[46]

In April 1903 Herzl, appropriately, used political arguments
with the imperialist Joseph Chamberlain: "we shall be used as
a small buffer-state. We shall get it not from the goodwill, but
from the jealousy of the powers! And once we are at El-Arish
under the Union Jack, then Palestine too will fall into the British
sphere of influence." Herzl then summed up Chamberlain's
reaction by saying: "That seemed to make quite a bit of sense
to him".[47]

When Herzl met the King of Italy, on January 1904, he tried
to interest him in the "Tripoli scheme: to channel the surplus
Jewish immigration into Tripolitania, under the liberal laws
and institutions of Italy." The King replied: "But that again
is someone else's home." "But the partition of Turkey is bound
to come", Herzl countered and ended with the words: "Italy
can do a lot for us, for the Sultan is afraid of Italy".[48]

The Italian monarch had a shrewd appreciation of an idea

[46]*Op. cit.*, p. 1367.
[47]*Op. cit.*, p. 1474.
[48]*Op. cit.*, p. 1600.

that Herzl had tried on the British, as the following exchange shows: "Napoleon had ideas about restoring the Jewish nation, Sire!" "No, he only wanted to make the Jews, who were scattered all over the world, his agents." "An idea I found in Chamberlain too." "It is an obvious idea", the King said.[49] With Herzl, as we have seen, it was a case of the Jewish people being offered as agents to any friendly European Power.

The same search for a powerful protector, whose prestigious name might also impress the reluctant Jewish millionaires, prompted Herzl's approach to Cecil Rhodes. He presented the Zionist plan as "something colonial" which would be "quite good for England, for Greater Britain too" and asked Rhodes "to put the stamp of your authority" on the plan. Incidentally he put Rhodes first on a list of "the figures in my chess game"— the others being the President of the United States, the King of England and the Czar of Russia.[50]

Indeed Herzl believed that a Jewish State in the Levant would benefit not just one of the European Powers, though he tried to enlist them in turn, but all Europe: "I spoke on the general advantages of the Jewish State for Europe. We would restore to health the plague-spot of the Orient. We would build railroads into Asia—the highway of the civilised peoples. And this highway would not then be in the hands of any one Great Power."[51]

The need for an European protecting power seemed inherent in Zionist thinking. Herzl had a poor opinion of France and she played no part in his calculations, but many years earlier Moses Hess had written: "France, beloved friend, is the saviour who will restore our people to its place in universal history... Do you still doubt that France will help the Jews to found colonies which may extend from Suez to Jerusalem... Frenchmen and Jews, there is no doubt they were created for one another."[52]

Herzl's willing subservience to the interests of the European

[49]*Op. cit.*, pp. 1599, 1600.
[50]*Op. cit.*, pp. 1194, 1179.
[51]*Op. cit.*, p. 338.
[52]Hess, in Hertzberg, *op. cit.*, p. 133, and in *Rome and Jerusalem*, letter 12.

imperial Powers is striking indeed. It has been argued, even by a critic of the Zionist movement, that Herzl's negotiations with these Powers were ineluctable and realistic since these powers dominated world affairs at that time.[53] This argument will be examined critically a little later, for there were other forces abroad in the world, forces of which Herzl was not unaware. Herzl had a vision of the emerging anti-colonialist Third World. He met, and was favourably impressed by, the Egyptian nationalist, Mustafa Kamel. He was equally impressed by "the striking number of intelligent looking young Egyptians who packed a hall in Cairo", during Herzl's visit there, to listen to a lecture on irrigation problems. "They are the coming masters," he noted: "it is a wonder that the British don't see this. They think they are going to deal with the fellahin forever."[54] He was able to see the British Empire as part of a general historical process and the dangers that threatened it: "along with freedom and progress they (the British) are also teaching the fellahin to revolt. I believe that the English example in the colonies will either destroy England's colonial empire—or lay the foundation for England's world dominion. One of the most interesting alternatives of our time. It makes one feel like coming back in fifty years to see how it has turned out."[55]

Judged within the framework of his own ideas Herzl was looking backward not forward when he confined his Zionist activities solely to bargaining with or supplications to the imperial European Powers. He was not compelled to this by the spirit of the times but rather by the essentially European and colonial character of the Zionist movement itself.

* * *

The rise of Asian nationalism

Zionist theoreticians when asserting the claim that Zionism is "the Jewish nationalist movement" argue that it could hardly

---

[53]Maxime Rodinson, *Les Temps Modernes, op. cit.,* p. 31.
[54]*Diaries,* p. 1449.
[55]*Op. cit.,* p. 1449.

be anything else, for through Zionism the Jews of Europe were merely responding to the all-pervasive spirit of nationalism that dominated European politics in the second half of the 19th century. Yet when attention is drawn to the openly pro-imperial policies actually practised by the Zionists the counter-argument is advanced, as mentioned above, that these policies could hardly be anything else because the imperial Powers then dominated the world.

If the first argument of Zionist nationalism is admitted, then the second one is inadmissible, and it becomes fair and logical to compare Zionism with other nationalisms, especially those of Afro-Asia, since the goal of Zionism was the creation of a state in Asia.

Even a cursory comparison of the chronology of Zionism with that of the Afro-Asian national movements, up to 1919, reveals that while the latter continuously asserted the nationalist claim for independence against the colonial powers, Zionism consistently remained a movement of co-operation with those same powers.

Zionism as an organised political movement emerged with the publication of *The Jewish State* in 1896 and the 1st Zionist Congress in 1897. Then followed Herzl's diplomatic efforts which gained no territory but did achieve the recognition of the Jewish community as a political entity by the British Government in 1903. After Herzl's death came a quiet period of "cultural Zionism" marked by the founding of the first truly Zionist colonies in Palestine in 1908 and ending with the victory of the "political Zionists" within the movement in 1911. When World War I began the Zionist movement was still confined to a small minority of world Jewry "and it was stagnating."[56] Yet when the War ended the Zionists had in hand a promise made by the British government, through the Balfour Declaration, that a National Home for the Jews should be established in Palestine which then became, to all intents and purposes, a British Crown Colony.

It may, of course, also be argued that Zionism cannot and

[56]H. Sacher, *Zionist Portraits and other Essays*, London, 1959, p. 22.

should not be compared with the Afro-Asian national movements because they functioned outside Europe, while Zionism
had to work within metropolitan Europe itself. But even within
Europe at the turn of the century there was a degree of anti-
imperial and anti-colonial feeling of which there is no reflection
in Zionist thought or action.

We have seen that Zionism appeared so late on the European
stage that it has been described as "the last" of European nationalisms. The hightide of European imperialism can be placed
between the Congress of Berlin in 1878 and the death of Queen
Victoria in 1901. In Britain at least the Boer War had produced
deep questionings of the imperial idea, and in 1902 J.A. Hobson
had produced his classic study of "Imperialism", parts of which
Lenin later adopted. The well-known philosopher Herbert
Spencer and many other lesser writers attacked imperialism
both in its moral bases and its practical efficacy and profitability.[57] There was a *fin de siècle*, "recessional" mood in politics as
much as in the arts. But neither the questionings of Gentile
anti-imperialists nor the fierce onslaughts of Jewish communists
made any impression on the respectful admiration that Zionist
leaders had for the European Powers.

In Asia the anti-colonial assault on imperialism had begun
even before the founding of the Zionist movement in Europe,
which is noteworthy, because one could expect a time-lag between the genesis of nationalist ideas in Europe and their emergence in Asia. As far back as 1882 there was an embryonic
nationalist movement in Egypt, and in India the National Congress was founded in 1885. The Filipinos were fighting the
Spaniards and the Americans in 1896, while in 1905 Sun Yat
Sen founded his national movement in China. A year later a
call for full independence was made in India and in 1907 the
first bomb was thrown by Indian nationalists. In that same year
two nationalist parties were started in Egypt. An uprising in
Indochina had to be suppressed in 1908. In 1911 the Young
Arab movement started in Paris and the pan-Arab Decentrali-

---

[57]A.P. Thornton, *The Imperial Idea and its Enemies*, London, 1959, chaps. II,
III.

sation Party was founded in Cairo. In 1912, China overthrew the Manchus and the Moroccans fought hard against the French Army. In 1914, the Al-ʿAhd organisation was formed in Damascus, and in the following year Arab nationalists made their presence felt in the firm demands of the Damascus Protocol. Despite the emergency conditions of the War, Indian nationalists were active in the Home Rule movement between 1914 and 1916 and in 1918 they sent an appeal to the Versailles Conference for self-determination and Dominion Status, culminating in a demand for full responsible Government in 1919. Egypt also demanded complete independence in 1919, and when it was turned down there was a violent and country-wide uprising. In the same year the Arab Congress in Damascus rejected the post-war settlement. In 1920 there were months of fighting by the Iraqis against the British and the first non-cooperation campaign of both Muslims and Hindus in India led by Gandhi.

During the 40 years, 1880 to 1920, the whole continent of Asia was seething with nationalist agitation or uprising which the imperial powers suppressed in one area only to see it break out in another.

Making every allowance for the Zionist leaders—for the different conditions obtaining at that time between metropolitan Europe and colonial Afro-Asia, for the difference in political criteria and outlook between their time and our present—making all such allowances, what can one justly expect them, as nationalist leaders, to have done, considering what the Asian nationalists were doing? That they should have made contact with the Asian movements? They had the opportunities but refrained from doing so: that they should have co-operated with them? —only the Jews in the communist movement attempted anything. Perhaps even these steps were too much to expect, for did the Zionists not regard Asia as uncivilised and barbaric? But if the Asian barbarians could stand up to overwhelming European power, and fight and die for their freedom, then it is fair to expect, from some nationalist fellow-feeling, that Zionist nationalists should have, at the very least, maintained a certain reserve, a decent distance, from the imperial powers: instead they threw themselves into the arms of the imperialists. The

Zionists might, at least, have made it plain that their co-operation was a matter only of policy and convenience; instead they made it very clear that they genuinely admired the European governments, and that they were willing to be useful and dutiful junior partners. And it is because of the example set by the Asian nationalists, but ignored by the European Zionists, that one can say that in its motivations Zionism was not nationalist, in its objectives colonial and in its methods pro-colonial.

The Zionist movement has to be placed against the turbulent Asian background because it was the events of these years that shaped the thinking of the Asian leaders who, in the 1930's and 1940's, passed judgement on Zionist policies in Palestine.

With Asian nationalism taking the anti-colonialist course, and with Zionism an important political factor in West Asia after 1920, a comparison between the two movements is inescapable. And from that comparison spring two questions. Why did Zionism before World War I have to be so subservient to the European Powers?—to which an answer has been given in our survey of Herzl's activities; and why did there have to be so close an association of Zionism with the imperial interests of Britain in the Middle East during and after World War I? The answer to that question requires an examination of the Zionist-British collusion that resulted in the issuing of the Balfour Declaration.

* * *

Weizmann and political collusion

The Balfour Declaration—a "declaration of sympathy with Jewish Zionist organisations"—was issued by the British Government on the 2nd November, 1917. It is only 119 words long, and its operative paragraph reads: "His Majesty's Government view with favour the establishment in Palestine of a national home for the Jewish people, and will use their best endeavours to facilitate the achievement of this object, it being clearly understood that nothing shall be done which may prejudice the civil and religious rights of the existing non-Jewish communities in Palestine, or the rights and political status enjoyed by Jews in any other country."

The declaration had disastrous consequences for the two parties involved. It was meant to ensure the imperial interests of Britain in the Middle East, and it ultimately destroyed them. It was, presumably, meant to provide a solution to the age-old Jewish Problem: its words became the politico-legal foundation for the State of Israel but the Jewish Problem remains, and to it has been added the Israel-Arab problem and the wider Israel-Afro-Asia problem.

Even the name of this document is incorrect because "declaration" implies a unilateral statement, whereas this formulation was the result of close collusive co-operation between the British government and a group of Zionists, led by Dr. Chaim Weizmann. A far more accurate title for it has been provided by a leading British Zionist, Lord Sieff, who was involved in the negotiations. He has described it as "the Compact of 1917 between Israel and Britain"; a more convenient form of words would be "the 1917 Balfour -Weizmann Compact".

Lord Sieff's description is given in his preface to the latest of a long line of books on the "Declaration". This is *The Unromantics, The Great Powers and the Balfour Declaration*, written by Jon Kimche,[58] which is of interest because it attempts to give an answer to the question: "Why did there have to be so close an association of Zionism with the imperial interests of Britain in the Middle East?" This is the answer provided: "The agreed fact of the condition of the world at the end of 1918 was the unchallengeable power and might of the British Empire. And the Zionists were its ally, were establishing themselves under the umbrella of this protective power. As were the Arab nationalists who had responded to British encouragement to break with Ottoman rule and follow the Sharif Hussein and Lawrence in the "Arab revolt". The Egyptian nationalists under Zaghlul Pasha, though continuing their struggle for independence, had reached this point only because of their effective collaboration with the British. The harsh reality of 1918 was that there could be no form of even embryonic national inde-

---

[58]Published under the auspices of the Anglo-Israel Association, London, 1968.

pendence for either Zionists or Arabs in the Middle East except in close association with one or the other of the ruling powers: either with the British or with the Turks. The fortunate ones —Arab and Jew—opted for Britain."[59] In a second passage, a few pages later, Kimche broadens the base of his explanation: "Under the conditions of 1917 and 1918, there was no future for any national movement which did not have the support of a great power. In order to obtain this support Weizmann was prepared to reinforce Britain's New Imperialism in the Middle East."[60]

Jon Kimche is a most able, experienced and devoted advocate of the Zionist case. It is, therefore, natural that he, while admitting Zionist-British collusion, should argue that that collusion was inescapable, that the Arabs under the Sharif Hussein and Zaghlul were also colluding, and that "any national movement" would have had to collaborate. Kimche's answer shows an awareness that Zionist collusion, in a nationalist context, needs to be explained, that it needs to be shown as not being anti-nationalist; and that is a gain for truth. But the answer given does not meet the question since it is historically inaccurate.

It is, quite simply, a gross misrepresentation to compare the written agreement between the British and the Sharif and the unwritten Compact between Balfour and Weizmann. The Sharif did not volunteer to serve and protect British imperial interests in the Middle East; Weizmann we shall see promising to do so repeatedly, for that was the very basis of the 1917 Contract. All that the Sharif asked for was aid to fight for the establishment of an independent Arabia: he was given the aid but subsequently tricked out of the independence. The British approached a hesitant Hussein; the Zionists approached a reluctant Britain.[61] The Egyptian nationalists never collaborated with the British and Zaghlul, who joined them in 1914, was Britain's implacable foe during the war years while Weizmann was proving his loyalty to Britain. In 1919 Zaghlul led a mass

---

[59]*Op. cit.*, p. 74.
[60]*Op. cit.*, p. 80.
[61]R. Storrs, *Orientations*, London, 1937, p. 173.

uprising against the British in Egypt. So did Gandhi in India. So did the Palestine Arabs in 1920. These events serve to show, in addition to the long story of Asian nationalist struggles up to 1920, that in that year there were at least three national movements which "refusing the support of a great power" fought it instead, because they did not accept "the agreed fact" of "the unchallengeable power and might of the British Empire". Kimche's words are thus immensely significant and useful in throwing light, from the Zionist angle, on the fundamental difference between the Afro-Asian nationalists who before and after World War I were fighting Imperialism—New or Old—and the Zionist leaders who went under its "protective umbrella".[62] At base it was a question of mental attitude. The Afro-Asian leaders—Gandhi, Ataturk, Zaghlul—had no feeling of political subservience towards Europe; the Zionist leaders as Europeans, and the political underdogs of Europe, could hardly be expected to feel anything else. This is the real answer to our question.

[62]The formula of argument used by Kimche—admitting Zionist-British collusion but alleging collusion by others—is evidently becoming standard practice in Zionist writing. Thus another Zionist advocate, the Rev. J. Parkes, in his *Five Roots of Israel*, page 63, writes: "It is quite true that the Balfour Declaration and the Partition decision came from Europe and America. But that only makes Palestine conform to the general pattern of the twentieth century Middle East" for Egypt—according to Parkes—was created by Cromer not Mohamed Ali, and the wealth of Iraq and the Gulf by Western oil companies. This is another example of post-colonial Zionist embarrassment but here, again, there is in fact no parallelism between the "Declaration" and the other developments. The Egyptian nationalists did not invite Cromer into Egypt as the Zionists did the British into Palestine, and the nationalists did not co-operate with Cromer, as the Zionists did with the British during the war and the Mandate, rather they opposed Cromer. And surely one cannot compare the process of taking oil out of Arab lands, at a handsome profit, with the process of putting Jews into an Arab land, in return for a handsome promise of Jewish support. Both Kimche and Parkes seem to rely on their readers' ignorance of Egyptian history. As for when Kimche writes of Egyptian nationalists under Zaghlul collaborating: the nationalists never did, though Zaghlul did but only till 1917. And Parkes ought to be aware that in Egypt, despite Cromer's economic reforms, there was strong political opposition from at least 1895 onwards. cf. Tom Little, *Egypt*, London, 1958, pp. 112, 129-130.

It now remains to examine the agreed fact of Zionist-British collusion and to see how the 1917 Compact came about.[63] This examination falls naturally into three parts: the Zionist offer of assistance, the British acceptance from a variety of motives, and the subsequent discussions and bargaining on details.

With the Balfour Declaration, as with most other important statements of policy, it is the underlying assumption that is important rather than the theoretical superstructure. The assumption, in this case, is contained in seven words which are the key to the Compact; these are "the existing non-Jewish communities in Palestine". In 1917 the Jews in Palestine numbered about 56,000, or 8% of the population, but in those seven words the Arab people of Palestine were relegated, once and for all, to a subordinate position. They were not something in themselves, they were non-something else, they were merely non-Jews. In the long text of the Mandate the words "Arab" or "Palestinian Arab" nowhere occur: there the 90% majority is called, a bit more politely, "other sections of the population", the Jews, once again, being *the* section of the population, the norm. What is as surprising as the emotional connivance those words reveal between European Powers and European Jews is the fact that the authors felt no need for concealment, a reflection, doubtless, of "the power and might of the British Empire". What these words clearly imply is that the British and Zionists were in on the Palestine business together; they were the "insiders"; the Arabs were "the others", the "outsiders".

Given this basic Zionist bias at the very outset everything that happened later in Palestine was merely consequential.

From the way in which the 1917 Compact was concluded that bias was inevitable.

The idea of using the Jews specifically in a political role in

[63]A large number of books have been written about the Balfour Declaration. The definitive study is Leonard Stein's *The Balfour Declaration*. Weizmann's *Trial and Error* has to be referred to but, in view of Weizmann's proven unreliability, this book in most instances is of interest in revealing what Weizmann believed happened, rather than what really happened. On points of detail Weizmann's text always needs to be checked against the corrections supplied by O.K. Rabinowicz, *Fifty Years of Zionism*.

Palestine had occurred to several persons long before the birth
of political Herzlian Zionism. On March 22, 1799, it is
recorded that Napoleon issued a proclamation inviting all the
Jews of Asia and Africa to place themselves under his banners
to re-establish ancient Jerusalem.[64] As we have seen, the King
of Italy, a century later, interpreted this act as an attempt by
Napoleon to enrol the Jews as his agents. There is some doubt
whether this proclamation was actually issued but, presuming
it was, this comment by a Jewish historian is most *à propos* to
later events: "Bonaparte, incorrigibly the man of his age, made
free use of the fashionable dialect and called the Jews a nation,
went indeed almost further and offered them a National Home.
That he offered it in someone else's territory was, perhaps,
inevitable but no less characteristic."[65] The use of the fashionable dialect of nationalism, the generosity with someone else's
territory and the recruiting of agents were all present once again
in 1917.

The first official British political connection with Jews in
Palestine would seem to date from 1839 when Palmerston asked
British consuls to afford protection to the Jews. No further
official British action was taken till Chamberlain met with Herzl
but the idea of a British-Zionist initiative was never wholly
forgotten. In the 1840's a former colonial Governor pressed for
Jewish settlement in Palestine to ensure Britain's line of communications to the East.[66] In 1852 Hollingworth's *Remarks
upon the Present Conditions of the Jews in Palestine* said that
the establishment of a Jewish state in Palestine was "not only
an act of humanity and justice but a political necessity...in the
safeguarding of the highway across Asia Minor to India."[67]
Sir Laurence Oliphant, in 1879, linked the idea of Jewish settlement with the need to ensure "the political and economic penetration of Palestine by Britain."[68] The construction of the Suez
Canal only served to heighten Britain's sensitivity towards the

[64]P. Guedalla, *Napoleon and Palestine*, London, 1925, *et. seq.*
[65]*Op. cit.*, p. 33.
[66]*Backdrop to Tragedy*, p. 136.
[67]H.M. Kallen, *Zionism and World Politics*, London, 1921, p. 49.
[68]*Backdrop*, p. 137.

area of Palestine and made her that much more receptive to schemes that promised to safeguard its security: one such scheme was Zionism.

Upon the declaration of World War I Zionists on both sides of the firing lines seized on the possibility that the war could further their cause.

In Germany, where Zionist Jewish leaders strongly supported the war aims of the Kaiser's government,[69] the President of the Jewish National Fund, Bodenheimer, presented a memorandum to the Foreign Ministry urging the creation of autonomous Jewish areas in Eastern Europe which would help in the establishment of a Jewish state in Palestine.[70]

In Britain there was the same anticipation. Even before Turkey entered the War in October 1914 Weizmann wrote that after victory he expected "that Palestine will fall within the British sphere of influence...we could easily move a million Jews into Palestine within the next fifty or sixty years and England would have an effective barrier (for the Suez Canal against any hostile forces which might come from the north) and we would have a country...an Asiatic Belgium."[71]

Thus from the very beginning Weizmann envisaged a combination of the interests of Britain and Zionism in the Middle East. And this was only the latest expression of something he had thought of as a boy of 12 years when he wrote: "Therefore the obligation lies upon us to find some place of refuge. Because even in America, where knowledge prevails, they will persecute us...All have decided that the Jew is doomed to death, but England will have mercy on us."[72]

But the first move towards Zionist-British cooperation did not come from Weizmann or any other member of the Zionist Organisation as such but from a pro-Zionist Jewish member of the British government itself, Herbert Samuel.

---

[69]J. Kimche, *The Unromantics*, p. 10. Among them was Nahum Goldmann, now President of the World Zionist Organisation.

[70]*Op. cit.*, p. 10.

[71]L. Stein, *op. cit.*, pp. 126-127.

[72]Crossman, *A Nation Reborn*, pp. 14-15.

On November 9, 1914 Samuel approached the British Foreign Secretary, Grey, and put to him the idea of "the restoration there (in Palestine) of a Jewish State." Samuel, like Herzl, immediately linked it with imperial interests. "I thought that British influence ought to play a considerable part in the formation of such a state, because the geographical situation of Palestine, and especially its proximity to Egypt, would render its goodwill to England a matter of importance to the British Empire." "I also said that it would be a great advantage if the remainder of Syria were annexed by France, as it would be far better for the state to have a European power as a neighbour than the Turk"— a direct continuation of Herzl's pro-European protectorate idea.

On January 28, 1915, Samuel presented his idea to the British Prime Minister, Asquith, who dismissed it with scorn. In March 1915 Samuel circulated his plan, in revised form, to a wider circle and in this memorandum he ruled out the possibilities, for Palestine, of annexation to France, remaining Turkish, internationalisation—or the establishment of an autonomous Jewish State, in favour of "a British Protectorate, with encouragement for Jewish settlement". The idea that Palestine might be ruled by its own people does not seem to have occurred to Samuel.

Samuel, in February 1915, had had a second conversation with Grey in which the latter appeared "very doubtful of the possibility or desirability of the establishment of a British Protectorate". Grey said "it might be possible to neutralize the country." Samuel answered this by masquerading as a spokesman not of the Zionists but of the Palestine Arabs, "five sixths of the inhabitants", about whom he "expressed a doubt" whether they "would accept such a government". Samuel went on: "I pressed upon him the danger of any other Power than England possessing Palestine, and the risk that an international government might end in some European state becoming dominant."

Samuel had several other meetings, some with Lloyd George and Weizmann, from which he concluded that "the idea of a Jewish State was impracticable...so long as the great majority

of the inhabitants were Arabs", for "to impose a Jewish minority
government would be in flat contradiction to one of the main
purposes for which it had been declared that the Allies were
fighting. At the same time it was not necessary to accept the
position that the existing population, sparse as it was, should have
the right to bar the door." Therefore "opinion was crystallising
in favour of something in the nature of a British Protectorate."[73]

Thus from the words of the man who was the original creator
of the 1917 Compact the following facts emerge: the initiative
came from the Zionists; the complete congruence of Zionist
and British imperial interests was accepted from the very start;
an Arab majority ruled out a Jewish State in Palestine; a British
Protectorate was second best but under it Jewish immigration
could change the demographic position.

However, despite Samuel's position and persistence, his initial
efforts came to nothing because of the military situation in the
Middle East. Early in 1917 when the army under Allenby
seemed likely to eject the Turks from Palestine the Zionists once
again took the initiative. On February 1, 1917 a memorandum was presented to Sir Mark Sykes, an Undersecretary to
the Cabinet, along with a request that the Zionist Organisation
be permitted to use the cable and diplomatic pouch facilities
of the Foreign Office, which was immediately granted.

On February 17, 1917 the first official conference was held
between Sykes and five Zionist leaders, which marked the British
government's recognition of the Zionist movement. Though no
clearcut decisions emerged from this crucial meeting there was
a complete meeting of minds between the British and the Zionist
representatives.

What were the ideas on the future of Palestine in their minds?
What did the Zionists have to offer the British?

The Zionist position was laid out in two letters from Weizmann to C.P. Scott, editor of *The Manchester Guardian*. On
November 12, 1914 Weizmann wrote: "should Palestine fall
within the British sphere of influence, and should Britain encourage a Jewish settlement there, as a British dependency, we

[73]H. Samuel, *Memoirs*, London, 1945, pp. 140-145.

could have in twenty or thirty years a million Jews out there, perhaps more; they would develop the country, bring back civilisation to it and form a very effective guard for the Suez Canal."[74]

The second letter, written in March 1915, was much more detailed and explicit. He begins by referring to Britain's reluctance to be involved in any new responsibilities and also to the idea that Palestine should not belong to any great power. He suggests "the middle course...the Jews take over the country; the whole burden of organization falls on them, but for the next ten or fifteen years they work under a temporary British protectorate...A strong Jewish community on the Egyptian flank is an efficient barrier for any danger likely to come from the north...England would have in the Jews the best possible friends, who would be the best national interpreters of ideas in the Eastern countries and would serve as a bridge between the two civilisations."

Weizmann refers to the "shying away" of Asquith from such plans and to the "hesitancies" of Grey, and concludes "it is clear that England's connection with Palestine rested on the idea of a Jewish Homeland in Palestine; but for the idea of a Jewish Homeland, England would not have entertained the thought of a protectorate—or later of a mandate—over Palestine. In short, England felt she had no business in Palestine except as part of the plan for the creation of the Jewish Homeland."[75]

The thought, therefore, in the minds of the Zionist leaders on February 17, 1917, was that they had to persuade a somewhat reluctant Britain, and Britain alone, to press for a Protectorate over Palestine; for with Britain they could strike the bargain— Jewish immigration under British protection, Jewish protection to a British-controlled Suez Canal.

No bargain of any sort could be struck with any of the other possible future rulers of Palestine: certainly not with the Turks; nor with an international regime; nor with the French. Neither the Turks nor the internationals nor the French stood in need-

[74]Weizmann, op. cit., p. 191.
[75]Op. cit., p. 225.

of Zionist protection for any of their Middle East interests from any imaginable danger. The Zionists had nothing to offer them—why then should they give the Zionists anything—like immigration—in return? With them there was no basis for a *quid pro quo*, but only with the British, hypnotised by the Suez Canal.

The basis of the Zionist-British bargain from the Zionist viewpoint was set out by Rabbi Gaster who presided over the February meeting (it was held in his house): "what Zionists in England and everywhere desired was a British protectorate with full rights to the Jews to develop a national life."[76]

British expectations were many-sided and were both long-term and short-term. The long-term considerations concerned Britain's imperial position in the Middle East. We are fortunate to have the imperial argument laid out fully and frankly by one of the important participants in these events. He was Herbert Sidebotham, military correspondent of *The Manchester Guardian*, one of the most influential journalists of his day and a convinced Zionist. In his book *England and Palestine*, published in 1918, Sidebotham had a chapter on "British Interests in Palestine" in which he wrote: "on the Indian analogy what we would seem to require for the better and less burdensome defence of Egypt is a State to do for this frontier what Afghanistan has done for India." This forward defence position in Palestine, "if inhabited by a people at the same stage of political development as ourselves would be no burden but a source of strength. The only possible colonists of Palestine are the Jews. Only they can build up in the Mediterranean a new dominion associated with this country from the outset in imperial work, at once a protection against the alien East and a mediator between it and us...beginning its second life as a nation with a debt of gratitude to this country as its second father....The fact that Jerusalem, the capital of Judaism, was also a capital of a Dominion of the British Empire, and won by British arms, could give this country a great beneficial influence in every country of the world where there is a community of Jews." Sidebotham did entertain the

[76]Stein, *op. cit.*, p. 372.

possibility of other protecting Powers. He was against any condominium and against partition. "Internationalization was a lesser evil." However, he looked kindly on the Americans: "the Jews and Americans get on well together...America in Palestine could never be a danger to Egypt", but he doubted whether America would be interested; which left Britain as the only practical alternative.[77]

These long-term imperial interests did not interest everyone in Britain's War Cabinet. Weizmann records that in March 1917 he had to explain to Balfour, who by then was Foreign Secretary, "the importance of Palestine from the British point of view, an aspect which was apparently new to him".[78] As far as the official record goes Balfour thought that the Declaration's main value was its propaganda effect: "we should be able to carry on extremely useful propaganda both in Russia and America".[79] This argument also had weight with the Prime Minister, Lloyd George, who later avowed "we were anxious to secure the goodwill of the Jewish community throughout the world on the side of the Allies...the Balfour Declaration was aimed to secure that valuable support".[80] The British hoped that a pro-Jewish declaration would enthuse the rich and influential American Jews for the war effort; that it would persuade the Jewish communists in Russia not to make a separate peace with Germany; and the Jewish merchants in Poland and the Ukraine not to sell grain to Germany when the separate peace was eventually made. (Though Asquith also ascribed to Lloyd George the motive of wanting to exclude France from Palestine.)

It has been said that Balfour and Lloyd George were further moved by religious considerations springing from their Protestant upbringing on the Old Testament stories. Lloyd George admitted this factor.[81] With Balfour there was an additional religious motivation—that of Christian guilt for anti-Semitic

[77]H. Sidebotham, *England and Palestine*, London, 1918, pp. 183-224.

[78]Stein, *op. cit.*, p. 157.

[79]*Op. cit.*, pp. 546-547.

[80]H. Sidebotham, *British Interests in Palestine*, London, 1934, p. 41.

[81]Guedalla, *op. cit.*, concluding remarks by Lloyd George, p. 47.

persecution of the Jews. Speaking in 1922 Balfour asked the House of Lords to "consider whether the whole culture of Europe, the whole religious organisation of Europe, has not from time to time proved itself guilty of great crimes against this race".[82]

This, then, was the tangled complex of ideas and motives on the British side in February 1917—defence, propaganda, religion, guilt. As Lloyd George said: "let us be quite frank—our motives were mixed...I am not going to pretend that there was not a certain element of interest in it too".[83] For a government of a country fighting for its life, and as hard-pressed as Britain was in 1917, we can be reasonably sure that interest came first.

We know for certain that interest did come first with the British official directly negotiating with the Zionists. Not only was Sykes, in general, an imperialist; he was, in February 1917, very much in need of Zionist assistance to reduce French influence in the Levant, which had been given a clear field of future advancement by an agreement that Sykes himself had concluded, a few months earlier.

It was at this point that the Zionist offer and the British acceptance moved from a passive congruence of interests to direct and active cooperation. The 1917 Compact was issued in November of that year, but it was a working proposition from February onwards.

Sykes, and Samuel too, were in an acutely embarrassing position that February morning for only they knew that the future of Palestine, about which they were negotiating with the Zionists, had been settled in a secret agreement made with France and Tsarist Russia in May 1916, which internationalised much of Palestine. This was the notorious Sykes-Picot Agreement that carved up the Ottoman Empire and for which no one has had a kind word. It is remembered as the classic example of diplomatic duplicity—but the British were nevertheless dissatisfied with its terms regarding Palestine.

[82]A. J. Balfour, *Speeches on Zionism*, London, 1928, p. 60.
[83]Guedalla, *op. cit.*, p. 47.

Even before the Agreement was signed Sykes, in April 1916, was proposing that Britain should acquire a position on the eastern Mediterranean by converting the international zone of Palestine into an Anglo-French condominium. By the spring of 1917 the British government had moved on to a position of wanting sole British control in Palestine.[84] This is where the Zionists came in useful, for they did not want to deal with anyone except Britain in Palestine.

At the February meeting Sykes complained about the French wanting a say in Palestine while they were "not entitled to anything there." He asked the Zionists to try and "induce the French to give way." The Zionist leaders had already questioned Sykes on whether there was an agreement with France and had been given evasive answers by him. Accordingly when asked to tackle the French they replied that it was up to the British government.

Nevertheless a Zionist representative, Sokolow, was appointed to contact the French. He was introduced to Picot on the very next day by Sykes and he then told Picot bluntly that "the Jews had long had in mind the suzerainty of the British government "which had championed their cause" and was the most successful of the colonial Powers and was therefore "the most fitted for developing a new colony."[85]

For a time there was something like a tug-of-war for the Zionists between Britain and France. France did in fact outbid Britain by giving Sokolow a declaration, on June 4, favouring the "renaissance of the Jewish nationality" in Palestine. But the French did not yield their claim to Palestine and the Zionists gave no sign that they were prepared to switch their allegiance from Britain to France. However, French opposition had been partly neutralised by the Zionists, and Britain to that extent was encouraged to go ahead on her own.[86]

With Sokolow heading off the French, Weizmann discussed the details of the Compact with British leaders. On March

[84]Stein, *op. cit.*, pp. 278-279.
[85]Stein, *op. cit.*, pp. 374-375.
[86]*Op. cit.*, pp. 394-421.

22, 1917 he and Lloyd George agreed that a condominium with France was unacceptable; Weizmann said that "international control" was a shade worse; but joint control with the Americans was acceptable.[87]

In an interview between Lord Robert Cecil and Weizmann on April 25, the Zionist-British strategy to scuttle the Sykes-Picot agreement was confirmed in all details. Weizmann reiterated Zionist preference for Britain and their objections to a condominium, internationalisation or French control. The French, he said, "would not leave the Jews to develop their way of life" and they would lean on elements—like the Catholic clergy and the Christian Arabs—unfriendly to the Jews. Cecil replied that it would strengthen the British position if the Jews of the world would express themselves in favour of a British protectorate. Weizmann agreed and promised to work towards that end, but only if the objective was to be "a Jewish Palestine under a British protectorate".[88] And so it was agreed.

The subsequent involved negotiations over the precise wording of the Declaration are of no direct interest. They delayed its issuance, as did also protestations from leading British Jews who were anti-Zionists. This opposition produced a letter from Weizmann to the British War Cabinet, on October 4, 1917, which set the seal on the Compact. It said, inter alia, *"we entrusted our national and Zionist destiny to the Foreign Office and the Imperial War Cabinet in the hope that the problem would be considered in the light of imperial interests and the principle for which the Entente stands."*[89] (Italics in the original.) This *cri de cœur* made it difficult for the British government to procrastinate the issue of the Declaration any longer.

The question as to who should control Palestine was in fact settled on the field of battle by the military victories of the British forces under Allenby: when he entered Jerusalem in December 1917 it was certain that there would be a Jewish national home in Palestine and—almost—certain that it would be under the

---

[87]*Op. cit.*, p. 383.

[88]*Op. cit.*, pp. 391-393; Weizmann, *op. cit.*, pp. 241-243.

[89]Weizmann, *op. cit.*, p. 258.

protector desired by the Zionists, Britain.

After the Declaration had been issued there was one more service that the British expected of the Zionists—and vice versa—which was assistance in getting the Zionist-British Compact accepted internationally at the Versailles Peace Conference. Zionist support was expected in the form of a clear declaration of Zionist preference for an exclusively British Mandate to offset French claims and objections.

This gave the Zionists some leverage on the British, and Weizmann used it when he found the British military occupation authorities in Palestine not very friendly towards the idea of a Jewish National Home. In a threatening letter to Balfour written in May 1918 Weizmann spoke of his plans to call a Jewish Congress in Palestine whose voice "will not pass unheard at the Peace Conference. But the possibility of formulating a clear, strong and representative demand will exist only if the Jewish People know that during the period of British occupation the foundations of the National Home have been laid in Palestine." The British authorities in Palestine evidently perceived the threat behind Weizmann's confident manner, for Allenby's Chief Political Officer, General Clayton, wrote of the danger of offending the Zionists and thus throwing Zionism "into the arms of America or, even worse, into those of Germany. Thus the death-blow would be dealt to pro-British Zionism, and at the same time to any hope of securing Zionist influence at the Peace Conference in favour of a British Palestine."[90] As put by Kimche: "the mighty empire had to have Chaim Weizmann's alibi."[91]

The counter-leverage of the British against the Zionists was the vague possibility of an American mandate over Palestine. The Zionists were sufficiently perturbed at such a prospect for them to produce, early in 1919, a pamphlet entitled *A Jewish Palestine: The Jewish Case for a British Trusteeship* in which the Zionists argued against the claims of all other governments. The arguments used against America were: first, "the average

[90]J. Kimche, *op. cit.*, pp. 61-63.
[91]*Op. cit.*, p. 78.

American has a natural belief in the superiority of the American
type" so that the American government tends "to give the
American image to the subject-peoples". Secondly, "democracy in America too commonly means majority rule without
regard to diversities of type or stages of civilisation or differences
of quality. . . . If the wide arithmetical conception of democracy
were to be applied now, or at some early stage in the future,
to Palestinian conditions, the majority which would rule would
be the Arab majority." Thus dismissing the "crude" concept
of one-man one-vote, the third Zionist argument, more reasonably, declared that "it would not be to the advantage of a
Jewish Palestine to compel Jews to intervene on its account in
American domestic politics." In view of the fact that massive
Jewish intervention in American domestic politics has subsequently become a major factor in Middle Eastern affairs this
last objection reads rather ironically.[92]

Zionist fears were unfounded, because America was not interested, and the French had already conceded defeat in Palestine
in return for a free hand in Syria.

In his recent book Kimche advances yet another reason why
the Zionists preferred Britain. Only Britain, he claims, would
recognise Jewish nationality, not the Germans, nor the French,
nor the Americans; because the British felt that Jews were always
foreigners, always remained Jews and hence, however distinguished, were never accepted as British by the British. This is one
more example of the Zionist theory that anti-Semitism can be
useful in advancing Zionism.[93]

On February 23, 1919, the Zionists made their presentation
to the Council of Ten of the Peace Conference in which they
asked for a national home in Palestine and proposed that "the
sovereign possession of Palestine shall be vested in the League
of Nations and the government entrusted to Great Britain as
Mandatory of the League."[94] This was, of course, accepted.

In his autobiography published in 1949, Weizmann claims

[92]Stein, *op. cit.*, pp. 61-63.
[93]Kimche, *op. cit.*, p. 70.
[94]Stein, *op. cit.*, p. 616; Weizmann, *op. cit.*, pp. 303-306.

—and he does so with a touch of pride: "It was the Jews who gave substance and reality to the idea of a British protectorate—which afterwards took the form of a Mandate—over Palestine."[95]

That is a perfectly just claim for the Mandate, indeed, was the "substance and reality" of the Zionist-British Compact of 1917.

It now remains to see what this flow of reason and feast of soul looks like from the east bank of the Jordan; in other words, to put the Compact into its setting in West Asia within the larger Afro-Asian framework.

Inevitably things look very different. For here we have the spectacle of the Zionists taking the initiative in drawing a somewhat reluctant Britain into the Middle East and working hand in glove with Britain to make that possible. Britain was already involved in "imperial work" in Egypt and India; by 1914 she was already facing strong nationalist resistance from both those countries. From any standpoint, except a short-sighted selfish one, it was clearly better to keep her out of further entanglements in West Asia, which in fact was the opinion of Foreign Secretary Grey in 1914. But the Zionists preferred Britain even though two other alternatives were available—an international regime for Palestine or a Mandate under America whose hands were, comparatively, far cleaner than those of Britain. The Zionists did not favour these two alternative protectors because they would have been democratic, basing themselves on the principle of self-determination, and therefore more likely to think in terms of a Palestine Arab majority and a non-Arab minority rather than of Jews and non-Jews. Nor could the Zionists have had much hope of changing the ideas of an international or an American regime because, as has been said, the Zionists had no bargaining counter to offer them as they had with their offer to protect British interests in the Canal.

There is little doubt that if the Zionists had joined the Arabs in their opposition to a British Mandate, Britain would have been excluded. Before an American Committee of Enquiry (the King-Crane Commission), representatives of the Palestinian

Arab majority had declared that they would prefer American assistance to British rule if full independence was not possible.[96] Only then would there have been the possibility of lifting the future of a part of West Asia out of the web of imperial interests. But the Zionists did the opposite and promoted and served imperial interests because they were at home within the imperial systems of Europe.

Not the least of the peculiar aspects of the Balfour Declaration, "one of the most improbable documents of all time"[97] was that it completely failed to achieve any of its short-term objectives. Perhaps because it took so long to formulate—8 months for 191 words—it came too late to have any impact on the Jews in Russia, either communists or wheat contractors; it did not noticeably enthuse American Jewry; and while it did excite Jews in some other countries this did not appreciably aid the Allied war-effort. French influence was removed from Palestine, not by the Zionists but by British promises involving Syria. If the Declaration had been delayed for another 30 days it would have been seen as unnecessary because of the advance of the army under Allenby.

Yet another of its peculiarities is the re-interpretation of the motives of its sponsors, especially Lloyd George. We have seen how categoric statements by Zionist leaders that their motivation was reaction to anti-Semitism have been explained away. So also with the British Prime Minister of the time. Asquith recorded that Lloyd George "does not care a damn for the Jews or their past or their future." Immediately after 1919 his exaltations over Zionism began to diminish and thereafter he made only two major statements concerning the origins of Zionism and the Declaration. One was to the effect that the Declaration had been issued in gratitude for Dr. Weizmann's discovery of an explosive at a time of dangerously short supply; the other claimed that the Declaration was promulgated in exchange for propaganda work, and for no other reason.[98]

[96]H. Howard, *The King-Crane Commission*, Beirut, 1963, p. 102.

[97]Koestler, *op. cit.*, p. 4.

[98]Sykes, *op. cit.*, pp. 120, 232.

The Zionists and pro-Zionists refused to accept his words: "to accuse him, as he accused himself, of a passing and rootless interest in the matter is unjustifiable."[99] And so two theories are produced: one, mildly psychoanalytic, is that he was embarrassed by the romantic impulse which led him to support Zionism;[100] the other that he so admired Hitler's solution of the problem of unemployment that he was turned away from Zionism.[101]

As part of the attempt to confer respectability on what was an "unromantic" bargain Zionists also stress the Christian aspect of the Declaration, or rather its roots in Protestant devotion to the Old Testament.[102] Perhaps there were messianic dreams and stirrings of conscience in the hearts and minds of Balfour and Lloyd George, but it is surely more correct to say, in the words of a British Gentile Zionist, that Britain, "invested what was in our own interest with a halo of international duty".[103]

In 1924 Weizmann wrote an anguished letter to Churchill, at a time when the future of the area was under review, in which he reminded him that though "you have set up a great Arab kingdom in Mesopotamia you will have to rely on the Jews for your loyal element . . . It is difficult to understand", he went on, "how one can build an Arab loyalty so near the vital communications across the isthmus of Suez. All one has heard of the Arab movement leads one to believe that it is anti-European."[104] Such sentiments led one of his British biographers to complain that Weizmann "assumed that one of the tasks of the Jewish nation would be to protect Britain's imperial interests on the Suez Canal."[105] But Weizmann was proven right in 1956 for, when the "anti-European" Arab movement did seem in Britain's eyes to threaten the Canal, Britain found that she could rely on the Jews in Palestine for her "loyal element".

[99]*Op. cit.*, p. 121.
[100]Koestler, *op. cit.*, p. 4.
[101]Sykes, *op. cit.*, p. 233.
[102]Zwi Werblowsky, *Les Temps Modernes*, p. 39.
[103]Sidebotham, *British Imperial Interests in Palestine*, London, 1939, p. 3.
[104]Crossman, *op. cit.*, p. 125.
[105]*Op. cit.*, p. 36.

And without the first collusion of the 1917 Compact there would not have been the second collusion of the Treaty of Sèvres in 1956.

In the meantime, for nearly 20 years, there was less spectacular daily collaboration between the British and the Zionists in Mandatory Palestine.

* * *

The period of the British Mandate

History will doubtless recall the 20 years between the two World Wars as the classic period of Asian and North African nationalism. It was in this period that the mass movements went fully into action on all fronts and fought their greatest battles—some violent, others non-violent. No victories were achieved during this time against the colonial powers for no colonial territory achieved real freedom—only a titular independence was conferred on a few countries. Yet if after World War II the colonial citadels collapsed in quick succession it was because of the hard battering, the sapping and the mining, to which they had been subjected during these two decades.

If the 20 years between 1900 and 1920 seemed turbulent they were almost tranquil when compared with the seismic turmoil that shook Asia and North Africa from end to end between the wars, from the Philippines and Indonesia to Tunisia and Morocco. When one takes in its trans-continental scope and its inter-continental basis the inter-war period becomes one of the most awe-inspiring in world history.

For the Arab countries the nationalist chronology is impressive enough. The period began with the large-scale uprising in Iraq in 1920. In 1921 Abdel Krim began his rebellion in Morocco, and Zaghlul was deported from Egypt. Three years later, in 1924, Zaghlul, then prime minister, was compelled to resign. 1925 saw the beginning of the Druse rebellion in Syria and the bombardment of Damascus by the French; the struggle in Syria lasted for the next two years. Lebanon became a republic in 1926, and in Morocco Abdel Krim finally surrendered. The Egyptian Parliament rejected a treaty offered by Britain in 1928 and was dissolved; the same fate overtook the assembly in Syria at the hands of the French in 1929. The Libyans fought the Italians in 1930, Syria was declared a republic, and treaty negotiations between Egypt and Britain broke down. There was yet another rebellion in Morocco in 1932, and in 1934 the constitution was abolished in Egypt. In 1936 British troops in Egypt were moved into the Canal Zone, and France concluded treaties of independence with Syria and Lebanon. There was "nationalist agitation" in Morocco in 1937 and in Tunisia in 1938.[106]

These events were only the highlights of a movement that, in some form or other, was active, in one Arab country or another, every single day.

Arab Palestine was not excluded from the general Arab nationalist movement; rather the opposite, because in Palestine there was not one but two foreign enemies—the British and the Zionists. Preoccupied as the other Arab countries were with their own struggles they could give little aid to Palestine except towards the end of the period. But on their own the Palestinians fought a good fight leading to a significant political success in 1939.

There was violence in 1920, 1921, 1929, 1933 and 1936, sometimes directed more against the Zionists, sometimes more against the British, sometimes against both. Zionist propagandists invoked the emotive trigger-word "pogrom", but to the Arabs it was a straightforward struggle to prevent the usurpation of their homeland by foreigners. The interpretation depends on the point of view.

The violence in 1936 reached such proportions that one British historian describes it as "The Arab Rebellion".[107] It began with a country-wide six month strike by the Palestinian community followed by three years of guerrilla activity: "by the middle of 1938 large areas of Arab Palestine were under rebel control."

---

[106]J. Romein, *The Asian Century*, London, 1962. The chronological survey of Asian nationalism on pp. 411 *et seq.* is as useful as it is impressive.

[107]J. Marlowe, *The Seat of Pilate*, London, 1959, p. 128. This is by far the best and most fair book on the Palestine Mandate.

The British figure for Arab casualties, which would certainly err on the side of moderation, was 1,600 killed for 1938 alone.[108]

The 1936 Palestinian rebellion has been described as "a peasant revolt, drawing its enthusiasm, its heroism, its organisation, and its persistence from sources within itself".[109]

Another historian writing at the time described it thus: "In April 1936 the Palestine Arabs declared a general strike which lasted for nearly six months, in spite of every attempt by the British authorities, through military force and reprisals, to crush it. Huge concentration camps grew up after the well-known Nazi pattern. During the last few months this has taken the form of a vast national movement, aggressively hostile to British rule, and gradually displacing it in large areas of Palestine, which passed under the control of the Arab Nationalists... The British Government has pursued and is pursuing a ruthless policy of destruction and killing, thereby seeking to crush the national struggle for freedom.... Meanwhile the whole Arab world is aflame with indignation, and the East, Muslim and non-Muslim alike, has been deeply affected by this brutal attempt to crush a people struggling for their freedom. These people have committed many wrong and terroristic deeds but it must be remembered that they are essentially fighting for national freedom".[110]

Those were the words of Jawaharlal Nehru, who, naturally, looked at these happenings from the Asian point of view.

What, it may be asked, were the Zionists doing under the British Mandate during these 20 years? In the words of Nehru: "They have preferred to take sides with the foreign ruling Power, and have thus helped it to keep back freedom from the majority of the people."[111]

Zionist-British collaboration took place at all levels. Within a general framework of mutual support there was specific collaboration on immigration, on military and security questions,

---

[108]Marlowe, *op. cit.*, p. 151; and Marlowe, *Rebellion in Palestine*, London 1946, p. 214. The very low figures quoted by Sykes, *Crossroads to Israel*, p. 185, would be ludicrous if they were not so obviously partisan.

[109]*Op. cit.*, p. 137.

[110]J. Nehru, *Glimpses of World History*, London, 1942, pp. 766-767.

[111]*Op. cit.*, p. 765.

in the day-to-day administration of the country, in legislation, land settlement, granting of concessions, and in politics.

In the inter-war years the Jewish community in Palestine was the only group in Asia which, through its recognised leaders and as a matter of policy, openly and willingly collaborated with an Imperial Power, in thought and deed.

Overall co-operation was, of course, the inevitable consequence of the 1917 Compact, for the Mandate was essentially nothing but the implementation of that compact. Even the Revisionist leader, Jabotinsky, was staunchly pro-British. The general lines of Jewish-British collaboration were laid down by the strongly anglophile Weizmann and the Jewish community in Palestine adhered to them, under its local leaders such as Ben Gurion. Though Ben Gurion always disliked Weizmann and his "too docile attitude towards the British" he agreed with him on this basic policy: "Co-operation with the mandatory government is a basic condition for the growth of our population and for the increase of our strength in the country."[112] After the end of the Arab general strike "Ben Gurion triumphantly called the pro-Zionist attitude of the British 'the greatest political success since the Balfour Declaration'."[113]

The most important and the most obvious aspect of collusion was the inflow of Jewish immigrants—what Ben Gurion called "the growth of our population". The figures speak for themselves. In 1919 the effects of the war had reduced the number of Jews in Palestine to about 55,000 or 8% of a total estimated population of 700,000. In the 1922 census the Jews were 83,000 or 11%; in the 1931 census 174,000 or 16%; in 1942 the figures were 484,000 or 29.9%.[114] And in 1948 at the time of partition and the creation of Israel, 655,000 or 36%.

In terms of actual numbers the Jewish population of Palestine

[112]M. Bar Zohar, *The Armed Prophet, a Biography of Ben Gurion*, London, 1967, p. 42. Since Bar Zohar is the first person to have been given full access to Ben Gurion's private diary and papers, it must be assumed that he is the 'official' biographer of the Israeli leader.

[113]*Op. cit.*, p. 59.

[114]*Palestine, a Study of Jewish, Arab and British Policies*, E.S.C.O. Foundation, Yale University, 1947, vol. 1, p. 404; vol. 2, p. 665.

increased by 600,000 during the Mandate and of this increase 484,000 were immigrants.[115]

Thus the British, despite bitter Palestinian protest, held open the door of Palestine and allowed the Jews to more than triple their numbers by the inflow of foreign Jews, 90% of whom came from Europe[116] during the first decade and 80% in the whole 1919-1948 period.[117]

And this massive influx was into the small area of Palestine with a total population, at the end of the Mandate, of less than 2 millions. Only because of the imposition of British power was this possible; during the period, the Zionists, with British assistance, accomplished a radical alteration in the character of Palestine's population, involving the physical importation of just under half a million human beings: a service for which the Zionists are not always as grateful as they might be.

The immigration figures dispose of two of the favourite Zionist myths—one very old and one more recent. The older myth is that of "the age-old longing for The Return to Zion"—the fundamental emotional basis of Zionism. We have already seen that during the first decade of the Mandate, with immigration perfectly free, out of a total world Jewish population of about 15 million only 77,000 Jews responded to the age-old urge to return to Zion. Between 1920 and 1924 13% of the immigrants left again and between 1924 and 1928 over 33% re-embarked.[118] In the second decade it was anti-Semitism in Europe, and that propulsive force alone, that brought Jews to Palestine. Without pressure, in the first years, there was low immigration—the figure for 1932 was 9,000; and as soon as pressure was relaxed the figures fell again, from 61,000 in 1935 back to 9,000 in 1937.[119]

The reason for the unattractiveness of Zion was that the doors of far-more-attractive America were still open: for the period 1933-1942 75,000 Jews went to America from Germany and

[115]G. de Gaury, *The New State of Israel*, London, 1952, p. 28.
[116]E.S.C.O., vol. 1, p. 407.
[117]de Gaury, *op. cit.*, p. 28.
[118]Sykes, *Crossroads to Israel*, London, 1965, p. 110.
[119]E.S.C.O., vol. 2, p. 665.

Austria, compared with about 50,000 to Palestine.

While this partially disposes of the second myth that a Jewish State is necessary for Jewry as a permanent place of refuge, this is disposed of completely when we compare the actual numbers of Jews who came to Palestine from areas of acute persecution, like Germany, with those from areas of general anti-Semitism like Poland and the Balkans. Hitler's persecution of the Jews was, after "The Return", the most powerful weapon in the armoury of Zionist propaganda, but between 1932 and 1935 less than 12% of immigrants were from Germany;[120] only in 1938 did it rise to just over 50%;[121] and for the whole Mandate period the figure for German immigration is only 12%; while from Poland it is 36% and from the Balkans 15%.[122]

The explanation for this strange situation is given by Sykes: "It seemed that the main Jewish effort was decidedly not concerned with the new drift of affairs in Germany...most of the Jews in Palestine were Slavs...the Slav majority saw to it that Slav preponderance was not lost in the suddenly changed circumstances of the Nazi era."[123] Thus showing that even in the direst circumstances the Zionist themselves were not free from what might (not unfairly) be described as racism.

The Jewish influx under powerful British protection which the Arabs felt themselves powerless to remove was one of the main reasons for the 1936 rebellion and gave it its edge of desperation.

As might have been expected the Jews gave military assistance to the British against the Arabs: "thousands of young Palestinian Jews were armed by the British and organised in territorial units to help keep order, thus becoming the nucleus of an official Jewish army" writes Ben Gurion's official biographer.[124] In addition there were the Special Night Squads organised by Orde Wingate in which "several of Israel's most distinguished military leaders, including Moshe Dayan, learned their first

[120]Sykes, *op. cit.*, p. 169.
[121]Barbour, *op. cit.*, p. 233.
[122]de Gaury, *op. cit.*, p. 28.
[123]Sykes, *op. cit.*, p. 169.
[124]Bar Zohar, *op. cit.*, p. 59.

military lessons."[125] Whatever the motives, and whatever the justification, the fact is that the Jews fought alongside Britishers against the Palestinian Arabs.

Zionist-British military co-operation was occasional and as required. Political collaboration, of necessity, was continuous. Once again we have the words of Ben Gurion to describe the general Zionist approach. In 1934 he had secret negotiations with some of the Palestinian leaders, with the result that "he had refused to support them in their struggles against the British and the French. In all sincerity he said...'We will not fight against the British; they have helped us, and we want to benefit from their help in the future. We are loyal to our friends.' Ben Gurion had even informed the British High Commissioner of his meetings, without naming the other side's representatives, and had been encouraged to continue his efforts."[126]

We have seen that, prior to the Balfour Declaration, the Zionists, both Jew and Gentile, had set their face against the application of the principle of self-determination. Zionist opposition to a democratic system of representative government based on that principle became all the more determined in Mandatory Palestine.

This policy made the Palestine Zionists unique in Asia in one more way. When the Asian nationalists did not have recourse to violent methods their political demand was for constitutional advance through the granting of greater powers to democratically elected assemblies. The Zionists actively worked against any such trend in Palestine, and since the British would not go counter to their desires, though these were of a minority group, Palestine made no advance towards self-government during the years of the Mandate. In Nehru's words "they (the Zionists) helped it (Britain) to keep back freedom from the majority of the people."

The opposition of the Zionists to self-determination in Palestine, following the Balfour Declaration, came in the form of asking for equal representation between the Palestinians, then

[125]Sykes, *op. cit.*, p. 222.
[126]Bar Zohar, *op. cit.*, p. 55.

numbering about 700,000, and the 12 million Jews throughout the world. In a letter to Churchill written in 1921 Weizmann said that he "objected to a proposal to establish representative institutions in Palestine which would mean, in present circumstances, a great preponderance of Arab members...this proposal to establish representative Government mocks us", because an Arab majority would naturally declare itself against the National Home and Jewish immigration. What Weizmann asks for is "a recognition of the principle of equal representation of Jews and Arabs in Palestine in any representative system that may be set up and a clear understanding that the interest of Jewry in the country is world-wide and not defined by the numbers of the present Jewish colonists"[127]—who were then 10% of the population.

This strange proposal became official Zionist policy and was seriously put forward in the pamphlet, also issued in 1921, by the Zionist Organisation of Great Britain. "One of the reproaches", it begins, "with which Zionism has been confronted, especially in Liberal and Labour circles, is that it precludes the immediate granting to Palestine of self-governing institutions. This is not correct"; what the Zionists wanted was a Parliament which "must represent *all* the elements concerned, not only those who have today the advantage of being on the spot...There are at the present moment millions of adult prospective settlers eager to devote their lives to the reconstruction of Palestine as soon as conditions will allow." They had to be taken into account because after the National Home was accepted "Palestine became the joint interest of two partners—the present inhabitants of the country on one hand, the Jewish people as a whole on the other. A Palestine Parliament...should be representative of both. Bold and enlightened statesmanship could easily find a form of self-governing institutions reconcilable with this principle."[128] The whole idea being as grotesque as the suggestion that "millions" of Jews were waiting to go to Palestine, the British quailed from "easily" finding a means of linking Palestine

---

[127]Crossman, *op. cit.*, pp. 127, 132.
[128]*Zionism, op. cit.*, Zionist Organisation, London, p. 13.

in a constitutional structure with Jews in Warsaw and New York.

Yet this tongue-in-cheek proposal had the desired effect of imposing a veto. The British in Palestine never offered to introduce representative institutions but only consultative bodies which gave the appearance of democratic government. With these the Zionists were ready and willing to co-operate, thus putting the Arabs in the position of saying "No"

In 1921 the Zionists accepted and the Arabs refused an Advisory Council in which all the members were nominated. In 1922 the Zionists accepted and the Arabs refused a Legislative Council in which the 12 elected Arab members were outnumbered, by two votes, by 3 elected Jewish members and 11 nominated officials. For 10 years the British did nothing on this political front. In 1932 a new High Commissioner, Wauchope, signified a desire to move towards self-rule in Palestine. In London the Executive of the Jewish Agency told him that they disapproved of his revival of the Constitutional issue and that a Legislative Council would go against both Arab and Jewish interests![129]

But Zionist wrath was truly aroused when it became known, in December 1935, that though the proposed Council was severely limited in its powers, it would contain 14 Arabs, both elected and nominated, and 12 other members, 7 elected Jews and 5 nominated officials.[130] This was only a very small first step towards self-government but it was too dangerous for the Zionists. Even before the plan was officially presented it was denounced by the Zionist Congress on the grounds that Palestine was the concern not only of the Jews in Palestine but of the whole of world Jewry.[131] The Arabs asked for time to consider this proposal but in view of the Zionist veto the British government abruptly abandoned the whole project, so that Palestine continued to be governed as a colony.

The manipulative and elastic views of the Zionists on the simple and straightforward principle of one-man one-vote are revealed in the evidence given by Weizmann before the Royal

---

[129]Sykes, *op. cit.*, p. 175.
[130]E.S.C.O., vol. 2, pp. 785-786.
[131]*Op. cit.*, pp. 782-783.

Commission in 1937. He asked that "if in due course Jews should form a majority in Palestine, no veto should be placed on Palestine becoming a Jewish state." The Jews did not seek to dominate the Arabs. Therefore if in the Legislative Council "the present Jewish minority were given an equal number of seats thereon with the Arab majority, the Jews, on their part, would never claim more than an equal number, whatever the future ratio between the Arab and Jewish population might become."[132] What, in fact, Weizmann was suggesting was a return to the 1921 proposal, giving the Zionists and the nominated officials, representing the basically pro-Zionist British Government, more votes than the Arab majority.

Thus while Palestine participated in the nationalist turmoil that swept over Asia in the years between the Wars, it was differentiated from Asia in that it achieved no movement towards self-government. Elsewhere some steps were taken in that direction, however reluctantly, however small. In Palestine the Zionist objection to self-determination was effective because the British accepted it as a veto, that being part of a general understanding, an overall collaboration, between the British and the Zionists in continuation of their 1917 Compact.

* * *

Vagueness of objectives and boundaries

In their confrontations with the Imperial Powers the Afro-Asian nationalist movements made their demands quite clear. They wanted autonomy or home rule or independence within certain recognised boundaries and within a certain time, and quite often precise time-tables were laid down. That is one thing that the Zionists never did.

It is not that they did not put forward their demands concerning the political status and the boundaries of the Jewish State, but rather that they presented numerous and conflicting demands to the same authorities at the same time, to the same authority at different times, and to different authorities at the

---

[132]*Op. cit.*, p. 801.

same time. We now know that this unusual political behaviour was part of a deliberate policy.

The policy of flexible opportunistic vagueness continues to the present day, for no one knows what lines on the map the State of Israel would be prepared to accept as its final, definite frontiers.

On May 12, 1948 ten members of "The National Administration" sat down in Tel Aviv to work out the fundamental principles and administrative organisation of the Jewish-controlled areas of Palestine. The Mandate was due to end in three days time and because of the fighting between Arab and Jew two members could not reach Tel Aviv from Jerusalem and one was abroad.

The most important question to be decided at this meeting was whether or not a Jewish State was to be declared, and though this had been the goal of the Zionist movement since 1897, there was much hesitation when it came to the point of crossing the last threshold. The alternative of accepting an armistice, which would have frozen the political and military situation, was long debated and when the vote was taken it was six against the armistice and four in favour; rejection automatically meant that the State would come into being. It was thus obliquely, in a secret meeting, and by a majority of two votes that the final decision to create the State of Israel was taken.

According to the account[133] given of subsequent proceedings by Zeev Sharef, Chief Secretary of the Israeli Government, the meeting some time later decided to use the formula of words "on the basis of the U.N. resolution" and not "within the frame of the U.N. resolution" as had been originally proposed. Next came the question of the boundaries of the State. Some members were in favour of announcing its boundaries. Ben Gurion was opposed. According to Sharef: "The point had no apparent importance" and when the vote was taken it was five to four in Ben Gurion's favour; a bare majority of one.

In the version of these events given by Ben Gurion[134] himself

---

[133]Zeev Sharef, *Three Days*, London, 1962, pp. 122-123, 132-133.
[134]D. Ben Gurion, *Israel: Years of Challenge*, London, 1962, pp. 40-41.

the discussion on the reference to the U.N. resolution was part
of the debate on the matter of boundaries, as it obviously must
have been. In his words: "The problem was whether to declare
the State without specifying its borders or to specify the borders
as fixed by the United Nations. I was opposed to specifying the
borders. I pointed out that no borders were named in the American Declaration of Independence and maintained that we were
under no obligation to designate them. To be sure, we had
accepted the United Nations decision, but there was no telling
whether the United Nations would back up its decision if we
were attacked or intervene in the event that our neighbours
attacked us and we defeated them."

A third, more recent account,[135] adds still further touches to
the picture of what was decided on May 12. Ben Gurion's
biographer Bar Zohar writes: "After much argument, the
Council decided on Israel" (as the name of the State, Zion and
Judea having also been proposed). "Another fierce argument
broke out over defining the frontiers." Ben Gurion argued
against such a step saying: "We are not obliged to limit the
frontiers of our State. The Arabs are making war on us. If we
beat them the western part of Galilee and the territory on both
sides of the road to Jerusalem will become part of the State.
If only we have the strength...why tie ourselves down?" Ben
Gurion, his biographer goes on, had no intention of keeping
to the territorial limits for the Jewish State laid down by the
United Nations. He was sure that opportunities of increasing
the territory would occur, and that Israel would eventually
attain the initial aims, even if it took centuries. Instead of making
empty statements about the historic frontiers of the Jewish
homeland, he said nothing but later moved step by step towards
his objectives. Why have his hands tied? "Some people would
say these hidden intentions smacked of imperialism, but others
have called it a sense of history."

Thus at the critical hour of the Zionist struggle we find the
Zionists hesitant and divided on whether or not to proclaim the
Jewish State and after debate and division, refusing to state its

[135]Bar Zohar, *op. cit.*, pp. 133-134.

boundaries. And the latter was decided notwithstanding the
fact that its legal basis was a U.N. resolution which, on this
matter of boundaries, the Zionists decided to flout.

These two issues—the exact nature of the political goal, and
the boundaries of any possible Jewish state in Palestine, were
matters kept deliberately vague by the Zionist movement from
its very inception. The decisions of May 12, 1948, and the way
in which they were taken, were entirely in character with the
preceding fifty years of Zionist history, but were entirely out of
character with the approach of Asian national movements to
these questions.

The 1st Zionist Congress in Basle in 1897 declared: "The aim
of Zionism is to create for the Jewish people a home in Palestine
secured by public law." In that first, most solemn, pledge by
the Zionist movement there was a deliberate deception.

The title of Herzl's original booklet was *Der Judenstaat* and
from its pages, as well as from his other writings, it is crystal
clear that Herzl was thinking in terms of a nation-state with its
own flag, government, armed forces and other prestigious paraphernalia. Yet two years after the appearance of Herzl's work
the Zionist movement stated that its ultimate objective was not
"a state" but "a home". Max Nordau was responsible for the
new formulation and his explanation for the change was: "I did
my best to persuade the claimants of the Jewish State in Palestine
that we might find a circumlocution that would express all we
meant, but would say it in a way so as to avoid provoking the
Turkish rulers of the coveted land. I suggested 'Heimstatte'
as a synonym for 'State'... This is the history of the much commented expression. It was equivocal, but we all understood
what it meant. To us it signified 'Judenstaat' then and it signifies
the same now... Now there is no reason to dissimulate our real
aim."[136]

Herzl himself was privy to this deception. He said, in private:
"No need to worry (about the phraseology). The people will

---

[136]An article by Nordau in 1920, quoted by Sykes, *Two Studies*, p. 160.
Nordau made a similar confession to Israel Zangwill, *Jewish Standard*,
28.1.1944.

read it as 'Jewish State' anyhow."[137]

There is some doubt as to who was being deceived. According to Ahad Ha'am it was not the Turkish government but the Western Jews who would have been frightened off by the ambitious boldness of the word "state".

Thus for the next 20 years the equivocal circumlocution of "a home in Palestine" remained the ostensible goal of Zionism. But not quite. In May 1917, five months before the Balfour Declaration, Weizmann introduced another vaguely-worded objective. He declared that it was not "safe statesmanship to say that the Zionists wanted a Jewish State in Palestine...the creation of a Jewish Commonwealth in Palestine is our final ideal...the way to achieve it lies through a series of intermediary stages."[138]

Whatever a "Jewish Commonwealth" may or may not mean, this "final ideal" had in fact already been abandoned for yet another, equally vaguely-worded objective.

In the memorandum which the Zionist leaders, including Weizmann, had handed to Sykes in February 1917, it was stated that Palestine was "to be recognised as the Jewish National Home". This expression was devised by Sokolow and expanded in the Declaration to a "National Home for the Jewish People."[139]

What did "a National Home" mean? It depended entirely on the person using the words. The Zionist leaders assured Sykes that it did not mean a Jewish republic and this assurance greatly influenced the British Cabinet in favour of the Balfour Declaration.[140] But at least two of the most important members of that Cabinet, Lloyd George and Balfour, had quite other, private, interpretations: in 1921 they have been quoted as saying that "by the Declaration they had always meant an eventual Jewish State."[141]

[137]J. de Haas: *Theodor Herzl*, Chicago, 1927, vol. 1, p. 194.
[138]Quoted in Sykes, *Two Studies*, p. 226.
[139]Stein, *op. cit.*, p. 369.
[140]Sykes, *op. cit.*, p. 225.
[141]R. Meinertzhagen, *Middle East Diary 1917-1956*, London, pp. 103-104.

Such being the differences in interpretation amongst British leaders, who were close to, and favourably disposed towards, the Zionists, the contradictions and variations in the latter's interpretations were, of course, even more confusing.

Sokolow, the coiner of the phrase, protested in 1919 that it was being "obstinately repeated by anti-Zionists again and again that Zionism aims at the creation of an independent 'Jewish State'. But this is wholly fallacious. The 'Jewish State' was never a part of the Zionist programme."[142]

But in that same year Weizmann was telling the Council of Ten at the Peace Conference that what the Zionists hoped for in Palestine was "a nationality which would be as Jewish as the French nation was French and the British nation British. Later on when the Jews formed the large majority they would be ripe to establish such a government as would answer... to their own ideals."[143]

In the same year Samuel revived the "Commonwealth" idea: Palestine, he said, "may become a purely self-governing Commonwealth under the auspices of an established Jewish majority."[144]

A few months earlier, when he was in Palestine in 1918, Weizmann had given the impression to the British Authorities there that what he hoped for was "a completely Jewish Palestine in fifty years and a Jewish Palestine under a British façade for the moment."[145]

And yet Weizmann made so many statements to the contrary that one of his most bitter critics makes it a particular point of reproach against him that while Herzl favoured the State conception Weizmann was against it![146]

It is not surprising that with this vagueness at its core the Balfour Declaration was not officially published and not officially referred to in Palestine during 1918 and 1919.

[142]Sokolow, *History of Zionism*, vol. 1, p. xxiv.
[143]Weizmann, *op. cit.*, p. 625.
[144]*Op. cit.*, p. 625.
[145]A secret note of Hogarth, August-September 1918, quoted by Kimche, *op. cit.*, p. 67.
[146]Rabinowicz, *op. cit.*, p. 33.

But in 1922 the British Government did finally give its public interpretation of the Declaration and of the Jewish National Home. In a White Paper it stated that this did not mean "an imposition of a Jewish nationality upon the inhabitants of Palestine as a whole" but that Palestine should become "a centre in which the Jewish people as a whole may take, on grounds of religion and race, an interest and a pride."

These words might have been interpreted as imposing considerable limitations on Zionist ambitions but the White Paper was nevertheless officially accepted by the Zionist Organisation.[147] The 1922 White Paper did, in fact, take Zionism back to the cultural-spiritual centre idea of Ahad Ha'am. But since, simultaneously the British were allowing Jewish immigration, which was what really mattered, the Zionists did not quibble over words.

The next occasion when the Zionists were given a chance to state their objectives and stake their claim was in 1937. In evidence before the Royal Commission Ben Gurion said that the Zionists did not want a Jewish State, for three reasons: "a State may imply the domination by the Jewish majority of the minority... (a Jewish state) would like to be a member of the British Commonwealth of Nations... we are unwilling, and it is not in our interest, that we should be made responsible for the Holy Places."[148]

The last time that the Zionists defined their goals before the creation of Israel was at the Conference in May 1942 in New York which adopted what was called the Biltmore Programme. There was complete agreement on one point: that all restrictions on immigration (introduced in 1939) must be removed and a Jewish majority in Palestine must be achieved as soon as possible. The political decision was "that Palestine be established as a Jewish Commonwealth". There was no definition of what these words meant but from Ben Gurion's speech it was clear that for him they meant a Jewish state. He rejected parity with the Arabs, as well as a bi-national state, because without a Manda-

---

[147]Sykes, *Crossroads*, p. 92.
[148]E.S.C.O., vol. II, pp. 801-802.

tory such a self-governing state would mean a permanent dead-lock.[149] This rejection plus the demand for a Jewish majority could only mean Jewish statehood—but no one would say so.

Ben Gurion's biographer rightly asks: "Why a Common-wealth and not a State?" and suggests the answer: "Its ambi-guity could not but assist a wily tactician like Ben Gurion. There were three possible meanings: an independent Republic, a Dominion within the framework of a community of nations, or a country belonging to a Federation of States. Any of these was acceptable to Ben Gurion."[150]

This official explanation of Zionist "ambiguity" in 1942 ena-bles one to define with some precision this continuing character-istic of the Zionist movement. In every national movement, as for instance in the Afro-Asian movements of the last two generations, there are zigzags, advances and retreats, "two steps forward, one step back". But the goal, a clearly stated desire for ultimate independence, has always remained steady. In the Zionist movement it was the goal itself that changed its character so that sometimes it was said to be independence in a Jewish State, sometimes semi-independence in a National Home and some-times not a state at all but a cultural home.

This was not only bewildering, it was deceptive, because despite these public statements the real, private, objective of the Zionist movement did remain constant: it was a Jewish State in Palestine. The various descriptions used were not adjustments to changing circumstances; they were camouflage. The Zionists did adapt themselves to their political circum-stances in one way: when these were favourable they described their objective of a Jewish State as a Jewish State; when cir-cumstances were not favourable they described their objective of a Jewish State as a Commonwealth or a National Home.

That this objective did not change is apparent from the fact that the one factor which was always regarded as all-important was continuing immigration into Palestine leading to the es-tablishment of a Jewish majority community, a basic reversal

[149]E.S.C.O. vol. II, pp. 1080-1085.
[150]Bar Zohar, op. cit., p. 68.

of the demographic pattern. Under questioning no Zionist ever denied this cardinal tenet of the Zionist faith, but the tenet was not put in the forefront until the end of the Mandate. Nor did the Zionists or their friends voluntarily draw the obvious conclusion that a Jewish majority in Palestine inevitably meant Jewish political power and economic control.

If this conclusion was not drawn it was because immigration was in such small numbers that a majority seemed to be a long way ahead in the future and nothing would be gained in the meantime by substantiating Arab fears: but this lack of immigrants was, eventually, taken care of by the anti-Semites, to use Herzl's words.

That deception was consistently practised is now admitted. Nordau referred to his "circumlocution" of 1897 in 1920. In 1906 Rabbi Solomon Schechter, then head of the Jewish Theological Seminary in New York, and a devoted Zionist, admitted: "That the language of the leaders was sometimes ambiguous and not quite definite in the declaration of this principle (an independent national life in Palestine) is owing to the boldness of the proposition and the environments in which these leaders were brought up, where everything Jewish was in need of an apology, rather than to any doubt about the final aim of Zionism, as conceived in the minds of the great majority of Zionists."[151] Christopher Sykes, a writer most friendly to Zionism, concludes that his father, Sir Mark Sykes, one of the truest and most influential friends the Zionists have ever had, was the victim of Zionist "double-dealing" in 1917.[152] Bar Zohar states that "ambiguity" in 1942 assisted Ben Gurion's tactics.

From beginning to end Zionism, thus, has the appearance of "a movement of questionable straightness" about its basic goal, about which no national movement worth the name should need to be deceptive.

But the goal of Zionism was such that it had to be deceptive, and increasingly so. For after 1919, and even for many years before, the Arab majority of Palestine objected to being con-

---

[151]Schechter in Hertzberg, *op. cit.*, p. 505.
[152]Sykes, *Crossroads*, p. 24.

verted into a minority. How could Zionism in an age of anti-colonisation and democracy and self-determination openly avow that that was its intention? As far back as 1882 Pinsker had warned: "We will still be charged with reckoning without our host. What land will grant us permission to constitute a nation within its borders?"[153] Arab Palestine was certainly not prepared to grant that permission.

For that reason and perhaps, too, because of "the environment in which these leaders were brought up" Zionism differs from a simple straightforward nationalist movement by being neither simple nor straightforward in its basic objective. The hesitancy in Tel Aviv on May 12th 1948 was characteristic and understandable.

Nor was Zionism any the more direct when it came down to a matter of detailed delineation of the boundaries of the Jewish State.

Since the Zionist leaders always considered that the land of Zion was, unquestionably, their inalienable property—for had not Herzl himself said that they were "the hereditary lords of the land?"—they always tried to claim for it the most extensive boundaries possible.

But these were adaptable to circumstances. Just as the Zionist goal was revealed or concealed according to developments so too did the boundaries of the Jewish state expand and contract depending on contemporary events.

One Zionist writer has provided a vivid image of the elasticity of Zionist border claims. Norman Bentwich said that "the Rabbis compared Palestine to a deer whose skin grows when it is well fed," (and, of course, shrinks when it is not.) "So with an increasing population the very area of the land will grow."[154] Lord Bacon said the same thing but rather more bleakly; "Appetite grows with what it feeds on."

Herzl himself negotiated in accordance with the deerskin theory. In 1898 he was asked about the boundaries of the

[153]Pinsker, *Auto-Emancipation*, p. 40.
[154]Norman Bentwich, "The Future of Palestine" in *Zionism and the Jewish Future*, p. 201.

Jewish state in Palestine, whether these would run as far north as Beirut or even beyond that. He replied "We will ask for what we need—the more immigrants, the more land.[155] But the question set him thinking and a few days later he discussed Zionist demands with a friend and noted: "Area: from the Brook of Egypt to the Euphrates.[156]

Zionist territorial demands are of three categories—the religious, the secular historical, and the political Zionist.

The religious demand is for the area mentioned by Herzl—from the Wadi el Arish to the Euphrates. This, it is claimed, is the territory "promised" by Jehovah to His Chosen People. The exact geographical limits have been, and still are, argued endlessly by the theologians but this is the area still claimed by the orthodox religious section within Zionism.

The basic secular historical demand is for the area of Palestine historically occupied by the Jews from Dan to Beersheba. The political Zionists would ideally like this area plus adjoining territory to meet such modern needs as a viable economy and military security. The economic argument takes in the area of Hauran (now in Syria) because of its fertile wheatlands; and the headwaters of the Jordan, the snows of Mount Hermon, the river Litani, the river Yarmuk and the Jabbok stream (all of these now in Lebanon, Syria and Jordan) to provide water for irrigation and hydro-electric power. The Gilead area east of the Jordan (now in Jordan) was to be included because it was the sole remaining source of wood, and Transjordan and the Negev were earmarked as the only areas still containing uncultivated territory.

Military considerations indicate the inclusion of the invasion route through the northern Bekaa (now in Lebanon), the Hauran and the Yarmuk, and the area through which runs the former Hejaz Railway, from Amman to Deraa, (now in Jordan)—the railway being necessary to supply the 'eastern front'.[157] In the South, the claims extend to Sharm el Sheikh and the Straits of

---

[155]Herzl, *Diaries*, p. 701.
[156]*Op. cit.*, p. 711.
[157]H.F. Frischwasser-Ra'anan, *The Frontiers of a Nation*, London, 1955, pp. 86-87.

Tiran; while parts of Sinai also invite annexation to provide a bulwark against "Egyptian aggression".

This, it might be thought, is stretching the deer skin very wide by adding to the more modest original territory of Dan-to-Beersheba areas many times its size—all of course for the most cogently argued reasons, such as to obtain "natural frontiers" or "secure borders" for the Jewish state. In 1916, for instance, Israel Sieff, now Lord Sieff, angrily insisted that the Jewish state without "the whole of the Hauran and Hejaz Railway" meant a restricted Palestine "without any hope of extension" and under threat from the Arabs, "which will make our position east of the Jordan precarious for all time."[158]

There were some who thought the deerskin might stretch even further. Grey, the British Foreign Secretary in 1914, asked Samuel whether Syria should not go with Palestine. Samuel prudently replied that Beirut and Damascus should not be included in the Jewish state because "they contained a large non-Jewish population which could not be assimilated."[159]

But there were others in 1916 who, though they were political Zionists, were still stirred by the dreams of Messianic Zionism: "There is no need for Palestine today to be confined to its historic borders and Jewish colonisation may extend to the whole territory which was contained in the Promise... From the Mediterranean to the Euphrates and from Lebanon to the river of Egypt... the plateaux of Gilead and Moab and the plains that stretch away to the Tigris and Euphrates may be reclaimed by Jewish enterprise and industry." Such were the dreams of Norman Bentwich[160] and in spite of them, or perhaps because of them, he was appointed the second highest legal authority in Palestine, the Attorney General, in the British Mandatory regime. (In fairness it must be added that Bentwich ended his dream with the words: "It is not expected that the Jews will be able to occupy and appropriate the whole country":—as a lawyer Bentwich doubtless used the words "occupy" and "ap-

[158]Kimche, op. cit., p. 27.
[159]Samuel, Memoirs, p. 141.
[160]Bentwich, op. cit., p. 201.

propriate" advisedly.

And the Gentile Zionist, Sidebotham, who looked at things from the military standpoint, urged that "the Jews must have Hauran and Bosra (which now lies well inside Syria) as a traffic centre from North to South and from Palestine to Mesopotamia. Here the Jewish state might find consolation for Damascus, should that famous city be beyond its attainment."[161]

Thus encouraged and inspired, in November 1918, the Zionists drew on their maps for the Jewish State in Palestine a territory which was considerably larger than the area finally allotted to mandatory Palestine. Outside those borders the Zionists claimed all of what is now southern Lebanon up to the Litani river, all the sources of the Jordan, the whole of the Hauran area in what is south-western Syria "to a point just south of the Damascus territory" southwards from there along, but west of, the Hejaz Railway to the Gulf of Akaba and from there to El Arish.[162]

Ambitious though this map was it was not the last word in Zionist claims. The deerskin was stretched once more. It was Samuel who proposed a northern boundary much farther into the Lebanon and this was accepted; so that the final map showed a line starting from a point just south of the port of Sidon, running to another point "some twenty kilometres south of Damascus," thence to Akaba. Most interesting was the new Zionist frontier in the south-west. Here the revised draft simply said that "this line would be determined by negotiations with the Egyptian government." Why? Because the Zionists held on to the hope that the Jewish state would not stop at the Biblical "Brook of Egypt" or the Wadi el Arish, but might be advanced to include the whole of Sinai.[163]

This enlarged map was presented to the 1919 Peace Conference and it has been described in some detail because there can be little doubt that it remains the ultimate objective of the Jewish State, an objective largely realised in the 1967 war. Thus, *after* the cease-fire was declared on the Syrian front during the hosti-

---

[161]Sidebotham, *England and Palestine*, p. 195, *et. seq.*
[162]Frischwasser-Ra'anan, *op. cit.*, p. 101.
[163]*Op. cit.*, pp. 105-108.

lities in June, 1967, the Israeli forces advanced rapidly to seize some of the headwaters of the Jordan and a good portion of the Hauran area; likewise after the cease-fire on the Egyptian front they advanced to complete the occupation of 99.9% of the Sinai.

Between November 1918 and March 1923 the Zionists and British, on the one side, carried on a prolonged tussle with the French and Arabs, on the other, over the question of boundaries. The Zionists and the British worked as a team—Samuel pressed the Zionist arguments on the British Delegation at Versailles, Felix Frankfurter, an American later to become a Supreme Court Justice, saw Balfour, Weizmann badgered Allenby and even the French Jewish philosopher Bergson was called on to help with the frontier question. It was during these negotiations that Zionist-British collusion was most clearly manifest. The basis was perfectly plain—the British were urged to ask for more land for their mandated territory by the Zionists who were eventually going to take it over as the Jewish State, and who wanted elbow room, economic assets and defensible frontiers for that state. The British, in turn, had no objections to promoting their own influence in the Middle East through Zionism by pressing the needs of their Zionist allies upon France.

Thus in November 1919 the British War Office told Sokolow that it would help to put the case for the eastern frontier; and Allenby, after seeing Weizmann, "sent a telegram to the cabinet supporting Zionist territorial aspirations on military grounds."[164] The British Foreign Office experts argued with the French that Jewish colonisation "needed the large land reserves of the south and east and the waters of the north for irrigation and power purposes."[165] These experts, in their official notings, used such phrases as "If such a territorial compromise should prove unattainable the Zionist desiderata might conceivably be met by an economic agreement with the French."[166]

In the Anglo-French Conference on frontiers that met in London from December 23, 1919 both sides openly stated that

[164]*Op. cit.*, pp. 119-120.
[165]*Op. cit.*, p. 123.
[166]*Op. cit.*, p. 123.

they were arguing for and against the Zionists, not a Palestine
Mandated to Britain. The French delegate Berthelot offered
that "one-third of the waterpower (of the Jordan) should be
allotted to the Zionists." In reply Curzon, bargaining for Britain,
"warned France that the Zionists, who insisted on a good northern frontier, were difficult people to deal with and might even,
by some arrangement with Feisal, make trouble for the French."
Curzon said it was necessary to provide for the needs of future
Jewish colonisation and not merely the requirements of existing
Jewish settlements, and that the Zionists needed land and water.
Berthelot commented that "they would soon want Damascus."[167]
To try and win over the French, Sokolow interviewed the President of France, and on Weizmann's request the eminent American Jewish Judge Brandeis telegraphed Lloyd George, with an
endorsement from President Wilson. Lloyd George replied
finding fault with Brandeis' geography—a sign that Lloyd
George's earlier Zionist enthusiasm was waning now that Britain
was sure of incorporating Palestine into its imperial system.[168]

A Zionist authority on this subject even argues that the Zionists could have forced the British to fight harder for better frontiers if they had threatened not to request the League of Nations
to grant the Palestine Mandate to Britain. "Britain's whole
moral and legal basis for claiming Palestine rested on her assumption of the role of protector of the Jewish National home, at the
request of the Zionist movement... The Zionist leaders, however,
were too firmly committed to the support of Britain for any such
moves. As a result they were too much taken for granted by the
British and completely alienated the French, who came to regard
the Zionist movement as a willing tool of British policy... The
Jewish leaders were genuinely grateful to Britain for her support
of the national home and there did not seem to be any other
power which would really be acceptable as mandatory for
Palestine."[169] But it should be remembered that the Zionists
were dependent upon the support of Britain, then in physical

---

[167]*Op. cit.*, pp. 125-126.
[168]*Op. cit.*, pp. 128-130.
[169]*Op. cit.*, pp. 131-132.

occupation of Palestine, to obtain a foothold in the country; too much pressure upon the British might not only be ungrateful but also dangerous.

The Compact of 1917 thus, in minor details, worked to the disadvantage of the Zionists to the extent that the British were ultimately not prepared to alienate France for the sake of the Zionists.

Nor, for that matter, were the Zionists prepared to alienate even a hostile France for the sake of Feisal. In 1917-18 the British told Weizmann that the idea of a Jewish National Home would be more acceptable to world opinion if he could get a "no-objection" certificate from the Arabs. This is what Weizmann, by making a vague, non-political definition of the National Home, seemed to have got from Feisal in what has been called the Feisal-Weizmann Agreement,* although Feisal inserted a proviso concerning Arab independence that completely nullified the practical value of the Agreement. Nevertheless Arab and Zionist leaders had put their signatures to a single statement and the world could, and did, misinterpret that as an Arab agreement.

Therefore when the Zionists began drawing their frontiers they at first stated that they would be Feisal's allies and would protect his access to the sea between Damascus and Haifa. Very soon this offer was drastically diminished to a promise of a free port at Haifa in return for right of communication to Mesopotamia.[170]

The bewildered and good-natured Feisal evidently continued to believe in Zionist good faith and in January 1919 sent two of his advisers to the Zionists suggesting that "an Arab-Jewish entente would be far preferable to British and French trusteeships in the Middle East and that the Semitic peoples should try to do without the West". In spite of frequent later reminders from the Arab side the Zionists gave no reply to this touchingly naive

---

*Feisal's accord with Weizmann, limited as it was, was still repudiated by the Sharif of Mecca (Feisal's father), the Syrian Arab Congress and the Palestinians.

[170]*Op. cit.*, p. 94.

suggestion.[171]

Later in 1919 Feisal again approached Weizmann with an offer to assist the Jews in Palestine if he would persuade the French to waive their claim on the interior of Syria. "Feisal was apparently playing with the idea of an entente of the peoples of Asia against the imperialist powers." Weizmann's reply was to offer to do his best while asking Feisal "not to interfere with the French in the coastal districts of Syria, saying that they could be removed from there later on."[172] It was from their coastal bases that the French removed Feisal from Damascus later on.

Thus despite strong and persistent French opposition to Zionist territorial claims, Weizmann preferred France to Feisal, for the squabbles of Britain, France and the Zionists were family squabbles between "insiders". Feisal and the Arabs were "outsiders" from Asia with whom the Zionists would never co-operate, least of all against Europe; and most definitely not against Britain which had been briefed to act as the Zionists' advocate. Feisal's gesture was one of pitiable ignorance.

Two conclusions may be drawn from this account of frontier negotiations. First, it was a long-standing and deliberate policy, beginning with Herzl himself, for the Zionists not to define the precise frontiers of the Jewish State. They were always kept fluid and negotiable, advancing when political—or military—circumstances were favourable, contracting when these were not. The map presented to the Peace Conference had one indefinite element—the frontiers with Egypt. Zionist claims expanded greatly in 1918 to 1921, but then had to accept contraction in 1922 and 1923. The Jewish State expanded in 1948 over the frontiers drawn by the United Nations, and in 1956 over the Armistice lines. It contracted back to those lines in 1957. In 1967 it has expanded once again: it is once more the skin on a well-fed deer. This is surely not the end either of contraction or expansion.

This being the attitude of Zionists towards their frontiers

[171]*Op. cit.*, p. 107.
[172]*Op. cit.*, p. 117.

before and after 1947 it was only natural that on May 12 of that year the founders of the State of Israel should deliberately refuse to mention its boundaries. But there is no other state in Asia which has drawn round it on the map not a continuous black line but a line of dots.

Second, for five years, from 1918 to 1923, the Zionists used all their considerable resources to obtain for themselves the frontiers they wanted. The frontiers they struggled for were not those of a National Home, or of a spiritual centre of Judaism, or a centre of Jewish culture. They were frontiers based on the political, economic and military needs of the Jewish State, which was to emerge from a temporary British Mandate. Therefore when, at any time after 1919, the Zionist leaders said that they were not aiming at a Jewish State, they were concealing their real political objective behind a cloak of deliberate deception. And that, again, is a form of political activity foreign to the Asian nationalist movements, for to them the goal of independence had to be openly announced and had to be respected.

The Zionist attitude to Arabs and Orientals

The dedication and assurance with which the Zionists went about their chosen task of capturing Palestine for the Jewish State was produced not only by the spurring of necessity, the sometimes desperately urgent necessity, for finding a refuge for the victims of anti-Semitic persecution, but also by the serene assurance that they as Jews and Europeans were superior to the people whose land they proposed to "acquire and appropriate". Indeed they felt themselves superior to all the peoples of the Orient and they stated their superiority quite clearly.

Beginning, as we always must, with the Founding Father, we find Herzl relegating to the Arabs the task of draining malarial swamps for the Jewish settlers: "such Arabs as are immune to the fever might be used for the work."[173] For the people of the Levant Herzl had a favourite description which, strangely, he wrote down in English not German. After saying that the land would be purchased from its present owners and on being

[173]Herzl, *Diaries*, p. 741.

asked who they were, he replied: "Arabs, Greeks, the whole mixed multitude of the Orient." And again during his visit to Palestine he wrote of the road being lined "with a mixed multitude of Arab beggars, womenfolk, children."[174] Like many another Zionist Herzl did not so much despise the natives as show indifference to their welfare: "the Arabs unmentioned in *The Jewish State*, barely noticed in his diaries, appear in *Altneuland* as willing and eager to join the 'Jewish Society' because of the material benefits accruing to them."[175] The tendency to regard local peoples as objects to be moved around was the base of one of Herzl's more "lurid" ideas: "we would rally on Cyprus and one day go over to Eretz Israel and take it by force, as it was taken from us long ago."[176] Yet Herzl had at least a feeling of paternalistic pity for the Arab farmer, for when in Egypt he commented: "the misery of the fellahin is indescribable. I resolve to think of the fellahin too, once I have power."[177]

Other Zionist leaders were quite as outspoken. Pinsker said that the Jew, "like the negroes, like women, and unlike all free peoples, must be emancipated. It is all the worse for them if, unlike the negroes, they belong to an advanced race."[178] We have already noted Nordau's claim for the Jew as being "more industrious than the average European, not to mention the moribund Asiatic and African."[179] And Schechter complains that the Jews are not even spared "the taunt of tribalism and Orientalism."[180]

It is a charitable assumption that the Zionist leaders, who were men of intelligence and sensitivity, must have had some qualms of conscience when contemplating the taking over of "someone else's home", to quote the words used by the King of Italy to Herzl. This could, perhaps, be the explanation why it became standard practice in Zionist apologetics to refer to

[174]*Op. cit.*, pp. 701, 743.
[175]Talmon, *op. cit.*
[176]*Diaries*, p. 942.
[177]*Diaries*, p. 1454.
[178]Pinsker, *op. cit.*, p. 21.
[179]Ben Horin, *op. cit.*, p. 241.
[180]Schechter in Hertzberg, *op. cit.*, p. 507.

Palestine in terms which made of it The Barren Land with the Invisible Population. It is, naturally, easier for one's conscience, and very useful for propaganda, to say that one is moving into a barren territory in order to improve it, and that one is not displacing anyone else because there is no one there to displace.

The Zionist myth that Jewish settlers made the desert blossom like the rose in Palestine dies hard and is not being allowed to die because it is still being used by the Zionists on the uninformed. In certain areas, like the Huleh Valley, the Jewish settlers have done good work in clearing swamps and everywhere there has been immense effort put into re-afforestation. But Palestine as a whole has never been a desert. It has always been a part of the Fertile Crescent, which was so named precisely because it was fertile. Many European travellers in the 19th century attest to the striking contrast between the fertility of Palestine and the barrenness of the lands to the east and south. Above all we have the clear, categoric testimony of the greatest geographer of Palestine whose work, constantly republished, is the classic standard work of reference on the physical conditions of the Holy Land. Sir George Adam Smith in his *Historical Geography of the Holy Land* remarks: "If Palestine be not a land of forests, it is a land of orchards"..."even at the season of its annual ebb the fertility of the whole land affords a contrast to the desert." That was written in 1894. In 1911 the world-famous American geographer Ellsworth Huntington wrote of "the fertile, well-watered strip of the Philistine coastal plain" in his *Palestine and its Transformation.*

Indeed one of the earliest and most respected of Zionist leaders, Sir Moses Montefiore, wrote in 1839, that "in the Holy Land (the Jewish settlers) would find a greater certainty of success; here they will find wells already dug, olives and vines already planted, and a land so rich as to require little manure."

Now and again of course Zionist leaders do fall into the contradiction of arguing, like the socialist Borochov, that the Jews had to go to Palestine because it was the only country with a good climate and a good soil that was "available", but also sparsely inhabited.

I still clearly recall the look of surprise on the face of General

Dayan, then Minister of Agriculture, when I asked him why, according to Israeli statistics, the export of citrus fruit, Israel's main product, was the same volume in 1958 as it had been 20 years before. It is not that Israel had been a laggard in production but that in the 1920's Palestine was already richly fruitful, and citrus trees do not produce fruit overnight.

The fact is that the Zionists came to Palestine not because it was barren but because it was fertile. When the Israeli poet Bialik writes of the need to "heal this desolate land of the leprosy of its rocks and the rot of its swamps" he is writing poetry, not accurate geography. Zangwill had coined the resounding slogan "A land without a people for a people without a land." This was immensely successful at the level of popular propaganda but for the more knowledgeable the inconvenience of the already existing population in Palestine required a somewhat more sophisticated form of explaining away. It is, of course, possible to try and wave a magic wand at the Palestinians with sentences like "The Arab population was about half a million; and the country was regarded as virtually uninhabited;"[181] but even at first glance such words seem strange, and the half million do not magically disappear. Hence recourse is had to a game of numbers.

Thus, writing in 1916, Bentwich admits that the density of population in Palestine was 70 per square mile; but from this is subtracted the urban population which leaves 25 per square mile in the countryside.[182] This is then compared unfavourably with 143 per square mile in Sicily at that time, and even when the figure for Palestine rises to 60 per square mile in 1940 it still does not compare with Italy's 138. (What is not mentioned is whether the figures for Sicily and Italy refer exclusively to the rural population.)[183] What is saddening, when it is not grotesque, is that Zionist Jews seem to see nothing wrong in invoking the argument for colonies based on the need for Lebensraum. If the Zionist argument from underpopulation and emptiness

[181]Introduction to Pinsker, *op. cit.*, p. 11, note.
[182]Bentwich, *op. cit.*, p. 201.
[183]Dov Barnir, *Les Temps Modernes*, p. 453.

justifies their colonising Palestine then Hitler's claims for German colonies and Mussolini's claims on Libya and Ethiopia were equally justified, by the same reasoning.

Just as the Zionists produced a "critical mass" theory for anti-Semitism—that this occurs automatically when the percentage of Jews in the population rises above a certain figure—so they seem to suggest a "critical non-mass" theory on population; below a certain figure a country is declared "virtually uninhabited" and is then open for colonisation. For Palestine it evidently made no difference whether this figure was 25 per square mile in 1916 or 60 in 1940, it still remained suitable for immigration.

The always unpredictable Nordau produced a brisk solution to this population problem: "The majority is Arab. How to get around it? At least 500,000 Jews should be *dumped* into Palestine without delay. This is the precondition of friendly relations with our Arab neighbours, of peace, of the country's preparation to become the Jewish National Home."[184]

Yet even Weizmann made the same improbable linking of mass immigration to good relations with the Arabs. He told Balfour in December 1918 that the plan was to settle "about four to five million Jews within a generation" and assured Balfour that despite this the interests of the non-Jews would be safeguarded.[185] Other people shared Balfour's doubts. The Pope asked Sokolow in 1917: "is there enough space in Palestine to carry out your plan?" to which Sokolow returned a skilfully evasive reply, "There is the possibility of reaching our goal." The Pontiff then queried "Are many Jews likely to settle in Palestine?" Sokolow again replied with a skilful and grandiloquent evasion, "The best, and those who have suffered most."[186]

Weizmann made changes in his guesses about immigration figures to the order of millions in the space of a month. The last estimate, given above, was less cautious than other estimates, though at present, not one but two generations after 1918, there are almost three million Jews in Palestine. It is clear that

[184]Ben Horin, *op. cit.*, p. 202.
[185]Weizmann, *op. cit.*, p. 637.
[186]Sykes, *Two Studies*, pp. 201-202.

on the all-important subject of immigration figures the Zionist leaders did not know what they were talking about; they had no idea how many immigrants there would be and so resorted to guesses. But they should have known, because in 1918, after 10 years of work by the Zionist Organisation, and after nearly 30 years of sporadic Zionist effort, there were just 12,000 Zionist settlers on the land. It was obvious that there was not going to be any rush into Palestine nor, subsequently, was there.

The vague talk about millions of immigrants served two purposes: it made the Jewish state seem that much more necessary and it answered the problem of how to reconcile the Palestinians to the Jewish influx: a quick massive injection and everything would be over. As Crossman said, the Zionists failed to settle the issue quickly by bringing in half a million[187] immigrants in the first few years.

If the Arabs were not going to be overwhelmed quickly then it was self-evident that they would begin to resist—as the inhabitants of any country would do if threatened by an influx of immigrants on such a scale, with such credentials and such objectives. (The recent British reaction to Commonwealth immigrants provides an interesting example of how the British themselves were later to react to foreign immigration on a much smaller scale). But the Zionist leaders, with a few exceptions, did not want to face the appearance of possible Arab resistance, and so they explained it away in several ways.

The "Nordau Plan", as it was solemnly called, did, however, have the merit of pointing out that the population problem in Palestine was not demographic but political. It was not a question of less Arabs and more Jews, but of good or bad relations between Arab and Jew.

There was no excuse for the Zionists evading the issue of the original population, for at least one very distinguished Jewish Zionist, and several Gentile Zionists, gave them ample warning.

The wise and prophetic words of Ahad Ha'am deserve to be recorded. In 1891 he wrote: "We abroad have a way of thinking that Palestine today is almost desert, an uncultivated wilderness

[187]See p. 19 above.

and that anyone who wishes to buy land there can do so to his heart's content. But that is not in fact the case. It is difficult to find any uncultivated land anywhere in the country...we abroad have a way of thinking that the Arabs are all savages, on a level with the animals, and blind to what goes on around them. But that is quite mistaken. The Arabs, especially the townsmen, see through our activities in their country, and our aims, but they keep silent and make no sign, because for the present they anticipate no danger to their own future from what we are about. But if the time should ever come when our people have so far developed their life in Palestine that the indigenous population should feel more or less cramped, then they will not readily make way for us."[188] Twenty years later he sounded the same note of warning: "many natives of Palestine whose national consciousness has begun to develop since the Turkish Revolution look askance, quite naturally, at the selling of land to 'strangers' and do their best to put a stop to this evil."[189]

A few other Zionists spoke out[190] but it was from the friendly Gentile Zionists that the really pressing warnings came.

Samuel told Grey in their very first conversation in 1914 that the Arabs numbered five sixths of the population and Grey warned the Zionists of this fact two years later. At Sykes' first meeting with the Zionist leaders, in 1917, he told them that they would have "to go carefully with the Arabs" He repeatedly cautioned them against chauvinism and urged them to work towards co-operation with Arabs and to look at things "through Arab glasses".[191] That other great pro-Zionist, Sidebotham, stated that "the Jews in Palestine will have to co-operate with the Arabs. With friendly relations between them everything is possible to the new Palestine. Without them nothing but

[188]Ahad Ha'am, quoted in a note on page 126 of H. Kohn, *Nationalism and Imperialism in the Hither East*, London, 1923. The original source is *Am Scheidewege*, Judischer Verlag, Berlin, vol. I, p. 86 *et seq.*

[189]Quoted in Stein, *op. cit.*, p. 90.

[190]See M. Pearlman, "Chapters of Arab-Jewish Diplomacy, 1918-1922" in *Jewish Social Studies*, New York, vol. VI, no. 2, pp. 123-154.

[191]Stein, *op. cit.*, pp. 621, 283-284.

failure."[192]

The pity was that sometimes these same Gentile Zionists, along with many others, gave the Zionist Jews a ridiculously exaggerated sense of their own importance. Sidebotham himself wrote that "the recalcitrant Arabs of Palestine might have been transferred to Mesopotamia in 1917."[193] And Smuts talked of the civilising mission of world Jewry.

It was the more flattering voices that the Zionists listened to, ignoring the words of cautionary advice on their relations with the Arabs. At first they tried to say that the Arabs were not there. But when the Arabs made their presence felt, by violence among other means, then a swamping wave of immigration was proposed. But though the British held the door open for the Zionists they could not summon up the immigrants. The next evasion was to deny that the Arab in Palestine was discontented at all. After paying a visit there in 1922 Einstein said that he "did not feel any Arab hostility to Jews in Palestine."[194] Einstein may be forgiven for not noticing such mundane facts but we have Nordau saying that "there is no real opposition from the Arabs. The fellah is peaceful." Arthur Ruppin, the greatest Zionist expert on Palestine, affirmed "there is not much to fear from the national jealousy of the Arabs."[195]

But since the continuing Arab agitation against the Zionists had to be explained it was blamed, in classical colonial phraseology, on "agitators". "The uproar" wrote Nordau, "is the work of unscrupulous demagoguery by hired agents;" and sounding exactly like a British district officer, Nordau says that the Palestinians were having "their minds poisoned by anti-Semitic agitators from Syria."[196]

Weizmann, too, fell in with this foolishness. Writing from Palestine in 1918 he was convinced that there would be no trouble from the Arabs because "their political centre of gravity is shifting towards the Hedjaz." The trouble came from "the

[192]Sidebotham, *England and Palestine*, p. 194.
[193]Sidebotham, *British Imperial Interests*, p. 4.
[194]Einstein, *op. cit.*, p. 42.
[195]Ben Horin, *op. cit.*, p. 201.
[196]*Op. cit.*, p. 202.

Christian Arabs, or so-called Syrians" who were anti-Zionist because they had been worked up by the Jesuits, French financiers, Turkish pseudo-Jews and what not.[197] This frightening fantasy shows so little grasp of the realities of Arab politics that one sees the point of an admirer's remark that perhaps Weizmann would have been wiser not to ignore Arab leaders.[198]

As late as 1927 a Zionist writer could assert that "Palestine was never a great centre for the Arabs and...has but little spiritual and cultural significance for the Arab peoples."[199] An historian of imperialism has aptly remarked that imperialists are usually most ignorant about their imperial possessions.[200] Jerusalem is, after all, one of the three most holy places in Islam, and the Arab hinterland did fight the Crusaders for 200 years over Palestine.

When all other explanations and evasions still did not diminish the Arab opposition then the only thing left to say was that the Arabs were being unreasonable: "what I do not deny is that the Arabs will necessarily become a minority in the country of Palestine. What I do deny is that *that* is a hardship", said Jabotinsky to the Royal Commission.[201]

The Zionist attitude towards the Palestinian was nothing less than a rejection of reality, perhaps because the reality was too ugly and upsetting. They certainly seemed determined to see only what they wanted to see. Other explanations, from the Zionist viewpoint, have been given for this introversion.

Zwi Werblowsky reports, on the authority of Buber, that Max Nordau, hearing for the first time of the existence of an Arab population in Palestine, ran to Herzl and said "I did not know that; but then we are committing an injustice!"[202] But Nordau, as we have seen, later completely overcame his scruples.

Perhaps the explanation for the Zionist myopia lies in a simple emotional response. Hans Kohn, most discerningly, writes:

[197]Weizmann, *op. cit.*, pp. 630-631.
[198]Berlin, *op. cit.*, p. 43.
[199]P. Horowitz, *The Jewish Question and Zionism*, London, 1927, p. 70.
[200]Thornton, *op. cit.*
[201]In Hertzberg, *op. cit.*, p. 562.
[202]Werblowsky in *Les Temps Modernes*, p. 391.

"To the Jews, especially the popular masses from Eastern Europe, Palestine was the Jewish country, 'Eretz Israel', a fantasy of their dreams and longings, the refuge of their souls for two thousand years, a land, therefore, where history stood still. The fact that the country was not barren, or that it had been inhabited for 13 centuries, had hardly penetrated Jewish consciousness. And suddenly, to their genuine amazement and comprehensible indignation, these Jews found their country, at whose gates they stood at last after the thousand years migration, occupied by aliens who disputed their right to it."[203]

This explanation might suffice for the ordinary Jew of Eastern Europe before World War I: sunk in his narrow orthodoxy he might have dreamt messianic dreams of Palestine in which there were no Arabs. But surely the Zionist leaders cannot be excused for not knowing about the Arab presence, after all the warnings given to them and after all their visits to Palestine.* These leaders, mostly agnostic, made use of the religious fervour of East European Jewry to provide Zionism with a moving force; they seem to have betrayed Jewry's secular dreams too, for having striven to get the Jews on the move, how could these leaders tell their followers that they were moving into a land already occupied by people who were hostile to their coming? So in public they said, variously: there are few, if any, Arabs; the Arabs are not hostile; only a minority is hostile; the hostility of the Arabs does not matter. We find much the same things being said by the British and French about the population of their colonies.

In private converse the European Zionist Jew revealed what he really thought of the Arab. When Einstein, who finally became aware of Arab hostility, asked Weizmann what he intended to do about the Arabs, Weizmann replied "What Arabs?" In 1917 the British Cabinet asked the Chief Rabbi of Britain for his opinion of the draft of the Balfour Declaration. The Rabbi, naturally, approved, especially of the reference to "the

---

*There is certainly no excuse for the British on this point, since there was a British consulate in Jerusalem from 1839 onwards.

[203]Kohn, *op. cit.*, p. 128.

existing non-Jewish communities" which he said was in line with
Mosaic legislation that enjoined the Jews to love "the stranger"
and even more "the stranger that dwelleth" with them. This
was at a time when there were perhaps 35,000 Zionist Jews
living among 700,000 Arabs in Palestine. But for many years
before the Palestinians had made plain that they did *not* love
these new strangers who were determined to make the Palestinians "strangers" in Palestine.

The Palestinians were, of course, native to the land, and at a
time when the people of the whole of Asia were refusing to be
treated as "natives" by the colonising European governments
the Palestinians were not going to accept similar treatment from
the Zionists, even if these were very conscious of the fact that
they came from Europe.

CHAPTER IV

THE PROCESS OF REJECTION

Early Arab reaction

It is one of the claims of the Zionists—it is almost a rueful boast—that it was Zionism that produced Palestinian nationalism. This is only partly true. Until quite recently this Zionist claim was generally accepted, but it has been set aside convincingly in two articles by Neville Mandel which prove that local Palestinian opposition to Zionism long antedated the official intrusion of the Zionist Organisation in 1918.[1] The initial Palestinian opposition was on a much simpler, more human and more fundamental level: it was the non-political opposition of the peasant to foreigners whom he saw buying up the land of his country. That the opposition was non-political at first only gives it greater significance by indicating that the ordinary Palestinian farmer instinctively recognised the danger of Zionist colonisation before he was told about it by his leaders; these leaders, perhaps, were awakened to Zionism by this peasant opposition.

This took the form of harassment and outright assault on new Jewish colonies, and there are records of such attacks dating back to 1886. These settlers were those pushed towards Palestine by the pogroms of 1881 in Russia and because of the sudden influx the Ottoman authorities forbade Jewish settlement in

[1]Neville Mandel, "Turks, Arabs and Jewish Immigration into Palestine, 1882-1914", in *Middle Eastern Affairs*, no. 4, Oxford, 1965, pp. 76-108; and "Attempts at an Arab Zionist Entente, 1913-1914", in *Middle Eastern Studies*, London, 1965, vol. I, no. 3, pp. 238-267. This section is very largely based on Mr. Mandel's important pioneering work, and, accordingly, will not be footnoted in detail.

1884. The regulations, were, however, regularly flouted by the Jews, with the aid of corrupt officials, and the support of the local representatives of the European Powers defending their Capitulatory rights on behalf of Jews coming from their countries. Thus from the start there was a special protective relationship between the European governments and the Jews in Palestine.

The first official Palestinian protest against Zionist intrusion was made on June 24, 1891 when some Jerusalem notables sent a petition to Constantinople asking for the prohibition of entry and land purchase by Jews. The Ottoman Government legislated to this effect, and once again the prohibitions were moderated following protests by the European Powers.

After the 1st Zionist Congress the Arab press generally did not note its significance except for the Islamic reformer, Rashid Rida, who predicted that the Jews might "take possession of your country and colonise it". A year later, in 1899, a distinguished Jerusalemite, in a letter to Zionist leaders, informed them that Palestine now had a non-Jewish population and asked them to leave it in peace.

The refusal of the Egyptian Government to provide Nile water for the El Arish settlement in Sinai in 1902 could be seen as early evidence of Arab objections to Zionism.

The clash between Zionism and the "awakening of the Arab Nation" was foreseen by Nagib Azoury in his book of that name published in 1905: "these two movements are destined to fight continually, till one defeats the other." And in 1906 because of Arab complaints the Ottoman governor of Jerusalem was replaced by one who rigorously enforced the restrictions against the Jews.

Soon after the Young Turk Revolution of 1908 the Zionists appointed the first representative of the Zionist Organisation in Constantinople, and a Zionist-backed newspaper began to appear there.

The Arab press now joined in the anti-Zionist effort. In 1909 *Al-Ahram* of Cairo attacked the Zionists and in Haifa a newspaper was founded in 1908 with the express object of opposing Zionism. Two newspapers, one in Beirut and the other in Damascus, joined the anti-Zionist chorus in 1910, indicating that the movement was already acquiring an Arab rather than a mostly Palestinian character. In that same year, 1910, there was widespread propaganda against Zionism in Palestine through the press, pamphlets and caricatures. The first booklet in Arabic on Zionism appeared in Haifa in 1911 and, even more importantly, a society called The Homeland Party was founded in the same year whose object was to hinder Zionist progress in Palestine.

The Committee of Union and Progress of the Young Turks had for some time looked more favourably on the Zionists as a possible source of financial aid for the bankrupt Turkish Treasury. Hence, despite strong Arab objections, the immigration and land restrictions against the Zionists were eased in 1913. But these steps had the opposite effect to the one desired, because they only increased violence against the Jews in Palestine and in 1914 anti-Zionist societies were formed in Jerusalem, Jaffa and Haifa as well as in Cairo, and Constantinople.

Some Arab nationalist leaders concluded a tentative agreement of mutual support with the Zionist Organisation in 1913 but it lasted less than six months.* In 1914, however, there was an attempt to bring about a meeting between Zionist and Arab representatives, but such was the caution and suspicion on both sides that it failed to materialise.

These manœuvres, however, produced a clear statement of the Arab attitude towards Zionism and a possible basis for understanding. Haqqi Bey al-Azm wrote, in 1913, that the Arabs were prepared to open their country to the Jews on condition that (i) they adopted the Arabic language, (ii) they were not economically exclusive; (iii) they became true Ottoman subjects, (iv) they eschewed politics; and (v) they took into account the Arab nation "which today or tomorrow is bound to rise again". In short, the Zionists were asked to de-Zionise themselves and to become merely Jewish settlers. The Zionists, naturally, ignored this offer.

In 1914 the senior Zionist leader, Sokolow, came to Palestine

*See p. 166 below.

with the object of examining Arab-Zionist relations. He used the usual Zionist arguments that the Jews were fellow Semites "returning home", that they could be of use to the Arabs in improving the land and would respect Arab culture. One Arab leader retorted that Sokolow's words were "very, very nice" but that the Jews did not act by them: they were an economic threat to the local people and—as the vanguard of a Great Power invasion—a political danger as well.[2] Sokolow met several Arab leaders in Palestine, Damascus and Beirut, but nothing practical emerged from his visit.

From this account of Palestinian opposition to Zionism it is clear that the danger it represented was clearly understood from early on and that the Arabs formulated well-thought plans to counter Zionism, as well as to try and reach an accommodation with it. No agreement was, or could have been, reached because Zionist and Palestinian interests were totally antagonistic.

Though at first non-political the Arabs' opposition to Zionism soon became political and was based "on patriotic grounds; it enlarged Great Power influence in the Ottoman Empire and risked the forfeiture of another province."[3] The links between Zionism and Europe were always clearly seen by the Arabs.

It is noteworthy that Christian Arabs were as prominent as Muslims in the attack on the Zionists, especially in the press: this has continued to be a feature of the Arab anti-Zionist-movement down to the present.

All the many and varied forms of Palestinian and Arab opposition were fully and promptly reported to the central Zionist Organisation in Berlin, that, presumably, being one of the tasks of the Zionist office in Constantinople. This Zionist awareness is proven by the fact that most of the new material used by Mr. Mandel came not from Arab sources but from the Central Zionist Archives, and from translations in the Jewish Press at that time.

Therefore, from 1908 onwards, at the latest, there was absolu-

[2]This particularly prescient observation is given in *Attempts*, pp. 253-254.
[3]*Immigration*, p. 107.

tely no excuse for any Zionist leader to claim either that there were very few Arabs in Palestine or that there was no serious Arab opposition to Zionism: the opposition was fairly well organised, very vocal and was present in Egypt, Lebanon and Syria, as well as in Palestine.

So when the Zionists later on expressed surprise at the extent of Arab opposition they were indulging in deception, either not to disillusion their followers or to disarm their Gentile friends.

There were at least two Gentiles who saw the situation in Palestine clearly. T.E. Lawrence, in 1915, in one of his intelligence reports writes: "Behind these German Zionist Jews is their enemy, the Palestine peasant".[4] And the good Zionist, Sidebotham, wrote in 1918: "the Arabs tend to feel towards Jewish restoration in Palestine as England would towards the restoration of ancient Welsh supremacy over Britain".[5]

But with their powerful Western backing the Zionists cared little for the Arab opposition. They took no heed of two pieces of wise advice offered to them by Arab leaders: "they should take into consideration the friendship of their neighbours, which is preferable to that of the distant stranger;"[6] and "Governments are transient and fluctuate; the people are the constant factor, and one must come to an agreement with the people."[7] They are as applicable to Israel today as they were to the Zionists over 50 years ago.

Rejection by other Asian nationalists: Gandhi and Nehru

When the first Palestinian peasant, standing on his native soil, perhaps somewhere in the uplands of Galilee, threw the first stone at the first Jewish settler because he did not like the looks of him, this sign of rejection was a forewarning of the great difficulties which would obstruct relations between Zionism and Asian nationalism.

An enquiry into the links between Zionism and Asian nation-

[4]Stein, *op. cit.*, p. 628.
[5]Sidebotham, *England and Palestine*, p. 211.
[6]Mandel, *Immigration*, pp. 99-100.
[7]*Op. cit.*, p. 105.

alist movements produces a negative finding: there were no links—of friendship, that is, only links of hostility. This was partly due to Zionism's hostile contact with and rejection by the local Asians, the Arabs, but partly also to the fact that the Zionists, despite several opportunities, did not seek to have relations with Asian nationalists; because the Zionists, at least, did not feel themselves to be in the same camp as the Asians: the Zionists were Europeans working with or manipulating other Europeans, the Asians were fighting Europeans.

If the Zionists had been interested there was a bare possibility that they might have made friendly connection with other Asian movements before World War I despite the Arab rejection. Without that interest the Arab rejection in time became a moral veto on any friendly association between Zionism and nationalist Asia.

If the British held open the door of Palestine for the Zionists the Arabs guarded the gate between Zionism and Asia, for after 1918 friendship with the Zionists would have meant the renunciation of friendship with the Arabs. No Asian seeking Zionist friendship could ignore loud Arab protests that they were being dispossessed by these Europeans and their European friends.

Yet the Zionists might have gained the friendship, or at least neutralised the hostility, of the Arab gatekeeper to Asia if they had exploited certain opportunities that were offered them. The chances of successful Arab-Zionist association were never bright but they became nil, because, once again, the Zionists were not really interested in Arab friendship: they had far more powerful friends.

One can only wonder what course Middle Eastern history would have taken if Herzl had continued to maintain contact with the Egyptian nationalist leader, Mustafa Kamel, who called on him, for the second time, in Vienna on March 24, 1897. This is the coldly calculating entry Herzl made in his diary on what might have been a truly historic meeting: "He is on another tour to create favorable feeling for the cause of the Egyptian people, who want to rid themselves of British domination. This young Oriental makes an excellent impression: He is cultivated, elegant, intelligent, eloquent. I note him down,

because he will some day probably play a role in the politics of
the Orient—where possibly we shall meet again. This descen-
dant of our erstwhile oppressors in Mizraim* is now himself
sighing over the sufferings of bondage, and his road leads him
past me, the Jew, whose journalistic aid he seeks. Since at
present I can do nothing for him, I assured him of my good
wishes. Although I did not tell him so, I feel that it would be
good for our cause if the English were forced to leave Egypt.
For then they would have to seek another road to India in place
of the Suez Canal, which would be lost to them or at least rendered insecure. At that point a modern Jewish Palestine would
be an expedient for them—the railroad from Jaffa to the Persian
Gulf."[8] Herzl could have given journalistic support to the
Egyptian struggle, but Zionist support of Egyptian aims would
have lost the Zionists their hopes of British protection, so Zionists
and Egyptians went their separate ways to meet again in the
Orient only as enemies. This small incident and these calculations of Herzl reveal how much Zionism was caught up in the
web of European imperial interests, from which it could never
break free to align itself with those trying to destroy the imperial
system.

To be noted in passing, and with surprise, is Herzl's identification of himself with the Children of Israel under Moses and
Mustafa Kamel with the pharaonic regime of Ramses II; the
weight of the burden of Jewish memory is great indeed.

The next chance of Zionist-Arab co-operation came many
years later, in May 1913, when the Zionists and some Arab
nationalist leaders, both disappointed with the Young Turk
regime, concluded an 'entente verbale' in Cairo. The two
clauses in this entente were recognised by both sides as an "exchange of services" to prepare the ground for an 'accord com-
plet'. But by August the fundamental differences between the
two movements, which had not been mentioned in the entente,
pulled the two parties apart and it became a dead letter. It
was altogether too much a marriage of convenience, too much

*The Hebrew word for Egypt.
[8]*Diaries*, p. 527.

a tactical move by both sides, to have ever amounted to anything.[9]

The next example of Arab-Zionist co-operation was the Feisal-Weizmann agreement of 1919. As has been said, the Zionists needed an Arab no-objection certificate and Feisal hoped for diplomatic and financial support from the Zionists. The Zionists got a rather qualified certificate from a puzzled and trusting Feisal but Feisal got nothing in return. He certainly hoped to, but when, as we have seen, he asked for Zionist support against France the Zionists preferred France, even though she was opposing their frontier demands at the time, to Feisal who was trying to draw up a working alliance with the Jews against the Europeans. However hard the French bargaining over frontiers had been, the French and the Zionists still had a common cause against Arab nationalism. Once again Zion opted for Europe.

What was perhaps the last opportunity for Zionist-Palestinian co-operation was lost in 1934 when Ben Gurion refused the proposal of Arab leaders to support the Arabs against the British and French.

Having failed with the Arabs, there is no record of the Zionists trying to make direct connections with any of the non-Arab Asian national movements in the momentous 20 years between the Wars, though a splendid opportunity was provided by the Congress of Oppressed Nationalities that met in Brussels in 1927.

This Brussels conference was the most important anti-colonialist gathering to be held prior to the Bandung Conference in 1955. Among the Afro-Asian leaders, later to be famous, who attended were Pandit Nehru, Ho Chi Minh, Mohammed Hatta, who became Vice President of Indonesia, and Leopold Senghor, now President of Senegal. In the full report which he made to the Indian National Congress party Nehru notes that 175 delegates attended, representing 134 organisations. In the long list of countries represented from Asia, Africa, Europe and North and South America, Nehru lists Egypt, Persia, Syria, Morocco and French North Africa but not Palestine. Yet a Zionist dele-

[9]Mandel, *Attempts*, pp. 244-252.

gation from either Europe or Palestine must have been present for Nehru reports: "the official languages were French, English and German. Among other languages used were Arabic and Chinese. An attempt to speak in Hebrew was stopped partly for lack of time and partly because few, if any, would have understood it." Only Zionists would have wanted to use Hebrew. But they must have felt out of place in this anti-Western gathering with its principal emphasis on "co-operation between the national-liberation movements in oppressed countries".[10] What is certain is that such Zionists as did attend did not maintain the contacts made with other delegations at Brussels, while the other Asian leaders did. There is mention of this conference in the histories of most Asian nationalist movements but it does not figure in the history of Zionism.

Not even the presence of delegations of Indian and Chinese Jews at Zionist Congresses could turn the eyes of the European Zionists to Asia, though a delegation of Shanghai Jews attended as early as the 6th Congress in 1903.[11] Indeed, when an appeal was made in 1933 for help in reviving the ancient Chinese Jewish community of 200 members who were Jews by birth but had forgotten Judaism, nothing was done by the Zionist Organisation and so indigenous Jewry in China finally disappeared.[12]

There was a particular reason why the Zionists should have been interested in China, and its nationalist movement. The Zionists had the sympathetic interest of Dr. Sun Yat Sen, the founder of modern China and of the Kuomintang party, who was also a Protestant Christian predisposed in favour of the return of the Chosen People to Palestine. In April, 1904, replying to a prominent Shanghai Jew, Dr. Sun Yat Sen wrote: "I have read your letter and the copy of *Israel's Messenger* with much interest and wish to assure you of my sympathy with your movement which is one of the greatest movements of the present time. All lovers of Democracy cannot help but support the movement

[10]*Indian Annual Register*, Calcutta, 1927, vol. I, pp. 204-205 and vol. II, pp. 152-159. Also Eudin and North, *Soviet Russia and the East*, Stanford, 1957, pp. 265-266.
[11]H. Dicker, *Wanderers and Settlers in the Far East*, New York, 1962, p. 67.
[12]W.C. White, *Chinese Jews*, New York, 1966, p. 157.

to restore your wonderful and historic nation, which has contributed so much to the civilization of the world and which rightly deserves an honourable place in the family of nations."[13] In this warmly-worded message the leader of the biggest Asian nation held out the hand of friendship to the Zionists. But there was no Zionist response, neither at the time nor later when Sun Yat Sen became President of China. Their failure to seize this golden opportunity is convincing proof that Eurocentric Zionism had no real interest in Asian nationalism as such.

During the 1920's and 1930's, despite the obstacles raised by the colonising governments, some contact was maintained between the Asian nationalist movements as, for instance, between India and some of the Arab countries, India and China, and Burma and India. In 1938 Nehru met Wafd Party leaders in Egypt and the next year that Party sent a delegation to India.[14]

If the hard-pressed Asian nationalists could do that much towards keeping in touch, the Zionists, with their greater resources and world-wide links, could have done far more. Ben Gurion represented the Zionist trade unions at several international socialist gatherings during these two decades but they were all in Europe: he never travelled eastwards.

Having neglected to benefit from the friendship of Sun Yat Sen, the Zionists tried and failed to gain the friendship of Mahatma Gandhi, the father of modern India.

Perhaps it seems out of character for the Zionists, who had previously demonstrated little interest in Asian national movements, to attempt to win over Gandhi. But the Zionists did not pursue Mahatma Gandhi merely because he was an influence in Asia, rather because he had a large following in the West. The Mahatma's opinions were valued and respected by both his friends and foes. He was, after all considered a saint by many, and his endorsement of Zionism would have given to the move-

---

[13]H. Dicker, *op. cit.*, p. 68.

[14]This subject is dealt with at greater length in Chapter I "Early Contacts Between the Nationalist Movements" of *Afro-Asia and Non-Alignment*, London 1966, by this writer.

ment a certain moral and ethical weight. But no such endorsement, or even an expression of sympathy with Zionist aims, was
forthcoming from him. Gandhi totally rejected the idea of
Zionism which produced the state of Israel. His opposition
remained consistent over a period of nearly 20 years and remained firm despite the skilful and varied application to him
of that combination of pressure and persuasion known as lobbying.

The Mahatma's wholly negative reaction to Zionism may
surprise some people who would assume that the man who
strove to win equality for India's outcasts would, out of com-
passion, be moved into a position of sympathy for the Jews, the
outcasts of European Gentile society, and consequently of support for the Jewish State. This did not happen for two reasons.

Firstly, Gandhi believed in seeing all sides of a question; it
followed that the Mahatma would reject the idea of establishing
the Jewish State in Arab Palestine without consideration for
the native inhabitants, even though the Jews in Europe were
being persecuted.

Secondly, the Zionists who approached Gandhi did not succeed in linking in the mind of the Mahatma the fate of European
Jewry with the creation of a Jewish state in Palestine. His
assessment of the problem of anti-Semitism and Jewish survival
in Europe was based on his own experience with non-violence,
first in South Africa, then in India, and on his belief in a multi-
religious society.

That the Mahatma's rejection of Zionism should have been
as categoric as it was is, however, somewhat surprising because
two of his closest colleagues in his political struggles in South
Africa were Jews, and Zionists to boot—Hermann Kallenbach
and H.S.L. Polak. It was this close, early connection which led
Gandhi to remark to two Zionist emissaries many years later,
"I am half a Jew myself."

Polak drifted away but Kallenbach remained dear to Gandhi
who said of his friend that Zionism was a passion with him to
which he had given a good bit of his fortune. Furthermore,
Gandhi had read all the Zionist literature that Kallenbach had,
so his was a well-informed opposition.

As far back as 1906 he raised the issue of the Jewish National Home in his magazine *Indian Opinion* in the course of a criticism of the local Jewish community. This community, he wrote, composed principally of refugees from East European pogroms, did not aid another persecuted minority, the South African Indians; they failed to appreciate the parallel between their former status in anti-Semitic areas in Europe and the position of Indians in South Africa.

Since the period in South Africa comprised the crucial, formative years for the Mahatma, this Jewish abstention was probably an influence that determined his later critical approach to Zionist ambitions in Palestine. And yet, even on the old South African score, Gandhi's attitude was justified. If he had lived beyond 1948, his disapproval of the local South African Jewish attitude towards that country's race problem would have been reinforced by the fact that only as late as 1962 did Israel support anti-apartheid resolutions in the United Nations.

The Zionists made no less than five separate attempts to persuade Gandhi into making a statement favourable to their cause in Palestine. The first was through Hermann Kallenbach. This good friend and dedicated Zionist visited Gandhi in India in 1937 and over a period of weeks tried to win him over to the Zionist cause. He failed, for reasons given with convincing clarity in an article written by the Mahatma in his magazine *Harijan* on November 26, 1938.

In the article, Gandhi wrote that his sympathies were all with the Jews, whom he had known intimately in South Africa and some of whom had become life-long companions. Through these friends he had learned much about the age-old persecution of the Jews: "They have been the untouchables of Christianity. The parallel between their treatment by Christians and the treatment of untouchables by Hindus is very close. Religious sanction has been involved in both cases for the justification of the inhuman treatment meted out to them." Apart from his friendship, Gandhi said, there was therefore a more common universal reason for his sympathy for the Jews. But this sympathy should not obscure the requirements of justice. Gandhi thought that the Jews, like other peoples of the earth, should insist upon

making their home in their country of birth, instead of demanding a country belonging to other people.

"Palestine belongs to the Arabs in the same sense that England
belongs to the English or France to the French. It is wrong and
inhuman to impose the Jews on the Arabs. What is going on in
Palestine today cannot be justified by any moral code of conduct.
The mandates have no sanction but that of the last war. Surely
it would be a crime against humanity to reduce the proud Arabs
so that Palestine can be restored to the Jews partly or wholly
as their national home.

"The nobler course would be to insist on a just treatment of
the Jews wherever they are born and bred. The Jews born in
France are French in precisely the same sense that Christians
born in France are French. If the Jews have no home but Palestine, will they relish the idea of being forced to leave the other
parts of the world in which they are settled? Or do they want a
double home where they can remain at will? This cry for the
national home affords a colourable justification for the German
expulsion of the Jews."

Gandhi admitted that the German persecution of the Jews
had no parallel in history. Nazism, he wrote, was propounding
a new religion of exclusive and intolerant nationalism; if ever
a war could be justified, then a war with Germany to stop the
persecution of the Jews would be.[15] But Gandhi prescribed an
alternative to violence against the Nazis: defiant, non-violent
resistance on the part of the German Jews. "If I were a Jew
and were born in Germany, and earned my livelihood there,
I would claim Germany as my home even as the tallest Gentile
German might, and challenge him to shoot me or cast me in the
dungeon. I would refuse to be expelled or to submit to discri-
minating treatment." He was convinced that even if a small
number of German Jews started to behave in this manner, the
rest would soon follow. He pointed out that the German Jews
enjoyed an advantage over the South African Indians in that
the Jews were a compact, homogeneous community, who would

[15] *Non-Violence*, p. 170 ff.

be supported in their protests by the whole of world opinion.[16] Gandhi was sure that Hitler would have to come to terms with them if the Jews practised *satyagraha* (passive resistance) en masse,[17] even though this might at first mean the sacrifice of hundreds of Jewish lives.[18]

The Mahatma's post-war attitude was summed up in a conversation he had with Louis Fischer, in which the Mahatma stated that the Jews of Germany had made the mistake of submitting passively to Hitler. When Fischer replied that the Jews could do nothing else, Gandhi affirmed that Hitler's killing of the Jews had been the greatest crime of the age. Nevertheless the Jews should not have offered themselves to the butcher's knife; "they should have thrown themselves into the sea" and committed harakiri rather than submit. When Fischer asked if Gandhi meant that the Jews should have committed collective suicide, Gandhi replied: "that would have been heroism. It would have aroused the world and the people of Germany to the evils of Hitler's violence, especially in 1938, before the war. As it is, they succumbed anyway in their millions."[19]

Lest this be thought too harsh a judgement it should be noted that when, concurrently with the trial of Adolph Eichmann, the Israeli Government arranged educational displays on "the holocaust" in Israeli schools, the younger generation of Israelis was neither moved nor impressed but merely enquired, with shame and indignation, why the German Jews had not fought back.

Gandhi and the young Israelis were echoing the sentiments of earlier Zionist leaders. After the 1903 Kishinev pogrom, Ahad Ha'am wrote, "I thought that this time we should see the truth. I thought we should realise that our first duty is to be men, to throw off our servility, to refuse to be slaughtered like sheep, to show our lords and masters that five million human beings are a force to be reckoned with when they are conscious of being

[16]*Ibid.*, p. 173.
[17]*Ibid.*, pp. 178-179.
[18]*Ibid.*, p. 218.
[19]*Gandhi and Stalin*, p. 50.

human beings and not dumb animals that can only look pleading-
ly at the slaughterer. But my hope was vain...I am surrounded
by the weeping of slaves and the clamour of fools."[20] In the poem
Bialik wrote after the same tragic happening, he too records his
humiliation at Jewish non-resistance: "great is the shame" were
his words.[21] Gandhi, during the ominous situation of the 1930's
and after the war when the extent of Nazi atrocities were known
was no harsher than Ahad Ha'am had been after the 1903
pogrom—or than the young Israelis in 1961.

Gandhi's discussion of the Zionist case, in its spiritual as in its
political aspects, drew forth anguished replies in February
1939 from two very distinguished Jewish scholars who had
settled in Palestine.

The better known of the two was the famous philosopher
Martin Buber, then Professor of Philosophy and Sociology at
the Hebrew University in Jerusalem. Buber's reply was pitched
on as many levels as Gandhi's original statement. The philosopher wrote of the link between the Jews and Palestine: "The
Land itself is holy and not a mere geographic tract...dispersion
without a living heart makes a people sick...the sanction for
Zionism is not only or necessarily in the Bible." He argued that
the return to the land of Palestine might solve the problem and
crisis of unbelief among the Jews. Buber enquired how and why
Palestine could be considered to "belong" to the Arabs; by the
right of conquest, presumably, but there had been many other
conquerors after the Arabs; whereas the Jews, using methods
of settlement far removed from conquest, were not said to have
any right of possession. There was a place in Palestine for both
peoples, Buber went on, "A part that might become free without
encroaching on the living room of others—a national home
where its people could live as a nation". Then he used the
"civilising mission" argument with a reference to the "present
hopelessly primitive state of fellah agriculture". From here he
proceeded to the mystic argument about God waiting to see
what people did with the territory He gave them. Buber con-

---

[20]Ahad Ha'am. *op. cit.*, p. 281.
[21]Quoted in Schechtman, *Rebel and Statesman*, Vol. I, p. 78.

cluded by pleading with Gandhi, "Help us to convert the heart of the Arabs". The Jews did not need British protection he asserted: "We do not want force. We should be able even to fight for justice but to fight lovingly".

The second writer, Judah Magnes, then Rector of the Hebrew University, claimed that *satyagraha* would not have worked in Germany for lack of publicity to stir up public opinion. Confusing suffering with non-violence, Magnes pointed out that Jewish history was full of martyrdom and that Jews had shown their readiness to suffer. He admitted that the Arabs were in the majority in Palestine in the sense that most farmers and landlords were Arabs and Arabic was the chief language spoken. But, he said, Palestine was different from England in being sacred to three religions, and also in that the Jews have yearned for Palestine. He continued: "Jewish life will always be lacking in an essential constituent if Judaism and the Jewish people have no spiritual and intellectual centre in Palestine." But he added that this centre "must take on the qualities of a National Home . . . so this Jewish centre cannot be composed only of priests and scholars but endowed with all the problems of life—political and social as well as religious and spiritual". He said that because the Jews had reclaimed the land and revived ancient Hebrew "in this sense the land also 'belongs' to them".

Magnes went on: "The record shows that in no single instance have the legalized Jewish forces in Palestine committed an act of aggression". He, too, said that the Jews had not wanted the Mandate nor did they need British protection, while at the same time admitting that Jewish defence units were "merged" with the constituted forces of the country.

Non-violence in order to be effective, he said, must be offered in front of a constituted authority and not in front of roving bandits. Magnes concluded, "There are very many who agree with you that we must not 'reduce' the Arabs. If I understand what you mean by the word 'reduce' I would give it as my opinion after many years in Palestine that the Arabs have not been reduced."[22]

[22]Martin Buber and Judah Magnes, *Two Letters to Gandhi*, Jerusalem, 1939.

Gandhi did not reply to these letters, as he had already discussed the points raised in them on several occasions before.

First, Buber's point concerning the "right" of the Palestinian Arabs to Palestine: Gandhi considered that the Palestinians were inhabitants, not conquerors, and that the Palestinians were the "natives" encountered by the Zionists when they arrived in the 1880's.

Second, Buber defined a "national home" as a "home where (Palestine's) people might live as a nation". This would indicate that he expected a large part of the Jewish people to make their home in Palestine, but if this came about, his assertion that there would be room for both Palestinian Arabs and Jews was impractical. The Mahatma was well aware of the size of Palestine and the density of its population.

Third, Buber attempted to convince Gandhi of the "civilising mission" of the Jews in Palestine; but Gandhi had already rejected the British claim to be carrying out such a mission in India, and had opted for Indian independence.

Fourth, Buber and Magnes make conflicting points about "British protection": they both say that the Jews did not want it, but Magnes then admits that the Jews had "merged" their forces with the British military force in Palestine. Magnes' statement about the Zionists not wanting the Mandate was wholly incorrect.

Fifth, Magnes' insistence on the Jewish yearning for Palestine was contradicted, as we have shown, by Jewish immigration figures.

Sixth, Magnes argues that the Jews had not been party to any violence in Palestine, a claim that the record of Jewish participation in Wingate's Special Night Squads during the "rebellion" of 1936-39 disproves.

Finally, Magnes accused the Arabs of being "bandits" before whom it was impossible to offer *satyagraha*. Gandhi would have replied that violence would never succeed in convincing the Arabs of the moral right of the Zionist case, which Magnes wanted to prove.

Sometime during the late 1930's the well-known American pacifist, John Haynes Holmes, on the request of Rabbi Stephen

Wise, tried and also failed to obtain from Gandhi a declaration favourable to Zionism.

The next Zionist attempt to convert Gandhi, in March 1946, was made by Sidney Silverman, the British Member of Parliament well-known for his advocacy of the cause of Indian independence. He was subjected to a rigorous interrogation which reminds one that Gandhi was, after all, a trained lawyer.

The Mahatma began the conversation by expressing his sympathy but explained that Silverman had come to the wrong person. In view of the methods being used by the Jews in Palestine, Gandhi might not be able to go very far towards supporting them. Silverman replied that there were small groups of hot-heads and terrorists in Palestine and that their actions were wrong. Gandhi went on to say that unless the Zionists did something towards gaining the support of Indian Muslims, little could be done. Silverman then asked whether Gandhi sympathised with Zionist aspirations to establish a Jewish national home, on the grounds that the Jews were the only nation on earth without a country.

"Let me try and understand the question", asked the Mahatma. Why do you want a national home in Palestine?"

"For two reasons. Because 650,000 Jews are already settled there and we cannot begin anew. Secondly because there is nowhere else we can go to."

"Are there not waste spaces enough in the world to receive you?" asked Gandhi.

"Palestine itself was a waste space when we went there", replied Silverman. "We are cynical enough to say 'that is how we got it in 1917'. No one else wanted it. Now that we have developed it they want to turn us out. What guarantee is there that it will not be the same elsewhere too? In Canada, England, South America—it is the same story everywhere. We are treated as unwelcome strangers."

"Excuse my ignorance. May I ask what the attitude of Russia is towards the Jews?"

"The Yiddish language is recognized and Jews have full citizenship rights. Russia is perhaps the only country where preaching race-hatred is penalized."

"Now suppose Russia absorbed all the Jews, would that solve your problem?"

"No more than the existing freedom of the Jews to settle down in the United States. Russia would not countenance any mass immigration of the Jews. On that issue its attitude is just like that of any other country."

"Then you mean to say you are not a nation but are trying to become one", observed Gandhi. "What about the Arabs?"

"We are like an uprooted plant living a distorted existence. We want to regain what we have lost. The Arabs stand to lose nothing thereby. We can settle with the Arab population. There is no difference between the Arab labourer and the Jewish labourer. The trouble is created by the Arab League."

"Now let me see. Would you allow Arabs to enter freely into Palestine?"

"Yes, but subject to the condition that it does not defeat the declared object of establishing a Jewish national home in Palestine."

"Then you want to convert the Arab majority into a minority?"

Silverman admitted that the status of the Arabs was affected to that extent and an injustice would be done to them. But he maintained that even if the Arabs lost their status in Palestine there would still be five independent kingdoms left which they could call their own, and with the addition of Syria and Lebanon there would be seven Arab states. "It means five per cent of injustice to the Arabs to avoid the denial of all justice to the Jews."

"So the Arabs do stand to lose something?"

"Something which they never had."

"Something which they surely had before the Jewish immigration into Palestine began in 1917."

"Yes, but that was under Turkish rule."

"So you want the Arabs to sacrifice something which you want for yourself?"

"We only want them to make a little sacrifice so that justice might be done to the general situation."

After a little further talk the Mahatma concluded, "I can

only hope a just solution will be found which will give satisfaction to the Jews. But after all our talk I am unable to revise the opinion I gave you in the beginning."[23]

The fifth and last attempt to convert the Mahatma was made by Louis Fischer who referred back to the Buber-Magnes letters and the Silverman interview. To Fischer, Gandhi is reported to have said, "The Jews have a good case. If the Arabs have a case in Palestine the Jews have a prior claim." This very considerable shift in his position, if it did take place, was promptly reported to the Zionists by Fischer, but the move was self-defeating. Referring to his talk with Fischer, Gandhi in another *Harijan* article in August, 1947, came down even more emphatically on the Arab side. "The Jews", he wrote, "have erred grievously in seeking to impose themselves on Palestine with the aid of America and Britain and now with the aid of naked terrorism. Why should they depend on American money for forcing themselves on an unwelcome land? Why should they resort to terrorism to make good their forcible landing in Palestine?"[24]

One cannot withhold a certain admiration for the persistence of the Zionists and for their skilful choice of spokesmen. The first serious attempt to capture the mind of Mahatma Gandhi was through a very close friend, Kallenbach; then two distinguished philosophers, Buber and Magnes, said their piece; then came a prestigious American disciple, Holmes; finally one of India's best friends in the British Parliament, Silverman, and an influential journalist, Fischer. In all these cases one sees the Zionists trying to get a grip on the smooth, hard granitic surface of the Mahatma's mind and failing to get any purchase. Lobbying, however skilful, has its limits and it did not get very far with Mahatma Gandhi because from first to last he insisted that Zionism was morally and politically wrong.

Gandhi's uncompromising hostility to Zionism sprang from his discernment that this movement was caught in a dilemma to which it had no answer. In a press interview in May, 1946,

---

[23]For information on this discussion I am indebted to Mr. Pyarelal, for many years the friend and Secretary of Mahatma Gandhi.
[24]*Non-Violence*, Vol. II, p. 117.

he said: "If it is just a political hankering then I think there is no value in it. Why should they hanker after Palestine?...If it is a religious longing then surely terrorism has no place. They should meet the Arabs, make friends with them and not depend on British aid or American aid or any aid save what descends from Jehovah." Thus in one stroke he dismissed the Zionist ideal, its violent methods and its dependence on external support.[25] Gandhi's use of the word "hankering" may seem unkind but others have used it in the same connection. The Regius Professor of History at Oxford has written: "If Zionism was the age-old hankering of the Jews for the Holy Land it was that hankering secularised."[26]

Underlying Gandhi's disapproval of Zionism were three basic attitudes. As an Asian nationalist leader he could not approve the forcible thrusting into Asia of a state populated by non-Asian immigrants. As an Indian he rejected the Zionist claim, so successful with soft-hearted liberals, that the whole world must share in, and pay for, the guilt of Nazi Germany's persecution of the Jews, because there had never been any anti-Semitism in India. As a Hindu believing in *swadharma*, the working out of one's own salvation, he rejected the almost total dependence of the Zionists on political and financial aid from Europe and America. To these attitudes the Zionists did not, and still do not have, any answer.

Other motives, some of them less charitable, have been advanced to explain Gandhi's determined anti-Zionism. An American writer mentions four:[27] his sensitivity towards Indian Muslim feeling; his objections to Zionist methods which were inconsistent with his way of non-violence; that "he found Zionism contrary to his pluralistic nationalism" which excludes the establishment of a state based solely or mainly on one religion;" and, fourthly, that he apparently believed it imprudent to complicate his relations with the British, who held the Mandate, by approving of Zionism.

[25]The interview was with a correspondent of Reuters, *Non-Violence*, Vol. II p. 243.

[26]Trevor-Roper, *op. cit.*, p. 20.

[27]P.F. Power: *Gandhi on World Affairs*, Washington, 1960, pp. 74 *et. seq.*

Gandhi was a politician as well as a saint but this last reason is politically improbable for there was no outright hostility between Zionism and Britain until 1945 and he had burnt his bridges with Britain with his "Quit India" movement in 1942. As far as Indian Muslim feeling is concerned, one can only remember that Gandhi told Silverman to contact Indian Muslims about Palestine as they, presumably, would be directly involved in the fate of their co-religionists in that country. But with respect to the argument that he was influenced by his sensitivity to Indian Muslim feelings, he replied, "I have said often that I would not sell Truth for the sake of India's deliverance. Much less would I do so for winning Muslim friendship."[28]

The Zionists were only interested in having the support of Gandhi, with his world-wide reputation; they made no attempt to contact the Indian National Congress, a fact which underlines their basic lack of concern with Asian Nationalism as such. The Congress consequently identified itself fully with the Arab nationalist movements in West Asia. As early as 1921 the Congress enunciated its pan-Asian approach to foreign policy in a resolution stating that "the destiny of the people of India is inevitably linked with that of the neighbouring Asiatic Nations and Powers." In 1922 it observed that unless "the Jazirat-el-Arab (the Arab world) were freed from all non-Moslem control there cannot be peace and contentment in India." Sympathy for Egypt was expressed in 1924, and in 1928 full sympathy was offered to Egypt, Syria, Palestine and Iraq in their struggle against Western Imperialism. Indian nationalists observed September 27, 1936 as Palestine Day, with meetings and demonstrations all over India. The possibility of partition of Palestine was specifically condemned in 1937 and 1938 and the Congress Party then said that it "appeals to the Jews not to seek the shelter of the British Mandatory and not to allow themselves to be exploited in the interests of British Imperialism."[29] Against

[28] Non-Violence, vol. I, p. 219.

[29] D. Chakrabarthy and C. Bhattacharya, *Congress in Evolution*, Calcutta, no date; also, B. Prasad, *The Origins of Indian Foreign Policy*, Calcutta, 1962, pp. 129 *et seq.*

some opposition from within the Congress Nehru, in 1939, had a resolution passed condemning Hitler's pogrom and offering asylum to Jewish refugees in India, but at the same time it again deplored that the Jews had "relied on British armed forces to advance their special privileges in Palestine and thus aligned themselves on the side of British Imperialism."[30]

That the Indian national movement should have such wide international interests was, perhaps, mainly due to the far-ranging sympathies of the young Jawaharlal Nehru. In one of the letters from prison, dated May 1933, to his daughter (later collected and published as his *Glimpses of World History*), Nehru made a comprehensive statement of his views on the Jews, Zionism and the Palestine problem. He begins: "The Jews are a very remarkable people...Rather conceited they were, thinking themselves the Chosen People. But this is a conceit in which nearly all people have indulged." After describing the long centuries of persecution in Europe he describes Zionism as "this call of the past which pulls them to Jerusalem and Palestine." Of the Balfour Declaration he says: "This declaration was made to win the good will of international Jewry and this was important from the money point of view. It was welcomed by the Jews. But there was one little drawback, one not unimportant fact seems to have been overlooked. Palestine was not a wilderness or an empty, uninhabited place. It was already somebody else's home...everybody who was not a Jew protested vigorously at the declaration." Nehru's socialist leanings are evident in his analysis: "It was really an economic question... they were afraid that the Jews would take the bread out of their mouths and the land from the peasantry." The result, he goes on, was conflict, with the British "generally supporting the Jews...The Arabs...have demanded self-determination and complete freedom." Nehru then quotes Arabs as saying that responsible Zionist leaders have urged that a Jewish State would guard the British road to India by counteracting Arab nationalism. "How India crops up in odd places!" is his comment. He concludes by saying that the British are playing the Jew

[30]D. Norman, *Nehru—The First Sixty Years*, London, 1965, vol. I, p. 619.

against the Arab and that the Jews seem to look forward to the day when they will be the dominant community in Palestine. "The Arabs tried to gain their co-operation in the struggle for national freedom and democratic government, but they rejected these advances. They have preferred to take sides with the foreign ruling power, and have thus helped it to keep back freedom from the majority of the people."[31]

Five years later, in 1938, when Nazi persecution had begun to impinge on the world conscience, Nehru gave two lengthy expositions of his views on Palestine in newspaper interviews. His denunciation of the Fascists was total, but he still kept his eye on the essentials of the Palestine case: "It was possible for a certain number of Jews to go and settle in Palestine in an atmosphere of peace and goodwill but when they went with the object of dominating the country they could hardly expect to be welcomed by the Arabs." Fundamentally, Nehru said, the problem of Palestine was for him a nationalist one: the Arabs were struggling against imperialist control and domination. "It was a pity that the Jews of Palestine, instead of aligning themselves with that struggle, had thought fit to take the side of British imperialism and to seek its protection against the inhabitants of the country." He reiterated this accusation of collaboration against the Zionists in the second interview, adding: "by doing so they had not even served their own interests, for British imperialism had had its day and was fading away. It was not wise for the Jews to risk the displeasure, not only of the entire Muslim world, but also of most Asian countries for this vanishing support."[32]

The fundamental incompatibility of Zionism with Asian nationalism could not have been expressed better than in the words of this famous Asian nationalist, who was also a liberal and most sympathetic towards Jewish suffering. But he, like Gandhi, never accepted the injustice that was perpetrated on the Arabs in Palestine. What even a far-seeing leader like Nehru

[31]J. Nehru, *Glimpses of World History*, London, 1942, pp. 762-765.
[32]Nehru in interviews with *The Hindu* newspaper, Madras, 1.5.1938 and 17.12.1938.

could not anticipate was that the Zionists would be able to slip under the protection of another Western umbrella—that of America—as soon as the British imperial umbrella was closed and furled.

A certain number of Jewish refugees from Europe—doctors especially—came and settled in India. And at one time Nehru lent his support to the idea of starting a new university that would be staffed wholly or mainly by refugee intellectuals; but the slow-moving British imperial administration did not follow up what was a promising idea.

If Asian nationalist leaders can afford to be condign in their condemnation of Zionism, it was and is because they have never been afflicted by anti-Semitism, and therefore are not crippled by guilt in their political judgements of this issue.

Thus in the two great decades of Asian national struggle we find slowly-increasing support and co-operation linking the various nationalist movements without there being the slightest trace of anything similar developing between Zionism, in Europe or in Palestine, and the Asian movements. This was because of the basic dissimilarity between these movements which found expression in the consistent anti-Zionism of Asian leaders like Gandhi and Nehru.

The argument for Zionism as an anti-colonial movement

The Zionists do not, of course, concede that there is any difference at all between their movement and those of Asian nationalism. On the contrary, and especially in the last ten years, they have asserted that Zionism, in its principles, and as a European phenomenon, was nationalist and that Zionism, in action, in Palestine, was both anti-colonial and non-colonial.

The "nationalist" aspect of European Zionism has been dealt with; it now remains to examine the latter claims based on its record in Palestine.

The claim that Zionism was anti-colonial is founded on the fact that from October 1945 to February 1947, a period of 16 months, the Jewish community in Palestine waged a campaign of violence against the British administration. The claim to non-colonialism is argued from the general character of the Zionist effort in Palestine.

The most recent, and the most cogent, argumentation of the case for and against Zionism's anti-colonialism and non-colonialism is to be found in two essays included in the volume on "Le Conflit Israélo-Arabe" published by *Les Temps Modernes*— "Israël, fait colonial?" by Maxime Rodinson and "La coexistence ou la guerre" by Robert Misrahi. Both writers are French Jews.

The events which led to the British-Zionist clash in 1945 were these: after 20 years of trying to work an unworkable Mandate, faced with a growing Arab threat to very substantial British interests, political and economic, in the Middle East, nagged with the doubt that perhaps the Balfour Declaration was an injustice, the British Government tried to even the balance in its 1939 White Paper. Its principal provisions were that there was to be no partition of Palestine, no Jewish or Arab state, but a bi-communal independent Palestine within ten years; 75,000 Jewish immigrants were to be allowed in during the following 5 year period; thereafter no further Jewish immigration was to be allowed "unless the Arabs of Palestine are prepared to acquiesce in it"; the purchase of land by Jews was somewhat restricted.

The Arabs generally welcomed the White Paper; the Zionist reaction was one of anger and dismay. Their feelings were justified, for the 1939 White Paper signified a unilateral alteration of the 1917 British-Zionist Compact, which is why "the commonest description of it by the Jews was 'betrayal', and it remains so today."[33]

Zionist criticism was particularly directed at the section on immigration. Between 1920 and 1929 the British had permitted a net increase in the Jewish population of 100,000 persons; thanks to the British doorkeeper the net Jewish increase by immigration between 1929 and 1939 was 222,500; to which a further 75,000 was to be added, giving a twenty year total increase by immigration of 397,500 on the Jewish population of

[33]Sykes, *Crossroads*, p. 237.

56,000 that was in Palestine in 1919. This was not enough for the Zionists, because the natural increase in the Arab majority would have kept the Jews permanently in the position of a minority.

What the Zionists decided to fight was this belated decision of the British not to allow the Arab majority to become a minority by unlimited Jewish immigration.

The outbreak of war overtook developments in Palestine and since it was being waged against their main persecutor, Hitlerite Germany, the Zionists were in an anguished quandary. The way out was provided by a paradoxical slogan thought out by Ben Gurion: "we shall fight with Great Britain in this war as if there were no White Paper, and we shall fight the White Paper as if there were no war."

What this meant in practical fact was that the Jewish community co-operated actively in the British war effort, while the Arabs did so passively. By the end of the war 27,000 Jews had enlisted in the British Forces with the clear understanding, among the Jews, that they were to be the trained nucleus of the future Jewish Army.

On the political front the Zionists in 1942, according to the Biltmore Programme, abandoned the objective of the National Home in Palestine for that of converting Palestine into a Jewish Commonwealth.

When, soon after the end of the war, the new British Foreign Secretary Bevin refused to be rushed into taking a final decision on the future of Palestine, the Jewish underground forces launched their campaign, in October 1945, with the object of wrecking the Mandatory Government or else forcing it to revert to a policy of promoting Jewish interests. During the succeeding 16 months, the underground movements inflicted damaging casualties on British soldiers and civilians. In the year 1946 the two Jewish armed groups, Irgun and Stern, "could boast, and they were the kind who could boast about murder, that they had killed 373 people in Palestine, of whom 300 were civilians."[34]

This was the "national" struggle of the Zionist Jews in Pales-

[34] *Op. cit.*, p. 366.

tine. It ended with a conference in which the British met with
Zionists and Arabs separately in London in January 1947.
In a final meeting between Ben Gurion and Bevin, the British
Foreign Secretary, a last attempt was made to revive the 1917
Compact on the old, familiar basis of Jewish protection for Bri-
tish imperial interests.

Ben Gurion's official biographer describes the concluding
exchanges. Bevin said that Britain only sought to keep the peace
in the Middle East. Ben Gurion replied: "And the Negev—
doesn't that interest you?" Bevin admitted that there was oil
in the Negev, and that there was a plan to build a canal... "but
every time we start to prospect or to drill, you come and poke
your nose in and you establish farming villages there". Ben
Gurion was ready to swear that a Jewish State in Palestine would
safeguard British interests. But it was obvious that there was no
hope of reconciling the two points of view.[35] Britain then decided
to refer the Palestine issue to the United Nations.

This conversation between Ben Gurion and Bevin was hardly
the conclusion that would be expected after an anti-British anti-
colonial campaign, for it shows that the Zionists to the very end
did not want to break completely with the British; it was the
British who broke with the Zionists. The Zionists would have
been quite satisfied to go back to something resembling the old
situation, the status quo ante 1939, with the British still in
possession but keeping open the gates of Palestine to the Jews;
they did not categorically demand something new, like total
independence from British rule.

Between 1942 and 1945 there had occurred a considerable
retreat from the Jewish Commonwealth idea of the Biltmore
Programme that was opposed by Weizmann and influential
sections among the Zionists in Palestine and America.

Accordingly when the decisive bargaining took place in
London the Zionists put forward not the single demand for independence but a choice of three alternatives: a Jewish State in
all Palestine; a continuance of the Mandate but as it was prior
to 1939; partition.

[35]Bar Zohar, p. 94.

According to the Zionist historian Harry Sacher, the Zionists did not wish the question to be referred to the United Nations. "They would have much preferred to come to terms directly with the Government. Mr. Ben Gurion, at the beginning of the talks, had defined their two purposes: to secure Jewish national revival, safety and independence in Palestine; and to re-establish British-Jewish friendship. The second alternative, the execution of the Mandate in its true spirit and intent, seemed to him the best hope. He was willing to forego mention of a Jewish State as the goal, and to leave the outcome to time. But this was not acceptable to the Government."[36] Thus according to their own accounts the Zionists did not choose independence; it was the British who left them with no other alternative.

Hence in assessing the "nationalist" character of the Jewish campaign in Palestine the decisive question is not "who was it against?" but "what was it for?" It *was* against the British, restricting immigration, but it was *for* uncontrolled immigration preferably under a continuing British Mandate.

The Jewish struggle was, therefore, not a nationalist struggle by colonial subjects but a rebellion by discontented colons. Since 1945 two similar rebellions have taken place: that of the colons in Algeria against France in 1962 and that by the British settlers in Rhodesia against Britain in 1965. The fact that the Jews were not of the same racial stock as the metropolitan power, as was the case in Algeria and Rhodesia, makes little difference. They were European settlers, not natives, who had settled thanks to a decision of imperial policy by an European power and under its protection, but for which no such settlement would have been possible.

Accordingly Rodinson's characterisation of the Jewish fight against the British cannot be faulted: it was an example of how tensions arise between the metropolitan power and the colony where the colons are often displeased by rules imposed by the metropole through legislation which they cannot control, or at least not entirely, and which often seems to them to be not adjusted to local conditions. This is especially the case when the

[36]H. Sacher, *Israel: The Establishment of a State*, London, 1952, p. 72.

metropolitan power, framing an international policy on a world scale, has to take into account the interests and aspirations of the local people[37]—of whom the colons are not a part.

Presenting the broader argument that the Zionist movement in Palestine was non-colonial, Misrahi claims that it was so because it was anti-British (which has been dealt with); because land was bought from the Arabs not taken forcibly from them; because the Arabs were not exploited; and because the movement was socialist in character.

Rodinson, in reply, points out that many colonial regimes do not indulge in land confiscation—the British did not do so in Africa or India; though, after independence Israel has confiscated Arab land on a vast scale.

The direct exploitation of the natives is also a not necessary factor in imperialism—it did not happen in Australia or New Zealand or in North America. The relationship between Jew and Arab was not so much one of exploitation as of domination, according to Rodinson.

Just how far Israel is really socialist will be discussed later. Rodinson mentions, in passing, the Arab contention that Israel appears to be a part of a world-wide imperialist system that economically exploits the Third World, functioning alongside the industrialised countries of Euro-America and Japan; and that she is heavily dependent economically on the capitalist powers of Euro-America.[38]

We have seen that the claim that Zionism is similar to the Asian nationalist movements, because like them it fought an "anti-colonialist" campaign, cannot be sustained. The various arguments to prove that Zionism is also non-colonial break on one rock-like fact; the State of Israel produced by Zionism became possible when the Palestinian majority was converted into a minority; the Palestinians did not consent to this reversal—they fought it as best they could. If the movement which brought about such a situation is described as non-colonial then words lose all meaning.

[37]Rodinson, *Les Temps Modernes*, p. 55.
[38]Misrahi, *op. cit.*, pp. 545-554; Rodinson, pp. 78-82.

The opening door: The Asian Relations Conference, 1947

In the spring of 1947 it did seem as if, after all, the Jewish State in Palestine might be welcomed into the Asian family. Despite all the harsh, but true, things said by the Indian Congress Party and by leaders like Gandhi and Nehru, a delegation representing Palestine Jewry was invited to attend the first pan-Asian gathering ever held in Asia—the Asian Relations Conference which met in Delhi from the 23rd March to the 2nd April.

The Zionists could have been permitted the thought that all was forgiven and forgotten between them and Asian nationalism, but events belied these hopes. At the Conference itself Indian opposition to the Zionist presence in Palestine was reiterated and, subsequently, Israel was not invited to any other semi-official or official Asian or Afro-Asian conference.

The Delhi meeting was ostensibly non-official and cultural-intellectual, which was why the task of organising it was given to a scholarly and neutral body like the Indian Council of World Affairs. In fact it was completely official. The moving spirit behind it was Nehru, who had recently become de facto Prime Minister and Foreign Minister of India; and no less than six cabinet ministers were included in the Indian delegation. There were numerous officials in several other delegations. No less than 27 countries from Asia were represented, plus Egypt, because of her links with Asia.

The invitation to attend an important conference of this character must have seemed a real political windfall for the Zionists, particularly welcome at a time when their future was very uncertain. In February the future of Palestine was handed over by Britain to the United Nations which, in March-April, had not yet decided on what to do. Only in June was it agreed to send yet another commission of enquiry to Palestine. In the interim this invitation to Delhi from nationalist India, hitherto so critical, must have seemed like a major political and propagandist break-through for the Zionists.

The explanation of this unexpected move, as given by the

organisers in the official conference[39] record, is that "the need to have different points of view represented at the Conference had to be borne in mind; it was obviously important, for instance, to have both the Jew and the Arab points of view from Palestine and the Kuomintang and the Communist from China". Given Nehru's incurable ability to see both points of view on any problem this explanation can be accepted as sufficient.

As surprising as the presence of the Zionists was the absence of the Arabs. The Jewish delegation numbered 10 members: the delegates from 7 Arab countries numbered 6 in all—5 from Egypt, and one observer from the Arab League representing the other six countries.

The Arab abstention was all the more surprising because the idea of having such a conference first came from Arab delegates to the initial United Nations Conference in San Francisco in 1945.[40] Why then did they stay away? It could be that they were sulking because the Zionists were invited. Or they were, perhaps, in a huff because, after suggesting this gathering, some governments received their invitations late. Or, what is most likely, they did not attend because they could not be bothered to attend, for the Arabs have always been and still are careless and inept in their international public relations. Even the Palestinian Arabs did not come, thus leaving the field open to the Zionist representatives, who included such distinguished scholars as Dr. Hugo Bergman and Dr. Alfred Bonne.

By contrast, the calibre of the Arab delegates—with the exception of one Egyptian woman representative—was mediocre. The Arab League representative knew no English and since there were no translation facilities, could have understood very little of what was said.

The harsh antagonisms of the Palestine dispute broke through the euphoric enthusiasm of the Conference at the plenary session on the second day. Making his formal address, Dr. Bergmann spoke of the Jews as "old Asian people" "settling down in our

[39]*Asian Relations*, New Delhi, 1948, p. 5.

[40]The Asian Relations Conference is dealt with at greater length in Chapters II and III of *Afro-Asia and Non-Alignment* by this writer.

old-new homeland". He said that the Jews had learned in
Europe "to appreciate logical reasoning, methodical thinking",
but Europe could not teach them the cooperation of religions
and races. He continued: "it is our hope that Palestine, notwithstanding present difficulties, will not go the European way
of 'solving', so to speak, problems by dispossessing populations",
though that is precisely what his people did to a million Palestinians just a year later. Bergmann repeated the familiar Zionist
claim to have transformed barren deserts to fertility, referred to
the revival of Hebrew, and concluded with the hope that the
Conference would open a new chapter in human history.

In a brief speech the Arab League representative referred to
Palestine as "more oppressed than any other country". The
Jewish community was "trying to take advantage as a special
minority under the defence of British bayonets. We object to
that and we hope you will stand by the side of right with us."

The real reply to Dr. Bergmann came from the Egyptian
woman delegate. She welcomed the Jews as settlers in the
Middle East "but we do not want British rule to be replaced by
that of European Zionists. We object to them as foreigners, as
Europeans, not because they are Jews. The Arabs must live
in Palestine. Palestine cannot belong any more to its original
(Jewish) inhabitants."[41]

Dr. Bergmann, quite reasonably, asked for the floor to exercise
his right of rebuttal, but Nehru, who was presiding, refused his
request and after a brief, angry exchange with him, Dr. Bergmann and his delegation walked out. Some of the Indian delegates hurried after them and persuaded them to return, and Dr.
Bergmann even shook hands with the observer from the Arab
League.[42]

When he closed that day's session Nehru referred to Palestine.
He once again expressed his sympathy with Jewish sufferings
but "at the same time it is also clear... that the people of India,
necessarily for various reasons into which I shall not go, have
always said that Palestine is essentially an Arab country and no

[41]*Asian Relations*, pp. 56-58, 63-64, 64-65.
[42]Press reports.

decision can be made without the consent of the Arabs". He hoped that after the withdrawal of "the third party" the question of Palestine "will be settled in co-operation between them and not by any appeal to or reliance upon any outsiders".[43]

This was an inauspicious beginning for the Zionists but it did not prevent them from taking an active part in the group discussions where, naturally, they did their best to publicise Zionist achievements in Palestine. This was particularly so in the groups handling the questions of "Agricultural Reconstruction" and "Industrial Development". The latter discussion was turned to such good propaganda effect that the report began by singling out, as prominent exceptions to the "low measure of industrialisation" in Asia "the Asian Republics (of the U.S.S.R.), Turkey, parts of Palestine and parts of the Middle East".[44] Even now Israel is only lightly industrialised and was still more so in 1947.

One minor oddity was Dr. Bonne's spirited advocacy of Esperanto as the new international language of peace and brotherhood.[45]

These gains for the Zionist delegation were offset by yet another political set-back when Mahatma Gandhi, who attended some of the sessions, addressed words of advice to the Arabs and the Jews. He appealed to the former to try and win over the Jews and he asked the Jews to abandon their terrorist movement because "he was quite sure they would get nowhere with violence".[46]

Zionist reactions to this Conference were necessarily an admixture of satisfaction and disappointment. *The Zionist Review* wrote that "the presence of Palestine Jewry brings home the fact that Eretz Israel is in Asia and that Jews have an important part to play in the regeneration of a Continent". But "Pandit Nehru's statement...is an indication that a great deal still remains to be done to bring home to Asiatic peoples the realities

[43] *Asian Relations*, p. 70.
[44] *Op. cit.*, p. 150, *et. seq.*
[45] *Op. cit.*, p. 204.
[46] Tendulkar, *Mahatma Gandhi*, Bombay, 1953, vol. 7, p. 431.

of Palestine—that the Holy Land is inseparable from the people of Israel".[47]

The door to Asia that the 1947 Conference seemed to open before the Zionists never opened any farther; if anything, it closed a little because India never again welcomed a Zionist delegation, and acceptance by the India of Gandhi and Nehru was something that the Zionists particularly desired.

The door to Asia for Israel remained ajar, but no more, and so in its relations with the continent this Conference, from the Zionist viewpoint, was inconsequential. Thereafter Zionist Israel remained firmly outside the mainstream of independent Asian countries.

Inter-continental aggression at the League of Nations and in the United Nations

After 1920 the fate of that part of Asia known as Palestine was decided not in Palestine by the Palestinians, nor in Asia by the Asians, but by the governments of Europe and of North and South America; at first at the League of Nations in Geneva and then in the United Nations at New York.

The act of aggression at the League was its acceptance in 1922 of the decisions to include the Balfour Declaration in the Palestine Mandate, and to assign that Mandate to Britain, originally taken by the San Remo Conference in 1920.

The act of aggression in the United Nations was the decision to partition Palestine adopted in November 1947.

It may be contended that the word "aggression" cannot be applied to these decisions because they were within the competence of such international organisations, and that in fact international organisations exist in order to take such decisions. This is an extremely debatable proposition in itself, but what is incontrovertible is that in these two instances the League and the U.N. took decisions that were unique in character and which have never been repeated. In the first case the League accepted a declaration of policy that was meant to change the demographic balance of a particular country leading eventually

[47]*Zionist Review*, London, 28.3.1947.

and inevitably to a change in sovereignty over it. In the second case the decision was to partition that country. In both cases the wishes of the majority of the people of the territory immediately concerned were set aside; in both cases the wishes of the majority of the governments in the area and in the continent concerned were ignored or set aside. At the League of Nations was begun, and in the United Nations was completed, the process of thrusting an alien political entity into Asia, against the wishes of Asia, by the governments of three other continents. "Inter-continental aggression" is not an unfair description of that process.

It is important to make the distinction, at least this once, that these decisions were taken *at* the League and *in* the U.N. and not *by* the League or the U.N. for, in effect, there was no such thing as *the* League and is no such thing as *the* U.N. In both bodies there were and are an international secretariat and a Secretary-General without decision-making powers. The decisions were and are taken by the member-governments, some of whom, in spite of equality of vote, carry more weight than others and tend to impose their will. This was emphatically so for Palestine in both the world organisations: it was Britain that got her way at the League and the United States in the U.N., and they did so by getting support from governments from every continent except the one directly affected. To blame an entire organisation for decisions taken by some of its members is inaccurate and unfair and is largely the result of vague phraseology. It is commonly acccepted usage to say that "the U.N. created Israel" or "the U.N. partitioned Palestine". Nothing could be farther from the truth; and the truth would be approximated to by the smallest possible verbal change, of one word: "Israel was created 'at' (or 'in') the United Nations", and not "by" it.

Britain had a far easier task in imposing her will on the League than the United States later had in the U.N. because the League was a far smaller and more manageable body. It was, almost completely, a white man's club. In this age of universality it comes as a shock to realise just how exclusive the so-called League of Nations was. During the 1947 U.N. debates, Zionist representatives harked back to the League decision on the Balfour

Declaration to say "the solemn pledge of 52 nations cannot be flouted".[48] That was a clever piece of propaganda because at the time when the League took its decision on the Mandate it had only 40 members. Its founding membership was 32 and of these only 6 were from Afro-Asia: India (as one of 5 British Empire representatives), China, Japan, Liberia and Siam; Hejaz was also included but fell by the wayside. Of the 10 other states invited to accede only one—Persia—was Asian. Therefore the Palestine decision in 1922 was taken when the League had only 6 Afro-Asian members. What chance, therefore, was there for the League agreeing to a request by the Palestine delegation in 1921 that the choice of a mandatory government should be decided by popular vote in Palestine?[49] The first Arab country to be admitted was Iraq, in 1932.

The League watch-dog over the mandatory powers, its Permanent Mandates Commission, had eleven members only one of whom, Japan, was from Afro-Asia.

Even when the League was at the end of its active life, in 1938, only eleven of its 58 members were Afro-Asian. Thus there was no possibility of a specifically Arab or Asian viewpoint on Palestine prevailing within a League of Nations so heavily weighted in favour of Europe and North and South America where opinion was favourable to Zionism.

Nor were things very much better, from the Afro-Asian viewpoint, in the United Nations during its early years after World War II. It was only after 1950 that the steady acceleration in the process of de-colonisation made the U.N. increasingly more representative of the world as a whole. At the Conference in San Francisco in 1945, at which the future structure of the U.N. was discussed, there were 12 delegations from Afro-Asia among a total of 50 countries. Two years later 57 countries voted on the partition resolution, 15 of them being Afro-Asian. The world organisation was still only a slightly less exclusive white man's club.

Such being the continental distribution of membership within

---

[48]D. Horowitz, *op. cit.*, p. 243.
[49]Esco, vol. I, p. 477.

the U.N. it was not surprising that there were only two Asian members—India and Iran—on the 11-member U.N. Special Commission on Palestine (UNSCOP) which was sent to look into the whole Palestine problem in June 1947. Its membership was actually supposed to be representative of the world: Sweden and the Netherlands represented western Europe; Czechoslovakia and Yugoslavia eastern Europe; the British Commonwealth had two representatives, Canada and Australia; and Latin America three, Peru, Uruguay and Guatemala. To give 18% representation to the continent directly involved was evidently considered fair—in 1947. That would hardly be the case now.

UNSCOP split along continental lines. When it submitted its findings, in August 1947, these consisted of a majority report favouring partition and a minority proposing an independent federal state. The majority of seven were the representatives from Europe and from North and South America; the minority of three were Yugoslavia from Europe and India and Iran from Asia. Australia abstained.

It has been pointed out[50] that the three Latin American votes, out of the seven for the majority report, represented more than 40% of the weight in favour of partition. Thus Latin America, 8,000 miles away from Palestine and divided from it by a sea and an ocean, a continent that had no connection with the Jewish problem, played a major part in the disposing of territory in Asia.

One of the most curious aspects of UNSCOP's findings was the twelfth and last of its general recommendations. A majority of seven had favoured the creation of a Jewish State which, since 1897, the Zionists had sought as a solution for the Jewish Problem. By a majority of nine, Uruguay and Guatemala excepted, UNSCOP destroyed this most fundamental tenet in the whole range of Zionist ideology. Recommendation XII said: "In the appraisal of the Palestine question it should be accepted as incontrovertible that any solution for Palestine cannot be considered as a solution for the Jewish problem in general." With

[50]E.B. Glick, *Latin America and the Palestine Problem*, New York, Herzl Foundation, 1958, p. 70.

these words the UNSCOP majority took the basic document of
the Zionist movement, Herzl's booklet, and separated its title,
"The Jewish State", from its sub-title "An Attempt at a Modern
Solution of the Jewish Question". Fifty years after Herzl the
UNSCOP members knew better. Hence the five members of
the majority who voted for Recommendation XII also voted
for a Jewish state while at the same time denying its Zionist
raison d'être. There could be few more perfect examples of
political illogicality.

India was represented on UNSCOP by a distinguished jurist,
Sir Abdur Rahman. Zionist feelings towards him are clear from
this description of him by Horowitz, the Jewish Agency liaison
officer with UNSCOP. "The Indian was corpulent and heavy;
with coarse pronounced features. He was openly and virulently
pro-Arab. His manner was forthright and tactless and he had
a narrowly juridical approach to problems."[51]

Asia's rejection of the Jewish State was made even more
clear and emphatic when the UNSCOP reports were debated at
the U.N. As Horowitz puts it: "The Asiatic bloc was solidly and
unitedly negative. The fact of our complete isolation on this
continent, into whose life we aspired to become integrated,
pained me especially, and I anxiously followed the attempts
to overcome the perverse situation."[52]

The "perverse situation" was this: in the General Assembly,
meeting as an Ad Hoc Committee on Palestine, a resolution
which sought to refer to the International Court of Justice
the whole question of whether the U.N. had any competence to enforce partition without consulting, or against the
wishes of, the inhabitants of Palestine was lost by only one vote.

That was "perverse" enough. Still more "perverse" was the
vote in the Committee on the partition plan. This produced
only a simple majority—25 for, 13 against and 17 abstentions—
but a two thirds majority was necessary in the General Assembly
for a question of this level of importance.

In this Committee vote not one Asian or African country

---

[51]G. Horowitz, *op. cit.*, p. 165.
[52]*Op. cit.*, p. 258.

voted for the creation of a Jewish State. With the exception of Cuba all the negative votes were Afro-Asian. Among the 17 abstainers were China, Ethiopia and Liberia.

Even at the Committee stage the pressure on the Afro-Asian countries by pro-Zionist governments, especially the United States, was already intense. The Philippines, for instance, did not vote in the Committee because its delegate, General Carlos Romulo, deliberately absented himself from its meetings for three or four days "so that no one should be able to get hold of him",[53] to compel him to vote in a way in which he did not approve; but he promised to be present for the vote in the Assembly. The Thai delegate was also in an embarrassing situation because a coup d'état had occurred in his country and he did not know whether the new government accepted him as its representative; so he, too, ceased attending the Committee meetings for some days, but was later persuaded to attend and voted against partition.

After the Committee vote, which spelled defeat for partition, and before the vote in the Assembly, six countries became the target for Zionist and United States pressure or, as it is called in U.N. circles, "arm-twisting". These were: Haiti, Liberia, the Philippines, China, Ethiopia, and Greece. The arm-twisting worked, for only Greece remained firm in opposition, moving, in fact, from abstention in Committee to a negative vote in the Assembly. China and Ethiopia continued to abstain, while Liberia moved from abstention to an affirmative vote and the Philippines, from what would have been a negative vote, to the affirmative.

Thailand did not vote because a telegram arrived in time to withdraw the credentials of her representative. Sir Mohammed Zafrullah Khan, who represented Pakistan, wrote of the incident: "whether that telegram came from the government of Thailand or from some other source we do not know."[54] These words reflect the general belief that extremely dubious means

[53]Sir Mohammed Zafrullah Khan, *Palestine in the UNO*, Karachi, 1948, p. 19.
[54]*Op. cit.*, pp. 9, 19.

were used to pressure delegations to vote against their better judgement and against their consciences.

The main source of pressure was the United States; without it the General Assembly would not have approved of the Jewish State by the required majority. This is attested to by the words of Horowitz, who as a senior Zionist diplomat took part in these activities. "America's line of action had swung in a new direction. As a result of instructions from the President (Truman), the State Department now embarked on a helpful course of great importance to our interest. The improved atmosphere swayed a number of wavering countries. The United States exerted the weight of its influence almost at the last hour, *and the way the final vote turned out must be ascribed to this fact*. Its intervention sidetracked the manipulation of the fringe votes against us."[55] (Italics mine.)

Just how great was the pro-Zionist "manipulation" is indicated by comparing the speech and the vote of the Philippine delegation. General Romulo was as good as his word; he did finally appear in the Assembly and made a strong speech against partition. He described it as a move towards "political disunion and territorial dismemberment" which would "turn us back on the road to the dangerous principles of racial exclusiveness and to the archaic doctrines of theocratic governments" and away from "the modern trend towards inter-racial co-operation and secular democracy". In conclusion he condemned "the territorial mutilation of the Holy Land".[56] Having made this speech General Romulo, who had to leave New York, left written instructions with his alternate delegate to vote against partition. Three days later the Philippine delegation voted for partition.

The delegation of Haiti underwent the same mysterious process of transformation; a clearly negative speech followed by an affirmative vote.

It was through such dubious "manipulations" that a favourable vote for the Jewish State was obtained in the United Nations.

[55]Horowitz, *op. cit.*, p. 301.
[56]U.N. Records, 124th Plenary Session of the General Assembly, 26.11.1947.

In that final vote only Liberia and the Philippines among Afro-Asian countries voted affirmatively; China and Ethiopia abstained; and of the 13 negative votes, 11 were Afro-Asian, the other two coming from Cuba and Greece.

No further evidence is required to prove that the Jewish State was thrust into Asia, against the wishes of Afro-Asia, by other continents—Europe, and North and South America. A clear case of inter-continental aggression.

On this issue Europe, east and west, communist and anti-communist, was united. In order to get the British out of a particularly sensitive area of the Middle East, Russia and her junior partners switched from their established, doctrinal hostility to Zionism to a policy favouring partition and the creation of a Jewish State. No sooner was the state created than they switched back to opposition.

From the Afro-Asian viewpoint the real villains of the piece at the United Nations were not the Europeans or the North Americans but the Latin Americans. The European and North American vote can be explained, though not excused, as an expiation of their anti-Semitic guilt. But that explanation does not apply to South America. A Zionist author has ascribed South American pro-Zionism to a belief in humanitarianism, Catholicism, the self-determination of peoples, the sovereign and juridical equality of states, and universality of U.N. membership.[57] If this explanation is true the Latin Americans can be accused of the most insufferable hypocrisy. Perhaps the most charitable explanation is to say that with their Hispanic background they are more susceptible than most to quixotry. Yet, quixotic or not, their vote was decisive: a Zionist publication was quite correct when it described their support as "the spinal column of the pro-Zionist bloc in the United Nations".[58]

It should be made clear that not all the Latin American states were pro-Zionist. Cuba voted against and Argentina, Chile, Colombia, El Salvador, Honduras and Mexico abstained.

The Colombian delegate was one who clearly saw the vote as

[57]Glick, *op. cit.*, Introduction.
[58]Quoted in Glick, *op. cit.*, p. 16.

inter-continental aggression: "No wonder", he said, "that the plan has had to come across the Atlantic in search of the supporters it has failed to find in the countries adjoining Palestine in the eastern Mediterranean, in western Europe, or in the distant Asiatic mainland."[59]

Not only the Latin Americans but almost all the pro-Zionist delegations at the U.N. in 1947 can be brought under the charge of hypocrisy. During the debates on the future of Palestine a resolution was put forward which asked all states to admit Jewish refugees on a quota system. It was defeated by a vote of 15 affirmative, 18 negative and 22 abstentions. The geographical distribution on this humanitarian vote was almost the exact opposite of the political vote on partition. Those countries that voted for partition abstained on accepting Jewish refugees; and those delegations that voted against the Jewish State voted for accepting Jewish refugees. It was only the latest expression of an apparent correlation: anti-Semites are often pro-Zionist, anti-Zionists are often pro-Semites. The Zionists had no complaints about this outcome: "It (the resolution) was denounced as gambling with the bitter lot of the refugees" wrote Horowitz.[60]

In taking up such a negative stand on the question of Jewish refugees the pro-Zionists and the Zionists were repeating in 1947 attitudes that they had adopted nearly 10 years earlier. In July 1938 a conference of 31 nations, none from Afro-Asia, met to discuss the problem of Jewish refugees. Of all these only the tiny Dominican Republic offered to accept 100,000 Jews. The U.S. agreed to accept Jews to the limit of its normal immigration quota for Germans of 30,000 a year; Britain made a promise of a similar amount and Australia agreed to 15,000 immigrants. That was all. Yet it was those very countries which refused to accept any Jews in 1938, and voted against receiving them in 1947, that were most enthusiastic about creating a Jewish State in West Asia.

Two types of people were satisfied with this outcome in 1938,

---

[59]U.N. Records, 127th Plenary Session of the General Assembly, 28.11.1947.
[60]Horowitz, op. cit., p. 301.

the Nazis and the Zionists;[61] the former because it revealed the hypocrisy of the democracies; the latter because "if the thirty one nations had done their duty and shown hospitality to those in dire need then the pressure on the National Home and the heightened enthusiasm of Zionism within Palestine, would both have been relaxed. Even in the more terrible days ahead they made no secret of the fact, even when talking to Gentiles, that they did not want Jewish settlements outside Palestine to be success-ful."[62] As a result of this Zionist indifference to non-Zionist refugees in 1938 tens of thousands, perhaps hundreds of thou-sands, of Jews who could have been saved were not saved.

The manipulated votes at the U.N. in 1947 which brought Israel into existence were based as much on Zionist ruthlessnesss as on pro-Zionist hypocrisy. Small wonder that the Arabs and the pro-Arab Afro-Asians were not able to prevent the success of inter-continental aggression committed against them. It is a point for reflection that today—when the U.N. more genuinely represents the whole world—a vote similar to that creating Israel would be utterly out of the question.

The reluctant acceptance

The Afro-Asians were not able to prevent the Zionists pushing their way, and being pushed by others, into their living room but they could and did refrain from asking the Zionists to sit down and make themselves at home. This is revealed in the reluctance with which Asian states established diplomatic re-lations with Israel.

No Asian state recognised Israel in 1948, the year of its birth. Four did so in 1949: Ceylon, Formosa, the Philippines and Burma. India and Thailand followed in 1950, Japan in 1952 and Nepal in 1960.

Diplomatic relations were developed even more slowly, and by both sides; though naturally Israel was far quicker off the mark than the Asians. She established consulates in the Philippines in 1950 and in India in 1951. A legation in Japan followed in

[61]Sykes, *Crossroads*, pp. 223-228.
[62]Sykes, *op. cit.*, p. 228.

1952, in Burma in 1953 and in Thailand in 1954. The first Israeli embassies in Asia were established in Burma in 1957 and in Thailand in 1958—ten years after the founding of the State.

Not till 1955 did any Asian countries send diplomatic missions to Israel: these were the Burmese and Japanese legations. And at the present time these two missions, now raised to embassy level, and a third embassy, that of the Philippines, are the sum total of Asian diplomatic representation in the Jewish State.

Asia has thus continued to give the diplomatic cold shoulder to a state that from the earliest days was recognised as being a foreign body.

CHAPTER V

CHINA AND INDIA TURN THEIR BACKS

Israel has had to pay a price for the direct and massive assistance that the United States has given her inside the United Nations and, even more, outside it. That price was a total denial of relations with the biggest Asian country—Communist China, that has now developed into a Chinese policy of virulent hostility towards Israel.

Because of the consistent hostility towards Zionism evinced by the Indian national movement there was little chance of normal relations developing between Israel and the second largest Asian country. But things might have been different with Communist China: it was a firm American veto that put an end to any such possibility.

Israel recognised the Peking regime in January 1950, that is, only a few months after the declaration of the People's Republic in October 1949. This was during the period when non-identification with either side in the Cold War was still the official policy of the Israel government. However, when the Korean War broke out in the summer of 1950 Israel gave full support to American actions in and through the United Nations which were, in the main, directed against China. This, naturally, ruled out the possibility of any relations developing between China and Israel.

For instance, Israel voted for resolutions authorising United Nations troops to cross the 38th Parallel, to brand China as an aggressor and to place an embargo on shipments of war materials to China and North Korea. Nevertheless one notes the curious fact that in a belated message of congratulation for Israel's Independence Day in 1952 the Chinese government wished

Israel "victory in the struggle for national independence, democracy and liberty",[1] which was a first indication that Communist China, unlike India, had not adopted an anti-Zionist line of thought and was open-minded about the State of Israel.

In December 1953, only a few months after the end of the Korean War, the first direct contact was made between Communist China and Israel and, most surprisingly, the initiative came not from Israel but from China. This move was made in Rangoon when the newly-arrived Israeli Minister, Mr. David Hacohen, paid his first formal call on the Chinese Ambassador. According to Mr. Hacohen's account[2] it was his Chinese colleague who first asked whether Israel would be interested in closer ties with Peking. A month later the Chinese Ambassador made a formal statement that China "wishes to form trade ties with the State of Israel. The intention is to seek imports from Israel," especially chemical fertilisers. It immediately occurred to Ambassador Hacohen that Israel could not ignore the embargoes on trade with China imposed by the United States and the United Nations; he told the Russian Ambassador that Israel "would not agree to circumvent them".

Despite these misgivings the Israelis suggested sending a trade delegation to China and, in June 1954, Chou En-lai himself, during a visit to Rangoon, confirmed China's acceptance of this suggestion. The Chinese later let it be known that the Israeli delegation's visit would be paid for by China and that it could stay as long as it pleased.

The visit actually took place in February 1955 and lasted for three weeks, at the end of which a general declaration was issued in which both sides expressed their willingness to have

---

[1] New China News Agency, 28.5.1952.

[2] D. Hacohen, *Burma Diary*, Tel Aviv, 1962. This present account is based on translated excerpts published in the magazine *New Outlook*, Tel Aviv, vol. 6, no. 9, 1963, pp. 29-44. Since the Chinese have not published anything on this strange diplomatic episode the question arises whether one can accept the Hacohen account as being veracious. I think one can, because Hacohen himself is a forthright personality and also because, in 1953, Israel would not have been likely to take the first step towards China, so far removed was she from the Asian scene.

trade relations.

In addition to commercial links the Israelis were equally, if not more, interested in developing diplomatic relations with China. They were encouraged in the belief by a statement made by Chou En-lai at the end of 1954 in the People's Congress that steps would be taken towards the exchange of diplomatic representatives by China with Afghanistan and Israel.

Two events put an end to any such possibility. The first was Israel's vote, in the United Nations General Assembly of 1954, abstaining on the acceptance of the Peking regime as the representative of China. (In 1950 and 1951 Israel voted affirmatively.) This was not a conclusive rejection, for even after it China expressed the hope for relations with Israel. What was conclusive was the refusal of the Israeli government to act quickly on repeated suggestions by Ambassador Hacohen to send an ambassador to Peking.

He is convinced that both these developments—the United Nations vote and the lack of action—were due to American pressure on the Israeli government.[3] In Rangoon itself Hacohen felt this pressure when, soon after his return from Peking with the trade delegation, he evaded meeting the American Secretary of State, Foster Dulles, then visiting Rangoon; officials in Dulles' entourage met him and advised him that it "was not worthwhile" for Israel to establish ties with a regime that was "about to fall"; a view with which Hacohen did not agree. Hacohen has said that what made Israel particularly vulnerable to American pressure was the fact that Israel's Ambassador in Washington was also her representative at the United Nations: he could not say or do anything in New York that would prejudice his mission in Washington.

In any case, nothing was done about establishing relations before the Bandung Conference in April 1955, and after that it was too late. At Bandung Chou En-lai subscribed to an anti-Israeli resolution though Hacohen was told that the Chinese leader "would have preferred not to say anything on this issue", "he did not mention Israel" and as a non-member of the United

---

[3]In conversation with this writer in Jerusalem in November 1965.

Nations was not bound by the United Nations resolution calling for the return of the Palestinian refugees: "relations between China and Israel had not been harmed in any way", Hacohen was assured.

But they had in fact been harmed, irreparably, by another development at Bandung: the first contacts made by Chou En-lai with a whole group of Arab leaders including the then Colonel Nasser. China suddenly realised that the Arabs were numerous, that they could be a force, and that they wanted friendly relations with China. Above all there was the realisation by China that the new Arab regimes were nationalist and wanted to break the hold of western imperialism on the Middle East.

Israel, closely tied to America, could offer no such promising possibility and so China decided to come down on the Arab side in the Arab-Israeli dispute.

After Bandung more than a year passed before the Arab governments, led by Egypt, opened diplomatic relations with China, for they, too, were under American pressure. According to one theory it was this move by Egypt that led Dulles to cancel the American offer of assistance in building the High Dam which eventually led to the Israeli-Anglo-French attack on Suez in 1956. China came out in total support of Egypt at that time and in the next few years political and commercial ties between the Arab states and China developed apace. Arab-Chinese friendship, or at least co-operation, was given definite, formal shape when Chou En-lai visited five Arab countries at the end of 1963 and early in 1964.

Since then China has adopted an openly anti-Israeli policy by giving some financial and military aid to the Palestine Liberation Organisation, which has talked of the destruction of the political structure of the State of Israel.

After 1956, when Chinese-Arab rapprochement became an accomplished fact, Israel continued with her vote of abstention on Communist China's representation in the United Nations. Only once, in 1961, did Israel vote in the affirmative but this was a transparent diplomatic device, because just prior to this vote she had supported the American proposal that the change in China's representation required a two-thirds majority; and when she voted affirmatively Israel was quite sure that there would not be such a majority. However in 1965, when the voting on this question became close, Israel switched from abstention to a negative vote, against Communist China. The new Israeli argument is that she now favours representation both of mainland China and of Formosa: "our principle that the United Nations should reflect existing reality applies both to China and Formosa. The fact is that there is a certain regime in the mainland. But it is also a fact that there is a certain regime on the island of Formosa",[4] to quote the Israeli Foreign Minister.

In voting against Communist China in the United Nations Israel has departed from the line taken by most of the Afro-Asian countries. But in doing so she has consulted her own national interests: she has continued to please the United States and she has not displeased Formosa, which, as a permanent member of the Security Council, has adopted a fairly neutral policy as between the Arabs and Israel.

Some regrets have been expressed in Israel (apart from the leftist parties) that the relations between her and Communist China are exclusively those of mutual hostility. In 1963 Ben Gurion said that "in a decade China will probably be among the most important countries in the world" and in 1965 he said that "the road to peace in the Middle East lay through Peking".[5] But if one is to judge by Peking's words and its ferocious attacks on Israel's neo-colonialism, especially after June 1967, the kind of peace sought by the Israelis will never obtain Chinese support.

The regret Israelis feel at China's rejection of the Jewish State turns to bitter disappointment and even angry denunciation when they talk of India's rejection of their state in the years since 1948.

For an Indian it is Israel's disappointment that is difficult to understand. Anyone familiar with the frequently expressed views of Gandhi and Nehru on Zionism would assume that an independent India guided by these men was bound to be un-

[4]A.S. Eban, *Israel in the World*, London, 1966, p. 22.
[5]Press reports, 9.6.1963 and 29.6.1965.

friendly towards a state created by Zionism.

Indeed the partition of India, totally opposed by the national movement, which was taking place in 1947 and 1948, at the same time that Israel was being created by another partitioning, added one more argument to Indian opposition to Israel.

Perhaps Israel's disappointment sprang from her own great desire to win acceptance by India. The approval of the India of Gandhi and Nehru would have given Israel a certain moral standing; it would also, in more practical terms, have given her full and respected membership of the Asian family with the international acceptance and diplomatic support that this would bring her. The invitation to the Asian Relations Conference in 1947, doubtless, also raised false hopes. And the private opinions of unrepresentative Indian diplomatic representatives at the United Nations in 1947 probably did likewise; Horowitz records[6] that the Indian delegation, and its leader Mrs. Pandit, were disgusted when they were asked to vote against the partition plan.

The policy of the Indian Government towards Israel from 1948 to the present has been entirely consistent with the views expressed by Gandhi and Nehru in the preceding decades. They did not approve of the basic idea of a Jewish State and hoped it would not come into existence. Since it has come into existence India has, realistically, recognised that fact; but she has not given approval and, moreover, has expressed her stringent disapproval of Israel's aggressive and expansionist policy towards her Arab neighbours, with whom, on the other hand, India's ties have become increasingly friendly.

Having voted against partition India also voted against Israel's admission to the United Nations because the state was created "through force of arms and not through negotiation".

India hesitated a great deal before recognising Israel in September, 1950 and when she did it was announced that this did not mean that she considered the frontiers Israel had at that time as being finally determined. A certain number of unnecessarily apologetic reasons for this action were given in

[6]Horowitz, *op. cit.*, p. 258.

the communiqué, especially the claim that non-recognition "would limit the Government of India's role as a possible intermediary between Israel and other states". These words showed that India entertained the hope, completely baseless, of being a possible peacemaker between Israel and the Arabs. Announcements made simultaneously that this act of recognition in no way affected India's friendship with the Arabs, or her policy on the Palestine question, destroyed any possibility of Indian peacemaking.

India was so nervous about hostile Arab reaction that it was not clearly stated whether the recognition was *de facto* or *de jure* or both, and confusion on this point continues to the present day. Since nothing was specified, Indian recognition was, in fact, both *de jure* and *de facto*.

Whatever hopes India may have entertained on her role in the Middle East, the more realistic reason for her recognising Israel was concerned with the Far East. India at that time was trying to propagate the idea that China would be less belligerent if she was accepted by the world and that this could easily be done by every country recognising her, because diplomatic recognition should not be interpreted as evidence of moral approval but merely as acceptance of fact. It would have seemed illogical for India to talk this way about China while conspicuously refraining from accepting the fact of Israel's existence. So she accepted it but gave no approval.

The withholding of approval was indicated by India's refusal to have diplomatic relations with Israel despite persistent Israeli efforts, supported by equally persistent pressure from the United States. A year after recognition Israel was permitted to open a consulate in Bombay but attempts since then to move this office to the capital, New Delhi, and to raise it to a consulate-general have failed because of Indian government opposition.

India's refusal to move any nearer to the Jewish state has been sharply criticised by Israelis and by pro-Zionist Americans. It has been denounced as an act of cowardice, of hypocrisy and of cynicism, as a betrayal of non-alignment and of India's proferred claim to consider issues on their merits. But in adopting an aloof attitude to Israel that is precisely what India has done:

she has considered the issue on its merits and has concluded that in principle, and for India's national interests, it is better to have as little as possible to do with Israel.

It is this consideration of principles and interests that Israel demands for herself but denies to India. No one thinks it cynical for Israel to give more importance to the United States than to the Asian colossus, China, but it somehow becomes cynicism when India rates 13 Arab countries as more important than the small single country of Israel, which has great propaganda and equally great nuisance value, but not much else.

There are, from the Indian viewpoint, many very solid reasons why she should prefer relations with the Arab states over those with Israel, and they have been listed, quite comprehensively, by Zionist and Israeli writers.[7]

These are: competition with Muslim Pakistan for the support, or at least neutrality, of the Muslim Arab countries, especially on the Kashmir dispute—taking into account the fact that the Kashmir issue is on the United Nations agenda and the Arab bloc numbers 13 votes; India's vital sea and air communications with the West run across the Arab lands—the Suez Canal being especially important for India; India's supplies of oil come, mainly, from Arab countries in the Persian Gulf area; there are sizable communities of Indian traders, most of them prosperous, scattered across the Arab world; in terms of domestic politics no representative Indian government can afford to ignore the strongly pro-Arab sentiments of India's 80 million Muslims; several Arab countries, such as the U.A.R., Syria, Iraq and Algeria are firm supporters of the policy of non-alignment with which India is identified; finally, and perhaps most important of all, are the increasing trade and commercial relations between India and the Arab area: the Arab countries are a large market of 100 million people for India's developing industries while India buys from the Arabs large quantities of cotton, wheat,

---

[7] R.V. Kozicki, "India and Israel, a Problem in Asian Politics", *Middle Eastern Affairs*, New York, May 1958; and M. Medzini, *The State of Israel and the Asian Nations, 1948-1949*, unpublished thesis of Georgetown University, Washington, D.C., June 1960, pp. 52-54.

rice, dates and phosphates: the only commodities India could buy from Israel are some fertilisers, industrial diamonds and false teeth, hardly a foundation for extensive trade relations. The trade figures speak for themselves: in 1964 India exported goods worth Rupees 500 million to the Arab countries and Rupees 800 thousand to Israel, while imports were valued at Rupees 840 million from the Arab world and at Rupees 4 million from Israel.

The government of India knows the value of the Arab world to itself and frames India's West Asia policy accordingly. The Arabs expect far more from an Asian country like India than, for instance, from even a friendly European country like Yugoslavia, which is a good customer of Israel and they would be deeply offended if India were to make any friendly move towards Israel; and it is not in India's interest to offend the Arabs.

But even if there were not an either-or choice to be made between the Arabs and Israel it is entirely possible that India would still not have diplomatic relations with the Jewish State, because there are several countries, larger and more important to India than Israel, with whom, for reasons of economy, India has not exchanged diplomats. Israel assumes that she has a special role and a special importance in the world; but that is an assumption which not every other government shares—especially in Asia.

According to an Israeli account[8] Israel on one occasion did come as near to establishing full diplomatic relations with India as she once did with China. Early in 1952 the then Director-General of the Israeli Foreign Ministry, Eytan, visited New Delhi and after talks with Nehru and others it was agreed that India should have a diplomatic mission in Israel, but, so it is claimed, Nehru's decision was not ratified by the Indian Cabinet, which sounds inherently improbable because at that time there was no issue on which Nehru as Prime Minister could not have got the Indian Cabinet to agree with him, provided he thought the issue was important enough for him to assert his authority. If there was a change of decision it emanated from Nehru and not the

[8]W. Eytan, *The First Ten Years*, New York, 1958, pp. 181 *et seq.*

Cabinet.

Since 1952 official relations between India and Israel have been virtually nil. A few students have been exchanged and an Indian mission studied the trade union and kibbutz movement in Israel, and its conclusion was that the kibbutz was not suitable for India: "Israel's experience is partly irrelevant and partly misleading."

One Israeli Cabinet Minister, for Labour, has been to India, but no Indian Minister has been to Israel.

Indian regulations, in fact, make it difficult for private Indian citizens to visit Israel and the Government has often stopped delegations of various sorts from going to Israel: the Israeli consulate in Bombay is very active in its propaganda work and is generous with its invitations. To a large extent the Indian government tries to undo the work of the consulate, and vice versa; only politeness, or inertia, explains the continuing presence of this office in Bombay.

The Indian government has also been turning down offers of assistance from the Israeli government: in 1964 it was an offer to establish a model agricultural settlement; in 1965 to teach "improved" farming techniques; and in 1966 to supply fertilisers.

Not unnaturally the Israeli press and government viewed India's election to the Security Council in November 1966 with mixed feelings and India in the Council has been as condemnatory of Israeli actions in 1967 as she was during the Suez aggression in 1956.

Yet the Government of India's approach to Israel has never been as bitterly hostile as that of the Chinese government. In 1958, and again after the 1967 hostilities, India has told the Arab states that they should accept the geographic and historical existence of Israel, without necessarily granting her diplomatic recognition. And this advice is not very welcome to the Arabs.

One development that has caused disappointed surprise and criticism of Israel in India has been the frequent complaints of ill-treatment made by Indian Jews who emigrated to Israel.

In 1951 there were about 20,000 Jews in India and of these

perhaps 8,000 left for Israel.[9] Their motive for leaving was partly religious and partly economic.

Even before the establishment of the Israeli consulate in Bombay the Zionist organisation sent officials to India who succeeded in persuading members of the Jewish communities in Bombay, where they are called Bene Israel, and in Cochin, to go to Israel. The leading expert on Indian Jewry notes that: "many Bene Israel hoped that migration to Israel—which in the absence of aggressive measures against Jews in India might be interpreted as an expression of Jewish solidarity and love of the Holy Land—would result in complete acceptance by other Jews. But migration has so far failed in its goal."[10] Another, more materialistic explanation, is that Zionist propaganda presented Israel as providing a richer, easier life for Jews than India's harsh environment could do.[11]

Most of the Indian immigrants have found some place for themselves in Israeli society but there were quite a few who, in the early 1950's, raised loud complaints of poor housing, poor food and unsuitable work in the more backward areas of Israel. What is more they claimed that these hardships were imposed on them as a result of colour consciousness by "the white skinned snobs", or European Jews. Using the familiar Indian tactic of passive resistance they went on hunger strikes in front of the Zionist Agency office in Jerusalem, demanding repatriation to India. They also aired their grievances in the Indian press just at the time when Israel was trying hard to obtain diplomatic relations with India. So embarrassing did these complaints prove that the Israeli government finally agreed to send several hundred immigrants back to India.

But the complaining continued, and when in 1960 this writer met with Indian Jews in Beersheeba some still grumbled about being given "jail work" and spoke of wanting to return to India.

In 1962, religious discrimination was added to the grievances of the Bene Israel when the Chief Rabbi of the Sephardic sect

[9]S. Strizower, *Exotic Jewish Communities*, London, 1962, pp. 48 *et seq.*
[10]S. Strizower, "The 'Bene Israel' in Israel", *Middle Eastern Studies*, London, vol. 2, no. 2, January 1966, pp. 123-143.
[11]Quoted in Strizower, *The Bene Israel*, p. 132.

promulgated a special directive that, because of doubts as to their Jewish authenticity, investigations "as far back as possible" should be made into the ancestry of Bene Israel contemplating marriage with other communities of Jews. The stipulation about the investigation going "as far back as possible" was limited only to the Bene Israel and was, therefore, discriminatory.[12] Once again there were sitdown and hunger strikes in Jerusalem and once again criticism of Israel appeared in the Indian press. Under considerable pressure the Chief Rabbi amended his directive to the satisfaction of the Bene Israel, but not before they had been reminded once more that they were not fully accepted in Israel.

It is noteworthy that one of the reasons given for the inability of Indian Jews to adapt to Israel is that: "Persecution is only known to them from hearsay; they have never experienced it. They have lived for many centuries on excellent terms with Hindus, Mohammedans and Christians".[13] In short, pure Zionist enthusiasm is not enough to make one feel at home in Israel; an essential ingredient is an experience of anti-Semitic persecution.

Israel is now more aware than previously of the importance of China and India in Asia and in the world. Looking into the future Ben Gurion has prophesied: "As Europe sinks, so Asia ascends. In (Asia) dwell the two most numerous races in the world—the races of China and India, between them making up almost one half of the entire human kind, and great not only numerically but also in ancient and original cultures".[14] But China and India have turned their backs on the Jewish State.

Therefore without acceptance by the two largest Asian countries, whether separately or jointly, Israel will never be able to feel herself a real part of the continent of Asia in which she is situated. Facing a joint rejection by China and India all that Israel could do to break out of her encapsulation in West Asia was to establish uncertain and changeable relations with countries around the Asian periphery.

[12]*Op. cit.*, note 20 on p. 143.
[13]*Op. cit.*, p. 132.
[14]Ben Gurion, *Rebirth and Destiny of Israel*, London, 1959, p. 454.

CHAPTER VI

THE ALIEN ALMOST AT HOME

The partial breakthrough

When, after achieving the State of Israel, its leaders looked east towards the continent in which they had placed themselves, they knew they faced a formidable task to get themselves accepted; but they also knew that they had to make the attempt or else accept the position of an unwanted foreign body—which they were not prepared to do. They realised now that Asia was becoming a potentially important force in world affairs. However slight the natural empathy between Zionism and Asian nationalism might be, Israel did not want to have an Asian bloc ranged against her in the future. But Israel wanted a formula which would allow her to keep her European complexion and her close links with the major Western powers as well as to obtain acceptance by Asia. She was not interested in making any attempt to adopt Asian nationalist attitudes towards the West, or towards racialism or anti-colonial struggles throughout the world. Least of all did she intend to make compromises on her attitude to Palestinian Arab rights, although this more than anything else could make her acceptable to the rest of Asia. In consequence, no ready acceptance of Israel by Asian nationalist governments was forthcoming.

Ben Gurion, Israel's first Prime Minister, and a student of Oriental thought, was particularly aware of the importance of, and the difficulties facing, Israel's Asia policy. "Less than all others", he wrote, "may we of Israel shut our eyes to the rise of Asia and its peoples", but, he went on, "we must not, we have no right, to renounce our European heritage."[1] Israel has never been able to escape from this basic sense of being European.

On the morrow of the Suez aggression, when all Asia was still condemning Israel, a somewhat chastened Ben Gurion remarked: "we must realise that the peoples of the Far East know nothing of the Bible and of Israel. They have just obtained their liberty and freed themselves from Europe, and every white man is already suspect in their eyes."[2] A few months later Mrs. Golda Meir, for long periods Israel's Foreign Minister, commented: "Israel considers herself an integral part of the Asian continent. There is no room for the Afro-Asians to be against us; perhaps our only sin is that we have white skins."[3]

Over and over again one finds the Israelis making the same facile excuses for Asian rejection—colour prejudice and lack of an Old Testament background.

The point needs to be made that Asians feel no colour prejudice against at least one indubitably European country, Yugoslavia, because she follows what Asians believe to be the right policy of supporting Asian nationalism while Israel, as we shall see, opposes it.

Israeli apologists seem to find nothing strange in such statements as: "Israel has succeeded on the whole in persuading the Bible-reared Europeans of the Jewish right to national self-determination in the Holy Land";[4] or "The very name 'Israel' is part of the Christian heritage... When the Jewish state was established and called Israel, it did not have to explain itself—except in Asia."[5] Israelis do not seem to find it curious, or derogatory, to claim that Europe accepts Israel not on her merits but because Israel's religion has been incorporated into Europe's religion.

Contemporary political motivations are also found by some Zionists for Asia's lack of understanding of Israel—all of them

[1]Ben Gurion, *Rebirth and Destiny of Israel*, p. 456.
[2]*Jerusalem Post*, 5.12.1956.
[3]*Ibid.*, 3.3.1957.
[4]*Ibid.*, "Israel Would Be Asia's Window to the West", article by I. Ben Zvi. 25.3.1956.
[5]Eytan, *op. cit.*, p. 181.

incidentally, the outcome of Asian inadequacy. These are listed[6] as: experience of colonial domination; a sense of economic and technical insufficiency and inferiority; general insecurity and a suspicion of all big powers; solidarity with other Asian countries; and a special devotion to the U.N. That Israel somehow is associated with big power colonialism and is opposed to the U.N. is itself a damaging implication; yet there are a few pro-Zionists who will say that Asian opposition is due to the fact that Asians see her as a creation of Western imperialism and that Israel's interests lead her to support European powers against Asian demands for self-determination.[7]

But, in general, Israeli thinking is that Asian unwillingness to accept Israel is due to Asia's mental or emotional shortcomings—and so much the worse for Asia.

To define their place in Asia is a definite problem for the Israelis. There are not many Israelis who would subscribe to this forthright definition: "Are we Europeans coming to Asia or are we Asiatics returning from a long sojourn in Europe? The answer is simply that we are neither. We are Israelis—a people with Asian ancestry, with a largely European upbringing, with historical ties with Jews living in the United States, South America and the Soviet Union."[8]

Ben Gurion himself would not accept that definition. For him "the State of Israel is a part of the Middle East only in geography, which is, in the main, a static element. From the decisive aspects of dynamics, creation and growth, Israel is a part of world Jewry."[9] And this, rather more official, definition recalls the image of the hydroponically-reared plant, its roots floating in a chemical solution, not embedded in the earth: if Israel is only geographically in the Middle East then she is in Asia only geographically.

Nevertheless because of Asia's importance Israel has tried to

---

[6]E. Ben Horin, "A Basic Outline of Israel's Position in Asia", *Hamizrah Hehadash, The New East, Quarterly of the Israel Oriental Society*, vol. VII, no. 4, 1957.

[7]These latter points are made by I. Ben Zvi and E. Ben Horin.

[8]*Jerusalem Post*, editorial, 20.4.1958.

[9]Ben Gurion, *op. cit.*, p. 489.

make friends with some Asian countries, and has achieved a variable degree of success.

It has been observed that Asia's acceptance of the Jewish State was slow and reluctant. In 1952, four years after Israel's establishment, it had 42 diplomatic or consular missions in Europe, the Americas and Australasia, but only two in Africa and just two in South and South East Asia—consulates in Manila and in Bombay.

It may or may not be a coincidence but Israel has made her quickest and easiest penetration in countries that are military allies of the West, and, specifically, with the United States. This was the case with the two Muslim countries of West Asia, with whom Israel established relations four years before she achieved anything in South or South East Asia.

Both Turkey and Iran had voted against the partition plan but both recognised Israel as an accomplished fact. This was at a time when both these countries, Turkey more than Iran, were totally dependent on America. Despite energetic Israeli attempts to develop every sort of link with Turkey, especially commercial ties, the Turks were never much at ease with the Jewish State. In the years immediately after 1948 Turkey was mentioned as the prime example of Israel's ability to get along harmoniously with an Asian country. The Suez aggression gave the Turks the opportunity for the withdrawal that they had been waiting for; they had only maintained a legation in Israel and in 1956 they withdrew their Minister; and since then Turkey has been represented by a fairly junior *chargé d'affaires*.

The Asian country with which Israel has the most important relations is Iran—relations that are shrouded in mystery and secrecy. When I sought detailed information on the exchanges between the two countries Israeli officials in Jerusalem told me that I would be sparing them embarrassment if I turned my attention to some other Asian country.

Both sides have evidently agreed not to publicise their close connection: Israel in order to please Iran, and Iran in order not to displease the other Muslim countries.

The story of the diplomatic relations between the two countries is curious enough. Iran granted *de facto* recognition to

Israel in March 1950 and an Iranian diplomat with a strange designation appeared in Israel: first called "Envoy Extraordinary to Palestine" he later became "Special Representative to the State of Israel". A year later, when Mossadeq came to power in Iran, the Iranian Consulate General in Jerusalem was closed, the *de facto* recognition was withdrawn and it was announced that all Jews in Iran were to be "compulsorily repatriated".

Soon after Mossadeq's overthrow friendly relations were resumed, and since 1953 there has been a whole series of agreements between Israel and Iran. Iran supplies Israel with all her oil, and in return Israel has undertaken the construction of roads and buildings, the raising of the yield of sugar beet and cotton, the rehabilitation of earthquake stricken areas and the provision of sewage systems. An immensely circuitous airline connection between Israel and South Africa passes through Teheran.

It is impossible to discover what the volume of trade is between the two countries, because since 1961 all mention of Iran has been dropped from the otherwise comprehensive statistics produced by the Israeli government.

Clearly there could not be this degree of intercourse without some form of diplomatic representation, and in 1960 the Shah announced that Iran had never ceased to recognise Israel. There have been stray references to an Israeli Mission in Iran, where the Israeli community is sufficiently numerous for there to be a separate school for its children.

In 1961 the Shah said that relations between Iran and Israel "were like the true love that exists between two people outside of wedlock. Iran is strengthening its ties with Israel, but for political reasons it cannot recognise Israel de jure."[10] The Shah's warm feelings for Israel are understandable, because one of Israel's technical assistance schemes in Iran is the provision of highly expert advice to the secret service of the Iranian police, which is one of the main props of the monarchical government.

Relations between Israel and the monarchical regime in Iran

[10] *Jerusalem Post*, 31.12.1961.

will continue to be good because they are based on a common hostility to Arab nationalism. But the link is not necessarily popular in Iran, where there were riots against co-operation with Israel in June 1963.

Israel made her real breakthrough into what may be called Asia proper, Asia outside her own West Asian area, through the sickly and now defunct organisation called the Asian Socialist Conference. The idea of a meeting of Asian socialists was first mooted at the 1947 New Delhi meeting, but nothing further happened till March 1952 when representatives of the Socialist Parties of Burma, India and Indonesia met in Rangoon and it was decided to call a Conference.

Burma had begun to show some interest in Israel on the ground that they were the only two countries in Asia where socialist parties were in power. In September 1952 the Secretary-General of Burma's ruling party visited Israel and was much impressed with what he saw. Therefore with Burma acting as the host to the Asian Socialist Conference it was natural that Israel should be invited, along with representatives from India, Pakistan, Indonesia, Lebanon, Malaya, Japan and Vietnam. The Israeli delegation was led by Moshe Sharett and R. Barkatt and because of their ability, and because they could speak for a government, it played a leading part in the deliberations.

What, at first glance, may seem surprising is that at this meeting, their first Asian conference, albeit an unofficial one, the Israeli socialists did not in any way minimise their connection with Europe but emphasised it. Instead of merging themselves in the Asian socialist movement they tried to get the Asian socialists to merge with the European-dominated Socialist International. This issue was one of the two main questions debated at the Rangoon Conference and on both of which Israel took an anti-Asian line.[11]

The Asian socialists assumed that they were meeting together to set up an organisation of their own: the preliminary conference in March had mentioned this as the main objective of

---

[11] *Three Years of Asian Socialist Conferences*, Bombay, 1956, and S. Rose, *Socialism in Southern Asia*, Oxford, 1959, chapters I and XIII.

the later, larger gathering. But Israel came near to upsetting the socialist applecart when her delegation suggested that any Asian socialist organisation should be merged with the Socialist International by becoming a regional member of that body. Since the International was older, larger, wealthier and better-organised a merger would have meant, in effect, that the Asian body would have been swallowed up. Israel was supported by the right-wing Japanese faction and by the Malayans. Strongly opposed to any such idea were the socialists from India, Egypt and Lebanon and, to a lesser degree, those from Pakistan, Indonesia and Burma itself.

The basis of this opposition was straightforward Asian feeling, coupled with a belief that the Socialist International was predominantly European, because of which it had not taken a firm enough line on anti-colonialism and neutralism. So strong was the feeling against it that a proposal was actually put forward to prohibit Asian socialists from becoming members of the Socialist International.

A compromise was reached between this proposal and the Israeli suggestion: a separate Asian socialist organisation was formed but it was decided that there should be liaison at all levels between the two bodies.

The second main subject discussed at Rangoon was neutralism. The Asian socialists, or at least those from the South Asian countries, have had their own distinctive approach to this issue: they have stood for aligned non-alignment, a Third Bloc organised on the lines of the other two.

Some delegations at Rangoon wanted a clear declaration associating Asian socialism with non-alignment. Again, this was opposed by the Israelis and the right-wing Japanese. Another vague compromise was approved which merely said that the Asian countries should not identify themselves with "so-called peace movements", or with any military system but should strengthen themselves and make up their own minds on problems of world peace.

The Rangoon Conference established a permanent bureau to carry forward its work, such as it was. On this body were represented Burma, India, Indonesia, Japan, Malaya, Pakistan and

Israel; with delegates of Yugoslavia and of the Socialist International. The latter body informed the Asians that for joint publications Barkatt of the Israeli delegation would represent the Socialist International.

Having tried and failed to divert the Asian socialist movement on two fundamental issues, the Israelis nevertheless succeeded in dominating the movement in the next few years, because of their greater financial resources. The political dividends accruing to Israel, in the shape of political contacts with several Asian countries, amply justified this investment.[12]

We have seen Herzl commenting that it was surely possible to buy up the Latin American republics. The Israelis did not quite buy up the Asian socialist movement but they certainly financed many of its activities. This was not just fraternal support born of socialist fellow-feeling because, as at the first Conference at Rangoon, the Israeli socialists either tried to get the Asian socialists to do something that they did not want to do or, as at the second conference in Bombay, to get them not to do something that they wanted to do.

The second, and last, Asian socialist conference could not have met at a worse time for the Israelis—on November 3, 1956, four days after the commencement of the tripartite aggression on Egypt. The representation at this meeting was at a very high level, but the air of importance this imparted was wholly spurious for the conference achieved nothing of any great practical significance. The Burmese delegation was led by the Prime Minister, and the Prime Minister of Ceylon also addressed the gathering; while the Indonesian and Israeli delegations were headed by former Prime Ministers, for Israel it was Sharett again. The fraternal Yugoslavs were again present, as were the Vice-President of Austria and a member of the Popular Socialist Party of Chile. This time the only Arab representative was from Algeria, possibly because the Suez crisis was at its height throughout the conference.

---

[12]That Israel to a very large extent financed the Asian Socialist Conference was confirmed to this writer by R. Barkatt in a conversation in Jerusalem, November 1966.

This issue, naturally, dominated the session. The original draft on West Asia—drawn up by India, Burma, Indonesia and Japan, was so condemnatory that the Israeli delegation could not accept it. This Israeli refusal amounted to a veto, not only because of a desire to maintain socialist solidarity but also because in the preceding five years the Asian Socialist Conference "had come to lean quite heavily on the Israeli party".[13] The Asian socialists, quite literally, could no longer afford to displease or expel the Israelis. When the wording was watered down the Israelis agreed to abstain, as did the Pakistan delegation in protest against the toning down; the Yugoslavs also raised strong objections.

While the Asian governments, in their capitals and at the United Nations, and their peoples in street demonstrations, were spontaneously condemning the aggressors, all that the Asian Socialists were able to say was: "Despite the earlier developments, the Conference strongly disapproves the encroachment and occupation by Israeli troops of Egyptian territory and appeals to the Israeli government to withdraw their troops within their borders." Thus an attack, 300 miles deep into Egyptian territory, becomes an "encroachment" to be "disapproved": that is a measure of the grip that the Israelis had on the Asian socialists.

The Israelis tried to strengthen their hold when they put forward a resolution on party organisation, which, among other things, proposed to set up a training centre for cadres, and a special fund to promote contacts and exchanges between members. The Israeli delegation assured a reluctant and sceptical gathering that it "felt confident that the money would be forthcoming from other unspecified sources".[14] The project was accepted in principle, but little came of it.

The climax of Israeli influence on, amounting almost to control of, the Asian socialist movement came at a meeting of the Bureau of the Secretariat held at Katmandu in April 1958. Though this was a mere 18 months after Suez a resolution greet-

---

[13]S. Rose, *op. cit.*, p. 248.
[14]*Op. cit.*, p. 253.

ing Israel on her 10th anniversary was passed while all resolutions congratulating the U.A.R. were rejected. Another resolution called for Israel's integration into the Middle East and condemned certain negative aspects of U.A.R. policy. It was also decided to send a delegation to the Middle East to study conditions, the itinerary and terms of reference of which were to be drawn up in consultation with the Mapai party, which represented Israel in the Asian socialist movement. Earlier in this Bureau meeting Pakistan had asked for the expulsion of Israel from the movement and was supported by Yugoslavia and Japan. But by the end of the meeting, the Yugoslav observer had been excluded, and the Pakistanis were talking of the necessity of an Arab-Israeli settlement; from which it is clear that the Israelis were able to get at least the eight socialist parties attending this meeting to say exactly what they wanted them to say.

Perhaps at this Katmandu conference the Israelis committed the mistake to which they are particularly prone—they overreached themselves, for the one-sided attitude of the participants towards the Arab-Israeli issue was unrealistic to the point of being grotesque. Whatever the reason, the Israelis were not able, on any later occasion, to stage-manage the Asian socialists quite so effectively. In fact the Asian socialist movement slowly faded away, though it has served the Israeli purpose by leaving a strong residue of pro-Israeli sentiment in the approach of Asian socialists to West Asia.

Israel made contacts with Asian political parties not only through the centrist Mapai and the Asian socialists but also through Israeli parties more to the left, such as the Ahdut Haavodah which, curiously enough, tried to establish relations with the centrist Indian Congress Party. An agreement of sorts was reached in 1959, though nothing seems to have come of it, but after its conclusion the Ahdut Haavodah representative, who was Yigal Allon, now Deputy Premier, expressed regret that Mapai and the trade union federation, the Histadrut, had made connections with the small and uninfluential Indian Socialist Party.[15] An earlier attempt at political bridge-building

[15] *Jerusalem Post*, 13.7.1959.

by Israel's leftists had proven singularly inauspicious. In April 1955, just before the Bandung Conference and in direct competition with it, a left-wing Afro-Asian meeting had been held in Delhi; from which later emerged the Afro-Asian Solidarity Movement. At this meeting Israel was represented by its Mapam, Adhut Haavodah and Communist parties, which apparently agreed to a resolution condemning "the aggressive policy of the ruling circles of Israel"; it was announced as having been passed unanimously. The three parties were strongly criticised in Israel for accepting this resolution, which could be one reason why there were no further political connections between Israel and Asia at the farther left section of the political spectrum. Asia's communists and "progressives" have always been, doctrinally, firmly anti-Israel.

The door to Burma having been opened at the Rangoon Conference, Israeli influence, trade and assistance flooded into that country. One gets the impression that Israel was determined to make Burma a showpiece of how beneficial relations with Israel could be for Asian countries. Starting in 1953, two years before diplomatic relations were established, and for the next ten years, a bewildering variety of contacts, on every plane and in every field of activity, rapidly materialised. There were visits and training missions to Israel of Burmese politicians, civil servants, officers and men and women of the armed services, social workers, farmers, technicians, trade unionists and industrial workers. In Burma Israel undertook to develop a million acres of jute, corn and soya beans; to assist in regional irrigation planning; to help in the management of plants for the manufacture of tyres, glass, ceramics and paint. Israel also agreed to conduct a geological survey of Burma, to establish a joint shipping line and to send experts, physicians and scientists to train Burmese students. A trade agreement in 1955 provided for an annual barter deal of 1 million dollars worth of Israeli manufactured goods against Burmese rice. Israel sold Burma a consignment of obsolete fighter planes and in 1958 agreed to supply her with bazookas and mortars. On the personal level, U Nu, in 1955, became the first head of government of any country to visit Israel, where he was given a most enthusiastic welcome;

which was all the more enthusiastic because U Nu, in a huff, cancelled a visit to Egypt when that country criticised his going to Israel. His visit was repaid in 1959 when the Israeli President went to Burma. Two years later he was followed by Ben Gurion, the student of Buddhist philosophy, who spent eight days in meditation in a Buddhist monastery. He visited the local synagogue soon after emerging but this did not blunt the criticisms of Jewish religious parties in Israel. Nor were they mollified when he explained the special importance of Burma as a centre of Buddhism, which was "a tremendous spiritual force in Asia".[16]

Soon after Ben Gurion's visit U Nu, in a gesture of reassurance to the Arabs, went to Cairo and in a joint communiqué with President Nasser urged the settlement of the Palestine problem on the basis of the U.N. Charter and the full restoration of the rights of the Arab people of Palestine. This was not at all to Israel's liking, especially since it came from what was then Israel's best friend in Asia. Ben Gurion described it as "an unpleasant surprise" at the time and, a little later, said that U Nu had been "tricked" by Nasser.

Trickery or no this was, for Israel, a cloud the size of a man's hand in the blue skies of its friendship with Burma.

Japan, in point of time, was the second Asian country that Israel set out to cultivate, and she has now taken over from Burma the role of Israel's best friend in Asia.

Israel was among the first countries to express readiness to establish diplomatic relations with Japan, even before the San Francisco Peace Treaty was signed in September 1951; "especially since none of the Arab States made a move to start any action of its own in Japan. Obviously it was also easier to deal with Japan because there were no Moslems in that country."[17] An Israeli Legation was installed at the end of 1952, but it took Japan over two years to reciprocate.

Israel's main objectives in Japan were commercial exchanges,

---

[16]Full details of Israeli-Burmese exchanges are given in M. Medzini, *op. cit.*, pp. 63-71; R.J. Kozicki, "Burma and Israel: A Study in Friendly Asian Relations", *Middle Eastern Affairs*, New York, March 1959, and *The Jerusalem Post*, especially for September and October 1961.

[17]M. Medzini, *op. cit.*, p. 57.

and by 1965 the two-way trade between them amounted to almost 50 million dollars.

Perhaps to Israel's surprise, cultural relations with Japan became almost more important than the commercial. This development was largely due to the influence of Prince Mikasa, a younger brother of the Emperor, who is a university teacher and a specialist in the Hebrew language and Biblical history. There is now an active Israel-Japan Friendship Association which has its own magazine, a Japan-Israel Women's Welfare Organisation, a Jewish Community Centre in Tokyo and even a small group of Japanese who adhere to Judaism. Most curious of all is the Japanese Kibbutz Association which has sent a couple of hundred young Japanese to Israel to study the kibbutz movement. Links have also been established between the trade unions and the socialist parties in both countries.

The Philippines is the only Asian country to have a treaty of friendship with Israel. It was signed by President Garcia in February 1957 and then sent to the Senate for ratification. Because of demands from the leaders of the Philippine Muslim community the final signing by the contracting parties was delayed for over a year. Despite this treaty, relations between Israel and the Philippines, though amicable, are not as extensive as with other Asian countries. A certain number of Israeli experts have been provided in the fields of irrigation, soil conservation and agricultural advice generally.

Israel's relations with Thailand, Cambodia and Laos blossomed vigorously in the late 1950's and early 1960's. In Thailand Israeli experts established a model farm near Bangkok and training schemes in co-operation, community development and local government. Experimental farms were also set up in Laos and Cambodia. In Cambodia country advisers have been provided to the Ministries of Commerce and Industry, to the National Bank, the co-operative movement, and the tourism industry. Besides carrying out a survey of natural resources in Cambodia Israel is participating in joint ventures for the production of soft drinks, salt and tobacco. Israeli experts are also working on the Mekong Valley Scheme, especially in the Cambodian and Laotian sectors.

Socialism was the link connecting Israel and Nepal, between which relations developed rapidly soon after Nepal recognised Israel in 1960. Israeli experts were sent to Nepal to advise and train on such varied subjects as co-operation, meteorology and handicrafts. A joint Israeli-Nepalese construction company undertook the construction of schools, a college, a hotel and the airport at Katmadu. The Israelis are also in charge of a scheme for forest clearance and two other settlement projects, each involving 1,000 families. Nepalese paratroopers have been trained in Israel.[18]

It is the military link that seems to have proved most effective with Israel's latest friend in Asia, Singapore. That small island republic has turned to Israel to provide it with a military mission to train its armed forces.

While the number of experts Israel can send abroad is necessarily limited she can provide training to a much larger number of Afro-Asian technicians in Israel herself. In 1965 it was estimated that at any one time there were something like 3,000 trainees in Israel—a surprisingly high figure considering Israel's small size.

The co-ordinating agency for most of the training programmes is the Afro-Asian Institute for Labour, Economics and Co-operation which began work in Tel Aviv in 1960. Apart from co-ordination, the Institute itself provides six month training courses in the fields of co-operation and trade union organisation. By 1965 875 trainees from 62 countries had attended 10 international courses and 15 seminars at the Institute.

It has become something of a showpiece for Israel, but in fact the Afro-Asian Institute is a joint Israeli-United States endeavour. The necessary funds to get it going were not forthcoming from Israel itself and so "It was decided that the Institute would be established and run jointly by the Histadrut and the United States trade union movement. Mr. George Meany, the Chairman of the Board of the AFL-CIO, was chosen as one of the co-chairmen...The Board of the Institute includes a number of

---

[18]*Ibid.*, pp. 104-120. Also information provided by the Israeli Ministry of Foreign Affairs.

prominent Israeli academicians. . . as well as Mr. Walter Reuther and other American union leaders.''[19]

Here once again, we have a compact of interests, this time at the semi-official level, between Israel and a Western country. After World War II the internationally-minded leaders of the American trade union movement were much concerned at the prospect of the trade unions of Europe, and later of the Third World, falling under communist domination. This is where the trade union training given by Israel was immensely useful, for not only was Israel in Asia, she was ostensibly socialist, but non-communist. The ideas proferred by Israel and her Afro-Asian Institute would be attractive to the Afro-Asians, but, from the American viewpoint, quite safe.

Thus even in her altruistic aid programme Israel, knowingly and deliberately, served as a help-meet of the West. Nor, as we shall see later, was this the only example of Israeli aid to Afro-Asia and Western interests working together.

Israel, as might have been expected, worked hard at keeping her Asian friendships in a state of good repair by exchange visits of dignitaries. The King and Prime Minister of Nepal, as well as successive Burmese Premiers, have been invited to Israel. The President of Israel has visited both Burma and Nepal; and a tour through South and East Asia by Sharett in 1956 was followed by similar tours of Israeli Foreign Ministers, Mrs. Meir in 1962 and Abba Eban in 1967.

The record of Israel's contacts with these Asian countries is quite impressive. That it was partly attributable to American pressure is an undoubted fact because America tried, and failed, more than once, to pressure India into friendliness towards Israel; and at least five of these countries—Turkey, Iran, Thailand, the Philippines and Japan, are very susceptible to American pressure. But that is only part of the explanation for Israel's success. Israel does have skilled advice to offer, her experts mingle with the people of the country, and being small her aid is, ostensibly, above suspicion. Indeed Israel has used the argument of her small size to appeal to other small countries like

[19]*New Outlook*, Tel Aviv, vol. IV, no. 3, January, 1961, pp. 60-61.

Nepal, Cambodia, Laos and Singapore. The ties of socialism have helped her in Nepal, Burma, Japan and Singapore. And with Singapore she has used the parallel that they are both surrounded by hostile countries of people of a different race and religion—Islam in both cases. According to one student of Burma the fact that both Burma and Israel were at one time ruled by Britain has given them a common inheritance in "the procedure and techniques of administration, educational methods, and service organisation,"[20] which partly explains the otherwise "strange sympathy" between them. With Japan it is on economics that Israel seeks to base an affinity—that both countries are hard-working, have a high growth rate and a large volume of exports.[21] In Burma Buddhism has been seen as providing favourable ground for friendship with Israel, and of South East Asia it has been said: "Buddhist kindliness and peacefulness, and a French cultural background are conducive to better and growing understanding of Israel's plans and problems."[22]

Though Israel's endeavours to gain Asian friendships were many-sided and were pursued with energy and intelligence, her attempts to break through her encapsulation in West Asia were only partially successful because she could make no headway with the non-Arab Muslim countries (Iran and Turkey excepted), nor with China and India, and even some of her friends were hesitant. What deprived Israel of any solid basis of friendship with Asia was the fact that on major political issues that dominated Asian thought and feeling Israel was on the side of the West against Asia. This disaccord on fundamentals threw suspicion even on Israel's programme of aid.

Pro-colonial votes and attitudes

In the hard and horrible present-day world it is not at all unusual for one government to give assistance to another govern-

---

[20]H. Tinker, *The Union of Burma*, Oxford, 1961, p. 361. Also W.C. Johnstone, *Burma's Foreign Policy*, Harvard, 1963.

[21]*Japan Times*, Tokyo, 15.5.1967.

[22]*Jerusalem Post*, 6.1.1957.

ment for which it has no real sympathy, or even such lack of
sympathy that it is trying to overthrow it: national interest often
prevails over friendliness or even ideology. Thus we have the
spectacle of communist states giving aid, including arms, to
feudal monarchies or right-wing military juntas, and such
regimes seeking this aid, while both sides are doing their best to
suppress or subvert the other's principles.

The communist states at least try to keep aid and subversion
in separate, not always water-tight, compartments—aid is a
matter between governments while subversion is the business
of the Communist Party, local or international. Thus the contradiction between aid and opposition is softened.

In the case of Israel and the Afro-Asian countries there is no
such softening of the contradiction: it is the Israeli government
that grants aid and it is the Israeli government that opposes the
Afro-Asians on de-colonisation, on the Cold War, on racial
discrimination, on self-determination, on disarmament—that is,
on every major international question in which the Afro-Asians
are concerned. On all these questions, it must be noted, the
communist bloc supports the Afro-Asians.

Even the ex-imperial powers, even capitalist America, do not
have such a consistently anti-Afro-Asian record as does Israel.

The only countries with a voting record similar to Israel's
are South Africa, Portugal and some of the smaller and more
extreme right-wing military regimes in Latin America.

But South Africa, Portugal and these Latin Americans do
not offer aid to Afro-Asia, and if they did it would be indignantly
refused. Israel's aid is not refused, because of a practical and
a propagandist factor. The practical consideration is the Afro-
Asian's need for aid; the propagandist factor is Israel's ability
not only to minimise her pro-colonial record but also to give the
impression that her aid programme has the most noble motivations.

We have seen that from very early on in the history of the
Zionist movement both Gentile and Jewish Zionists anticipated
that a Jewish State in Palestine would serve as some sort of
intermediary between East and West, a bridge between Europe
and Asia. We have also seen that several Zionist leaders inter-

preted this role as the Jew bringing European "civilisation" to the "barbarian" east. After the establishment of Israel, in the post-colonial age, that sort of vocabulary is no longer used. Israel, it is said, is a bridge between the "developed" and the "developing" countries, or between technologically "advanced" Europe and less technologically advanced Afro-Asia; Israel's European background is thus made to appear not a liability, but a positive advantage to Afro-Asia.

In the words of Ben Gurion: "Israel regards it as a historic privilege—and therefore a duty—to assist newly freed peoples".[23] Every Israeli who has anything to do with the aid programme echoes those sentiments. A tone of patronage is often, though not invariably, present in these Israeli statements; but if we set that aside what we find is a modernised, secularised version of the old myth of the Chosen People which has a special "mission" to fulfil in the world. Now it is no longer the religious truth of monotheism that is the message of Israel, but the scientific truths of technological advancement, which Israel, as the only country of Europeans in Asia, is uniquely fitted to carry to the Third World.

The Afro-Asians would seem to have accepted this exalted motivation as the explanation for Israel's aid programme, because they have no qualms in accepting her assistance despite her thorough-going anti-Afro-Asian attitude at the United Nations. But with this attitude why should Israel want to help countries with which she is basically at odds? Obviously not out of a sense of altruistic mission, but because aid is politically useful in disarming Afro-Asian opposition. Of governments, as of individuals, it is true that friends are helped because they are liked, and people who are disliked may be helped to conceal the fact of dislike and to prevent a reciprocation of dislike. Nothing else can explain the sharp contradiction between Israeli economic aid and Israeli political opposition to Afro-Asia.

When Ben Gurion spoke of Israel's privilege and duty "to assist newly freed peoples" he was obviously only thinking of economic assistance because Israel, at the U.N., did her best to

[23]M. Pearlman, *Ben Gurion Looks Back*, London 1965, p. 179.

prevent many Afro-Asian people from becoming free.

The first big problem of de-colonisation that the U.N. faced was the struggle of the Indonesians against the Dutch, which so stirred the whole of Asia that Nehru called a special Asian conference in Delhi, in January 1949, to consider the matter. But because of "the traditionally good relations between the Dutch and the Jewish people and the valiant record of the Dutch during the Second World War when many of them helped Jews at the risk of their very lives"..."Israel preferred to abstain from participating in the acrimonious debate on the Indonesian problem".[24] Israel also abstained on the Afro-Asian resolution supporting Indonesia on West Irian. Israel, because of her historical connection with Europe and her role vis-à-vis world Jewry, found herself in a dilemma. And because of the very nature of the Jewish state, being in Asia but not of it, Israeli solidarity with Asian national movements was sacrificed to safeguard Israel's umbilical link with Europe and the interests of Jewish communities in the Diaspora.

It was the latter consideration which caused Israel to abstain for 12 years from condemning South Africa's apartheid policy: not even Jewish memory of racial persecution prevailed against the interests of South Africa's large and very prosperous Jewish community. Only the Israeli government's almost desperate desire to win the friendship of the new states of Africa obliged her to switch from abstention to a condemnation of apartheid which was, nevertheless, much criticised in Israel.

Having opposed the application of the principle of self-determination in Palestine all through the 1920's and 1930's it might have been expected that the Zionists would accept it after Israel was established, as no longer presenting a danger to the Jewish community. But they evidently do not believe in taking any risks for in 1952, when the U.N. General Assembly adopted a resolution supporting the principle of self-determination of peoples by 40 votes to 14, Israel was one of 6 countries that abstained.

The Zionists could not accept the principle of one-man one-

[24]Medzini, *op. cit.*, pp. 75, 77.

vote before 1947 and today they continue to oppose it. When in the 16th Session of the General Assembly, in 1961, an Afro-Asian resolution called for this democratic procedure to be applied in Southern Rhodesia, Israel abstained.

Israel likewise abstained on other Afro-Asian resolutions demanding the prohibition of the use of nuclear weapons, the suspension of nuclear tests, and the de-nuclearisation of Africa—thus increasing Arab fears that she was keeping her hands free for the possible use of nuclear weapons said to be under construction at her secret nuclear plant at Dimona.

Even though Israel eventually supported anti-apartheid resolutions she is flouting the U.N. embargo on trade with South Africa. Her national airline, El Al, is one of the few that flies into South Africa and most of the diamonds for Israel's important diamond-cutting industry come from South Africa.

Needless to say Israel has voted against all Afro-Asian resolutions giving support to the liberation movements in the Arab North African countries, Tunisia, Morocco, and Algeria. With France her principal supplier of arms Israel could show no sympathy even for the heroic Algerians. As a result of these votes the Jewish communities in these three countries were placed in jeopardy. But whereas Israel rated Dutch or South African Jews above Indonesian or African nationalists she rated France above North African Jews.

The voting record of Israel at two U.N. General Assemblies, the 15th and 16th in 1961 and 1961-62, has been analysed[25] and this analysis shows that Israel has the second highest coincidence of voting with the United States of all Middle East and North African countries (Turkey has the highest); the lowest coincidence of all these states with the Communist bloc; and, with Turkey, either the lowest or second lowest coincidence of voting with the Afro-Asian groups: in the 15th Session Israel voted only 69 times, out of 145 votes, with the Afro-Asians (Turkey 81), and in the 16th Session Israel's figure was 59 out of 125 votes (Turkey 55).

[25]*Middle East Record*, The Reuven Shiloah Research Center, Tel Aviv University, volumes I and II, 1960, 1961.

There could be no clearer, more conclusive, proof of how far removed, in her political interest, is Israel from the Afro-Asians.

Against this factual background Israel's programme of aid to Afro-Asia appears not as "a duty" or "a mission" but merely as the economic price paid for political shortcomings.

So antagonistic were Israel's interests to those of the Afro-Asians at the U.N. that she considered a defeat for them a victory for herself. Speaking of the 1955 Assembly, following the Bandung Conference, Ishar Harari, a Member of the Knesset and a member of Israel's U.N. delegation, said: "The most significant development in our favour was the defeat of the Bandung Conference countries on practically every issue brought before the General Assembly".[26] And that has remained true for the subsequent Assemblies.

Even on issues involving particular Asian countries Israel has not hestitated to take a pro-colonial position when it has suited her interests. Evidently despairing of India's friendship the Israeli press could not bring itself to express any approval of India's military take-over of Goa in December 1961. Whatever the rest of the world may think of this action it was enormously popular throughout Afro-Asia. But this Afro-Asian feeling was not shared by Israel. There the newspapers were non-committal on the substance of the issue but reproached India for hypocrisy and double standards. (The Israeli press later revealed that Israel was selling small arms to Portugal, which were certainly used against the freedom fighters in Angola and Mozambique.) When, in October 1962, China attacked India she received sympathy, if not support, from many countries, not excluding Russia. All that the Israeli press could do was, once again, to bring an accusation of double standards against India.

Despite her pro-colonial votes and attitude Israel continues to have some friends in Afro-Asia. This cannot be ascribed only to the effect of her aid programme, for pro-Israeli feeling is strong in India which receives no Israeli aid. Here we have evidence of the power of Israeli propaganda, of the projection

[26] *Jerusalem Post*, 21.1.1956.

of the myth, or rather the myths, of Israel. And on no occasion was this persuasive power more clearly demonstrated than when Afro-Asia, by and large, forgave Israel for her flagrant collusion with France and Britain in the attack on Egypt in 1956.

* * *

The Suez collusion forgiven

The whole story of close, co-ordinated collusion between Israel, France and Britain for their attack on Egypt in October-November, 1956, is now known.[27]

It is now crystal clear that but for French and British military support, Israel would not have made a full-scale attack across Sinai. It is equally clear that without Israeli military collaboration France and Britain would not have attacked.

What is still not absolutely definite is whether Israel took the initiative in asking France to join in an attack, or whether this initiative came from France. Nutting is unclear on this point;[28] but, according to Robertson, it was Israel which took the first step, on September 23, 1956, when General Dayan went to Paris with "a clear invitation to France to help Israel fight a defensive war"; also "Israel had canvassed for help, found it, and now thought in terms of preventive war".[29] Bar Zohar ascribes the initial move to the French who, early in August, put the question to Peres, of the Israeli Defence Ministry: "If we make war on Egypt, would Israel be prepared to fight alongside us?" Without hesitation Peres answered "Yes". But that was still only a reply to a conditional question. Bar Zohar agrees with Robertson that the crucial decision was made, not by any French leader, but by Ben Gurion in a cable to Peres in Paris "late in September" "which gave a new turn to the

---

[27]The most full and authoritative account of the Suez episode is given by Bar Zohar in his official biography of Ben Gurion, *The Armed Prophet*. Also most revealing are the accounts given by T. Robertson, *Crisis, The Inside Story of the Suez Conspiracy*, London, 1964, and A. Nutting, *No End of A Lesson*, London, 1967.

[28]Nutting, *op. cit.*, p. 57.

[29]Robertson, *op. cit.*, pp. 134, 137.

whole affair. Israel had officially come into it".[30]

Bar Zohar is even more emphatic in his assertion that, whoever made the first move, the final, crucial decision to attack depended on Ben Gurion: "He was in a very strong position; it depended on him, on his decision, whether or not there would be a Suez war, and so he could dictate his conditions".[31]

At the secret conference at Sèvres, from 22nd October, Ben Gurion dictated his conditions for the pretext Israel would provide to France and Britain; they were accepted in writing and so the decision to launch the Suez war was taken.

Compared to the collusion in this Treaty of Sèvres of 1956 the collusion of the Compact of 1917 seems child's play: but without the Balfour Declaration there would have been no Suez War, for one element in the earlier compact was protection for British interests in the Suez Canal area by a Jewish State. Thirty nine years later, in very different circumstances, the Jewish State did what it could to provide that protection, and failed.

If the tripartite plot failed to wrest control of the Suez Canal from Egypt it was due, in large measure, to very vigorous and vocal protests from the countries of the Third World.

Yet these protests were directed far more at the French and British than at Israel. An exculpatory summing-up by an Indian socialist leader presents an accurate picture of what happened: "Though Israel began the attack (on Suez) she did not suffer in any way. Rather the idea that the State of Israel had come to stay was strengthened in the international world".[32]

We have seen how the Asian socialists, at their Conference in Bombay during the Suez crisis would say no more than that they "disapproved" of "the encroachment" of Israeli troops. But when they turned to Britain and France they declaimed against this "cynical and unprovoked intervention" and "their aggression against Egypt" in "a flagrant violation of peace",[33]—as

---

[30]Bar Zohar, *op. cit.*, pp. 219, 221.

[31]*Ibid.*, p. 225.

[32]J.B. Kripalani, Foreword to J. Blumenthal, *The Significance of Israeli Socialism*, London, 1958, p. 8.

[33]S. Rose, *op. cit.*, p. 249.

fine an example of double standards of judgement as one could hope to find.

Not all the Asian governments were unequivocally on Egypt's side on the legal issues arising from her nationalisation of the Canal. At the Suez Canal Conference in London in August, 1955, five Asian countries—Pakistan, Turkey, Japan, Ethiopia and Iran (all military allies of the Western Powers), voted for the Western proposal to persuade Egypt to accept international supervision of the Canal; while three—India, Indonesia and Ceylon—supported Egypt.

Of course once the military attack was launched much more support for Egypt was forthcoming, but it took the form of attacks on Britain and France, rather than on Israel. This was true both of the Japanese and the Indian press. And at a huge public meeting in Delhi called by the Congress Party, the Party President made no mention of Israel but only castigated Britain and France. One of India's leading national figures, Mr. C. Rajagopalachari, denied that there had been collusion and asked for an international guarantee of Israel's frontiers.

There were several reasons for this strange deflection in the condemnatory attacks of the Afro-Asians. It was partly a question of habit: it was normal to think the worst of the ex-imperialists, and so the worst was thought and said. It was partly a question of size: compared to Britain and France Israel seemed a minor element, and so it was thought that if she was a partner she could only be a very junior partner. Finally, it was partly a question of lack of information: it was only some time later that Israel's major part in the conspiracy became known, and by that time indignation had cooled.

Hence no lasting blame attached to Israel, a state in Asia, for her part in providing the pretext for, or even actually drawing in, two European powers to attack an Afro-Asian country. Nehru saw it as a turning back of the clock of history, the re-invasion of Asia by Europe, but not many other Afro-Asians had his historical vision, and not even he branded Israel for being the Iago to a couple of blundering Othellos.

The final irony is that while the Suez affair did not turn Afro-Asia away from Israel as much as it should have, it definitely turned Israel away from the Third World for after 1956 Israel abandoned all pretence of neutralism and strove strenuously to make herself, formally and openly, a military ally of the West.

* * *

Israel opts for the West

The attempts that Israel made, after 1956, to incorporate herself into the military structure of the West were only the most recent, and perhaps the most successful, of repeated efforts to become a Western military outpost. Since 1951 Israel has tried to obtain a military alliance with the U.S. alone, with Britain alone, with France and Britain, with America, Britain and France jointly, with NATO, and with three local allies of America—Ethiopia, Iran and Turkey, with the blessings of the U.S. and of France: from what is known the last-mentioned effort seems to have been the most successful.

From what is not known for sure, but may be guessed at from the present close diplomatic and military collaboration between the U.S. and Israel, the Jewish State has at last succeeded in obtaining a working agreement, if not a formal defence treaty, with the United States.

What is surprising is not that Israel tried to become a military vassal of the West—for that was inevitable—but that her attempts were not more successful much earlier.

The whole history of the Zionist movement linked Israel with the Western bloc of countries, and communism's rejection of Zionism repelled her from the Eastern bloc. Despite the communist countries' support for the creation of Israel, and a timely supply of Czech arms in 1948, the Zionists and communists continued to be wary of each other: Bar Zohar even writes that "(Israel's) flirtation with the Soviet Union lasted no more that a year, the year of the War of Independence".[34] Although this is an extreme assessment of the communist policy change, there is no doubt that the communist support of Zionism was short-term and directed at removing the British presence from Pales-

[34]Bar Zohar, *op. cit.*, p. 181.

tine. After which the communists resumed their coolness to
Zionism and Israel.

Setting aside all the political, historical, cultural and sociological considerations, one has only to mention a single set of
figures to show that Israel could never be anything but pro-
Western. Israel, in the period 1948-1962, when her population
was growing from three quarters of a million to two-and-a-third
million people, received from American Jewry the gift of 1
billion dollars, in cash or kind; plus half a billion dollars in
purchases of Israeli government bonds; plus a quarter billion
dollars invested in enterprises in Israel. Up to the present Israel
has also received a billion and a half dollars in personal restitu-
tion from West Germany and three-quarters of a billion dollars
as reparations.

Considering Israel's complete dependence on this massive
Western charity it is very much to her credit that even for two
years, 1948-1950, the new state of Israel should have attempted
"a brief venture in neutrality".[35] Under the pressure of the
Korean War Israel moved from "neutrality" to what she called
"non-identification"; and then, as the pressure increased, from
non-identification to identification—with the West. In Korea
Israel gave her complete support to American policy.

According to one apologist it was "in December 1950 under
the specter of general war (that) Israel was reported to be study-
ing the possibility of an outright alliance with the West".[36]
That "specter" did not drive other more vulnerable countries
into the arms of the West but that it had this effect on Israel
is true, for early in 1951 "Israel began secret negotiations for
her first military pact with the West".[37]

The Western representative was the British Commander-in-
Chief in the Middle East who wanted Israel to supply air and
naval base facilities and to develop her arsenals and repair
workshops. According to Ben Gurion's biographer, Bar Zohar,

---

[35]N. Safran, *The United States and Israel*, Cambridge, Mass., 1963, pp. 219
et. seq.

[36]*Ibid.*

[37]Bar Zohar, *op. cit.*, p. 182.

(who is able to quote conversations verbatim) "negotiations developed in a friendly spirit". Ben Gurion at the time wrote to the British Foreign Secretary that Israel could not enter the Commonwealth "but we should like to establish relations with you on the lines of those between you and New Zealand"—which is the same thing. Just when "it seemed that Israel would become Britain's first ally in the Middle East", "this fine dream was shattered" when the Conservatives replaced the Labour Party in the British Government, and the then pro-Arab Anthony Eden filed away the project of a military alliance with Israel.[38]

In 1954 the Israeli government approved a secret service operation in Egypt (which was later to have a great impact on Israel's domestic policy through the notorious "Lavon Affair"), the object of which was "to prevent the British from leaving the Canal Zone--or rather, to make them change their minds" for a British withdrawal was not thought to be in Israel's interests. The plot misfired and the British withdrew.

Hence in the following year Israel turned from Britain to America and "the talks continued...throughout 1955". According to Bar Zohar "at first there was a gleam of hope...Israel was prepared to give military bases, but in exchange wanted guarantees for her frontiers and her security. In the end the United States proved to be lukewarm. What the Americans really wanted was some unilateral agreement which would give them the bases they required and the right of intervention in Israel's military policy". Not even Israel could agree to this.[39] These negotiations began in secret, but towards the end of 1955 the then Israeli Foreign Minister, Sharett, began to talk about them publicly in what seemed to be an attempt at putting pressure on America. In October he stated that "we feel more urgently entitled than ever before to a security treaty with the United States", and when he was succeeded by Mrs. Meir she spoke of Israel "pleading" for such a treaty.[40]

[38]*Ibid.*, pp. 182-183.
[39]*Ibid.*, p. 202.
[40]*The Times*, London, 21.10.1955 and *The Jerusalem Post*, April and May 1956.

In the next year, 1956, Israel swung back from America to Europe and colluded with Britain and France at Suez, in the third successful, but temporary, military alliance between her and the West.

It was only about six months after the final tidying-up of all the consequences of the Suez aggression that Ben Gurion took Israel over a watershed in her relations with the world. Despite Israel's military successes Ben Gurion realised that Arab hostility had only been increased; Israel had to have a powerful protector, and this could only be found in the West. At that time he committed Israel irrevocably to the Western camp.

This policy was not wholly popular inside Israel. Weizmann had favoured non-identification; so, too, had the leftist parties. The internal stresses created by Ben Gurion's foreign policy initiative broke surface only in January 1958 when, because of a cabinet crisis, Ben Gurion resigned and reconstituted his coalition government ostensibly because of a scandal caused by a leakage of news about a plan to buy arms from West Germany. The real cause of the crisis, however, was a debate between the "pro-European" and the "pro-neutralist" factions in the government regarding Israel's basic foreign policy orientation.

This was a conclusive confrontation, and when they won, the pro-Europeans took Israel into the West and, necessarily, out of Afro-Asia.

The arguments pro and con were described in detail in three articles that appeared at the time in the well-known French newspaper Le Monde, under the significant title Israël, Etat Occidental?[41] Putting his point of view to the French journalist, Ben Gurion said that he condemned neutralism. He recalled the incompatibility of communism and Zionism, and said that neutralism would mean capitulation to the Soviets. He was against the neutralisation of the Middle East, including any ban on the supply of arms. To get arms from the West Israel had to support the West—France on Algeria and the United States by accepting the Eisenhower Doctrine. The pro-Europeans contended that Israel "whether it wants it or not is, by its situa-

[41]Le Monde, 1, 2, 3, January, 1958, by Eric Rouleau.

tion, an advance post of Western defence in the Middle East"; "it is the natural frontier of the Free World". Who, then, is to be the guarantor of Israel? Not Britain; not the U.S., because earlier attempts to enlist her aid had failed; and France was out of the question (because of Algeria). Therefore geography had to be bypassed, and Western European military organisations had to be extended to the Middle East to include Israel. What Israel wanted was a general alliance with NATO as a whole. The Baghdad Pact had not sealed Western Europe's south-east flank against Russia, because it was too weak an organisation. That gap could be filled by Israel.

The pro-neutralists in Israel were to be found mainly in the Mapam and Ahdut Haavodah parties on the left, with some supporters in the centre and on the right. The best-known single pro-neutralist was, and still is, Nahum Goldmann, President of the World Jewish Congress. They argued that neutralisation would end the exhausting Middle East arms race. It also should not be assumed that Russia would be eternally hostile: a policy of neutrality could lead to Russia permitting its Jews as well as those of Eastern Europe to emigrate to Israel: hundreds of thousands of Jews had been let out of Eastern Europe during 1948-1950 when Israel had been neutral.

Fortunately, or unfortunately, the pro-neutralists in Israel were weak and confused. Goldmann himself is an American and, despite his position, not well known in Israel. The Mapam and Ahdut Haavodah compromised their neutralism when they did not leave Ben Gurion's government either over Suez or over the Eisenhower Doctrine or over the purchase of West German arms. Lacking firm leadership the pro-neutralists were pushed aside.

Though this debate went on in the early months of 1958, Ben Gurion's approaches to the West had taken place, as said, some six months after the end of the Suez crisis, in the late summer of 1957.[42]

In August Ben Gurion opened his diplomatic campaign by suggesting to Dulles that the U.S. should encourage pro-Western

[42]These events are described in detail in Bar Zohar, *op. cit.*, pp. 256-258.

Turkey and Iraq to attack Syria, which was then under some influence from its local communists.

When Russia in turn threatened Turkey, and America issued a guarantee of Turkey's frontiers, Ben Gurion asked for something similar from Washington. In October Mrs. Meir proposed to Dulles that there should be co-ordination between America, NATO and Israel, a guarantee for Israel, against Egypt and Syria, in return for which Israel was prepared to provide ports and airfields in case of emergency.

Simultaneously, through France, Israel asked NATO to guarantee her frontiers. Israel's representatives pressed their demand at a NATO Council of Ministers that met in Paris in December 1957.

Both America and NATO rejected the Israeli offer.

Thus by the time the debate on Ben Gurion's foreign policy developed publicly in Israel the most important moves had already been made.

Undaunted by the rebuffs received Ben Gurion, in the early months of 1958, shifted from the idea of a collective NATO guarantee to possible bilateral agreements with West European countries. In the Knesset Ben Gurion announced that negotiations were under way with three countries, one of them being France.[43]

As late as March 1958 Ben Gurion was still saying that since "other countries in the Middle East have guaranteed frontiers", such as Turkey, there was no reason why Israel should not have them.[44]

At the same time the indefatigable Prime Minister was pursuing another project, with far more success. After the formation of the United Arab Republic in February 1958 Ben Gurion turned to all the other countries in the area that might feel threatened by Arab nationalism. Bar Zohar records the result of Ben Gurion's cogitations: "Ethiopia was becoming increasingly alarmed at Nasser's expansionist policy. Turkey feared the Arab enemy on her southern frontiers, and Iran was engaged in a territorial dispute with Iraq. The total population of these countries and that of Israel was greater than all the Middle East states combined. Why not try to bring about a common alliance?"[45] The necessary approaches were made and the results were: "all were promising, though Turkey was showing some hesitancy".

Yet, Ethiopia, Turkey and Iran were Afro-Asians; the Western umbrella was, in Israel's eyes, still necessary, and could be unfurled over the four, three of them Western allies, if not over Israel alone.

In May 1958 Dayan spoke to Field-Marshal Montgomery towards this end and the Field-Marshal approved and promised to speak to President Eisenhower. In July Ben Gurion sought President de Gaulle's blessings: "if your Government looks upon this attempt with a favourable eye, it would be of great help".

Ben Gurion also asked directly for the all-important backing of the United States. In a letter to Eisenhower he wrote: "The first stages of this plan are already meeting with success. But two things are dependent upon American support: the political, financial and moral aid and the inculcation of the feeling in Iran, Turkey and Ethiopia that our efforts have the agreement of the United States."

De Gaulle sent "a non-committal reply. But reaction from the United States was favourable. The 'peripheral pact' was born—without official proclamation, without ceremonies to sign it. But it was the facts, the deeds that matter; and the alliance was to have a long life". The American reaction was favourable because, after 1957, the U.S. realised that, despite American support at the time of the Suez crisis, President Nasser was not going to move away from his position of non-alignment between America and Russia.

Yet a "peripheral pact" was only peripheral, even if it did have America's blessing. Five years later, in 1963, when Egypt, Syria and Iraq agreed to bring the very short-lived "Arab Federation" into being, Ben Gurion tried once more to obtain

---

[45]Bar Zohar, *op. cit.*, pp. 261-263.

the direct protection of the Western powers. He wrote to President Kennedy suggesting a defence treaty; the supply of a large quantity of arms; and paradoxically, the disarmament of the Middle East.

He once again approached President de Gaulle asking whether the time had not come "to seal the great friendship between our countries by a political treaty of military aid". Both Presidents said "No". At the same time, on the political front, Israel was seeking membership, or associate membership, of the Council of Europe and, in the economic field, was trying to become a member of, or be associated with, the European Common Market.

At the point of time to which this account has brought us, 1963, how do we find Israel situated in relation to the continent of Asia in which she found herself? Supported by the West she had been thrust into and established on Asia's western rim. Encapsulated by the enmity of her immediate Arab neighbours she had tried to establish friendly links with the areas of Asia beyond the Arab belt. Here she met with rejection too, from a large, hard core of countries—from the Muslim states, from China and from India. Despite a vigorous programme of aid, despite Western good offices, Israel could establish only peripheral relationships both in West Asia and in East and South-East Asia.

So she turned from Afro-Asia, because the Third World could not offer her what she wanted: "no power concentration offering an adequate substitute for the Western or the Soviet bloc in the matter of pacification, security or of economic and technological assistance and progress."[46]

She turned back to the mother-continents of Zionism, to Europe and North America, and made repeated efforts to gain their military protection, but with only limited success; for the West was more conscious of the growing importance of Afro-Asia than was Israel, and it was not ready to displease Afro-Asia by befriending an Israel that was ever more clearly seen as a hostile foreign body. Israel may have become a "Western defence bastion", "a Westernised, pro-Western, highly-develop-

---

[46]Bar Zohar, *op. cit.*, p. 293.

ed, highly efficient, resolute national state in the dismal morass of the Middle East".[47] For men like President Kennedy and President de Gaulle that was not enough.

So making a virtue of necessity the most eloquent of Israel's advocates, Abba Eban, announced, as early as 1956, "if Israel is now separated from the Middle East, we owe that separation not only to the hostility of our neighbours but also to the very essence and nature of our own national movement. We are separate from the region and will remain so separate by an act of our own will".[48] The facts of political life thus enforce on Israel the realisation that "the very essence and nature" of Zionism sets her apart from Asia.

But if she is not a part of Asia, and she is refused the formal position of an outpost of the West, what then is Israel? The answer, in the words of Abba Eban, is: "Israel not as a Middle Eastern country, but as a Mediterranean country".[49] And as a Mediterranean country Israel looks down the length of that sea, to the West, not eastwards towards Asia.

The drawing away of Israel and Asia was mutual. For even if the Asian governments were not aware at the time of Israel's frantic efforts to ally herself with the West, the essential foreignness of the Zionist Jewish state was clear to them, and, from 1955 on, they too drew back.

[47]Shahtai Rosenne, "Basic Elements of Israel's Foreign Policy", *India Quarterly*, Delhi, no. 4, 1961.

[48]John Connell, *Israel: Western Defence Bastion*, Anglo-Israel Association, London, 1963, p. 4.

[49]M. Davis, (ed.) *Israel: Its Role in Civilisation*, New York, 1956; *Nationalism and Internationalism in Our Day* by Abba Eban, pp. 121, 122.

CHAPTER VII

ASIA DRAWS BACK

The Afro-Asian and Non-Aligned Conferences

Asia's drawing back from Israel was a product of the process by which Asia tried to draw together. This began in 1954 when five South and South-East Asian countries met at Colombo to discuss mutual problems. Almost absent-mindedly they proposed a larger Afro-Asian gathering which eventuated as the famous Bandung Conference of 1955. A preparatory meeting for Bandung was held at Bogor, near Jakarta, late in 1954. At Colombo, Bogor and Bandung there was some discussion, and even controversy over whether or not Israel should be invited. After Bandung it was accepted that Israel would not be invited to any conference of Afro-Asian or non-aligned countries, but at these subsequent gatherings controversy continued as to how strongly Israel should be condemned. Reviewing the negative role Israel played in the deliberations of these meetings one sees her as a continuing cause of differences among Afro-Asians, small but too irritating to be ignored. It is also noteworthy that at each successive conference the condemnation of Israel is ever more strongly worded.

At Colombo[1] Mr. Muhammad Ali, the Pakistani Prime Minister, introduced a draft resolution that damned Israel root and branch: it condemned the establishment of the State of Israel as a violation of international law; it also condemned Israel's aggressive policy towards her neighbours; and it expres-

---

[1] The details of this conference given below are taken from the official minutes prepared by the Ceylonese civil servants who comprised the secretariat of the Conference. The documents were circulated privately.

sed grave concern for the plight of the Arab refugees.

Commenting on this draft Mr. Nehru said that India had always had great sympathy for the Arab cause. But since India had recognised Israel it was difficult for him to say that her creation was a violation of international law. Furthermore, attempts that the United Nations were making to settle this problem would be prejudiced by the Pakistani resolution.

Prime Minister U Nu of Burma, which by now had developed very friendly relations with Israel, suggested that the Pakistani draft should be toned down. Ceylon and Indonesia expressed no opinion one way or the other.

Mr. Muhammad Ali then said that he would be satisfied if the resolution condemned aggression in Palestine and expressed sympathy with the victims of aggression; and the matter was referred to the drafting committee.

In their final discussion of this matter the five Prime Ministers deleted two paragraphs proposed by Pakistan, retaining only an expression of deep sympathy for the Arab refugees. What is surprising is that in their discussion the Premiers expressed doubt whether the United Nations had reached a formal decision that the Arab refugees should be returned to their original homes, which, of course, the U.N. had done in a resolution passed as far back as 1948 and repeated annually since then. Hence it was decided to delete any reference to decisions of the U.N. in the final communiqué.

This text stated: "Examination of the situation in the Middle East has caused the Prime Ministers the gravest concern as regards the sufferings of the Palestine refugees, and they urge the United Nations to restore all the rights of these refugees in Palestine. The Prime Ministers expressed their understanding of the situation of the refugees, and expressed the hope that a just solution of the Palestine problem would be reached as soon as possible."

Thus five Asian leaders, making what they believed to be an original proposal on Palestine, recommended that "all the rights" of the Palestinians should be restored; and even Burma had to go along with this strong formulation. But that these leaders, and their advisers should have been ignorant of what the U.N. had already decided is indicative of just how inept Arab publicity had failed to inform friendly countries on the principal Arab problem.

The decision to exclude Israel from meetings of the Afro-Asian conferences was in effect taken in mid-air somewhere over the Kra Peninsula around 1 p.m. on December 27, 1954.[2]

The Colombo Conference having approved the idea of a general Afro-Asian conference the Prime Ministers agreed to meet at Bogor, to work out the practical details. Mr. Nehru flew to Indonesia in an aging Dakota he affectionately referred to as "my bus", and at Rangoon he picked up U Nu. During the flight the two leaders discussed the forthcoming conference, and it was over lunch that the question of inviting Israel was dealt with. Preliminary meetings had already revealed that there was definite opposition to Israel's presence.

Nevertheless, because of the close "socialist" links established between Israel and Burma, U Nu told Mr. Nehru that if Israel, a country in Asia, were not invited to an Afro-Asian conference, then Burma might not attend. Mr. Nehru agreed that Israel ought perhaps to be invited, but pointed out that if she were present the Arab states would stay away, which would mean that almost the whole of West Asia would be absent. The conference would then become so unrepresentative that India would have to reconsider whether her own attendance would be worthwhile. After this display of pressure and counter-pressure U Nu was aware that even though Burma was one of the sponsors of the conference there was no possibility of Israel being invited just on Burma's say so.

There were differences of opinion on extending invitations to only two countries, China and Israel. After a preliminary discussion[3] the matter of an invitation to Israel was temporarily dropped because there was no general agreement. Burma and Ceylon were in favour of inviting Israel; Pakistan and Indonesia were

[2]Information on this episode was provided by a member of Mr. Nehru's party who wished to remain anonymous.

[3]Details of the closed sessions were obtained from a variety of official, anonymous sources.

opposed; India said that on the basis of the geographic principle Israel should be invited, but that India "was not prepared to face the contingency" of the Arabs not attending because of Israel.

In the final discussion on the subject Indonesia reiterated her objection to Israel's presence while Burma, notably subdued, said she had no objection. Ceylon proposed that the Arabs should be approached and reasoned with, but Indonesia said this was pointless since their view was known and the Arab League had recently issued a warning that an invitation to Israel would be considered an unfriendly act. Pakistan pointed out that the Arabs were still legally at war with Israel because they were only bound by a cease-fire, and then repeated the Indian argument that inviting Israel would jeopardise the success of the conference since the Arabs would stay away. Summing up, Mr. Nehru argued that though such an invitation might be justified he did not think the matter should be pressed against the wishes of the Arab countries. Burma agreed with this view, and it was so decided.

Two points are noteworthy in this discussion. After his mid-air conversation with Mr. Nehru, U Nu did not repeat his threat of staying away in support of Israel, though he did make such a threat when there was talk of Formosa being invited; clearly the Indian counter-threat had given him pause. With Burma, Israel's Asian friend, lukewarm in her advocacy, Israel's chances of admission were slight indeed. It could be argued that the five Prime Ministers did not decide this question on the merits of the case but, as certain Burmese newspapers said, had let themselves be blackmailed by the Muslim bloc led by Pakistan. This is unfair to Pakistan which had used the same argument as India, that Israel's presence would wreck the conference. The Arabs, in fact, did impose a veto and they did so because Israel was an alien in their midst. At Bogor the leaders of South and South-East Asia accepted the validity of this Arab feeling.

The Israeli press tried to explain away this setback and in the process made a most significant confession. As the *Haaretz* newspaper put it, the non-invitation to the Bandung Conference was hardly a loss because discussions at that meeting would be vague. The only well-defined subjects would be "colonialism, racialism and national sovereignty" which were not of great importance to Israel. These subjects were, of course, of paramount importance to the Afro-Asians.

The discussion of the Palestine problem at the Bandung Conference will be described at some length[4] because this was the only official meeting of Afro-Asian (or Non-Aligned) governments at which the heads of delegations gave their views on the substance of this question; at all subsequent gatherings the leaders only dealt with it in cursory fashion when they discussed the wording of the final communiqués.

The discussion began with the presentation of two draft resolutions, one by Afghanistan and the other by the Pakistan representative, Prime Minister Muhammad Ali. The final text adopted was almost identical with that of the Afghan draft; the Pakistan proposal in its original form asked only for the implementation of the U.N. resolution on the Palestine "refugees". Both delegations supported their resolutions with brief but vigorous speeches.

The main presentation of the Palestine case was made by a Palestinian, Mr. Ahmad Shukairy, who had been included as a member of the Syrian delegation. Happily Mr. Shukairy, on this occasion, restrained his natural tendency towards bombast and made his point with incisive effectiveness.

He began by asking, "What is the nature of the problem? Is it a boundary dispute? Is it a dispute between two States? Is it a conflict between two conflicting ideologies? Certainly not. The problem involves a people and their homeland...It is the national existence of a people that is at stake...the people of Palestine have been subjected to a process of extinction as a nation...This is not a matter of a change of regime, or a change of government, or a coup d'etat. This is a matter of the displacement of a people...The Arabs of Palestine are entitled to the

---

[4]References to, and quotations from, the discussion on Palestine are taken from the verbatim text, prepared by the Conference secretariat and circulated privately.

full exercise of self-determination in their homeland." Referring to the right of the Palestinian "refugees" to return home, Mr. Shukairy said that he did not base his case on the U.N. resolution because this was an inherent right: "the United Nations does not restore this right: it only recognises this right." He then went on to make the point that, at that moment, Israel owned by law only six per cent of the land area under its control and commented, "I know that some of you are amazed by this statement; I see it in your faces." And he then made the further statistical point that "the Arab people of Palestine have been reduced, during a period of only 30 years from 94 per cent of the population to 10 per cent." "Israel, "he went on, "does not belong to Asia. Israel does not belong to Africa" because, he asserted, it was produced by Zionism which is an imperialist movement created in Europe. Mr. Shukairy concluded: "No student, no scholar of history can point out in any period so unique a tragedy of a whole people thrown out of their land and compelled to live in camps as refugees."

The Iraqi delegate (Dr. Fadhel Jamali) made the usual reiterative speech but the Lebanese representative (Dr. Charles Malik) gave a warning, to become familiar at other conferences, that the Arabs would not feel a real part of the Conference and would be estranged "from the general Afro-Asian community" if a forthright resolution were not passed.

In view of subsequent developments the speech by the Iranian delegate (Dr. Ali Amini) was surprisingly firm: "what has been done in Palestine is not only tantamount to colonialism but is worse" because the Palestinians had been "rooted out" of their territory.

This was followed by three very brief interventions from Turkey, Jordan and Egypt. At Bandung Egypt was represented by Colonel Abdel Nasser, still wearing his officer's uniform. His statement, and this was the sum total of his remarks on Palestine, was limited to two procedural sentences: "Mr. Chairman, I agree with the Delegation of Jordan regarding the amendment of the Resolution made by Pakistan. There is no difference between the Afghanistan resolution and the Pakistan proposal and I support the Afghanistan proposal."

Mr. Nehru spoke next and in his speech, after referring to "the tremendous tragedy" of Palestine, he asked, over and over again, "what can we do about it? How can we help, apart from expressing our views and moral sympathy?" To which he made the bleak answers, ". . . the Conference cannot do anything about it. . . I have no suggestion to offer"; he made no reference to U.N. resolutions as offering any solution. In his usual discursive, rambling fashion Mr. Nehru raised the question of the forces that lay behind Zionism, which "it may be assumed is an aggressive movement. . . Surely no one is going to say that Zionist imperialism is strong enough, powerful enough to shake the world, in spite of everybody?. . . What then is behind it? Who is behind it? We do not give enough consideration to this aspect of the question. Zionism may sometimes be strong, aggressive as it often is, but surely it is not strong enough to carry on this aggressive attitude for these long years. Therefore we should understand the forces behind the movement. I do not indicate them". Having said that, he then added, "Obviously it becomes a matter of power politics, a matter which concerns the Big Powers whether they be within the United Nations or outside. . . It is much more than a local situation."

Eighteen months later a specific, if partial, answer was provided to Mr. Nehru's question, "What is behind Zionism?" when Britain and France colluded with Israel in the attack on Egypt.

U Nu, speaking for Burma, gave his pessimistic answer to Mr. Nehru's first question, "What to do about Palestine?" He wondered whether "where the mighty nations failed the Asians and Africans who are weak both militarily as well as in the economic sense can succeed." America, Britain and Russia were silent on the non-implementation of the United Nations resolution calling for the return of the Palestinians to their homes "so I doubt very much that where these mighty nations have failed we can succeed." Accordingly, he asked the Conference to limit itself to a compromise resolution which would not "force us to do what is really beyond our capacity" because Burma had "not only diplomatic relations with the Jews but also so many economic, cultural and political ties with the Jews, just as much as we have friendly ties with the Arabs." He proposed a "compromise" resolution that called for "direct negotia-tions."

Mr. Zorlu of Turkey took U Nu sharply to task for his defeatist suggestion that "the moral force behind this committee was not sufficient to lend support to the proposal. This is not entirely true...the moral force and the potential that we represent cannot be lightly minimised."

At this point the discussion became a debate between the Arab delegations and Mr. Nehru. In the course of his remarks the Indian Prime Minister had referred, in passing, to the five million Jews killed in Europe during World War II. He had also expressed surprise that Mr. Shukairy should have said that a negotiated settlement was not possible. He argued that "some time or other, whether you are enemies or whether you have fought a war, there must be negotiations. There is always some kind of settlement...After all, one can settle things either by compulsion, that is by pressure, or by negotiation."

The initial Arab response was made by Dr. Malik who said that the story of the Jewish massacre was just "Zionist propa-ganda". So also was the claim that the Arabs were refusing to negotiate: they were quite prepared to negotiate on the basis of the U.N. resolutions.

Mr. Shukairy made a fuller reply to Mr. Nehru. He did not deny the fact of Jewish persecution: "I hate it", he said, "but the question is can persecution be cured by committing another flagrant injustice, by another persecution...by expelling a people from their homeland?" He went on to deny that there was any basis of negotiation with Israel on the three elements of the Palestine problem, "the problem of refugees, the territorial question and Jerusalem". Israel, he said, adamantly refused the repatriation of a single "refugee"; it rejected the interna-tionalisation of Jerusalem; and as regards territory, it said "what we gained by war we will give up only by war." The Arabs, he concluded, were asking the conference to reaffirm the ina-lienable rights of self-determination and repatriation and of enjoyment of property.

Something of a breach had developed here between the Arabs and the Indian delegation, which the Secretary-General of the

Arab League later ascribed to an Arab "misunderstanding".[5]
Later that evening a group of Arab leaders called on Mr. Nehru
and the misunderstanding was quickly cleared up. In the next
morning's session Mr. Nehru explained exactly what he had
meant. His reference to Jewish persecution "was of course no
justification for the Jews coming to Palestine...Because the
Jews were persecuted in certain countries, it does not mean that
they should persecute others...in spite of the sympathy that
was felt for the Jews no one wanted them in any other country
and so they were automatically pushed out." On the need for
a negotiated settlement, he stood his ground because, as he said,
he had been "trained under Mahatma Gandhi...always to be
ready to talk to the enemy."

At this morning session the drafting committee produced the
formulation on Palestine that forms part of the final communiqué. It says: "In view of the existing tension in the Middle East,
caused by the situation in Palestine and of the danger of that
tension to world peace, the Asian-African Conference declared
its support of the rights of the Arab people of Palestine and called
for the implementation of the United Nations resolutions on
Palestine and the achievement of the peaceful settlement of the
Palestine question." In this the only change from the original
Afghan proposal is the final reference to the U.N. To this,
in a brief interjection, Mr. Chou En-Lai wished to add the words
"under the conditions of excluding intervention by outside
forces" because foreign intervention was the root cause of the
trouble over Formosa as over Palestine; "we are suffering from
the same cause as the Arab countries", the Chinese delegate
said. Having made his point, he did not press for its acceptance.
Burma suggested two changes to give priority to peaceful negotiations over the implementation of U.N. resolutions, which
certainly would have been more acceptable to the Israelis,
but having made his point, U Nu also did not press for acceptance.

Two points may be made on the questions raised by Mr.
Nehru. When he argued that there had to be either war or a

---

[5] A.K. Hassouna: *Report on the Bandung Conference.*

negotiated settlement he was presenting a false set of alternatives because twenty years of Arab practice has shown that there can be a state of no war, no peace, no negotiation. Also he seemed to see Zionism as a movement that was used by the Great Powers, while, as we have seen, it is more accurate to see Zionism and the Great Powers as forces that cooperate and that use each other.

There are several points of interest concerning the discussions on Palestine at the Bandung Conference—apart from the fact that, fifteen years later, the debate on whether or not to negotiate a settlement still has contemporary relevance. Thus, there were comparatively few speakers and not even all the Arab states took part, with Tunisia, Yemen and the Sudan maintaining silence, and Egypt and Saudi Arabia limiting themselves to brief procedural remarks. And of the non-Muslim countries only India and China, briefly, spoke in support of the Arab viewpoint. Summing up the outcome of the discussion, the Egyptian delegate, Colonel Nasser, on his way home, remarked, "It is just a resolution. However, it has some moral value".[6]

The real importance of Bandung, however, was in what it began rather than what it did. It was at Bandung that East Asia, Asia, South-East Asia and West Asia got to know each other for the first time. Partly because of inert Arab diplomacy countries like Cambodia and Laos had had little chance of learning, at first hand, the Arab case on Palestine, but this situation was somewhat remedied at Bandung. The bridges built at Bandung between the two halves of the Asian continent were of the greatest importance, especially those between China and the Arab states. And along with this coming-together came Asia's first, and definitive, refusal to accept Israel as part of Asia, or of Afro-Asia. At Bandung the Afro-Asians took their stand alongside the Palestinians and thereafter Israel had no chance of ever being included in any of their official or unofficial gatherings. The first, rather mildly worded resolution at Bandung could only become more and more denunciatory at subsequent conferences; and so it was.

[6] *The Hindu*, Madras, 28.4.1955.

Israel and the Israeli press put a correct estimate on the adverse importance to them of the Bandung Conference. Moshe Sharett, the then Israeli Prime Minister, sent a message to the Conference Chairman, the Indonesian Premier, expressing "astonishment" and "regret" that the Conference had discussed Israel while she had been excluded.[7] The Israeli newspapers showed much interest in Bandung and only a few of them continued to take the line that since the main problem on the Conference agenda was confrontation with the West which did not concern Israel directly, Israel's non-invitation was not to be regretted. Most newspapers expressed concern in varied ways: it had been proven that socialism was not enough of a basis for relations with Afro-Asia; "our isolation is still total"; the "utter political and psychological isolation of Israel" had been demonstrated; "our pro-Western school of thought is wrong" and, perhaps most significantly, "Israel appears as a foreign body in the Middle East".[8]

After Bandung the countries of Afro-Asia have never again met in a Summit Conference, nor are they ever likely to. Two tortuous preparatory meetings, at Foreign Minister level, were held in Algiers in June and October 1965, which could only agree on indefinite postponement. The reaction of the Israeli press to this failure is clearly indicative of the estrangement of Israel from the Afro-Asian group. Satisfaction was expressed that the Afro-Asians were not going to meet again and that things were very different now from what they had been at Bandung. One newspaper hailed "the decline and disintegration of the Afro-Asian World"[9] and another referred, with gratification, to "the social, economic and military weakness that lies behind the vigorous speeches of most Afro-Asian leaders".[10] In short, after ten years, Israeli commentators accepted the assumption that what was bad for Afro-Asia was good for Israel.

By this time the functions of the geographical Afro-Asian group

[7] *The Statesman*, Calcutta, 24.4.1955.
[8] Israeli press review in *The Jerusalem Post*, April 24 to 28 1955 and *Zmamim*, 22.4.1955.
[9] *The Jerusalem Post*, 5.11.1965.
[10] *Haaretz*, Tel Aviv, 5.11.1965.

had been taken over by a new political grouping of countries brought together by a common allegiance to the policy of non-alignment. The two groups very largely overlapped, for while not all Afro-Asians were non-aligned almost all the non-aligned were Afro-Asians: when the first Summit Conference of twenty five non-aligned states was held in Belgrade September 1961, only two of them, Yugoslavia and Cuba, were not from Afro-Asia.

There was, of course, no question of Israel being invited to Belgrade as a non-aligned country because even though formally she was not a member of a bloc or a pact her basic allegiance with the West was apparent by 1965. Her attempts to enter NATO were not generally known but, on the other hand, her collusion with Britain and France in 1956 was ample proof that Israel was not a part of the ex-colonial Third World.

After the Belgrade Conference the Israeli press expressed far more satisfaction than it did after Bandung and there was some justification for this feeling. At the time of the Conference the problems that held the world's attention were many and serious —Russia's resumption of atomic testing, acute tension in Berlin where the infamous wall had just been erected, the aftermath of the French attack on Bizerte, Algeria and Angola and the struggle for power in the Congo. By contrast the Palestine problem, which was in one of its quiescent periods, seemed to have become one of that group of insoluble problems (like Kashmir) which the world had simply learned to live with.

Consequently, with the exception of Guinea, only the Arab representatives, excluding Algeria, mentioned Israel and Palestine in their general statements. The only discussion on the issue took place in the committee drafting the Conference communiqué, and it went along familiar lines. The Arab delegates suggested a strongly-worded formula which Burma and to a lesser extent Yugoslavia tried to soften; even India, represented by Krishna Menon, supported the soft line. However, when the heads of delegations came to put their finishing touches to the draft, President Tito and Mr. Nehru moved away from the Burmese position to some extent. The Israeli press, while thanking U Nu for his support, expressed disappointment at the attitudes of the Presidents of Yugoslavia, Guinea and Mali and of Mr. Nehru.

The paragraph on Palestine in the Belgrade declaration was just a bit stronger than that of Bandung whereas, after the Suez collusion, it might have been expected that it would be firmly critical of Israel. The text read: "The participants in the Conference condemn the imperialist policies pursued in the Middle East, and declare their support for the full restoration of all the rights of the Arab people of Palestine in conformity with the Charter and resolutions of the United Nations."[11]

Comparing this with the Bandung resolution we see that the reference to a "peaceful settlement" was eliminated and there was now mention of "the *full* restoration of *all* the rights" of the Palestinians. More significant was the placing of the Palestine issue within the context of "imperialist policies" in the Middle East because it was this line of thought that has come increasingly to the fore in subsequent conferences.

It was very much in evidence in the communiqué of the Second Non-Aligned Conference held in Cairo in October 1964, with the result that this communiqué was described by Israeli Foreign Ministry experts as "one of the worst resolutions" ever passed on the Palestine problem.[12] In the intervening four years between the Non-Aligned Summits the Third World had become decidedly more militant in mood and more aware of the threat of neo-colonialism, a tendency that continues down to the present. For this reason, and also because the Second Conference was held in an Arab capital, it was inevitable that the reference to Palestine would be more sharply worded. But because the membership had been increased, unwisely, from twenty-five at Belgrade to forty-seven at Cairo, there were more numerous objections to the hardening attitude on Palestine. Thus in the drafting committee, eight countries made reservations on the wording of the draft communiqué: these were Ceylon, Liberia, Chad, Togo, Nigeria, Tanzania, Nepal and Burma (the Israeli

[11]Yugoslav Government: *The Conference of Heads of State or Government of Non-Aligned Countries*, Belgrade, 1961, p. 258.
[12]*The Jerusalem Post*, 12.10.1964.

press reported that there were eleven such countries, adding Cambodia, Ethiopia and Senegal). But at the concluding session all of them, except for Nepal and Burma, publicly withdrew their reservations amid acclamation, which prompted the Israeli press to say that Israel's friends followed a two-faced policy. The Second Non-Aligned Conference stated that it "condemns the imperialistic policy pursued in the Middle East and, in conformity with the United Nations Charter, resolves:

"1. To endorse the full restoration of all the rights of the Palestinian Arab people to their homeland and their inalienable right to self-determination.

"2. To declare its full support to the Arab people of Palestine in their struggle for liberation from colonialism and racism".

This represents by far the most pro-Palestinian and anti-Israeli position adopted by the Afro-Asian Non-Aligned countries. The first operative clause concedes the right to repatriation and the right to self-determination for which Mr. Shukairy had asked nine years earlier in Bandung; and the second clause is noteworthy for its designation of the Palestinian struggle as being one of "liberation" and for its bracketing of Zionism with "colonialism": "liberation" and "colonialism" are powerfully evocative words for Afro-Asians, though in opposite senses. In 1964, the Palestine question was still as quiescent as it had been in 1961; there was no special particular reason why the Cairo resolution should have been so much stronger than that of Belgrade except that this change represented a growing ground swell of opposition to the Zionist state which had been gathering momentum over the years.

By the time the Non-Aligned countries held their Third Summit Conference in Lusaka in September 1970, there was one very special reason why the Afro-Asians should be critical of Israel: this was Israel's continued occupation of Arab territory seized during the fighting in June 1967. Consequently, the Lusaka resolution is longer and more openly condemnatory than anything adopted hitherto.

A fairly mild resolution on the Palestine problem was introduced by Ethiopia in the political committee where the deputy heads of delegations—usually Foreign Ministers—represented

their countries. This was soon overtaken by a far stronger formula presented by Iraq. After long debate in committee this
resolution was actually adopted by the political committee
where, according to the Israeli press, only twenty six delegations
out of the sixty two present, took a "moderate", that is pro-
Israeli stand.[13] This was a remarkable decision because, for the first
time, the Afro-Asian Non-Aligned countries meeting at Foreign
Minister level, agreed to recommend the application of sanctions
against Israel if she continued to refuse to evacuate occupied
Arab territory. Because of a delay in the issuance of the final
communiqué, the news was sent round the world that the Lusaka
Conference had agreed to sanctions. However, when the heads
of delegations met to consider the communiqué, as recommended
to them by the political committee, there was the general feeling,
even among the pro-Arab delegations, that the call for sanctions
went too far, in terms of what the Non-Aligned countries could
get the rest of the world to accept and to implement. The
recommendation was, accordingly, changed from "sanctions"
to "adequate measures", a considerably weaker recommendation but not as much as may be thought when read in the context
of the entire resolution; which is also noteworthy for the fact
that for the first time "Israel" as such is mentioned by name
as being the subject, or rather the target, of the resolution.

The text of the Lusaka resolution as finally approved is as
follows (with the original wording passed by the political committee in brackets):

"The Heads of State or Government of the Non-Aligned
countries re-affirm previous resolutions adopted by the non-
aligned countries which have drawn attention to the dangerous
situation in the Middle East, as well as to the fact that continued
Israeli occupation of the territories of three non-aligned countries constitutes a violation of United Nations principles, a
challenge to the aims of non-alignment and a grave (serious)
threat to peace; consider it impermissible for Israel to keep
the territory of three sovereign and non-aligned countries under
occupation and continually to pursue the policy of the flagrant

[13] The Jerusalem Post, 17.9.1970.

use of force and to use the occupation of these territories as a means of pressure for imposing solutions; reiterate the inadmissibility of the acquisition of territory by force and call for the immediate withdrawal of Israel from all Arab territory occupied after 5th June 1967; declare that full respect for the inalienable rights of the Arab people of Palestine is a pre-requisite to peace in the Middle East; call for the full restoration of the rights of the Arab people of Palestine in (to) their usurped homeland, and reaffirm their support in their struggle for national liberation against colonialism and racism; reiterate the necessity of abiding by and implementing U.N. resolutions adopted in this regard; express their support to the efforts of the Special Representative of the Secretary-General of the United Nations to implement the Security Council resolution of the 22nd November, 1967; deplore Israel's obstruction of these efforts aimed at establishing peace based on justice and, in particular, its interruption of the talks undertaken by the U.N. Special Representative in carrying out the task entrusted to him by the Security Council resolution; recommend to the United Nations that it take adequate measures against Israel (recommend the application of sanctions under Chapter VIII of the United Nations Charter against Israel) if it persists in disregarding efforts to establish peace based on justice and in refusing to evacuate occupied territory in accordance with the Security Council resolution."

This long, detailed and strongly condemnatory resolution is a far cry indeed from the short, vague and anodyne wording that emerged from Bandung: in fifteen years the Afro-Asian governments, whatever their reservations, could not but take a public stand against Israel.

Just how fundamental this Afro-Asian opposition to the Zionist state is becomes evident when we note one small but most important change made in the wording of the resolution by the heads of state. The Foreign Ministers had agreed to "call for the full restoration of the rights of the Arab people of Palestine *to* their usurped homeland" but the heads of state altered one word which makes it read "the full restoration of the rights of the Arab people of Palestine *in* their usurped homeland". This means much more than the right to return: it means that the Afro-Asian heads of state accept that there is a national, "inalienable" bond between the people of Palestine and the territory of Palestine and this recognition in turn means a movement towards the concept that the Zionist state erected on that territory must be replaced by, or dissolved into, a Palestinian national entity. Afro-Asian rejection of Israel can go no further.

The four conferences dealt with were official governmental gatherings. Unofficial meetings of the various Afro-Asian organisations were strongly critical of Israel many years earlier than the official ones. Thus the forty eight countries represented at the First Conference for Afro-Asian Solidarity stated, in Cairo on January 1, 1958, that "the State of Israel is an imperialist base that threatens the progress and security of the Middle East" and the Conference declared that it supported "the rights of the Arabs of Palestine to return to their homeland". In succeeding years gatherings of Afro-Asian journalists, jurists, youth organisations and women roundly condemned Israel in uncompromising terms at conferences held in Guinea, Indonesia, Algeria, Tanzania and Ghana.

In January 1966, the Afro-Asian Solidarity movement widened into the movement for the solidarity of the peoples of the three continents, South America being added. The first Tricontinental Conference, held in Cuba, resolved that:

"1. The Conference regards Israel as being essentially imperialist in its nature, aggressive and expansionist in its aims, racialist in its composition and Fascist in its ways and means.

"2. The Conference regards Israel, the State of the Settler, as a base of imperialism and an instrument in the service of colonialist aggression, penetration and economic, political and cultural infiltration on the Three Continents.

"3. The Conference regards the right of the Palestinians to liberate their homeland as a natural extension of their inalienable right to legitimate self-defense."

Not much, in the way of condemnation of Israel, could be added to these angry, forthright statements.

The majority of the governments of Afro-Asia are, presently, right wing or middle-of-the-road; the Afro-Asian Solidarity

Movement is frankly leftist. But whether their government is a traditional monarchy, a moderate republic or an agitational "progressive" organisation, the Afro-Asians seem to have at least two things in common—they are nationalistic and they are anti-Israeli, and the two feelings seem to go together, and to an increasing degree. Because, the closer the nationalistic Afro-Asians draw together, the more they extrude the Zionist state. And this has been true even of the countries in Asia and Africa to which Israel has shown special friendliness, such as Burma and Turkey and Ghana.

Propinquity and withdrawal

A definite pattern is discernible in Israel's relations with some of the Afro-Asian states: the greater the friendship for them displayed by Israel, the less friendly to Israel do these countries eventually become, as they develop in confidence and self-reliance. To judge by what has happened over and over again in the Third World, for a country with independent standards of judgement to know Israel well is to draw back from her.

(And, the same rule seems to apply to individuals in their relations with Israel: witness the fact that the United Nations Mediator Count Folke Bernadotte and the United Nations Chiefs of Staff, Generals Bennike, Burns and Von Horn, who had a great deal to do with Israel, all ended by feeling antagonistic towards her.[14] It has become almost axiomatic that officers of the United Nations Observer Corps, however friendly they are to Israel when they arrive, and they usually are, are anti-Israel at the end of their tours of duty.[15]

What is under examination here is not the usual ups-and-downs that are a normal part of relations between governments, as between individuals, but the process we are referring to begins with an initial period of very busy and extremely cordial rela-

[14]For Count Bernadotte see M.E. Jansen, *The United States and the Palestinian People*, Beirut 1970, Chapter III; General E.L.M. Burns, *Between Arab and Israeli*, London 1962, Beirut 1968; and General Carl Von Horn, *Soldiering For Peace*, London 1966, record their authors' experiences.
[15]Von Horn, *op. cit.*, p. 283.

tions between Israel and a second country. Such friendly relations last for anything between five and eight years; then there comes a drawing-back by the Afro-Asian government. This rapidly gains momentum, so that ten or twelve years after Israel made her advances towards the Afro-Asian country, the relationship is nothing more than diplomatically correct; and, as far as can be observed, the connection remains at this purely formal level even though there is no open breach.

One study of Israel's relations with the developing countries makes mention of the "closing down prematurely of joint ventures in Burma, Ghana and Tanzania",[16] which is really a reference to the withdrawal of friendship by three countries that Israel wooed with particular ardour.

As we have seen earlier the change in Burma's attitude was signalled in 1961 when U Nu, in his last year of office, paid a visit to Cairo. The change in attitude towards Israel became increasingly evident after 1962 when the military regime of General Ne Win came to power: the flow of visitors and trainees dwindled to a trickle and eventually halted altogether; and what was particularly galling to the Israelis was that their joint ventures in Burma were nationalised as part of the programme called "the Burmese Way to Socialism".

The swooping dip in Burmese-Israeli relations is clearly indicated in their trade figures: in 1964 Israeli imports from Burma were valued at $700,000; by 1967 they had fallen to $1,000 and Israeli exports to Burma which stood at $1.4 million in 1964 had fallen to $4,000 in 1967.

The withdrawal of Turkey was more gradual than that of Burma. After the 1956 Suez aggression, Turkey withdrew the Minister from her Legation in Israel and since then has never been represented by anything but a chargé d'affaires, sometimes of junior rank. In January 1965 the Turkish government let it be known that it was going to loosen its ties with Israel. The 1967 fighting gave Turkey the occasion to take another step away from Israel and in 1969 Turkey unilaterally denounced her trade agreement with Israel. The volume of trade between

---

[16]L. Laufer: *Israel and the Developing Countries*, New York 1967, pp. 143-144.

them was, in any case, dwindling: Israeli imports of $ 5 million in 1966 had dropped to $ 2.3 in 1968 and exports of $ 8.2 million fell to $ 3.6 in the same period.

The first shock of rejection of Israel by Africa came when Ghana, Guinea and Mali joined with the U.A.R., Algeria and Morocco in the Casablanca Conference of 1961 to issue a communiqué very critical of Israel. Israel was especially hurt at the conduct of Ghana and Guinea which she had been courting assiduously—in fact, Ghana represented Israel's break-through point in Africa as much as Burma had in Asia. Israel's relations with Mali and Guinea never recovered from this initial rebuff and those with Ghana went into a steady decline. With the then President N'Krumah's strong emphasis on Africanism it was inevitable that Ghana would terminate her joint ventures with Israel, and this in fact happened when Ghana took over the Israeli share in a shipping line and a construction company.

Much the same thing has happened in Tanzania where early enthusiasm and joint ventures have given way to nationalisation and a bitterly hostile attitude, especially after 1967.

That it is not merely Israeli expansionism and occupation of Arab territory that is responsible for the process of withdrawal is shown by the case of Ceylon. Even though Israel has maintained a legation in Colombo, the Ceylonese government has always kept a certain distance between itself and Israel: in 1960 it withdrew the accreditation of its non-resident Minister to Israel. Then in 1970, three years after the 1967 battle, a new government in Ceylon, under Mrs. S. Bandaranaike, broke off all diplomatic relations with Israel in what was almost its first official act after taking office. Why so?

The explanation is to be found in the fact that this government was more leftist or radical and less pro-Western than its predecessor. The same reasons operated in Burma and in Guinea. And they are operating today to influence the Middle East policy of the Indian Prime Minister, Mrs. Indira Gandhi, a policy which is more frankly anti-Israel than was that of her father, Mr. Nehru. India's interests in the Middle East have not changed in the last five years, nor have the Arab states increased their leverage on India (rather the opposite) and yet India's policy

has become more antipathetic to the Zionist state; and much of
this change had come before June 1967. The explanation is to
be found in the increasing radicalisation of Indian political
thought and feeling. Nowadays to be an Afro-Asian radical or
leftist implies, automatically, an anti-Israel position.

In Burma what also worked against the Israeli link was a
growth of indigenous feeling—it was "Burmese" socialism that
General Ne Win was trying to introduce; just as it was "African"
socialism that brought about the "premature" closing down of
the Israeli joint ventures in Ghana and Tanzania.

In all these cases—Burma, Guinea, Ghana, Tanzania and
Ceylon—what we also see impinging on the Israeli connection
is a growth in local self-confidence. That this increase in a
desirable quantity should assume an anti-Israel aspect is due
to the very effusiveness with which Israel proffers her aid. Over-
anxious to find openings in a generally aloof or hostile Afro-Asia,
Israel has swarmed in with a multiplicity of aid projects at the
first opportunity. This has tended to give the impression to the
local people that they are being taken over by foreigners, telling
them what to do and how to run their own country. And then
such Israeli aid has also given an erroneous impression to the
Israeli public who come to feel that their aid is the main, or sole,
prop for certain Afro-Asian countries—and this too is resented
by the Afro-Asian recipient governments when they come to
hear of it.[17] But the Israelis need to make overmuch of their
assistance, in fact and in their propaganda, because this aid
is not based on calculations of mutual benefit or feelings of philanthropy but on the politico-psychological necessity of escaping
from isolation.

Since the United States is the major representative of what is
called "the West" to be anti-Western is to be anti-American:
and to be anti-American is to be anti-Israel since America is the
sponsor and supporter of Israel. Even allowing for the fallacy
of *post hoc ergo propter hoc* there seems to be a correlation between
the two antipathies. There can be no other explanation for the
following recurrent phenomenon: a country friendly to the

[17]M.E. Kreinin: *Israel and Africa*, New York 1964, p. 178.

United States becomes hostile and soon after also takes a hostile attitude towards Israel, having earlier been friendly with the Zionist state. This has happened with Turkey, the Philippines and Cambodia, where the anti-American-cum-anti-Israel change-over was particularly well defined. It can safely be predicted that the same thing will happen in Japan where signs of the linked withdrawal process are already apparent.

Thus it is propinquity with Israel, with the essential nature of the Zionist state, that produces the reaction of withdrawal in Afro-Asian states motivated by indigenous nationalism and by growing self-reliance and self-confidence. The opposite is also true. Analysis of the voting record in the United Nations reveals clearly that Israel's best friends in Asia and Africa and Latin America are, in the vast majority, the small, the weak, the helpless and those that are tied economically and militarily to powers outside of Afro-Asia.

Confirmation by the United Nations voting record

We have seen how Afro-Asian and Non-Aligned conferences, official and unofficial, gradually hardened their stand against Israel. It may be argued that the final communiqués of these conferences did not represent the actual feeling or policy of each individual government towards the Palestine problem because member-states could be affected by the general atmosphere of a conference and also by the need to maintain a consensus, since no votes are cast at such meetings. Hence the only way in which a country could register its actual opinion, negatively, was by entering reservations privately which, as we have also seen, some countries occasionally did on the clause concerning Israel.

For these reasons the voting record of the United Nations General Assembly probably represents a more clear and honest picture of the real policy of the Afro-Asian states towards Israel and the Palestine problem. In the roll-call votes governments take up public positions, and in New York the Afro-Asians can do so coolly and deliberately for there they are in a world setting, unaffected by the local scene or by regional or continental enthusiasms.

Therefore the votes of the Afro-Asian states at the United Nations on the various issues arising from the Palestine problem present us with a clear and accurate scale on which to measure the exact degree of *public* support they give to, or withhold from, the Arab states or Israel. This is particularly true with respect to the votes cast in the General Assembly subsequent to the Middle East conflict in June 1967, and particularly just after the fighting when feelings were running high and both Arabs and Israelis were urging their friends to stand up and be counted.

In this Special Session of the General Assembly convened to deal with the results of the June battle, three resolutions of importance were voted on. There was the Non-Aligned or Afro-Asian resolution which called for the unconditional withdrawal of Israeli forces from Arab territory occupied during the battle. This was supported by the Arab countries. Then there was its direct competitor, the draft put forward by the Latin American countries (excluding Cuba) which linked Israeli troop withdrawal to a cessation of the state of belligerency existing between the Arab states and Israel and which, therefore, was favourable to the Israeli viewpoint. And finally there was the resolution on Jerusalem which declared invalid Israel's unilateral annexation of the Jordanian sector of the city.

The votes on these three resolutions, when put together, give us a three-part scale of pro-Arab, intermediate and pro-Israeli positions. The pro-Arab and pro-Israeli groups can further be subdivided into "completely" and "strongly" pro-Arab and "strongly" and "very strongly" pro-Israel. (The Arab states are not included in this classification).

In the 1968 regular Session of the General Assembly three resolutions of substance once again came to the vote. The first was an innocuous draft from the United States which sought an extension of the mandate of the United Nations Relief and Works Agency for Palestine Refugees. This was passed by a vote of 101 in favour to none against with one abstention, Israel. A slightly more strongly worded resolution with a reference to persons "at present displaced...as a result of the June 1967 hostilities" went through by a vote of 88 to none. No conclusions can be drawn from these two votes despite the unusually large number of abstentions, absentees or non-participants in the latter vote.

More revealing was the vote on a six-power resolution, the operative clause of which called upon Israel to accept without delay the return of the 1967 "refugees". On this draft the vote was 91 in favour, one against, Israel, and nine abstentions, Botswana, Colombia, Dahomey, Dominican Republic, Jamaica, Ruanda, Togo, Uruguay and Venezuela.

The first really controversial resolution was one put forward by five powers—Afghanistan, Indonesia, Malaysia, Pakistan and Somalia—which did not come to a vote in the Assembly because it failed to receive the required two-thirds majority in committee, which voted 44 in favour, 42 against with 22 abstentions. This draft called for the appointment of a custodian "to protect and administer Arab property in Israel".

The second controversial resolution with a revealing voting pattern demanded "respect for and implementation of human rights in occupied territory". In no uncertain terms it deplored the violation of human rights and the disregard for fundamental freedoms in Israeli occupied territory, asked Israel to stop blowing up Arab homes and proposed that the United Nations should appoint a committee of inquiry composed of three member states to investigate conditions in the occupied territories. This particularly pro-Arab resolution was adopted by the Assembly, 55 votes in favour, 23 against and 41 abstentions.

These votes can also be broken down into the categories used in Table I.

A comparison of the tables for 1967 and 1968 (Tables I and II) shows a definite, even a decisive, shift of sympathy away from Israel towards the Arabs. Thus the 1967 voting totals of 44 pro-Arabs, 8 intermediate and 51 pro-Israelis become 55-17-25, respectively, in 1968, which means that Israel lost exactly half its votes. This radical change was due to two blocs shifting their votes: 11 European votes moved from the pro-Israeli to the Intermediate section and 12 Latin American votes likewise moved from the pro-Israeli section, with six of these becoming pro-Arab. It is significant that this change for the worse in

TABLE I – *Voting on the Three Resolutions Considered by the Special Session of the General Assembly—Summer 1967*

	PRO-ARAB VOTING			
	Completely	*Strongly*		TOTAL
ASIA	Afghanistan, Ceylon, Cyprus, India, Indonesia, Malaysia, Pakistan	Burma, Cambodia, Iran, Thailand, Turkey, Japan		13
AFRICA	Burundi, Congo (Brazzaville), Guinea, Mali, Mauritania, Sengal, Somalia, Tanzania, Togo, Uganda, Upper Volta, Zambia	Nigeria, Cameroun, Congo (Kinshasa), Sierra Leone		16
EUROPE	Russia, Yugoslavia, the eight countries of the Communist Bloc	Finland, France, Greece, Spain		14
LATIN AMERICA	—	Cuba		1
NORTH AMERICA	—	—		Nil
TOTAL				44

EUROPE	Sweden	1
THE AMERICAS		Nil
TOTAL		8

PRO-ISRAELI VOTING

	Very Strongly	*Strongly*	
ASIA	—	The Philippines	1
AFRICA	Central African Republic, Dahomey, Kenya, Liberia, Malawi, Ruanda, South Africa	Botswana, Ethiopia, Gabon, Gambia, Ghana, Lesotho, Madagascar	14
EUROPE	Iceland, Italy, Malta, Portugal	Austria, Belgium, Denmark, Ireland, Luxembourg, Netherlands, Norway, United Kingdom	12
LATIN AMERICA	Barbados, Bolivia, Colombia, Jamaica, Uruguay	Argentina, Brazil, Chile, Costa Rica, Dominican Republic, Ecuador, El Salvador, Guatemala, Guyana, Honduras, Mexico, Nicaragua, Panama, Paraguay, Peru, Trinidad and Tobago, Venezuela	22
NORTH AMERICA	The United States	Canada	2
TOTAL			51

TABLE II – *Voting on the Three Resolutions on Palestine Considered by the Regular Session of the General Assembly—1968*

PRO-ARAB VOTING

	Completely	Strongly	TOTAL
ASIA	Afghanistan, Ceylon, China (Formosa), India, Indonesia, Iran, Malaysia, Maldives, Pakistan	Burma, Cyprus, Japan, Nepal, Philippines, Singapore, Turkey, Thailand	17
AFRICA	Burundi, Congo (Brazzaville), Guinea, Mali, Mauritania, Senegal, Somalia	Cameroun, Central African Republic, Chad, Ghana, Ethiopia, Kenya, Nigeria, Niger, Uganda, Upper Volta, Tanzania	18
EUROPE	Yugoslavia, Russia, and seven countries of the Communist Bloc	Greece, Portugal, Rumania, Spain	13
LATIN AMERICA	Cuba	Chile, Honduras, Mexico, Peru, Trinidad and Tobago, Venezuela	7
NORTH AMERICA			Nil
TOTAL			55

		TOTAL
EUROPE	Austria, Belgium, Denmark, Finland, France, Iceland, Ireland, Italy, Luxembourg, Norway, Sweden, United Kingdom	12
LATIN AMERICA	Argentina, Barbados, Brazil, Uruguay	4
NORTH AMERICA	Canada	1
TOTAL		17

PRO-ISRAELI VOTING

	Very Strongly	*Strongly*	TOTAL
ASIA			Nil
AFRICA	Botswana, Dahomey, Togo, Ruanda	Equatorial Guinea, Gabon, Gambia, Ivory Goast, Lesotho, Liberia, Madagscar, Malawi, Mauritius, Swaziland	14
EUROPE			Nil
LATIN AMERICA	Colombia, Dominican Republic, Jamaica, Haiti	Bolivia, Ecuador, El Salvador, Nicaragua, Panama, Paraguay	10
NORTH AMERICA		United States	1
TOTAL			25

TABLE III – *Voting Records of United Nations Members on the Palestine Problem: Consistent Positions in 1967 and 1968*

PRO-ARAB VOTING

	Completely	*Strongly*	TOTAL
ASIA	Afghanistan, Ceylon, India, Indonesia, Malaysia, Pakistan	Burma, Cyprus, Japan, Thailand, Turkey	11
AFRICA	Burundi, Congo (Brazzaville), Guinea, Mali, Senegal, Somalia	Cameroun, Nigeria, Tanzania, Upper Volta	10
EUROPE	Russia, Yugoslavia and seven Communist Bloc countries	Greece, Rumania, Spain	12
LATIN AMERICA	—	Cuba	1
NORTH AMERICA	—		Nil
TOTAL			34

INTERMEDIATE VOTING

EUROPE	Sweden	

PRO-ISRAELI VOTING

	Very Strongly	*Strongly*	TOTAL
ASIA	—	—	Nil
AFRICA	—	Botswana, Gambia, Gabon, Lesotho, Dahomey, Liberia, Malawi, Madagascar, Ruanda	9
EUROPE	—	—	Nil
LATIN AMERICA	Colombia, Jamaica	Dominican Republic, Ecuador, El Salvador, Nicaragua, Panama, Paraguay	8
NORTH AMERICA	—	The United States	1

Israel's position in the voting owes little or nothing to the Afro-Asian group whose voting record remained strikingly consistent for these two years: in 1967 the figures were 29 pro-Arab, 7 intermediate and 15 pro-Israeli votes and in 1968, 35-0-14, respectively. The 1968 figure of 14 pro-Israeli votes is not, however, in fact, Afro-Asian but only African and out of the 15 pro-Israeli Afro-Asian votes in 1967 only one, the Philippines, came from Asia. Thus, in Asia, the continent on which Israel was brought into being, Israel has no solid base of support while in Africa Israel has a firm bloc of 13 or 14 staunch supporters.

If we superimpose the voting tables of these two years we can distinguish the persistent positions of United Nations members towards the Palestine problem.

Thus the consistent voting record at the United Nations in 1967 and 1968 was 34 pro-Arab, 1 intermediate and 18 pro-Israeli.

Three resolutions came to the vote in the 1969 General Assembly. Two of these concerned the continuation of the mandate of UNRWA and special assistance to the organisation; these were passed without a dissident vote. The really controversial resolution was an omnibus one which, perhaps unfortunately, combined references to humanitarian, human rights and strictly political issues. Thus its text made mention of the recognition "that the problem of the Palestinian Arab refugees has arisen from the denial of their inalienable rights under the Charter of the United Nations and the Universal Declaration of Human Rights", going on to state that their plight had been "aggravated by the reported acts of collective punishment, arbitrary detention, curfews...", it recalled earlier resolutions asking Israel "to accept the return of the 1967 refugees" and "reaffirmed the inalienable rights of the people of Palestine".

The voting on this resolution was of an unusual pattern—48 in favour, 22 against and 47 abstentions. Its all-inclusive nature probably lost it some votes but precisely because it was all-inclusive the votes for it and against it necessarily represented very firm policy positions either in complete support of the Arabs or in complete support of Israel.

Thus we reach the surprising, but factual, conclusion that on the Palestine issue, the Arabs have twice as many all-out supporters as does Israel.

A comparison of these various tables reveals that the continents most friendly to Israel were North America and Latin America, the latter being particularly important at the United Nations because of the number of its votes. Africa was almost exactly equally divided in its sympathies, while Europe, if anything, tended to favour the Arabs, especially after 1968. Indeed from the two last tables we note that while outside of the Communist Bloc, Yugoslavia was prepared to give full support to the Arab position there was not a single country in Europe that was ready to give equal support to Israel; and Europe is the mother-continent of Zionism. The least friendly continent to Israel, clearly and consistently, is Asia, the continent on which Israel was brought into existence by the votes of other continents.

At the United Nations where the democratic, if unrealistic, principle of "one nation, one vote" obtains it does not really matter, as far as the final result is concerned, which country votes on what side. But it should disturb Israel (and gratify the Arabs) that all the African—and most of the Latin American —states strongly supporting Israel are minuscule and unimportant. The Arabs have Nigeria and Tanzania on their side while Israel's four most staunch supporters—Malawi, Botswana, Lesotho and Swaziland—are utterly dependent on the racialist regime in South Africa (which as we shall see is one reason why they support Israel). Israel's largest African supporter is Madagascar, with a population of six million people: in Africa, too, Israel, the off-shore state, is supported by an island state as in Asia Israel has received the support of Singapore, the Philippines and Japan, all lying off the mainland. Among Israel's African friends are those with foreign military alliances and foreign military bases on their territory—Ethiopia, Madagascar, Chad, Gabon and the Ivory Coast.

Having established how the Afro-Asian countries, as well as those of other continents, took up *public* positions in the United Nations for or against the Arabs or Israelis, it now remains to try and discover why they should have adopted these positions.

Pro-Arab motivations

We will deal first with the African and Asian countries which supported the Arabs against Israel.

These countries may be divided into two broad groups, each with certain generalised motivations. The first is the "India-type" and India, of course, Ceylon, Burma, Malaysia, Cyprus and Nigeria all come under this heading. This type is nationalist liberal, non-aligned, pluralistic and secular. And, the second can be called the "China-type" and includes Communist China, which is the prototype of the group, along with such countries as Burundi, Congo (Brazzaville), Guinea, Tanzania and Cuba. These are the communist or "progressive" countries.

The India-type. The characteristics of the India-type were laid down many years ago by Mahatma Gandhi and Jawaharlal Nehru. Gandhi's feelings about Palestine included that of Asian solidarity. And, it is this feeling of Asian solidarity expressed so many years ago by Gandhi that motivates Afro-Asian leaders today, particularly because of the fact that the Palestinian people, to whose interests Gandhi gave primacy, have, after a 20 years' absence, reemerged as a main contestant in the struggle for Palestine. Because the Palestinian partisan groups have newly commanded the attention of the world the present generation of Afro-Asians, like other peoples elsewhere, have come to realise, as Gandhi did earlier, that the Palestinians are an Asian people resisting displacement by people from outside Asia. And the prognosis for Palestinian popularity is good because the more the Palestinians resist the greater will be their appeal to and the greater will be the response of Asian solidarity.

The feelings expressed by Nehru at Bandung are much stronger in Afro-Asia today as Israel's dependence on the former imperial powers and on the friends of these powers, especially the United States, has become increasingly clear. For if colonialism in Afro-Asia is dead, the fear of neo-colonialism is not. The anti-colonial experience of most of the Afro-Asian countries militates against Afro-Asian sympathy for Israel, particularly after June 1967. For the whole of Afro-Asia, with the single exception of Thailand, has experienced foreign occupation and Israel has become a foreign occupying power over large areas of Arab territory. Nor has Israel been a particularly gentle occupier: the mass arrests, the curfews, the deportations, the destruction of houses to which Israel's military government has had recourse are all too familiar to the Afro-Asians and evoke in them a very particular revulsion. This not only shows up in governmental votes at the United Nations but it is very evident in increasing anti-Israeli feeling in the press and public opinion. The emergence of the armed Palestinian resistance movement after March 1968, has been a major factor swinging Afro-Asian opinion towards the Arab cause because the Palestinian resistance evokes memories of the national liberation movements which secured independence for the various Afro-Asian countries.

One of the points made against Zionism by Mahatma Gandhi was that it was based on, and openly encouraged, a double loyalty in the Jewish communities throughout the world. And Gandhi's objection to double loyalties was based on his own experience and his knowledge of the composition of Asian countries. For the danger of a minority claiming double loyalty is very real to many countries in Afro-Asia, in Kenya and Nigeria and Malaysia, Thailand and Indonesia. In these countries there are both large indigenous minority groups and communities of overseas Indians and Chinese. The example of Palestine where a minority was allowed to grow to the point where it claimed a state of its own through partition is an especially dangerous precedent for these Afro-Asian countries. In some of these states the minorities have followed the Zionist example and have demanded that they be given separate states through partition. Thus the history of Palestine from 1920 to 1947 and the story of the Zionist struggle and the creation of the state of Israel serves as a warning to Afro-Asia rather than an example to be followed.

The Afro-Asian countries beset with minority problems are trying to solve their problems by working towards a secular, pluralistic society. Israel's insistence on the fact that she is a "Jewish state" and that its Jewishness must be preserved (and now against the Palestinian demand for a pluralistic, secular, democratic state), pushes the Zionist state in exactly the opposite direction from the Afro-Asians, towards a racial-religious exclusivity.

Gandhi put his finger on this sensitive point when, in conversation with the British Zionist Member of Parliament, Sidney Silverman, he asked, "Would you allow Arabs to enter freely into Palestine?" And was given the answer, "Yes, but subject to the condition that it does not defeat the declared object of establishing a Jewish national home in Palestine." If the Mahatma put the same question to the Israeli authorities today the answer given to him, as it has been to several international organisations, would be a categoric "No". It is for this reason that the Palestinians strike a responsive chord among Afro-Asian audiences when they say that their political objective is the creation of a multi-racial, multi-religious democratic secular state in Palestine for this is precisely the goal of several Afro-Asian states.

We can find five reasons why the India-type Afro-Asian countries should have a basic predisposition against Israel. First, Israel is non-Asian in origin and population, second, she was created and is now sustained by foreign imperial or pro-imperial powers, third, she has opposed liberation movements in a number of Afro-Asian countries (Algeria being just one example) as well as Afro-Asian non-alignment, fourth, she is an occupying power and fifth, Israel exemplifies minority double loyalty and denies the possibility of a pluralistic society. Although these may, at a glance seem vague or generalised motivations, they made their impact on Afro-Asian public sentiment in the months immediately after the June 1967 battle. And this showed just how important and how positive the revival of historical fears and memories can be.

The China-type. While the India-type of Afro-Asian countries is more pro-Arab than anti-Israel, the China-type is more anti-Israel than pro-Arab. There are three reasons why the China-type adopts an anti-Israel position. First, that Israel is considered an integral part, a bastion, an outpost, of America's neo-colonial empire; second, that Israel is becoming, if it has not already become, pro-capitalist, if not capitalist; and third, that Israeli "socialism" has long since lost its revolutionary fervour and is now frankly anti-revolutionary.

This left-wing, "progressive" approach to the Palestine problem has recently permeated the West through the adoption of the Palestinian cause by the New Left. In Afro-Asia leftist pro-Palestinianism, however, dates back to 1955. Then the progressives or left-wing leftists of Afro-Asia came together for the establishment of the Afro-Asian Solidarity Movement, making its headquarters in Cairo. The Movement organised innumerable conferences which brought together the progressive anti-colonialists of Egypt, Algeria and Syria, from the Arab side, with those of India, Indonesia, Ceylon and of Guinea, Mali and Tanzania, from Afro-Asia. Though few in number the progressives of Afro-Asia, many of whom discovered the Arab cause through contact with Arab progressives, have considerable influence in their respective countries because they are to be found in key positions both in their governments and in the fields of publicity and education.

The convention in New Delhi, in November 1967, of an International Conference in Support of the Arab Peoples gave new impetus to the pro-Arab, anti-Israeli policy of the progressives. Although those foregathering came mostly from the Afro-Asian Solidarity Movement, there were, in addition, representatives, mostly left-wing, from countries in the other four continents: Argentina, Australia, Brazil, Canada, Finland, Italy, Panama, the United States and Yugoslavia, among others. Many liberation movements from Africa also sent representatives. The conference produced three very lengthy documents, totalling 4,000 words, the gist of which was that imperialist Israel should withdraw from Arab territory and that the Palestinian people should have the right to return to their homeland.

This Conference was important because it drew into the Palestinian cause not only people of the communist left but also those of the non-communist progressive left, or the "New Left".

The thinking of the China-type differs considerably from that of the India-type. The India-type criticises and condemns Israel for her links with the United States because American policy towards the Afro-Asian countries and their aspirations is not, in Afro-Asian eyes, sufficiently sympathetic. For the China-type the question is much more basic: for him the United States is the hated enemy which must be fought and defeated. Israel is the close ally of the United States and therefore is an enemy which must be actively opposed. The progressive Afro-Asian argues that there is an umbilical link between imperialist America and its Middle Eastern colonialist outpost and points to the massive financial assistance given to Israel by American Zionists, to the most up-to-date military hardware provided by the United States government to Israel and to the thoroughgoing diplomatic support of Israel by America in the United Nations, all this as evidence of this link. For the progressive the enemy is a trinity of countries—the United States, West Germany and Israel. And, the near total identification of Israel with America, for which Israel works so hard and which she so proudly proclaims, is guaranteed to earn the Zionist state the angry hostility of some progressive Afro-Asian governments and of a very wide circle of leftists in Afro-Asia, of intellectuals and political activists.

Israel had an excellent line of approach to Afro-Asian leftists and socialists through the appeal of Israeli socialism. But ample information is available from official Israeli sources, and from the leftist opposition inside Israel, to show that the socialist sectors of Israel's economic life are shrinking before the advance of the private sector. The kibbutz movement is on the wane, and has been for some time, and the same is true of the Histadrut. It has been argued that the influx of massive funds from German compensation and reparation payments began the process of converting Israel from an austere, pioneering socialist state into a reasonably affluent Levantine country, not all that different from neighbouring free enterprise Lebanon. The fact remains that after the fighting in June 1967, the main international effort to make good Israel's losses did not take the form of an appeal to socialist brotherhood and belt-tightening but rather the convening of two well-publicised conferences in Israel of several hundred Jewish millionaires from all over the world. And when the communiqué of the first of these conferences recommended that Israel should retain the occupied Arab territories because this would be economically beneficial to Israel, the Afro-Asian progressives began to see Israel not merely as an outpost of colonialism but also as a colonising force in herself.

Because of her vitally important connection with the United States, Israel cannot very well present herself as a "revolutionary" or "progressive" state. She has even to play down her socialist background. But the newly emerged Palestinian resistance movement not only says that it is socialist but goes further and claims that it is both revolutionary and progressive. Whether it is justified or not and whether it is useful or not the Palestinians no longer refer to their resistance movement as a national liberation struggle but only as "the Palestinian Revolution". Therefore, when it comes to supporting the revolutionary forces in the Middle East, Afro-Asian progressives and the New Left of Europe and America automatically exclude Israel and turn towards the Palestinians. "The Palestinian Revolution" uses the familiar talk of the international leftist movement; and it has adopted the same familiar heroes—its operations bear the code names of Guevara and Ho Chi Minh. With the gradual waning of leftist interest in Viet Nam there are signs that Palestine, willy nilly, is taking its place as the prime cause of progressives in Afro-Asia and for the New Left in Europe and America.

Hitherto socialists, the more orthodox variety from both Europe and Afro-Asia, held views favourable to Israel. But, for the last three years it would seem that only the old guard of the orthodox Western socialist groupings continues to support Israel (and that because of Western guilt feelings for the decimation of the European Jewish community rather than Israel's socialism) while the more individualistic progressives and "New Leftists" have been drawn to the Palestinian resistance movement because of its revolutionary aspect. These younger leftists, moved by revolutionary and socialist brotherhood, are also jarred by the Israelis' insistence on the preservation of the exclusive Jewishness of their state and attracted by the demand of the Palestinians for a non-racialist, non-sectarian state in Palestine.

Common motivations of the China-type and the India-type. There is another set of motivations common to both the China and India-types of Afro-Asian countries and these motivations begin with economics.

It is becoming increasingly true that the world is no longer divided according to politics between East and West but, according to economics, between North and South—a concept that the Yugoslavs first put forward. There are two countries which, because of their affluence and advanced social structure, are part of the developed North: these are Japan in the East and Israel in the West. But while the affluence of Japan is a consequence of internal economic endeavour, that of Israel is derivative from the affluence of other countries in the Northern sector. Whatever might be the precise origin and nature of Israeli affluence the fact remains that this affluence sets Israel apart from the underdeveloped countries of Afro-Asia. Israel faces the same publicity problem that Western countries face: the more successful Israel is in making herself known the wider becomes the gap of understanding and identification between her and people from the very different economic and social background of Afro-Asia. Thus a commission sent by the Government of India to study the Israeli kibbutz movement reported that, as far as India was concerned, the kibbutz was "partly misleading and partly irrelevant."

In the ideological phraseology of the Chinese, Afro-Asia is part of "the world village" while Europe and America are "the world city"—and so is Israel. In short, the economic structure of Israel is the exact reverse of that of most Afro-Asian countries.

Not much attention has been paid to these aspects of Israel's make-up but, in fact, it is Israel's non-agricultural, industrialised affluence that wholly sets her apart from the mainstream of Afro-Asian life. And since the gap between the rich and the poor is widening on a global scale so, too, does the gap between Israel and Afro-Asia. This development rather than the political antagonisms of today will govern the relationship between Israel and Afro-Asia in the future.

The Afro-Asians also fear Israel because of her undetermined frontier policy. Israel has been very reluctant to put forward peace proposals but in every Israeli plan that has been put forward unofficially there are new territorial demands involving acquisition of territory as a result of military victory. Such claims run counter to two cardinal principles which the Afro-Asians hold, namely that existing frontiers should be respected and that aggression should not pay. In no other part of the world is it so vital to maintain the sanctity of new and fragile frontiers, frontiers which can be altered only at the risk of letting loose countless antagonisms. It was for that reason that the African states, in their first summit meeting in 1963, solemnly pledged that all existing frontiers were to be accepted even though they were colonial boundaries and often cut through ethnic and tribal units. Likewise, India and Pakistan in 1965 set a precedent when they both withdrew from territory taken in that year's fighting. The principles that frontiers must not be changed and that aggression must not pay play an increasing part in Afro-Asian evaluation of the Palestine problem after July 1967, when it became evident that Israel was trying to achieve new and enlarged frontiers.

In their speeches at the United Nations and in a whole series of bilateral communiqués, the governments of Afro-Asia have reiterated, with almost monotonous regularity, that Israeli troop withdrawal should be prompt, total and unconditional, that *faits accomplis* cannot be regarded as definitive and the use of force cannot justify territorial gains or provide political advantage. Even the unofficial allies of Israel, Iran and Ethiopia, have made these points at the U.N. and elsewhere. These unexceptionable principles may be no more than principles for the well-established states of Europe but such principles express the very real, practical policies of the Afro-Asian governments and are founded on most genuine anxieties. Until Israel withdraws behind fixed and mutually agreed frontiers, Israel will represent an unsettling factor to practically every single Afro-Asian state. European realists may say that national boundaries have always been established by force but these words fall on deaf ears in Afro-Asia where there is a belief that we live in a changed and more ordered international community.

As specific examples of this belief we may quote the cases of three very different and widely separated Asian countries—Japan, Ceylon and Turkey. Turkey, over the years, has displayed considerable friendship for Israel; Ceylon maintained a cool and detached attitude towards both the Arabs and Israel; and Japan, while friendly towards Israel, declared that she adopted a position of "absolute neutrality" during the fighting in June 1967. Yet, within a matter of weeks, these three countries were demanding that Israeli troops should withdraw unconditionally and that there should be no *fait accompli* based on military conquest.

This nationalistic Afro-Asian reaction (even from countries most friendly to Israel) against the political consequences of and the territorial situation resulting from the Israeli military victory was also due to the discovery by Afro-Asians that Israel was not the underdog in the Middle East; Israel was not, as many had thought, David but rather a military Goliath. Thus, the natural sympathy people who once were underdogs accord others in that same position was transferred from the Israelis to the Palestinians. A new David emerged to confront the Israeli Goliath and this was the Palestinian resistance.

"Nothing succeeds like success" is a truism which does not seem to apply to military success. Because of the ease and swiftness of their military victory, the Israelis have begun to display a degree of self-assurance that is not far removed from arrogance. Israel's leaders have spoken in terms of "chastising" and "punishing" the Arab states which support the Palestinian resistance movement. This tone, cold and school-masterish, brings back to the Afro-Asians memories of their former colonial masters and it was just this attitude that the Afro-Asians found particularly distasteful. Then when Israeli leaders, as they often do, go further and talk the language of the mailed fist, with threats of more military action and further conquest and still further expansion, they convert the reluctant respect Afro-Asians might have felt for Israeli military prowess and the quick victory in 1967 to alarm and indignation.

In brief, what Israel runs counter to, especially after June 1967, is a basic Afro-Asian nationalist feeling. It is this visceral feeling that leads countries like Burma, Japan and even Thailand to resent Israel's bullying words and bullying actions and her air of arrogant superiority based on armed strength. In terms of social respect in Afro-Asia the warrior has always come some way behind the teacher and the priest; whereas in the New Sparta that Israel shows signs of becoming, the teachers and the priests are being rudely elbowed aside by the man at arms.

Sectional motivations of the Afro-Asians. It is obvious that Islam, and the key centralising role of the Islamic University of Al-Azhar in Cairo, makes a major impact on the policy of the Afro-Asian Muslim countries toward the Palestine problem. Those countries with sizable Muslim minorities are also considerably influenced by Islamic ties. The effect of this Islamic impact is to make the Asian countries pro-Arab and the African countries less pro-Israel. In Africa, the countries influenced by the Islamic factor are Mauritania, Somalia, Nigeria, Niger, Guinea and Mali; and in Asia, Turkey, Afghanistan, Pakistan, the Maldive Islands, Malaysia, Indonesia and, to some extent, India. In Turkey the deep Islamic feeling of the countryside has, during the past four or five years, gradually counteracted the Turkish government's initial friendliness towards Israel.

It is unfortunate for Israel that her major military prize, and one which she has sworn never to give up despite world-wide exhortations, is the city of Jerusalem whose Muslim shrines make it the third holiest place in the Islamic world. The furore caused in Muslim countries by the burning of the Aqsa Mosque brought about the calling of an Islamic conference in Rabat and the establishment, by the conference, of a permanent Islamic Secretariat. The Muslims of Afro-Asia consider Israel, at least indirectly if not directly, responsible for the burning of the Mosque and thus it is impossible or extremely difficult for any Afro-Asian country with a sizable Muslim community to be anything but antagonistic to Israel as long as Israel remains in occupation of the Holy City. Such is the strength of feeling among Turkish Muslims for their holy places in Jerusalem that the Turkish government, for which secularism has been a guiding principle since Mustafa Kemal, was obliged to attend the Islamic conference. Indeed, it would seem that among many Afro-Asians and in a number of Afro-Asian countries, as in the world at large, there is a stronger feeling of loyalty towards a holy city than there is sympathy for, and understanding of, the Palestine problem itself—of which the future of Jerusalem is but one aspect.

Economic considerations motivating the Afro-Asians. Although it is doubtful that economic considerations play any large part in the policies of Afro-Asian governments towards the Palestine problem, economic interests would incline the Afro-Asians towards a pro-Arab stance. This is true because the Afro-Asians should find it far more advantageous to protect their large and important interests in the Arab world rather than to establish economic relations with Israel which can only be smaller in scope than those with the Arab countries and which involve the importation by Afro-Asian countries of products that can be purchased from any other industrialised Western country.

From the economic point of view there is, of course, no comparison between the resources and demands of the Arab countries and those of a single, quite small country like Israel. Thus the 100 million Arabs represent a huge market for the industrial or the semi-industrial products of such countries as Japan, Hong Kong, Singapore, India and Pakistan. And potentially the Arab world offers the opportunity of even greater expansion. Likewise important and large-scale oil and petro-chemical industries are being developed through the joint efforts of Iran, Kuwait and Saudi Arabia, on the one hand, and Pakistan, Japan and India, on the other.

Set against this, Israel's imports from Asia in 1966 amounted to a mere $ 52 million and its exports to $ 74 million. But of the exports, 90 per cent was a single commodity, industrial and polished diamonds. In 1968 the import figure had dropped to $ 50 million while the total of exports stood at $ 103 million;

thus Afro-Asia has an adverse balance of trade with Israel. In any case the total trade figures for Afro-Asia are a very minor part of Israel's commercial relations; the global figure for exports was $639 million and for imports $1,088 million. Afro-Asia is the source for less than 5 per cent of Israel's imports and takes 16 per cent of her exports.

The land, sea and air communications of East Africa and South and South East Asia with all of Europe and with the East Coast of North America run across the Middle East. That conditions in the Middle East should be such that these lines of communication are kept open is a major political and economic interest of all the countries in the above mentioned area. Only when the Suez Canal was first closed in 1956 did the countries of South Asia in particular wake up to the fact that peace in the Middle East was of vital importance to their economies. Because of the second closure of the Canal, since June 1967 the countries of East Africa and South and South East Asia have had to pay an additional 15 to 20 per cent on the price of imports from Europe and the West and the cost to Europe and the West of the exports of these Afro-Asian countries has risen by a similar amount. The never very robust economies of these Afro-Asian countries were not adapted to take this new and heavy burden, and this burden was imposed on them because of the presence along the Canal of Israeli troops – a presence that all of these countries have condemned and asked to be removed. This amounts to a very positive economic grudge that these countries have against Israel.

It must be recognised that the economic interests of the Afro-Asian countries bordering the Indian Ocean involve the Arab states in a positive sense, but Israel only negatively, insofar as she can halt oil supplies and break communications. Thus the Afro-Asians have very strong economic interests in the Eastern Arab area in normal times of peace, interests involving trade, economic cooperation and communications. Israel, however, really comes into the economic picture only as a disruptive force.

Public policy and private dealings. In the preceding sections we have seen that nationalist sentiment and historical experience, ideology and various general political and economic considerations are the primary motivations for Afro-Asian states adopting a pro-Arab Palestine policy. The measure we have used to determine just how friendly the Afro-Asians are to the Arabs has been the Afro-Asians' voting record at the United Nations. Then what we have actually been discussing is the *public* policy or posture of the Afro-Asian states. This may be called their "declaratory policy" and it may be distinguished from their "action policy", that is to say the policy they follow in their direct bilateral relations with Israel. In many cases, "declaratory policy" seems to be in contradiction with Afro-Asian "action policy". That there should be such a contradiction between private and public, between domestic and international, may seem, at first glance, ambivalent or even hypocritical. But such contradictions are common form in public as in private life and in relations between states as between individuals and in the case of relations between Afro-Asian states and Israel the contradiction is not as sharp as it might first appear.

The contradiction is readily apparent. If we glance at the list of consistently pro-Arab countries (Table III), we see that the six Asian countries which are "completely" pro-Arab do not have diplomatic relations with Israel and are thus consistent in their hostility. But the African countries which are also, in their United Nations votes, "completely" pro-Arab and both the Asian and African countries which are "strongly" pro-Arab, without exception, maintain full diplomatic relations with Israel. Indeed, some of them like Tanzania, Thailand and Japan have friendly, and in the case of Japan, cordial, relations with Israel.

This contradiction has not, of course, escaped the notice of the Israelis, particularly in their relations with African states. When some ten years ago countries like Ghana and Guinea, with which Israel was then on friendly terms, joined the so-called Casablanca group in condemnation of Israel, public opinion in Israel was shocked and disappointed and the Israeli Foreign Ministry delivered protests and asked for explanations. But since then the Israelis seem to have learned to live with the fact that "the very countries that have had strong bilateral and technical cooperation ties with Israel have often voted for anti-Israel positions".[18]

Thus the Israelis have learned to absorb public affronts and have adopted the attitude that it is the cordial bilateral relationship that matters while antagonistic votes at the United Nations can be safely regarded as being merely "declaratory". It may be true that the votes of some of the smaller African states at the United Nations are merely high-flown gestures, but there are other Afro-Asian countries whose votes at the U.N. coincide with "action" or interstate policy. And, it can be argued that all countries whose voting record is "completely" or "strongly" anti-Israel pay the price in one important respect: Israel is uniquely able to influence publicity media around the world, especially in the West, so that countries critical of Israel can expect to, and do in fact, come in for more critical attention from the media than they perhaps deserve.

Cyprus provides us with a good example of how declaratory policy overlaps with action policy. Immediately after its pro-Arab and anti-Israel votes in the 1967 United Nations General Assembly Special Session, about 30,000 Israeli tourists cancelled their visits to Cyprus en bloc, a heavy blow to Cyprus tourism which is a major sector of the Cypriot economy. Then the Israeli government let it be known that there would be a resumption of the flow of Israeli tourists to Cyprus in 1968 if the Cypriot government would modify its voting at the United Nations. President Makarios replied that this could not be done. Nevertheless Israeli tourists did return to Cyprus in 1968.

Setting aside President Makarios' evaluation of the rights and wrongs of the Palestine question, the consistency of his policy can be explained by the fact that, at that time, Cyprus was under considerable military pressure from Turkey. To support Israel would have meant supporting the principle that aggression can pay and would have been extending an open invitation to Turkey to attempt an invasion of Cyprus.

Among the Afro-Asian countries which are "completely" or

[18] *The Jerusalem Post*, 21.7.1967, "Why the Arabs and India failed to swing the Afro-Asian vote" by David Kimche.

"strongly" pro-Arab are several that have the same congruence of policies as Cyprus and for the same reason. These are India, Pakistan, Somalia, Burma, Thailand, Turkey, Japan and Nigeria. For all of these countries a "declaratory" policy against military aggression and expansion is real, live "action" policy.

If there is a contradiction in the policy of some of these countries and if they are able to get away with it, then it is because neither Israel nor the Arab states are in a position to demand or impose any exclusivity in their friendships. It has just not been possible for either side to apply against the other anything like a Middle Eastern "Halstein" doctrine. Israel, however, does receive some help in this respect from her more powerful Western supporters, particularly the United States. Thus it is Israel's friends who help to close the gap between "action" and "declaratory" policy with respect to certain vulnerable Afro-Asian states (and especially the micro-states of Africa). These powerful friends see to it that, to a certain extent at least, countries are not allowed to get away with maintaining a friendly interstate "action" policy while following an unfriendly international "declaratory" policy. The more independent and nationalist a country is, however, the less is the gap between the two policies.

Pro-Israeli motivations

The pro-Israeli motivations of the Afro-Asian countries may be designated as positive and negative.

Positive motivations of the Afro-Asians. The first and most obvious motivation has been hinted at in the preceding section; that is that Israel takes the trouble to make herself known. She has established diplomatic missions, promptly, in even the smallest of the Afro-Asian states and these missions are staffed by dedicated and efficient diplomats. Cleverly produced publicity material is widely distributed by the Israelis and there is a constant flow of delegations of various types to and from Israel so that interest is maintained continuously.

By contrast, the Arab states do not exert any comparable effort. This is partly due to lack of funds and personnel; partly to the fact that the Arabs do not see the importance of Afro-

Asia and instead expend their energies on trying to convert the unfriendly West. The main Arab reason, however, is that they are so convinced of the justice of their cause that they do not see the need to present their case to peoples whom they assume are already their friends.

The Israelis take no friendships for granted. As newcomers to the Afro-Asian scene, they have to make their case and they do so with assiduous energy. And, naturally, some Afro-Asians respond positively to the Israeli advances because Israel is obviously going out of her way to make this effort.

Israel's programme of technical assistance in Afro-Asia has been conspicuously successful. This is a two-way system with Israeli experts going abroad and Afro-Asian technicians being trained in Israel itself. In 1965, it was estimated that at any one time there were 3,000 trainees in Israel, a surprisingly high figure considering Israel's size.

The services of Israeli experts are available to Afro-Asian countries in a great variety of fields; furthermore, they are really expert in their subjects, are hardworking and live and work alongside the local people without that aloof separateness that marks experts from most other countries (with the exception of the Peace Corps). The services of these experts are not given free, but they accept salaries at local rates. The Israeli expert is, therefore, with good reason, looked upon as a valued friend in many Afro-Asian countries and earns a great deal of credit for his country. The Israeli Foreign Minister was being no more than strictly factual when he said, in January 1967, that the technical assistance programme was "the largest single activity" of his Ministry, adding that it had "released Israel from her regional isolation and saved her from any danger of provincialism."

In addition to technical assistance Israel has gone in for quite large-scale joint commercial enterprises with several Afro-Asian states. Israel contributes both expert advice and financial backing to such schemes which have been undertaken in Cambodia, Burma, Nepal, and Iran as well as in Ghana, Kenya and Tanzania. These projects include such varied endeavours as soft drink and tyre factories, the construction of airports and water supply systems, joint shipping lines and the development of tourism and hotel industries.

Despite her own dependence on external financing, Israel has provided loans and grants to several countries, all of them in Africa. Although no details are available on the size and purpose of this financial assistance, the recipients of such aid are known—Ghana, Ivory Coast, Kenya, Malawi, Nigeria, Sierra Leone, Tanzania and Upper Volta.

As befits a martial country, Israel has provided military and police training and has also supplied arms to several Afro-Asian states. These are Congo (Kinshasa), Ethiopia, Kenya, Madagascar, Sierra Leone, Tanzania and Uganda in Africa and Burma, Iran, Nepal and Singapore in Asia. This military assistance is of particular importance in Afro-Asia where the armed services potentially or actually are the governing authority. In those states where the military is in power, help in increasing their efficiency may mean their remaining in power—a signal service indeed. Israel's assistance to Ethiopia and Iran is of a special nature. In Ethiopia the Israelis are training the Ethiopians to combat the guerillas of the Eritrean Liberation Movement and in Iran the Israelis cooperated with the Iranians in assisting the Kurdish rebels in their fight against the Iraqi government before a peace settlement was reached in 1970.

There are of course ties which have been built on emotions as well as those motivated by material considerations. It is the general pro-Zionist and pro-Israeli bias of Afro-Asian socialists that accounts for the friendship between some orthodox Indian socialist parties and Israel, and for the impact that Israeli socialism has made on the ruling parties of Kenya and Tanzania. Then Israel exerts a strong emotional pull on several of the Afro-Asian leaders who are a part of the Judaeo-Christian tradition.

The religio-emotional mainspring of Zionism, the factor that is said to give it validity and legitimacy, is Old Testament prophecy which the Zionist movement claims to have fulfilled. Zionism thus has roots in Judaic-Christian belief, and this religious basis of the Zionist state has attracted certain Afro-Asian leaders while it has no significance for others. The Afro-Asian leaders whose religious backgrounds are Hindu, Buddhist,

Confucianist and so forth and for whom Biblical prophecy has
no meaning, feel no attraction to that quasi-religious political
movement that is Zionism. But there are those who hold the
belief that the creation of Israel by Zionism is justified as the
fulfilment of Biblical prophecy. One such leader is President
Banda of Malawi who is a very devout elder of the Church of
Scotland and who sent Israel a message of support during the
crisis of June 1967. Another Gentile Zionist is the Emperor of
Ethiopia who takes his title "the Lion of Judah" very seriously
indeed. It was not surprising therefore that after the capture of
Jerusalem by Israeli troops the bishop of the Ethiopian church
in that city should have sent his congratulations to the Israeli
Army, adding, "I was always convinced that the God of Abraham and David would keep His promises to Israel."

The endless stream of Afro-Asian leaders who are brought to
tour Israel see much that is to be admired in that country. Israel
gives a strong impression of being an efficient, well-organised,
bustling country whose people know what they want and how
to get it. All this is in marked contrast to what is to be observed
in practically every other country of Afro-Asia. Much of Afro-
Asia may be politically hostile to the West but the whole area
is striving desperately towards westernisation. The majority
of the people in Israel may now be Afro-Asian in origin but the
texture of daily life, personal values and national ideals of Israel
are all Western. Thus Israel seems to have achieved what Afro-
Asia is striving towards. The fact that this has not been achieved
through westernisation but through western implantation eludes
most of these leaders, especially those from Africa. They and
their peoples continue to feel genuine admiration for Israel's
determination, her military strength and her success in achieving
her national goals.

The further fact that even though most Israelis are light-skin-
ned they generally do not behave towards the Afro-Asians with
the arrogance or condescension Afro-Asians have come to expect
of the white man gives a personal dimension to the feeling of
admiration these Afro-Asians have for Israel.

Negative motivations of the Afro-Asians. It is obvious that the

Afro-Asian countries may support Israel because of shared fears and common enemies as well as through admiration and real friendship. The proverb popularly ascribed to the Arabs, "The enemy of my enemy is my friend", has universal application.

For example, it is said, and there is probably a measure of truth in it, that black Africa feels friendly towards Israel, the enemy of the Arabs, because of the African memory of Arab slave traders who, for centuries, raided across the Sahara into all the countries of West and North Central Africa. Certainly the Israeli representative in the United Nations Trusteeship Committee, in the meeting of October 9, 1967, referred to this African feeling against Arab slavers, and was sharply rebuked by the Tanzanian delegate for what was called a "mischievous and impertinent" attempt "to drive a wedge" between Arab Africa and Black Africa.

Then in countries where there is political anti-Muslim feeling, the Arabs, as the originators of Islam, are also disliked. Ethiopia is just such a case, for the Muslim peoples of Eritrea and Somalia have been fighting the Ethiopian Imperial government which has, as we have seen, obtained Israeli assistance for opposing the rebels. So also in India the most vociferous supporters of Israel are Sikh and Hindu religious parties which are openly and violently anti-Muslim. (The Hindu Jan Sangh Party, which gives Israel most support in press and Parliament, was responsible for the assassination of Mahatma Gandhi whom they considered was too pro-Muslim.)

In some of the small states of West Africa the ruling elite is Christian while Islam is steadily gaining ground among the people. Here a fusion of anti-Muslim and anti-Arab feeling takes place to produce pro-Israeli sentiment. Hence in May, 1967, the National Youth Movement of Sierra Leone passed a resolution declaring, "we support the Israeli people in their just struggle against Arab imperialism and Islamic domination". A similar case is Chad where a Muslim majority is now fighting to wrest the reins of power from the hands of a non-Muslim minority.

The support given by Egypt and, latterly, Algeria, to subversive "progressive" opposition movements in some of the conservative African states has made friends for Israel. This is true of Malawi and Congo (Kinshasa). And by supporting the Somali people, the U.A.R. succeeded in antagonising both Ethiopia and Kenya. Ethiopian antagonism was increased still further by Sudanese and Syrian help to the Eritreans.

The progressive Arab states have also scared off a lot of the conservative African governments by their loose talk about "Arab socialism", for example the governments of Liberia, Malawi, Gambia and Madagascar. Turkey also found this propaganda disturbing. Israel, of course, also claims that she is socialist but she does not threaten to export her socialism as do the progressive Arabs.

In March 1967 the Israeli Foreign Minister made a tour of some countries in South East Asia and coverage in the Israeli press of the tour indicated that Israel had discovered a common factor between herself and some of these countries: they all were small and isolated by hostile neighbours. These countries with whom Israel shares geopolitical isolation are Laos, Cambodia, Nepal, Ethiopia and, very much in evidence these days, Singapore.

Future trends in Afro-Asia

Looking to the future, the question that concerns us is this: are there likely to be any changes in the interests and policies of the Afro-Asians in the Middle East which would make them more, or less, pro-Arab or pro-Israel?

As far as we can see, the pro-Arab, anti-Israeli trend that began to emerge in Afro-Asia late in 1967 when it became apparent that Israel had become an occupying power (and a similar change in European attitudes began in the spring of 1968) is bound to grow stronger.

This prediction is made on the basis of the calculation that the motivations which make Afro-Asians pro-Arab—Asian solidarity, nationalism, non-alignment, historical memory, non-aggression and the principle of territorial integrity—are more deep-rooted, enduring and positive than the motivations that make other Afro-Asians pro-Israel. There is a limit to the effectiveness of a policy of paying court, of technical asssistance and extending loans and aid; there is a limit to the amount of admiration one can feel for military success and efficiency; there is a limit to the impact of shared hostilities; and there is a limit, too, to Western influence, which, in fact, is already waning in Afro-Asia. Israel's vital "Peripheral Pact" with Turkey, Iran and Ethiopia is a temporary structure: Turkey has already drawn back a considerable way, and the policies of Iran and Ethiopia are personal to the Shah and the Emperor, who is a man full of years.

In the long run Israel can only find acceptance in Afro-Asia if she secures the acceptance of her immediate neighbours in West Asia. But that seems farther off than ever.

The Indian popular reaction and reversal in 1967

The popular reaction—and the reversal of that reaction in India to the crisis caused by the Second Battle for Palestine in 1967 is of interest for a variety of reasons. Firstly, because according to Israeli sources, India led the diplomatic attack on Israel at the United Nations. Secondly, India has always been a prime political and propaganda target of the Israelis: their viewpoint has been expressed, widely and effectively, by a very active Israeli Consulate in Bombay aided by the India-Israel Friendship Society founded in 1964. Thirdly, varying opinions on this issue were freely expressed in the Indian Parliament and the Indian press so that ample material for study is available. Fourthly, these opinions are common to many other Afro-Asian countries. And, lastly, the division of opinion was so deep and violent that it shook the Indian government and almost reached crisis proportions. On the 1967 Middle East issue the government of Mrs. Indira Gandhi faced the same challenge to its authority as, reportedly, did the governments of Yugoslavia, Czechoslovakia and Poland.

The challenge arose from the fact that while governmental policy was pro-Arab there was widespread popular criticism of this policy represented in the press and in Parliament.

When Mrs. Gandhi succeeded to the Indian Premiership

early in 1966 there was some speculation in Zionist circles that she might soften India's official attitude towards Israel. The reason for these hopes is unclear but, in the event, they were disappointed: "The first five months of Mrs. Gandhi's Premiership were marked by an unmistakable hardening of this (anti-Israeli) attitude in comparison not only with the Nehru era but even with the immediately preceding Shastri regime."[19] The Indian Premier spelt out her attitude very clearly during a visit to Cairo in 1966: "Our support is not only due to our traditional friendship towards the Arab people but to our belief in and commitment to secularism and to the principle that states should not be carved out or created on the basis of religion. We are deeply concerned at the human suffering caused to the Arab Palestinian refugees and support their right to return to their homeland."

India had a direct involvement in the 1967 Middle East crisis: she was a member of the Security Council, an Indian general commanded the U.N. Emergency Force in Gaza and Sinai, and a battalion of the Indian Army was a part of that Force. When fighting broke out on the 5th June the Israelis attacked the positions occupied by the Indian contingent both with artillery fire and air strafing: fourteen Indian soldiers were killed, twenty-one were wounded and nineteen were reported missing. After ten days Israel expressed condolence and offered to pay compensation but the Indian Government rejected both the regrets and the compensation.

Speaking in Parliament Mrs Gandhi described this incident as "a cowardly attack...wanton, deliberate and without provocation." Much sympathy for the victims was expressed both in Parliament and the press but, significantly enough, Israel was not really held blameworthy. In fact, there was opposition in Parliament to a move to condemn Israel for this attack on the ground that the Indian troops should have been moved out of the battle zone earlier.

All this was due to the fact that many Indian political parties

[19]Joseph B. Shechtman, "India and Israel" in *Midstream*, New York, August-September 1966.

and newspapers had already adopted an anti-Arab stance during the weeks in May when the crisis was developing. In a debate in the Lower House of the Indian Parliament on the 26th May only the Communist Party supported the pro-U.A.R. stand of the Government. One right wing party, Swatantra, representing big business, said that India should be neutral between the Arabs and Israel; the other right wing group, the Hindu religious Jan Sangh, totally pro-Israel, accused the Government of being "a war-monger"; while the left wing Praja Socialists were also of the opinion that India had gone too far in backing the U.A.R. And during these attacks the members of the ruling Congress Party did nothing more than maintain an uncomfortable silence. Yet they did more when the debate moved to the Upper House where they actually criticised their own Party Government for being too hasty in support of the U.A.R. Little wonder that on May 29 the Israeli government took the unusual step of issuing a statement saying that it was impressed by the degree of Indian popular sympathy, misrepresenting anti-Arab feeling for pro-Israeli sympathy.

The next day several members of Parliament put questions as to whether President Nasser had thanked India for the support she had given him so far, and why he had only given thanks to General de Gaulle.

The day after hostilities commenced several members of the Parliamentary Executive of the Congress Party criticised the Indian Foreign Minister's statement that the very existence of Israel created tension. Both the Deputy Leader and the General Secretary of the Executive advised a more neutral stand.

On June 7 and 9 there were angry clashes in the Indian Parliament between the Jan Sangh and Communist Party members. On the latter date these became so unruly that Parliament had to be adjourned, but not before one Jan Sangh member accused the Government of converting India into the fourteenth Arab state.

On June 16 M.P.s asked if the United States might not reconsider its food aid to India because of the Government's anti-Israeli policy.

The debate went rumbling on for several more weeks for on

July 20 it was reported that there had been heated exchanges between Prime Minister Gandhi and members of the
Congress Party Parliamentary Executive. Some of the members
later admitted that the Party was split on this issue and claimed
that many, perhaps most, of its members were opposed to the
Government's policy. Things had reached such a pass that Mrs.
Gandhi felt obliged to threaten a General Election so as to obtain
a popular mandate on the question (which she would not have
got). Two days later, amid rumours of opposition to her Middle
East policy from the Deputy Prime Minister (who was also the
Finance Minister) as well as from the Defence Minister, Mrs.
Gandhi denied that there were rifts in her Cabinet over this
issue.

After this date Middle East events gradually faded out of
India's internal politics but enough had happened to indicate
that opposition to the government's Middle East policy was
sufficiently widespread to bring its very existence into jeopardy.

And while it fought off these attacks from outside and inside
its own ranks in Parliament the Indian government looked in
vain for any substantial support from the Indian press. Apart
from a few, small, communist and progressive publications
every major Indian newspaper was critical of official policy.
The editorialists produced a variety of arguments to support
their case: India, they argued, had departed from non-alignment by her one-sided support of the Arabs and had thereby
forfeited any chance of playing the part of peace-maker, which
she had done in various disputes in the past; it was also said that
Realpolitik made it prudent for India to be friendly with a militarily strong Israel who would be a reliable ally; opposing Israel,
they went on, would bring India into disfavour with Israel's
friend, the United States, which could affect its economic aid
to India and be productive of unfavourable publicity; it would
also make it difficult for India to obtain financial assistance from
private sources because of the influence of Zionist financiers
in international banking circles. To some extent these warnings
were proven true because President Johnson did show his displeasure with India's pro-Arab policy, and private Jewish

emporiums in New York cancelled orders for several million dollars worth of Indian handicrafts.

Parliamentary and press opinion both affected and was affected by popular sentiment. What the sentiment was is shown in an opinion poll taken in August 1967 in four principle Indian cities.[20] Even though the wording of the questions was biased in favour of Israel the figures are too striking not to be accurate in a general sense. While 24 per cent of those questioned thought that India should continue to support the Arabs, 49 per cent believed that both the Arabs and Israel should be treated at par. Taken according to political parties the poll revealed that 37 per cent of the communists polled gave the government greatest support, followed by the socialists—with 28 per cent; only 25 per cent of the Congress Party members polled supported their own government with the two right wing parties giving 17 per cent and 15 per cent of their polled support to the government. Except for the communists a majority of the supporters of the four other parties favoured India taking a more neutral position.

What was truly significant for future developments is that while a majority of the respondents said that Israel had risen in their estimation no individual or party was prepared to vote even one per cent in favour of India giving support to Israel and not supporting the Arabs.

Thus, despite all the angry debates and the bitter criticism of official policy Indian popular feeling on the 1967 crisis was revealed as being, very definitely, not pro-Israeli even though it was greatly dissatisfied with the totality of India's commitment to the Arabs: it was critical of the Arabs but it withheld support, completely, from Israel.

This rather lopsided attitude indicates that the average Indian expressed his opinion not on the basis of a calm analysis of the Middle East crisis (for in that case the statistical probability is that at least 10 per cent should have favoured a pro-Israeli policy) but rather on the basis of emotional prejudice— a pre-

[20] *The Statesman*, Calcutta, 14.8.1967; the poll was made by the Indian Institute of Public Opinion.

judice which did not involve the Israelis at all but which did involve the Arabs.

In India this prejudice is a deep and long-standing anti-Muslim hostility, which goes back to the time of the 17th century Moghul Emperor Aurangzeb. More recently, it has to be remembered, the Indian sub-continent was partitioned, as far as the Muslim community was concerned, on the basis of religion into the states of India and Pakistan. And in September 1965 India and Pakistan had fought a war which the propaganda on both sides represented as being a "Jihad" and an "anti-Jihad".

By mid-1967 the opinions of almost all non-Muslim Indians on an issue involving the Muslim Arabs was strongly influenced by this anti-Muslim emotion. This was true of all sections of the populace—politicians, businessmen, journalists, soldiers—and it underlay even the most rational explanations they put forward to justify an anti-Arab attitude.[21]

There was one political group that was not at all concerned with concealing the fact that its anti-Arab stand was due to anti-Muslim feeling. This was the Jan Sangh. During the crisis its mouthpiece, a weekly quaintly titled "The Organiser", was full of articles and cartoons praising Israel and jeering at the defeated Arabs, to which was added the occasional anti-Russian jibe. Thus one heading proclaimed "the rights of Israel to Jerusalem are infinitely stronger and juster than the rights of Russians over German or Polish territory" or "a Jewish state in the heart of Islam cannot be considered such an atrocious crime as the demolition of the Visvanath by Aurangzeb and the erection of a mosque on the site." In an interview with this weekly the Israeli Consul, playing up to his readership, claimed that the Arabs "behave like savages...you do not know what Muslim fanaticism can do."

Yet even a journal with such strident views came out, in its issue of the 9th July 1967, with the unusual double headline

---

[21]Several Indian political commentators referred, at that time, to this anti-Muslim bias: N.C. Chaudhuri quoted in *The Jerusalem Post*, 24.7.1967, "Why Delhi is Pro-Arab" and C.P. Ramachandran in *The Observer*, London, 12.6.1967.

"Arabs Should Recognise Israel: Israel Should Become Asian." This referred to a meeting of the Central Working Committee, the highest executive body, of the Jan Sangh Party which produced a five-point resolution on the Middle East situation. These points were that the Arab countries must relinquish all intentions to annihilate Israel; "Israel must also realise that it is basically an Afro-Asian state and so instead of allowing itself to be used just as an instrument of Western diplomacy, it should play a respectable and purposeful role" in building up the region; "but for this it will have to reorient its attitudes, cease looking Westwards and develop altogether a new personality"; Israel must help generously in the resettling of the uprooted Arab refugees; the Suez Canal and the Gulf of Aqaba must be open to ships of all nations; Israel should withdraw its forces from all occupied areas.

There is more to comfort the Arabs than Israel in this resolution from the most anti-Muslim, anti-Arab group in India. And this is so because however strong anti-Muslim prejudice may be, an equally strong, or even stronger, basic nationalist feeling makes it impossible for even the Jan Sangh to approve of Israel as an alien body in Afro-Asia. Hence its advice that Israel should cease being an instrument of the West and should become Asian.

Within Afro-Asia the impact of anti-Muslim feeling on the Arab-Israeli issue extends far beyond India. Similar feelings productive of the same political reaction are to be found in many states of West Africa, in Kenya and Ethiopia in East Africa, and in Burma, Singapore and the Philippines—in fact in almost every country where there is a sizable Muslim minority. One notable exception is Cyprus.

On the more rational plane there were several other, but less potent, reasons to explain why Indian popular reaction should have been so anti-Arab. To a certain extent Indian national pride was involved, because of the belief that India had surrendered her freedom of action in the Middle East by timidly yielding to the Arab veto against her having any contact with Israel. Because of a prickly national self-consciousness the point was also made that while India had stood by the Arabs during the Suez crisis, the Arabs had refrained from supporting India when she fought China in 1962 or Pakistan in 1965. There was also, as we have noted, considerable disappointment, based more on nostalgia than realism, that India by supporting one side had lost the chance of once again playing the international peace-maker. All these complaints, too, are to be found in the Afro-Asian countries: at one time or another the Emperor of Ethiopia, President N'krumah and President Kenyatta have all fancied the role of Middle East mediator, and have felt disappointed when discouraged by the Arabs.

The pro-West and anti-socialist groups in India were not displeased to witness the defeat of the U.A.R. and Syria because, for them, these countries had become dangerously leftist, and, even more dangerously, under Russian influence.

The officers of India's armed forces, looking at events from a strictly military standpoint, expressed much admiration for the swift efficiency of the Israeli military machine.

More intangible but more important was the effect on Indian public opinion of the attitude of Western-educated intellectuals among India's politicians, bureaucrats, businessmen and publicists. Many of these, when at universities in Britain and America, had been greatly influenced by their Jewish professors, several of whom were also Zionists. The prime example, for the English speaking world, is Harold Laski at the London School of Economics whose views (on the Middle East among other things) helped to mould the political ideas of at least two generations of the intellectual elite not only in India but in such countries as Burma and Ceylon, Kenya and Ghana. Doubtless, thinkers like Raymond Aron have had the same effect on students from the Francophone countries of Afro-Asia.

Also when India, and other Afro-Asian countries, were struggling for their independence a good many of the friends and supporters in the metropolitan countries of these freedom movements happened to be Jewish and Zionist; the British Member of Parliament Sidney Silverman is a case in point. The Afro-Asian nationalists whom such people had helped in their days of need have felt under an obligation of gratitude, after achieving their independence, when their old friends have interceded with them on behalf of Israel. It was not easy even for someone like Mahatma Gandhi to resist this type of emotional appeal from a person like Silverman.

One has to recognise that the Jewish impact on the Afro-Asian intellectual has been so strong that many of the latter have taken over the guilt feelings of the West towards the Jews, even though their own countries have been wholly innocent of anti-Semitism. We caught a glimpse of this emotional transference in Mr. Nehru's reference to the Nazi persecution of the Jews in his remarks to the Bandung Conference.

Thus there was a whole complex of reasons why Indian public opinion should have favoured Israel rather than the Arabs in 1967. They were so varied that the wonder is that public opinion was not even more pro-Israel. If it was not it was because the very nature of the Zionist state ran counter to an Indian national feeling that was part of a wider Asian, or Afro-Asian, feeling of continental identity and self-respect.

Because of the strength of this feeling a reversal soon took place in Indian public opinion. We have seen that this was apparent in the Jan Sangh Party as early as July 1967. It became quite general, in the press and among politicians of all parties, by September and October of that year, by which time it was clear that Israel was not going to withdraw from the Arab territories she had overrun and, instead, was settling down as an ocupying, colonialist power. Few, if any, of India's major newspapers have anything favourable to say of Israel now: the very same editorialists who expressed admiration of Israel in 1967 now habitually apply to her such epithets as "arrogant", "ruthless", and "belligerent". Israel's harsh occupation policies and the emergence of the Palestinian resistance movement have aroused Indian national feeling to the extent that Israel at present has far fewer friends and apologists in India than she did before June 1967. Mrs. Gandhi's government no longer comes under attack in Parliament when it takes a pro-Arab stand in the United Nations. One of the most influential friends Israel has lost is the internationally known figure Jay Prakash Narayan, a disciple of Gandhi who has often been mentioned as a possible future President of India. Because of his socialist views he was for many years a staunch advocate of closer Indian links with Israel which he visited several times and to which he arranged visits by groups of young socialists. But by the middle of 1968 Israel's presence and behaviour in the occupied territories were too much for him and he pronounced a magisterial indictment of Israel as a Jewish and Zionist state.[22] This was a noteworthy but typical example of the reversal in Indian feeling of the favourable feeling of 1967.

As the voting in the General Assembly reveals, a similar reversal in opinion, and for the same reason as in India, has come about in many other Afro-Asian countries. But more so in Asia than in Africa where Israel, despite her anti-African policies, continues to have friends.

The difference with Africa

It was in 1960 and 1961 that the majority of African states south of the Sahara received their freedom from Britain and France. Yet it was only a few months later in the United Nations General Assembly at the end of 1961 that eleven of those new states, along with Liberia, rushed in where angels may well have feared to tread and tabled a resolution asking for direct negotiations between Israel and the Arab states.

This resolution was warmly welcomed and strongly supported by Israel and equally strongly opposed by the Arabs. Even though it was defeated, the tabling of this pro-Israeli resolution may very well raise the question as to how Israel, having failed to gather significant support in Asia after ten years of effort, was able to win so many African states to her side in a little over a year.

Before answering the "why" and "how" of this question it may clarify matters if an account is first given of just how different have been the relationships of Asia and Africa with Israel in such matters as United Nations voting, diplomatic connections, trade and aid.

The analysis of the votes of the United Nations revealed that

---

[22] *The Hindustan Times*, New Delhi, 11.5.1968.

while not a single Asian state was prepared to adopt a position very strongly or strongly in favour of Israel there were around eight African states which were prepared to do so; to which could be added another four or five states only a little less pro-Israeli. The group of half a dozen Asian and half a dozen African delegations who can always be depended upon to vote with the Arabs is matched by a dozen or so African delegations which can be relied on to back Israel. They are not the same countries that introduced the 1961 resolution, because there have been both additions and subtractions, but the nucleus is now formed by such countries as Malawi, Botswana, Lesotho, Swaziland, Ivory Coast, Gabon, Dahomey, Liberia and Madagascar.

The numerical difference between the two continents in terms of diplomatic connections with Israel is also very evident. In 1967 Israel had diplomatic, trade or consular missions in eight Asian countries only but in 27 countries in Africa.

While the population of Africa is a sixth of that of Asia, Israel's exports to Africa were a third of those to Asia. More striking is the figure for Israel's imports: in 1964 the figure for imports from Asia was $ 18 million which in 1968 had risen only to $ 19 million; but for Africa the figure in 1964 was already $ 27 million and this, in 1968, went up to $ 30 million. Apart from South Africa which is, by far, Israel's most important trading partner in Africa, most of Israel's trade is with countries of the conservative group—Gabon, the Ivory Coast, Ethiopia—that are Israel's political friends.

The distinction made by Israel herself in her approach to Asia and to Africa is particularly clear in her programme of technical assistance. In one year, 1966, there were 406 Israeli experts serving in various African countries (compared to 25 in 1958) while 728 Africans were training in Israel. The cumulative total of African trainees up to 1966 was 4,358 and by that year 2,000 Israeli experts had served in Africa. For Asia, however, the cumulative figures up to 1966 were 1,000 Asians trained or training in Israel and 100 Israeli experts in all with service in Asia.

Having illustrated the degree of difference, in certain areas, in Israel's relations with Asia, on the one hand, and Africa, on the other, we may now try and find the reasons as to why Israel was able to achieve the wide acceptance in Africa that eluded her in Asia, and in particular, why this came about so quickly. One reason is that Israel did not make her way into newly independent Africa on her own initiative or on her own merits: from the start she had powerful foreign sponsors. It will be recalled that all through the 1950's France and Britain were, politically and militarily, confronting the forces of Arab nationalism represented, in particular, by the U.A.R. and Algeria. Before and after the Suez aggression the U.A.R. fought its battles with Britain and France not only in the Middle East and Algeria but also in Africa by giving aid to nationalist movements in many countries, from Guinea to Togo to Kenya and Rhodesia. Consequently when the time came, in 1960 and 1961, for Britain and France to make their major withdrawal from Africa they, and the United States, pressed their advice on the new, and in most cases, inexperienced, states of black Africa, to accept Israel as a substitute, as a Western-type state that would be a safe, useful and disinterested friend. Clearly these three countries had every reason to sponsor the cause of Israel in black Africa as a counterweight to the quite rapid growth of Islam and to the influence of radical Arab political ideas which followed the southward movement of Islam. And Israel, of course, was only too ready to be sponsored.

Hence it is that Israel finds her best friends among the small, weak, conservative African states that are most closely linked economically and even militarily, with France (Ivory Coast, Chad, Gabon, Madagascar) or with Britain (Gambia, Sierra Leone) or with the U.S. (Liberia). And since it was France that had the most serious quarrel with the Arabs, because of Algeria, it was France that sponsored Israel most vigorously; which is why Israel has many more friends in the French-speaking group than in the English-speaking area of Africa.

If powerful sponsorship gave Israel easy entry into independent Africa, Israel took every advantage of this head-start by rapidly building up a network of relationships with the new states. They were naturally pleased with the interest in them being displayed by Israel which contrasted with the relative inactivity of the Arab countries. Israel has as many, and perhaps more, diplomatic missions in Africa than all the Arab states put together.

Also, as we have seen, the economic and political interests of the Asian countries link them positively to the Arabs but, for the most part, only negatively to Israel. The reverse seems to be true for most of the black African countries (except for those in East Africa, not including Ethiopia) whose political and commercial interests in the Arab world are very slight, while they do have positive interests, especially commercial, linking them to Israel.

Soon after achieving their independence, the African states split into the radical Casablanca group (in which black Africa was represented by three states—Ghana, Guinea and Mali) and the far larger conservative Brazzaville group which ultimately included no less than 21 countries. From the beginning the Arabs were associated with the African radicals because the U.A.R., Algeria and Morocco were members of the Casablanca bloc. Hence, and quite apart from Western advice on this matter, it was natural for the conservative Africans to feel sympathy for the enemy of the Arab countries that were allied to their African opponents. Conservative regimes in Africa would instinctively be suspicious of the Palestinian liberation movement which describes itself as a "revolution". And all the more so because, unlike the Asian states, most of the Francophone African countries never had liberation movements of their own, but merely had their freedom conferred on them, as a gift.

And, as a final reason for Israel's acceptance by Africa, one cannot ignore Israel's insidious attempts, which still contrive to perpetuate the identification of the modern Arab with the Arab slave trader of the past. This may be resented in some progressive African countries but it certainly strikes a responsive chord in other, more traditional, African communities.

Any account of how Israel has forged links between herself and the African countries would have to comprise a long list of aid programmes and of joint ventures.[23] Briefly, twenty of the thirty technical co-operation agreements entered into by Israel are with African states, 60 per cent of Israeli experts serving abroad and 60 per cent of Israel's foreign aid budget are allocated to Africa. And even though Israeli aid amounts to only 0.05 per cent of the total aid received by Africa it produces dispropor- tionate results, particularly in the area of foreign policy, because of the care with which the Israelis select their aid projects and the thoroughness of their execution.

Yet the types of aid which probably bring Israel most influen- ce in African countries are precisely those about which Israel is most secretive.

The first of these is Israel's assistance in building up the military and police forces of African states. The full list of coun- tries[24] having received such aid up to 1966 is: Cameroun, Central African Republic, Chad, Congo (Kinshasa), Dahomey, Ethiopia, Ghana, Ivory Coast, Kenya, Malawi, Nigeria, Sierra Leone, Tanzania, Togo, Uganda, and to these must be added Madagascar.[25] Ghana, Nigeria and, probably, Tanzania, have dropped out of this group, which means that Israel now supplies military and para-military assistance only to the con- servative and moderate governments which, as the U.N. voting record shows, are its firmest friends in Africa.

Even though one pro-Israeli writer[26] attempts to draw a veil of decency over the programme by saying that "because of their sensitive nature few details of military and police training prog- rammes have come into the open", the basic facts of what sort of military aid Israel is supplying to each of the countries listed

[23]Details may be found in the special African supplements published, usually annually, by *The Israeli Economist* monthly, Jerusalem; also in an article on the subject in *Le Monde*, Paris, 3 and 4 September 1967; and in Leopold Laufer, *op. cit.* and M.E. Kreinin, *op. cit.*

[24]Sanford Silverburg: *Israel Military and Paramilitary Assistance to Sub-Saharan Africa: A Harbinger for the Role of the Military in the Developing States*, Master's Thesis, American University, Washington, D.C., 1968, pp. 50-75, quoted in *Tricontinental* magazine, Havana, November-December 1969.

[25]Mentioned in L. Laufer, *op. cit.* and *Le Monde*, 3.9.1967.

[26]L. Laufer, *op. cit.*, p. 170.

above has "come out into the open". Thus aid is very varied: the training of officers, and paratroopers in particular, in Israel; Israeli officers on training missions in Africa; setting up of military academies; the establishment of youth battalions; and special courses for marine, airforce and police cadets.

Certain aspects of this military aid merit special attention. There is the sale of arms (Israel has a small but flourishing arms industry) including a Finnish mortar manufactured under licence in Israel, and Israel's own famous "Uzi" sub-machine gun which has been supplied to "several presidential guards in West Africa";[27] one of these is the Ivory Coast.[28]

Then there are the "special forces" for counter-insurgency operations that are trained and led into action by Israelis. The two countries in which this has been done are Chad and Ethiopia: in 1967 two Israeli advisers were killed in Chad and in 1970 the Eritrean resistance fighters claimed to have killed some Israelis in battles with the Ethiopian Army. It is in Ethiopia especially that the Israelis have done considerable counter-insurgency work: in 1967 it was reported that 20 Israeli officers were assigned to this mission.[29] (It will be recalled that Israel is giving the same type of military assistance to her other imperial ally, Iran, where she has advisers in the Shah's intelligence service.)

The importance of the military aid Israel is giving to the new African states can hardly be overestimated. Because a military take-over of the government is a possibility in almost every African state, to train army officers is to train the possible future rulers of these countries who will, at least, retain friendly feelings for the country that provided them with the military expertise that led to political power. Such is the case with President, then General, Mobutu of Congo (Kinshasa) who did his paratroop training in Israel.

Also all these conservative regimes are under pressure from reformist or radical forces. Any country, such as Israel, which

[27]*Le Monde*, 5.9.1967.
[28]Silverburg, *op. cit.*
[29]*Le Monde*, *op. cit.*

increases the deterrent efficiency of the watchdogs of these regimes, such as the presidential guards and the special forces, helps directly to maintain the regime in power. It would be unnatural if such rulers did not feel merely grateful but deeply indebted to Israel.

Yet another significant, and semi-secret, form of Israeli assistance to Africa is the arrangements by which Israel acts as the conduit for third countries to pass on aid incognito. The chronicler of Israel's relations with the developing countries once again remarks discreetly on this third country participation, "details on the extent of this type of cooperation are not readily available",[30] a sure sign that is not only embarrassing but also important. As we have seen, from the outset Israel's aid programme for Afro-Asia was used as a "front" by Western organisations; hence the financing by American trade unions of the Afro-Asian Institute in Tel Aviv, which is the key institution in Israel's Afro-Asian training programmes.

This indirect third party participation has been widened to include the financing, by other countries, of what are supposed to be Israeli assistance programmes in Africa: all that Israel supplies is the expert manpower. Israel may have tried to keep these dubious arrangements secret, for obvious reasons, but the theory behind them has been expressed openly: "a free world state wishing to enlarge its assistance flow to Africa might channel some part of it through Israel because of Israel's special qualifications and demonstrated acceptability to many African nations";[31] the assumption being that the "free world state" might not itself be of "demonstrated acceptability". Or again, "If there is *any* (italics mine) 'realistic' motive in Israel's program of foreign aid it is probably to be found in the hope that it will draw tangible rewards from the United States by serving, coincidentally with her own interests, the same objects that that country seeks to promote through its aid program".[32] Despite this assertion by a former Israeli citizen that the principal mo-

[30]Laufer, *op. cit.*, p. 9.
[31]Arnold Rivkin, *Africa and the West*, New York, 1961, p. 89.
[32]Nadav Safran, *The United States and Israel*, Cambridge, Mass., 1963, p. 267.

tive of Israel's aid programmes is to draw "tangible rewards", not from the states aided, but from the U.S., nevertheless some rewards are forthcoming for Israel, at least in Africa, from the grateful objects of "Israeli" aid.

Our Israeli source does lift the veil sufficiently to mention U.S. support for Israel's youth programmes in the Central African Republic and Dahomey; French assistance to youth projects in the Ivory Coast; "and Great Britain and West Germany have reportedly given assistance to projects elsewhere in Africa";[33] at which point the veil of vagueness descends.

Clearly third party financing of Israel's aid programme must be very extensive because to quote our source again, "Israel's achievement in having more than half its effort financed from non-Israeli sources is probably unique".[34] A safe enough claim, for few other countries would be prepared to accept credit for aid programmes financed by other governments whose identity is so suspect that it has to be kept secret.

That a country like Israel, totally dependent on masssive foreign charity, should itself give away money to other countries may not seem credible or creditable; but so it is. Israel has, in fact, made loans and grants to African countries about which, again, not much is known: "the Israeli government has published no statistical information on its loan and grant activities".[35] Only the names of Israel's African debtors are known: Sierra Leone, Nigeria, Ghana, Liberia, Ivory Coast, Tanzania, Malawi, Kenya and Upper Volta; at least five of these countries remain among Israel's staunchest supporters. Here again Israel was, in effect, merely passing on funds from third parties presumably because of her greater "demonstrated acceptability".

Last but not least among the methods by which Israel has won African support must be mentioned the generosity shown to various African leaders: gifts that would be "unconsidered trifles" in other circumstances assume importance to leaders of micro-states. The practice is, to some extent, mitigated by the

[33]Laufer, *op. cit.*, p. 23.
[34]*Ibid.*, p. 62.
[35]*Ibid.*, p. 138, note 2.

fact that, at least in private, Israeli officials talk freely of this practice.[36]

There would be nothing to criticise in the friendship shown for Israel by certain African states—it could be agreed that they were merely consulting their national interests—if it were not for the fact that on two vital issues Israel follows policies that are basically, fundamentally anti-African, that is against the interests of the entire continent.

The first of these is her covert support to secessionist movements. At the very first Summit Conference of the Organisation of African Unity, in 1963, it was agreed unanimously that the existing boundaries of all states must be respected even though, as we have said, these were colonial relics and did not conform to ethnic, tribal or geographic norms. The African governments realised that if the Pandora's box of frontier rectifications was opened, chaos and anarchy and conflict would be the order of the day from one end of the continent to the other: secession was, therefore, totally ruled out. Hence it was that when the Ibos of Nigeria made their secessionist claims for a so-called "Biafran" state all but four of the 41 African states opposed the move. But among the foreign forces giving clandestine aid to the Ibo rebels was Israel which wanted to weaken the central Nigerian government because that government had shifted its policy away from its earlier, pro-Israel stand. When the Ibo rebellion was finally crushed, the Israeli Foreign Minister announced, with sorrowful pride, that this tragedy would not have come about if other countries had given as much assistance to the Ibos as Israel had.

A second secessionist movement being supported by Israel is in the southern Sudan, again with the avowed object of weakening the anti-Israeli central government in Khartoum. Uzi sub-machine guns have been found in the armouries of the rebels; these have been funnelled to them through neighbouring Uganda where the Israelis are in charge of all military training.

It is in her relations with the racialist regime in South Africa

[36]Information on this was given to the author, in amusing detail, by a former senior Israeli diplomat with experience in Africa: the mink coat, I learnt, was always acceptable despite its unusability in Africa's climate.

that Israel runs counter to the basic national and human interests of the governments and peoples of the African continent.
The present government in South Africa is, as is well known,
based on the premise that, under the law of God, all men of
colour, blacks and browns, are inferior to the white man and
the laws of the white man in South Africa are intended to keep
the non-whites in a permanent position of inferiority. This
state, and those who support it, offend the fundamental human
dignity and human self-respect of the individual African, and
Israel is among South Africa's warmest friends and supporters.

It might be argued, to the contrary, that Israel has voted
against South Africa on the apartheid issue at the U.N. (though
she did so in 1962 only after eleven years of wavering) and she
also does not have any diplomatic relations with that country.
Against these gestures must be set the fact that Israel is in continuous contravention of the U.N. resolution asking member
states not to have any trade or commercial relations with the
apartheid regime. The Israeli national airline El Al flies to
South Africa and Israel was so determined to maintain this
air link that before 1967, the planes used to fly an immense
detour around the Arabian peninsula on the Teheran-Nairobi
sector. Israel's trade with South Africa is steadily on the increase and is now one fifth of her entire trade with the continent.
Impressive as that is, the figures obviously do not include the
raw diamonds that Israel buys "almost exclusively" from South
Africa.[37] Just how important this trade in diamonds is for
Israel is demonstrated by the fact that cut and polished diamonds
comprise no less than two-fifths of Israel's total exports.[38]

Israel's biggest stake in South Africa is the 100,000-strong
Jewish community there which is strongly Zionist and very
wealthy.[39] In the ten years from 1951 to 1961, this community
had contributed $ 20 million to Israel. But this figure was far

[37]*Le Monde, op. cit.*

[38]Table 1/4 in the annual *Statistical Abstract of Israel.*

[39]In the following section I am much indebted to Richard P. Stevens:
Zionism, South Africa and Apartheid: The Paradoxical Triangle, Palestine Liberation Organisation Research Centre, Beirut, 1969. Dr. Stevens' essay is a
valuable, pioneering piece of research.

surpassed in June 1967 when South African Jewry contributed
$ 30 million and also sent 861 volunteers to fight in Israel, the
second largest of all foreign contingents (520 volunteers came
from the five million American Jews). Even during peace-time
South African Jewish reserve officers have been permitted to
undergo military training in Israel, a procedure officially contrary to law.

The sending of volunteers and the remittance of funds were
special privileges accorded to the South African Jewish community and for them a price, naturally, had to be paid. That
price was the moral and ideological collusion between the anti-
Semitic doctrine of apartheid and the doctrine of Zionism:
a collusion that was practised not only in South Africa but everywhere else by the Zionist organisation.

The South African Boers of the Nationalist Party who have
enforced apartheid have always been strongly anti-Semitic:
during World War II they openly expressed their sympathies
for Hitler and for his anti-Semitic Nazi creed. On the other
hand, Zionism, the product of Jewish persecution in Eastern
Europe, has professed opposition to all forms of racial discrimination. The two beliefs appear, therefore, essentially anti-
thetical—except in the racialist state of South Africa after the
formation of the Zionist state (which has itself enforced apartheid
between Jews and non-Jews in Palestine).

Dr. Richard Stevens has described how, before 1948, the
Jewish community in South Africa and the Nationalist Party
existed in a state of mutual hostility. The establishment of
Israel brought about a change because the Bible-reading Boers,
many of them Gentile Zionists, saw in this event a fulfilment
of Biblical prophecy and the racialists among them "saw the
success of the Jews against the Arabs as a victory of White over
non-White".[40] The Jewish community made a parallel change
of policy and criticism of the racialist policies of the Nationalist
Party was replaced by fulsome praise. When Premier Malan
retired in 1954 he was accorded the highest honour of South
African Jewry by having his name inscribed in its Golden Book

[40] *Ibid.*, pp. 7 ff.

as recognition of his "contribution to better racial understanding (*sic*) in South Africa." His successor was presented with a silver plate. It was a Jewish attorney who prosecuted Nelson Mandela, the well-known black South African nationalist leader in 1968. Even the Sharpville massacre in 1960, which evoked condemnation around the world and from many individuals and groups within South Africa, was passed over in silence by the Jewish community. Instead, a few months later, a leading member of the community said that "a majority of us are supporting the Union Government's policy in connection with apartheid".[41]

When Israel voted against South Africa in 1962 the Nationalists promptly resumed their attacks on the Jewish community and on Israel. The then Prime Minister, Dr. Verwoerd said that the Jews "took Israel from the Arabs after the Arabs had lived there for a thousand years. In that I agree with them; Israel, like South Africa, is an apartheid state". The special concessions granted to Jewish organisations to send funds and goods to Israel were rescinded.

The South African Jewish community made amends in the only way it could—it strongly criticised Israel's vote both in South Africa and abroad. Representatives from the community spoke out in favour of the South African government's policy not only in South Africa and in Israel but also in America where some of them lectured under the auspices of B'nai B'rith, otherwise well-known for its championing of liberal causes.

This conflict of views was resolved by a compromise. The South African government was given to understand that Israel was obliged to continue her anti-apartheid vote in the U.N. because of her growing interests among the independent African states but that all the widespread variety of Zionist organisations around the world would refrain from any criticism of apartheid.

Thanks to this concordat an informal understanding was firmly established between South Africa and Israel. The South African press supported Israel during the 1956 and the 1967 crises. And, as we have seen, South Africa's vote at the U.N. was always cast for the most strongly pro-Israeli resolutions. And the four

[41]*Ibid.*, p. 19.

African states that are virtually captives of South Africa—
Malawi, Botswana, Lesotho and Swaziland—vote the same way
and do so, if not wholly, then at least partially because of South
African pressure.

At the end of 1970 a new triangular disposition of forces
seemed to be emerging in Africa, according to which the African
friends of Israel—the Ivory Coast, Gabon, Dahomey and Madagascar—came out openly for the beginning of a friendly
dialogue with South Africa. Whether this striking coincidence
of friendship was the product of accident or design time alone
will reveal.

The gap between "action" policy and "declaratory" policy,
at least as regards Israel, seems especially wide in Africa. While
Israel has been consolidating her friendships with a dozen African
states, despite her friendliness with South Africa, these same states
have joined with every other country in the Organisation of
African Unity to condemn South Africa and to condemn Israel
with increasing severity.

Recognising that any attempt to get an anti-Israel resolution
through the O.A.U. might split the infant organisation, the six
Arab members of the Organisation tactfully refrained from
raising the issue in the first Summit Conferences of the O.A.U.
But in September 1967, the Fourth O.A.U. Summit, to the surprise of even its Arab members, held a special debate on the
Middle East crisis and passed a strong resolution declaring that
it stood fully behind the U.A.R. and promised to work for the
evacuation of all territories of the U.A.R. occupied by a foreign
power—namely, Israel. The Ministerial Committee of the O.A.U.,
in February 1968, went even further to express its solidarity
with all the Arab countries occupied by Israeli forces and called
for the immediate and unconditional withdrawal of these forces.
The O.A.U. Summit Conferences of 1968 and 1969 only repeated
the 1967 formula but in September 1970, the Summit accepted
the Ministerial Committee's formulation by calling for the
withdrawal of Israel's forces from all occupied Arab territories.

At the same time some of these same African countries have
voted for strongly pro-Israeli resolutions at the U.N. Israel was
herself at first alarmed at this seeming contradiction but has

shrewdly decided that what really matters are her cordial bilateral relations with certain states and not the mass condemnations of the O.A.U.; just as what matters is her bilateral understanding with South Africa and not Israel's condemnatory vote against apartheid in the U.N.

The slow hardening of the O.A.U. attitude is not entirely hypocritical, for it reflects the increase in anti-Israeli sentiment among some of the larger, leading African states: one-time friends of Israel like Nigeria, Tanzania and Zambia are now anti-Israel and not merely in a vocal sense. It is because of this withdrawal that Israel's friends in Africa, with the exception of Ethiopia, are confined to the smaller states.

This could be the beginning of a belated realisation by the more important and independent African states that there can be no real friendship between them and Israel which is based on a racial doctrine and which maintains friendly relations and cooperates with the racialist states of southern Africa.

CHAPTER VIII

ISRAEL: A COLONY OR A COLONISER

In this survey of the relationship of Zionism to Asian nation-alism, and of the Zionist state to the nationalist states of Asia and Africa, we have found that some Asian nationalist leaders repudiated the Zionist movement because of its European origins and its acquisitive colonialist nature; later, some of the new states of Asia opposed the creation of Israel because of the way in which she was thrust into a reluctant Asia by non-Asian powers; then we have seen how some of the emerging countries of Asia and Africa turned away from Israel after her establish-ment because of what she did to the Palestinian expellees and because of her pro-Western and anti-Afro-Asian policies. More recently, after June 1967, yet other Afro-Asian countries have opposed Israel because of what she had become, an occupying military power. Looking into the future one can venture the prophecy that still more Afro-Asian countries will find them-selves opposing Israel for what she will become—not just a foreign colony but, in her own right, a coloniser.

There has been a tendency, even among Arab political ana-lysts, to underestimate Israel by describing her scornfully as nothing more than a dependent Western colony or bridgehead. This has never been true, because a congruence of interests has always been in operation between the Zionists and their various European backers: the only thing that was open to doubt was who was taking more advantage of whom at any one particular time. Since, perhaps, about early 1957 Israel has been on her own, or has at least felt that she could stand on her own, but always, of course, with the massive financial, political and propaganda support of the world-wide Zionist movement that has always to be taken into account. But since June 1967 Israel, in terms of political power, has really moved into the "take-off" stage: She is not merely capable of standing on her own feet, she can, rather more than less, decide where those feet should lead her in the years to come.

This opinion is, admittedly, in the realm of conjecture because not only is it hazardous to venture a guess about Israel's future, it is difficult enough to see the Jewish State as it actually, presently, is.

This is so because, by her very Zionist nature, Israel has to be thickly encrusted with myths. Without the myths the Zionist movement would have been too alarming and repellent; without the myths the Zionist state would be too disillusioning.

An extremely percipient observer of the Israeli scene, Dr. Ferdynand Zweig, in his book *Israel: The Sword and the Harp*,[1] lists the following as "The Basic Myths of Israel": The Myth of the Holy Book, of the Holy Land, of the Redemption, of the Continuity of Israel, of the Return, of Fulfilment, of the Exile, of the Special Creativity of Israel, of Israel as the Embodiment of Jewry, of the Founding Fathers, of "Solving the Jewish Question", of the Centrality of Israel, and of "the Fuller Jewish Life". Thirteen basic myths may seem an unusually heavy burden for a small West Asian country of three million people, and Dr. Zweig mentions that the native-born Israelis feel the mythical weight. However, some relief is provided by the fact that all these myths "can be summarised in one belief, the belief in the uniqueness and miraculousness of Israel", no more, no less.

But since Dr. Zweig says that these "myths...are factors towards social and national integration", "that they are helpful in mobilising the Christian world and other international support" and, last but not least, that they are "instrumental in forming Jewish opinion, and in encouraging Jewish immigration and Jewish financial support" one may wonder whether produc-

---

[1]London, 1969, p. 70 *et seq.* Though basically sympathetic to Israel Dr. Zweig's book contains some of the most honest, acute and dissillusioning analysis of Israeli society and politics.

ing such intensely practical and profitable results, these beliefs are genuine myths or just the products of far-sighted and intelligent Zionist propaganda.

Despite their mundane outcome these myths are, with their panoply of capital letters, very grand myths indeed. It is far more modest, secular, day-to-day myths that have shrouded the current reality of Israel from Afro-Asian eyes, the more so because these myths were specially directed at Afro-Asian sensibilities. They may be listed as follows—without capitals: the myth of Israel as a socialist state which is based on the sub-myth of the kibbutz and of the Histadrut; the myth of Israel as an example of civilised modernity; and the myth of Israel as the democratic exception in a non-democratic area.

From the amount of propaganda disseminated one would imagine that rural Israel was covered with kibbutzim from end to end. The facts are quite otherwise as is revealed in such publications as *The Economy of the Israeli Kibbutz* by E. Kanovsky and books on the kibbutz by M. Spiro and D. Leon.[2] The number of people in the kibbutzim has remained stationary at about 80,000 for the past ten years which means that, while in 1949 the kibbutzim represented six per cent of the Jewish population, they now contain only three per cent. The kibbutzim share of the cultivated area fell in ten years from 45 per cent to 32 per cent and is continuing to fall. Above all the kibbutz is a museum piece because the movement is slowly dying out for lack of fresh recruits and a loss of moral impulse. The kibbutz worker is no longer the Israeli ideal and because of this the kibbutz has been forced to deny its basic principles by having to take on hired labour. More important for the countries of Afro-Asia is the fact that the kibbutzim have never paid their way because they were never designed as economic enterprises. As Kanovsky writes, "The standard of living in the kibbutz has been largely divorced from their current profitability".[3] Dr. Zweig argues that both the kibbutz and the Histadrut are institutions that

---

[2] E. Kanovsky, *The Economy of the Israeli Kibbutz*, Harvard, 1966; M. Spiro, *Kibbutz*, New York, 1963; and D. Leon, *The Kibbutz*, Tel Aviv, 1964.
[3] Kenovsky, *op. cit.*, p. 79.

are unsuitable for export to Afro-Asia, a conclusion reached
15 years ago by an Indian government research committee.

The part of the Histadrut in the economic life of Israel has
also been vastly exaggerated, leading to the mythical belief
that it plays a major, determining role. A study of *The Public
Histadrut and Private Sectors in the Israeli Economy* by H. Barkai[4]
proves conclusively that in terms of contribution to domestic
product and of number of persons employed, the private sector
in Israel is overwhelmingly more important than the Histadrut.

With the dissolution of these two sub-myths nothing substantial is left of the main myth of a socialist Israel. It is hardly
surprising that Dr. Zweig, who has every sympathy for Israel,
should state categorically, "Israel is a showpiece of Western
capitalism in developing countries".[5]

The Israeli myth of civilised modernity is negated by the
fact that it is a religious state,—it has been unable to achieve
that essential prerequisite for modernity—a secular separation of
religion from government. In any religious state, like Israel,
citizens of religions other than the dominant one cannot but be
second class citizens. This classification has been codified by
the Israeli government's answer to the question, "Who is a Jew?"
Setting aside a ruling of its own Supreme Court, the Israeli
government decreed that only those born of Jewish mothers and
those officially converted to the Jewish faith can be Jews and
as such citizens of something called the Jewish nation and by
that token automatic citizens of the state of Israel. The main
Zionist impulse was said to be the need to bring about the heal-
ing communion between the Jewish people and the Land. But
it is not the Land, not even the Holy Land, that brings with it
any claim to citizenship as is the case in such diverse countries
as India, Greece and the United States. In Israel citizenship
comes through the womb and the synagogue, through blood
and religion. These archaic criteria are contrary to the concept
of a modern state.

[4]The Falk Project for Economic Research in Israel, Sixth Report, Jerusalem, 1964.
[5]F. Zweig, *op. cit.*, p. 300.

As for the myth of Israel's democracy, this is brought into serious question by the depressed position of two groups—the Arab minority and the non-European Jewish immigrants who are the majority. The full extent of the oppression and discrimination practised against these groups is fully documented in *The Arabs in Israel* by Sabri Jiryis, in the various publications of the Sephardic Council and in such economic studies as *Income Differentials in Israel* by G. Hanoch.[6] The cumulative evidence of these writers leads to the inescapable conclusion that the exclusively European Ashkenazi Jew, who is now probably a minority group, has a virtual monopoly of power and influence in Israel's public life.

For the very special benefit of Afro-Asia there is the further myth that Israel, in course of time, will become Afro-Asianised because the majority of Israel's population is now of Afro-Asian origin. This myth ignores the fact that Israeli society is not, as it has been called, a pressure cooker in which every ingredient is homogenised together, it is, rather, a one-way obstacle course in which only those who succeed in getting over the hurdles of Europeanisation come out as winners. It is an Eastern Jewish scholar in Israel who has best debunked this particular myth.[7] There is also the stark statistical fact that Eastern Jewry has completed its contribution to the population of Israel. From now on immigrants can only come from the West, from Russia and the United States. It is not without significance for the future that in 1970, for the first time ever, the United States supplied the largest single group of immigrants to Israel, over 6,000 persons.[8]

With all the various heroic and comforting myths stripped away, what is left? What, in fact, is the actual aspect of Israel today as seen by Afro-Asian eyes? It is a colonialist coloniser,

---

[6]S. Jiryis, *The Arabs in Israel*, The Institute for Palestine Studies, Beirut, 1968; and G. Hanoch, *Income Differentials in Israel*, The Falk Report, Fifth Report, Jerusalem, 1961.

[7]Nessim Rejwan, "The Two Israels, A Study in Europocentrism", *Judaism Quarterly*, vol. 16, no. 1, 1967.

[8]*The New Tork Times*, 23.10.1970.

a mini-imperial power. The founding fathers of Israel threatened
and cajoled the then colonial and imperial powers into implant-
ing a Jewish colony in Palestine, but now that colony, at one
remove, in the second generation, is doing its own independent
colonisation which makes of it an imperialist state, though perhaps a mini-imperialist, because, by global standards, the scale
is small.

According to analysts of the political phenomenon called
imperialism, it has distinct "moral", economic and psychological
characteristics, and Israel today displays them all. The "moral"
characteristic is that the imperialist must believe that he has a
duty, an obligation, a mission to rule "the lesser tribes without
the Law" for their own good. Apart from the consistent con-
descending Messianism of the Zionists and the Israelis there is
an abundance of declarations by Israeli leaders, before 1967,
of how much better off were the Arabs inside Israel compared to
their brethren in the Arab countries; and, since 1967, of how
beneficial in terms of prosperity, law and order, the Israeli
occupation regime has been to the Palestinian inhabitants of
the West Bank of the Jordan. We have already referred to the
economic argumentation in favour of Israeli expansion that was
contained in the report of the Jewish millionaires' conferences,
held in Jerusalem in 1967 and 1968, which advised the retention
of the occupied areas because of their profitability arising from
their resources of minerals and oil and tourism. But the analysts
of imperialism are agreed that the psychological urge towards
empire is the most important characteristic of all. Hobson
refers to it as "kilometritis, or milo-mania, the instinct for control of land", and Schumpeter provides this definition:' 'Imperialism is the objectless disposition on the part of a state to unlimited forcible expansion."[9]

Once again there is no lack of evidence that in Israel today
there is the "unbounded will to conquest". It is not only the
young "hawks" who have spoken of Greater Israel: even a man
reputedly as "mild" as Levi Eshkol did so when he was Prime

[9] J.A. Hobson, *Imperialism*, London, 1938, pp. 212-213; J. Schumpeter,
The Sociology of Imperialism, New York, 1955, p. 6.

Minister.[10] The present boundaries of Israel, the cease-fire lines
of 1967, fall short of the Zionist map submitted to the Versailles
Conference in the East and in the North. But the areas being
mentioned as objects of future Israeli expansion lie beyond the
frontiers of the Versailles map—there is talk of the Nile Delta,
of Amman and Damascus. One recalls the vivid simile of Norman Bentwich comparing the extent of the future Jewish state
to the skin of the deer that contracts or expands according to
the hunger or appetite of the animal.

Such is the reality, and since it is an Israeli reality a concealing, beguiling myth has to be woven around it. Dr. Zweig
refers, aseptically, to "The Mystique of Violence" in Israel
but attempts reassurance in these words: It is true that the Israeli
"is a warrior now, but not a warrior with a field-marshal's baton
in his knapsack, but rather one with a staff of a prophet in his
hand."[11] How, it may well be asked, how do these poetic words
apply to the Israeli pilot dropping his canisters of napalm on
Egyptian schools and factories and on Jordanian farms and
towns?

The Zionist state of Israel from its very inception was a foreign
object in the body of Afro-Asia: today this object is the cause of
widespread disturbance. If it resists absorption into a democratic, secular Palestine, or if it defies encapsulation within the
boundaries set for it by the United Nations, then the only likely
reaction to it will be rejection.

[10] *The International Herald Tribune*, Paris, 30.10.1967.
[11] Zweig, *op. cit.*, pp. viii-ix.

INDEX

Abdel Krim: 123

Abdul Hamid, Sultan: 17, 62, 83, 95, 96, 97; negotiations with Herzl, 90-91, 94

Afghanistan: 13, 113, 207; at Asian and Afro-Asian meetings, 254; at UN, 273, 274, 276, 278; ieasons for attitude towards Israel, 290

AFL-CIO: 230

Africa: 74, 167, 189, 236, 255, 284, 292; Jewish population, 9, 108; reasons for attitudes towards Israel, 297-300, 307, 324; relations with Israel, 235, 267, 269, 271, 295, 310-318, 322-323; and UN voting on Israel/Palestine, 274-275, 276-280

Afro-Asia: (see Asia)

Afro-Asian Conference (1955): (see Bandung Conference)

Afro-Asian Institute for Labour, Economics and Cooperation: 230-231, 316

Afro-Asian nationalism: (see Asian nationalism)

Afro-Asian Solidarity Movement: 227, 266, 284-285

Al-'Ahd Party: 102

Ahdut Haavodah Party: 226, 227, 245

Alexander II, Tsar: 54

Algeria: 12, 188, 245, 261; and Anglo-French policy in Africa, 312; at Asian and Afro-Asian meetings, 224, 266, 283; and Casablanca group, 269, 313; Israel fails to support, 236, 244, 284; relations with India, 212; supports opposition movements in Africa, 299

Algiers Conference (1965): 260

Ali, Mohamed (Viceroy of Egypt): 106n

Ali, Muhammad (Prime Minister of Pakistan): 250-251, 254

Alkalai, Yehudah: 47, 54, 58, 69

Allenby, General E.H.H.: 111, 117, 118, 121, 145

Allon, Yigal: 226

Altneuland: 150

America: (see Latin America, North America, South America, United States)

Amini, Ali: 255

Angell, Norman: 88

Angola: 237, 261

anti-Semitism: 23, 72, 96, 128; "critical mass" theory, 69-70, 153; Gandhi's views, 170, 180; peculiar to Europe, 53, 89, 184, 309; root of Zionism, 14, 45-51, 58, 76-78, 81, 121; and success of Zionism, 54, 55, 66, 127; used by Zionism, 52-53, 74, 119

Arab Congress: 102, 147

Arab League: 178; and Afro-Asian meetings, 191-192, 253, 258

Arab nationalism/nationalists: 102, 104; and Anglo-French policy in Africa, 312; common hostility of Israel, Iran, Turkey and Ethiopia, 222, 246; and Indian National Congress, 181; in Palestine, 124-125; and Zionist appeals to British, 122, 182; Zionist failure to support, 167; and Zionist Organisation, 162, 166

Printed in Beirut by

HEIDELBERG PRESS – LEBANON

DATE DUE